Praise for *Security Architecture for Hybrid Cloud*

Security Architecture for Hybrid Cloud provides a wealth of information to assist IT and security professionals, from strategic leadership to architects to engineers. It provides concrete, practical, and comprehensive information about how to plan, design, build, and operate secure IT environments and solutions. The information is well-structured, the writing precise and easy to read, and provides numerous concrete examples to illustrate the points. I will find a prime spot on my bookshelf for this book and expect it will be a valuable reference in my work.

—*Sarah Brown, Principal Cyber Security Lead,*
NATO NCI Agency

Security Architecture for Hybrid Cloud distills the collected wisdom of many skilled practitioners with thousands of successful cloud deployments, and provides an in-depth look at architectural thinking based on this experience. The authors explain why architectural thinking is essential for larger-scale systems and applications, some frameworks and patterns to avoid starting from scratch each time, and how to take a balanced and iterative approach for secure design and implementation. It's a must-read for anyone responsible for the security, scalability, availability, and usability of complex systems.

—*Chris Dotson, Distinguished Engineer,*
Author of Practical Cloud Security

This book provides comprehensive and accessible coverage of architecting for security that will become a standard reference in its field.

—*Paul Krause, Emeritus Professor, University of Surrey*

This book is an excellent reference for anyone responsible for integrating security into a solution architecture.

—*Peter Vincent, Enterprise Security Architect, IBM*

This book is an invaluable resource for anyone looking to secure their hybrid or public cloud infrastructure, offering comprehensive best practices and actionable guidance.

—*Professor Bart Preneel, Head of Computer Security and Industrial Cryptography (COSIC), KU Leuven*

This book is an essential read and reference for any discerning Architect. Security considerations are, at a minimum, an essential consideration in all solutions and enterprises, so are of worthy note for all Architects. At one level, this work provides essential guidance for those seeking to ensure the viability and validation of the security elements of their solutions, as well as guiding the vital efforts of governance required to assure enterprises of their overall security. At the same time, dedicated security professionals who seek to build upon proven robust practices in their security solutions will gain strong insights as to how solid architectural thinking will reinforce their expertise. A book that will only become more and more relevant.

—*Paul Homan, Distinguished Engineer and Architect Profession Lead, IBM*

In an era where cyber threats are constantly evolving and becoming increasingly sophisticated, it is imperative that the next generation of cybersecurity professionals possess the skills and knowledge to enable them to design and deliver effective security for the cloud. The popularity of architectural thinking for security among students underscores its significance as a foundational pillar of cybersecurity education. This excellent book serves as a valuable resource for students and will further enhance their learning. I would recommend it to anyone keen to learn more about security architectures in the cloud.

—*Professor Steve Schneider, Director of Computer Science Research Centre, University of Surrey*

As security concerns evolve rapidly and zero-trust models become increasingly prevalent, *Security Architecture for Hybrid Cloud* provides a structured approach that is valuable for all software architects; not just security professionals.

—*Murat Erder, Author of* Continuous Architecture in Practice

Tackling IT Security for a complex system is daunting, but this book gives an excellent overview of the wide range of topics which you will need to consider, and how you should approach it.

—*Kevin Robson, IT Architect, IBM*

Security Architecture for Hybrid Cloud

A Practical Method for Designing
Security Using Zero Trust Principles

Mark Buckwell, Stefaan Van daele, and Carsten Horst

Beijing · Boston · Farnham · Sebastopol · Tokyo

Security Architecture for Hybrid Cloud

by Mark Buckwell, Stefaan Van daele, and Carsten Horst

Published by O'Reilly Media, Inc., 1005 Gravenstein Highway North, Sebastopol, CA 95472.

O'Reilly books may be purchased for educational, business, or sales promotional use. Online editions are also available for most titles (*http://oreilly.com*). For more information, contact our corporate/institutional sales department: 800-998-9938 or *corporate@oreilly.com*.

Acquisitions Editor: Simina Cali	**Indexer:** BIM Creatives, LLC
Development Editor: Melissa Potter	**Interior Designer:** David Futato
Production Editor: Beth Kelly	**Cover Designer:** Karen Montgomery
Copyeditor: Tove Innis	**Illustrator:** Kate Dullea
Proofreader: Piper Editorial Consulting, LLC	

August 2024:   First Edition

Revision History for the First Edition
2024-07-25:   First Release

See *http://oreilly.com/catalog/errata.csp?isbn=9781098157777*

978-1-098-15777-7

[LSI]

Table of Contents

Part I.   Concepts

Part II. Plan

Part III.　Design

Preface

Twenty-five years ago, colleagues from the US traveled to the UK to help us develop a method and course to train a new cohort of security architects. Back then, most of the systems we dealt with were midrange or mainframes running a variant of Windows or Unix, and most of the networks were internal or private. The internet, cloud computing, containerized applications, Agile working, automation, and AI are examples of the tremendous change the world of information systems has gone through.

 Hybrid Cloud for Simplicity

We will refer to hybrid cloud throughout for simplicity. Where you see "hybrid cloud," also read that it could include multiple cloud services or be "multicloud."

While many things have changed, the main security architecture concepts we created 25 years ago have remained constant. We started out with the following standard set of concepts:

- Guiding principles (or security design objectives), based on protection from loss of confidentiality, integrity, and availability, set the stage for how to apply security controls.

- A set of security domains, which we then called subsystems, to group the security controls.

- Threat modeling examined data in transit and at rest to identify threats and countermeasures to protect the data. (Although we didn't call it threat modeling in those days and used ideas from the Common Criteria (*https://oreil.ly/zRlfE*) to describe the technique.)

- Network segmentation of a data center using zones and firewalls.

- A controls framework based on the Common Criteria protection profiles, providing a requirements catalog for security controls.

- Documentation and testing provided assurance of the security controls implementation.

We cover these concepts in this book, but many things have changed. One major change that has had a significant impact on architectural thinking is the move to hybrid (using both on-premises and cloud) and multicloud. It's becoming a standard platform architecture for many organizations, but it has multiplied the number of different technology platforms and the number of security policies to apply.

Threats have expanded, technology platforms are becoming increasingly complex, and protection mechanisms have become more sophisticated. Organizations now use many different technology platforms and service providers that enforce many different security policies using different technologies. It presents an enormous challenge to architect effective security in such a complex environment.

 ### What Are Artifacts?

One word you will hear often is the term "artifact." The term represents content, such as a diagram or table, created during the architectural thinking process. Combining artifacts into a document or presentation describes an architecture for a solution. Some artifacts depend on the creation of other artifacts. An artifact dependency diagram is useful to describe the set of all artifacts and their dependencies.

We've updated the method from 25 years ago to include techniques to handle the complexity of hybrid cloud and tested it over the past seven years with over 1,000 IBMers and MSc students. The current method reflects changes in industry context and improvements in architectural thinking, including:

- An artifact dependency diagram shows the architectural thinking domains and the dependencies between artifacts.

- Integration of zero trust principles throughout the method.

- Integration with other architectural thinking and project management techniques including design thinking, Agile practices, and DevSecOps.

- Consistency of the architecture diagrams to describe the functional components and deployment architecture.

- Introduction of new artifacts describing the complex shared responsibilities of hybrid cloud and new cloud architecture diagrams.

- Introduction of new control frameworks to use as requirements catalogs, including the National Institute of Standards and Technology (NIST) Cybersecurity Framework, NIST SP 800-53 Security and Privacy Controls for Information Systems and Organizations, and Cloud Security Alliance (CSA) Cloud Controls Matrix (CCM).
- Addition of new techniques for functional requirements definition, including design thinking and user stories.
- Introduction of updated techniques for threat modeling as the industry has developed new practices.
- Segmentation of networks has transformed into microsegmentation as it's become easier to configure networks with virtual private cloud networking.
- Acceleration of the architectural thinking process through the use of architecture patterns and deployable architectures.
- Extension of the method to include security operations process and procedure definition, including threat detection and response.
- Inclusion of traceability for requirements, architecture decomposition, and threats to support demonstration of compliance, and threat detection and response.

Security architecture has an important role to play throughout the different phases of the design and delivery of an information system. This book will focus on the artifacts and techniques for designing security that can overlay existing methods used in systems and software development. Utilizing methods and artifacts to clearly communicate the necessary security controls during implementation will introduce rigor. We want to enable you to apply this thinking to whatever development methods and practices you are already using.

Think of this as your "kit bag" of tools and techniques to pick up and use where necessary. Don't feel as though you need to rigidly apply everything in this book. More importantly, this book should instill the right systematic architectural thinking to embed security into systems so that you can effectively protect the processing of sensitive assets. We expect many of you will create your own techniques to supplement what we describe.

For security architects, although your primary goal is to mitigate risks by protecting valuable assets, this doesn't mean you should override the other qualities required of a solution, such as performance, availability, resilience, or cost. While your role is primarily to protect the business, you also need to be cognizant of the other drivers in your organization.

Audience

We've written this book for anyone who is architecting security controls and designing the integration of them into an information system. Architectural thinking for security isn't only for a security architect; it's the responsibility of all architects designing an information system. It's why this book is suitable for anyone involved in architecting systems.

We currently teach these concepts and techniques as a part of cybersecurity degree modules for UK NCSC-certified MSc degrees at two universities in the UK. The book incrementally builds on the concepts and techniques throughout, making it suitable for use in teaching. It's thanks to the past students who asked for a book to study that we authored this book.

We're assuming that you already have some broad understanding of information systems and cloud computing. Some hands-on experience will enable you to make good architectural decisions. Architects don't learn by drawing diagrams; they build their expertise through the practical delivery of applications and infrastructure. Many practicing architects worldwide use this approach.

Contents of This Book

This book takes you through the architectural thinking process, from understanding the context of the solution, requirements gathering, architecture definition, and the definition of security operations to secure the running of a workload or application. A discussion of each technique enables you to more effectively communicate the security characteristics for each part of the solution.

As a roadmap to the architectural thinking process, we've developed an artifact dependency diagram describing the phases of developing an architecture through a sequence of artifacts.

To support the learning process, the book has a case study to demonstrate the step-by-step development of the artifacts that are part of a solution.

Chapter 1 contains a discussion setting the context, explaining how different roles can use the method, and outlining the chapter structure for the book with an artifact dependency diagram to follow.

Conventions Used in This Book

The following typographical conventions are used in this book:

Italic
> Indicates new terms, URLs, email addresses, filenames, and file extensions.

Constant width italic

Shows text that should be replaced with user-supplied values or by values determined by context.

This element signifies a tip or suggestion.

This element signifies a general note.

This element indicates a warning or caution.

Using Figure and Table Examples

Supplemental material (figures, etc.) is available for download at *https://securityarchitecture.cloud*.

If you have a technical question or a problem using the supplemental material, please send email to *support@oreilly.com*.

This book is here to help you get your job done. If you wish to use content, and that use falls outside the scope of Fair Use Guidelines, (such as selling or distributing content from O'Reilly books, or incorporating a significant amount of material from this book into your product's documentation), please reach out to us for permission, at *permissions@oreilly.com*.

We appreciate, but generally do not require, attribution. An attribution usually includes the title, author, publisher, and ISBN. For example: "*Security Architecture for Hybrid Cloud* by Mark Buckwell, Stefaan Van daele, and Carsten Horst (O'Reilly). Copyright 2024 Mark Buckwell, Stefaan Van daele, and Carsten Horst, 978-1-098-15777-7."

O'Reilly Online Learning

 For more than 40 years, *O'Reilly Media* has provided technology and business training, knowledge, and insight to help companies succeed.

Our unique network of experts and innovators share their knowledge and expertise through books, articles, and our online learning platform. O'Reilly's online learning platform gives you on-demand access to live training courses, in-depth learning paths, interactive coding environments, and a vast collection of text and video from O'Reilly and 200+ other publishers. For more information, visit *https://oreilly.com*.

How to Contact Us

Please address comments and questions concerning this book to the publisher:

O'Reilly Media, Inc.
1005 Gravenstein Highway North
Sebastopol, CA 95472
800-889-8969 (in the United States or Canada)
707-827-7019 (international or local)
707-829-0104 (fax)
support@oreilly.com
https://www.oreilly.com/about/contact.html

We have a web page for this book, where we list errata, examples, and any additional information. You can access this page at *https://oreil.ly/security-architecture-hybrid-cloud*.

For news and information about our books and courses, visit *https://oreilly.com*.

Find us on LinkedIn: *https://linkedin.com/company/oreilly-media*

Watch us on YouTube: *https://youtube.com/oreillymedia*

Acknowledgments

Without the help of co-instructors, MSc students, and class participants over the years, the development of the techniques within this book would not have been possible. Thank you for attending classes and providing feedback to help enhance the documented techniques and artifacts. A special thanks to Pete Vincent, who has been on this journey since the start and leads course delivery at the University of Warwick.

We owe the opportunity to create the course and method to Martin Borrett and Julian Meyrick, who gave us the challenge of building an MSc degree module for the Warwick Manufacturing Group (WMG) at the University of Warwick.

Without the ongoing encouragement and support of Srini Tummalapenta, we couldn't have developed and shared the method with a global audience. The sponsorship and adoption of the method for internal reference architectures helped spread and develop the concepts.

The book took a few other people besides the authors to make it a reality. Many thanks to the technical reviewers, Murat Elder, Paul Krause, Kevin Robson, and Pete Vincent. Each reviewer brought their unique experiences to challenge us and provide great suggestions for some vital improvements. Many thanks to the fantastic O'Reilly team, including Simina Calin, Melissa Potter, Greg Hyman, Kate Dullea, Tove Innis, Beth Kelly, and the many others behind the scenes.

Acknowledgments from Mark Buckwell

Thank you to Professor Helen Treharne at the University of Surrey, who took a chance by allowing the delivery of an MSc degree module that was fully managed by myself and Theo Cudjoe. I couldn't have delivered the module without the support of Dr. Andrew Crossan and Professor Steve Schneider, who provided continuous encouragement and patience in answering my questions on the teaching of a degree module.

I am grateful to my co-authors, Stefaan and Carsten. Their relentless dedication over late evenings and weekends, together with their invaluable ideas, have enabled the delivery of a book that I believe is groundbreaking for cybersecurity solution design and delivery.

Finally, I want to thank my family, especially my wonderful wife Lizzie, who put up with me spending so much time on weekends and evenings writing the book, and my children James and Sarah, who were always there to support and encourage me. If you encounter any strange characters in the book, it's due to my cat Mittens, who kept me company by sitting on my keyboard while demanding her dinner.

Acknowledgments from Stefaan Van daele

I would like to thank my co-authors, Carsten and Mark, for the many interesting exchanges of ideas and viewpoints on security architecture during the creation of this book. I learned from each and every interaction. Additionally, writing a book as a security consultant means spending even more hours behind a glaring laptop screen. Therefore, I would like to thank my wife, Rita, for supporting me throughout this entire journey and for bearing with my absence on many occasions, whether I was upstairs just staring at an empty screen looking for inspiration or typing like a woodpecker on my keyboard. I would also like to thank my two daughters, Karlijn and Lise, for being my biggest supporters even as they followed the journey a bit from a distance.

Acknowledgments from Carsten Horst

In addition to the previous acknowledgements, I'd also like to thank all of the clients I worked with, whose projects and problem statements helped me gain the necessary experience to write this book. Thank you also to Kreshnik Rexha for his always very constructive input. The creative collaboration with my co-authors, Mark and Stefaan, has, throughout the whole writing process, been a significant inspiration for me. I'd also like to thank my wonderful wife, Christina, and my daughters, Clara and Caroline, whose admirable tolerance for activities such as writing books seems to have no limits.

Concepts

To introduce the book, we outline foundational security techniques and their use, and we discuss the different architect roles and how they relate to security architecture. We elaborate on the concepts of zero trust and the role of architectural thinking in the solution development process. Finally, we clarify the difference between enterprise and solution architecture, where this book is focusing on the solution architecture. This builds the foundation before we go into the stages of the solution lifecycle.

Introduction

Security often gets simplified down to selecting security controls or countermeasures that prevent loss of confidentiality, integrity, and availability. However, the integration of the controls is just as important as selecting the controls. A series of architectural decisions, informed by the sensitivity of the data and the context of the environment around the system, guides the integration of the security controls.

There are publications providing useful guidance on the design and implementation of cybersecurity technology, the use of software architecture methods, and the application of cloud security services. However, there is a need for a repeatable and consistent way of approaching the architectural thinking for the secure design of an information system hosted on hybrid cloud.

There is a need to clearly communicate the architectural thinking practices and provide assurance that the controls deployment is effective and comprehensive. In a regulated environment this is particularly important, as there needs to be transparency, starting with the design of the security controls through to the assurance mechanisms used to demonstrate compliance.

This book will take you through a step-by-step process to architect security into a solution that resides on hybrid cloud. This first chapter will set the context for the rest of the book by describing:

- The need for effective integration of the foundational security techniques
- The type of architect who should use the architectural thinking described within this book
- How the structure of the book uses an artifact dependency diagram as a roadmap to architectural thinking for security

Once you have read the introductory chapter, you may wish to skip to a chapter that's relevant to the current stage of your architectural thinking. However, we encourage you to start at the beginning, as the end-to-end method helps you understand the traceability of requirements, architecture decomposition, and threat modeling leading to detection and response. Once you have read the end-to-end method, the book will be a useful reference to dip into to refresh yourself on the techniques as you work on the security for a solution architecture.

Let's start by discussing the foundational security techniques for effective integration of security and compliance into hybrid cloud solutions.

Foundational Security Techniques

There are many different security controls used to protect data from loss of confidentiality, integrity, and availability. Foundational security techniques integrate the controls into a system. However, each of these techniques or concepts is normally discussed independently and the ones chosen tend to be the favorite of the loudest stakeholder or solution provider. None of these techniques alone is enough to design, build, and run a secure system.

In this book, we integrate four foundational security techniques into an end-to-end method:

- Compliance management
- Data-centric security
- Secure by design with threat modeling
- Zero trust architecture

Figure 1-1 shows how these techniques integrate together to form the foundation of the method we will discuss.

At the center of the diagram are the three architectural thinking techniques we will use to embed security into the architecture of a solution. This is all supported by the demonstration of compliance shown around the outside.

Compliance takes a static, unfocused approach to security, but data moving through a system is dynamic as it's processed while in transit, at rest, and in use. Let's start with the technique, which focuses on the transaction flows and processing of data.

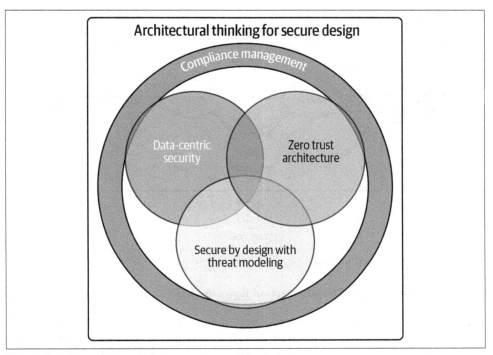

Figure 1-1. Foundation techniques

Data-Centric Security

Data-centric security puts a focus on analyzing the flow of data through a system from the start of a transaction to the end. At each stage of the journey, we consider the security controls needed to protect the transaction flow in transit, at rest, and in use.

The diagram in Figure 1-2 shows the flow of data as it passes through a system:

In the diagram, the shopper initiates a transaction to order some goods. The box represents the organization, and the outer ellipse represents the boundary of the system processing the data. Within the system, there are three interconnected subsystems that process the data. The dotted line represents the transaction flows that transport the data through the subsystems and require protection.

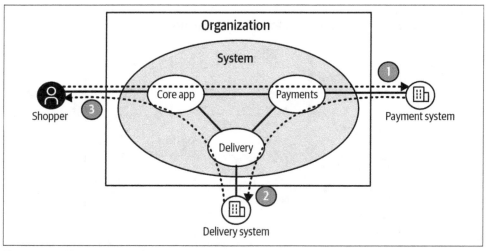

Figure 1-2. Data-centric security

Let's walk through each of the transaction flows in order:

1. The order is first passed as a transaction flow from the shopper to the "Core app" subsystem. When the order is ready to complete, the flow continues onto the "Payments" subsystem and out to an external payment system, as shown in flow 1.

2. After completion of the payment, the transaction returns to the "Payments" subsystem and moves on to the "Delivery" subsystem to connect externally to arrange for delivery, as shown in flow 2.

3. After the arrangement of the delivery, the confirmation of the order is then returned to the "Core app" subsystem and the person who placed the order, as shown in flow 3.

At many of the steps in this transaction flow, processing and aggregation of data are taking place, increasing the value of the data and the need for increased controls. At all stages of the transaction flow, we need to consider the security controls to protect the data from loss of confidentiality, integrity, and availability.

Once we understand the transaction flows we can move on to secure by design.

Secure by Design with Threat Modeling

Secure by design uses threat modeling as a way to identify risk-based security controls directly to transactions and data that move through a technology product or system.

In their paper, *Shifting the Balance of Cybersecurity Risk: Principles and Approaches for Secure-by-Design and -Default* (*https://oreil.ly/TYB8z*), CISA and other national security organizations define secure by design to mean where "technology products are built in a way that reasonably protects against malicious cyber actors successfully gaining access to devices, data, and connected infrastructure." It means that engineers need to embed security in the design of a software or hardware component through an assessment of the risk by carrying out threat modeling.

Threat modeling identifies specific threats and builds on security policies, practices, and processes that don't specifically address the risks to sensitive data. You can extend the practice to the examination of the application and infrastructure architecture for the identification of risk-based controls.

To ensure the identification of all sensitive data, we use a systematic architectural thinking approach for the examination of all the important data flows and transactions. Threat modeling practices need to work at scale across multiple computing platforms in a hybrid cloud environment.

We will discuss threat modeling further in Chapter 6, including recent approaches such as MITRE ATT&CK (*https://attack.mitre.org*) (Adversarial Tactics, Techniques, and Common Knowledge).

Zero Trust Architecture

Cloud computing and the use of mobile devices challenged the traditional concept of a perimeter-based security model. Traditional "castle and moat" security models assumed, after data passed through the perimeter, that everything inside a system could be implicitly trusted. The change in thinking started with the Jericho Forum (*https://oreil.ly/TkScf*) in 2007 releasing the Jericho Forum Commandments (*https://oreil.ly/UKNzr*) for a deperimiterized world where it's assumed a network perimeter doesn't exist.

John Kindervag, from Forrester Research, then came up with the term "zero trust" in 2010 and developed the phrase "never trust, always verify." He identified zero trust as a model that removes implicit trust within a system boundary and continuously evaluates the risks by applying mitigations to business transactions and data flows at every step of their journey. The phrase "assume breach" is also often associated with zero trust and comes from the phrase "assume compromise" used by the US Department of Defense in the 1990s.

The approach requires a combination of technologies, processes, practices, and cultural changes to be successfully implemented. It involves a fundamental shift in the way organizations approach cybersecurity.

Zero trust basics

The zero trust model assumes that all business transactions and data flows, whether originating from inside or outside the network, are potentially malicious. Every interaction in a business transaction or data flow must be continuously validated to ensure that only authorized users and devices can access sensitive business data. In effect, it moves the perimeter from the system boundary to the point at which identification, authentication, and authorization take place, resulting in identity becoming the new perimeter. The whole concept often gets simplified down to the "never trust, always verify" principle, but it's more than that.

Zero trust architecture requires a cultural shift that emphasizes the importance of security rather than just compliance throughout an organization. This means that implementing a zero trust architecture involves not only the deployment of specific technologies but also the development of processes and practices that promote a data security-first mindset across the organization, building on the *data-centric security* approach we discussed earlier.

When architecting and developing security for a system, an architect should follow a set of principles, tenets, or simply a way of thinking to apply zero trust. Zero trust isn't an end-to-end method, and a comprehensive approach requires integration with other architectural thinking techniques.

Zero trust principles

Organizations offer guidance in publications, including the US National Institute of Standards and Technology (NIST) SP 800-207 Zero Trust Architecture document (*https://oreil.ly/LBFUI*) that has a set of zero trust architecture tenets and the UK National Cyber Security Centre (NCSC) Zero trust architecture design principles (*https://oreil.ly/y_cR_*).

> **Zero Trust Network Architecture Principles**
>
> Don't get confused by "zero trust *network* architecture principles" that are used by solution providers to describe their products; they are a subset of the overall zero trust principles.

Throughout the book, we show zero trust tenets and principles embedded in the method. We've created five higher-level guiding principles in Table 1-1 mapped to the tenets and principles. We've brought them back to the familiar phrases you might see in marketing.

Table 1-1. Zero trust tenets and principles mapping

Guiding principles	NIST SP 800-207 Zero Trust Architecture tenets	UK NCSC Zero Trust Architecture Design Principles
Data-centric security	1. All data sources and computing services are considered resources.	1. Know your architecture including users, devices, services, and data. 2. Know your user, service, and device identities.
"Never trust, always verify" or Identity verification + Access control + Least privilege + Microsegmentation	3. Access to individual enterprise resources is granted on a per-session basis. 4. Access to resources is determined by dynamic policy—including the observable state of client identity, application/service, and the requesting asset—and may include other behavioral and environmental attributes. 5. All resource authentication and authorization are dynamic and strictly enforced before access is allowed.	4. Use policies to authorize requests. 5. Authenticate and authorize everywhere.
Data protection everywhere	2. All communication is secured regardless of network location.	7. Don't trust any network, including your own.
"Assume breach" or Continuous monitoring	5. The enterprise monitors and measures the integrity and security posture of all owned and associated assets. 6. The enterprise collects as much information as possible about the current state of assets, network infrastructure, and communications and uses it to improve its security posture.	3. Assess user behavior, service, and device health. 4. Focus your monitoring on users, devices, and services.
Zero trust component selection		8. Choose services which have been designed for zero trust.

We then come to the need to demonstrate compliance, not just against the policies, practices, and processes but against the threats we've identified.

Compliance Management

An organization uses compliance management processes to show it's following a set of rules, regulations, or standards given by external organizations, such as governments and industry bodies. The process ensures that businesses follow these strict requirements for operational risk, security, privacy, and resilience.

Compliance management includes checking that an information system meets a set of policies, practices, and processes for the organization. They may only cover a subset of the security controls needed to protect sensitive information, as they often represent a minimum level of security that organizations must meet to avoid fines or legal penalties.

Often, the security team can't keep up with changes in technology, new system vulnerabilities, emerging threats, or advanced attack techniques, resulting in slow or delayed updates to security policies and standards. In some cases, it takes a security incident to force improvements in protection to cope with new types of attacks or security vulnerabilities not previously identified or blocked.

The continuous raising of the compliance bar sometimes requires the implementation of new controls, even if the risk doesn't justify the increased controls. There are additional costs from the increased compliance, and the protection may still be ineffective for the most sensitive data.

Compliance Is Not Security

Compliance is not security, and you won't achieve compliance without security. We've seen many organizations where there is significant investment spent demonstrating "noncompliance" through compliance checking, control reviews, and audits, but little investment takes place in security. Focus on security with traceability to demonstrate compliance.

In Chapter 4, there is a discussion on compliance validation techniques, including traceability to demonstrate compliance, and in Chapter 10, a discussion on compliance assurance techniques.

Let's continue with a discussion on the users of the foundational security techniques in the industry today.

Users of the Security Techniques

The techniques or models that we discuss in this section are often primarily used by different types of security professionals, with the result that each of the different users promotes their own favorite technique. The integration of these techniques isn't often written about or practiced as an integrated set of techniques.

So where do we see these techniques used today?

Data-centric security
> We've seen architects overlay colored data flows for architecturally significant data flows, but it's not something we see regularly. Sometimes it's used for security, and other times it's just for showing the transaction flow.

Secure by design with threat modeling
> Secure by design is mostly referenced for the development of a software product using the software development lifecycle. It discusses the use of a threat model as part of the design of a product. Since the release of *Threat Modeling: Designing for Security* (*https://oreil.ly/myCZF*) (Wiley) by Adam Shostack in 2014, software

developers (or engineers) are more likely to use threat modeling as a technique during software development. We see the technique mostly used in software development rather than used for the end-to-end design of a whole application, system, or system of systems.

Zero trust architecture
Many different organizations are adopting zero trust architecture, but solution providers dominate where they use the technique to sell products that tend to focus on one domain, such as network security, identity management, or threat management.

Compliance
Compliance is often the focus of risk and compliance organizations in many regulated industries. We suspect it's because it's easier for auditors, consultants, and executives to think about a series of checklists that don't require the deep technical background necessary to use other techniques.

This book will take you through a method that will integrate each of these techniques together, but before we talk about a method, let's consider who should be architecting security into a solution.

Architect Roles for Security

Architectural thinking is the primary role of an *architect*. However, it's a skill also used by consultants and software engineers engaged in making architectural decisions. We will discuss further in Chapter 2 how architectural thinking fits with consulting and engineering.

Architectural thinking for secure design is also not only for security architects; a wide range of architect roles need to apply security to the development of an information system. Architects developing infrastructure or applications should adopt this method, not just security architects.

In Agile development, there is a need for a hybrid role called a *security champion*, who will have both architectural and engineering skills. They should be able to use this method to advise the developers on embedding security into DevSecOps.

A range of different architect roles should use architectural thinking for security techniques, including:

- Security architect
- Infrastructure and application architect
- Security champion

Let's continue by discussing each of these architect roles and how they should be using the method in this book.

Security Architect

A security architect is an architect with a specialty in security, compliance, and risk management. We've split the role of a security architect further into four categories: enterprise security architect, solution security architect, product security architect, and advisory or consulting security architect. Each role has a common set of security skills but a different focus with additional skills and experiences:

Enterprise security architect
> A security professional who is a specialist in enterprise architecture and produces enterprise-level guidance on the application of security to an enterprise. They develop an enterprise architecture and guiding principles to align with the security strategy and guide the development of security in solution architectures.
>
> They must have a good understanding of current threats and the direction of the industry, as well as excellent communication skills, to align the enterprise with the enterprise security strategy and architecture.
>
> If you have this role, this book contains some overall guidance on enterprise architecture in Chapters 2 and 3. Together with the rest of the book, these chapters enable an enterprise security architect to understand the architectural thinking for secure design process so they can provide the right inputs to support architects in the solutioning of security.

Solution security architect
> A security professional who is a specialist in the development of solution architectures for security in specific projects or initiatives within an organization. For example, they may develop an architecture for a specific solution, such as a privileged access management service.
>
> They must have a deep understanding of specific threats and risks associated with the technology and a good understanding of the organization's enterprise strategy, enterprise architecture, policies, standards, and guidelines.
>
> In addition, they need to have all the skills of infrastructure and application architects in resilience, scalability, and operations, as they will be developing the architecture for a security application.
>
> They will work closely with engineers, developers, testers, and project managers. They need to have excellent communication skills to explain security concerns to non-technical stakeholders.
>
> If you have this role, the whole of this book provides the security-specific architecture activities needed for a security solution, but generic architecture

techniques, available in other software and application architecture publications, will supplement the techniques discussed in this book. The end of this chapter contains references to other useful publications.

Product security architect

A security professional who is a specialist in the development of a security product or suite of products. They're often specialists in a specific security domain, such as identity and access management or threat detection, with a deep understanding of the products' software and hardware requirements.

They will be responsible for the development of the architecture for a security product and will work closely with the development and testing teams. For the product to be quickly adopted, they will need to understand how it fits into an enterprise environment and the benefits it delivers.

They will need great communication skills to explain the benefits of the product to the product management team, which will market and sell the solution.

If you have this role, the whole of this book provides the security-specific architecture activities needed for a software product, but generic architecture techniques, available in other software architecture publications, will supplement the techniques discussed in this book. The end of this chapter contains references to other useful publications.

Advisory or consulting security architect

A security professional who is a specialist who advises an organization on how to integrate security controls into its infrastructure and applications. They work with the lead or chief architect for the project and sometimes with architects of other disciplines to embed security into the solution developed.

They need to have a good understanding of not only industry best practices, regulatory requirements, and security technologies but also infrastructure and application architecture solutions. The architect has "T-shaped" skills with a deep security understanding and a wide range of skills related to information systems.

They need to be able to talk about security with a wide range of stakeholders, including those who aren't technical and those who work on the specific implementation of the security controls and have deep engineering skills.

If you have this role, the whole of this book provides the security-specific architecture activities needed for an infrastructure or application architecture, and the artifacts will need to overlay the architecture developed by an infrastructure or application architect. The end of this chapter contains references to other useful publications that will enable you to better support the architects you are advising.

If you are an architect for an information system, think about what role you have in integrating security into the solution architecture. The question isn't whether you are responsible, but to what extent.

Infrastructure and Application Architect

There are many projects or initiatives that don't need the benefit of a specialist security architect, the infrastructure or application architect will need to integrate security into the solution. The infrastructure architect might be designing a cloud platform, while the application architect might be designing a payments platform that's hosted on the cloud platform. In both cases, security will be the responsibility of these architects. This book will help them with the architectural thinking for secure design needed in their roles.

Security Champion

In an Agile or DevOps development environment, a security champion may take on the role of an advisory security architect. In this case, the security professional will have a mix of architectural thinking and engineering skills that enable them to get into the details of advising a developer on how to develop code securely. Further detail on this role is in Chapter 10.

Contextual Roles and Responsibilities

All the roles need to understand the end-to-end architectural thinking process and the artifacts involved. Each role's responsibilities for leading or assisting in the development of artifacts will vary. As technical leaders, they will need to adapt their responsibilities depending on the context of the organization, product, project, or program.

Now that we've talked about the foundational security concepts requiring integration into a method and the architect roles, let's move on to a discussion of the structure of the book that will enable an effective walkthrough of the method.

Book Structure

The book has a series of chapters that build a security architecture using techniques to develop artifacts throughout the book. Each chapter focuses on specific artifacts and techniques, giving you the opportunity to also use the book as a reference manual. Each chapter will highlight techniques that support zero trust. To help reinforce the learning from the book, we've included examples of artifacts based on the case study contained in Appendix A.

Artifact Framework

Let's start with looking at the framework used throughout this book, followed by the detailed artifact dependency diagram.

In Figure 1-3, we show a framework for the architectural thinking that's used to develop a security architecture. Each block on the diagram represents a grouping of related artifacts.

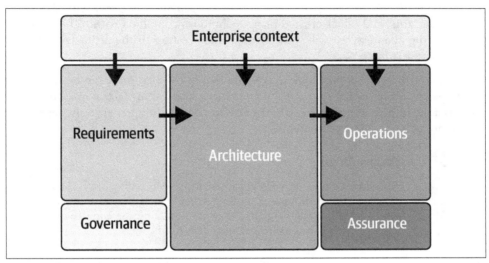

Figure 1-3. Artifact framework

At the top, we have the *enterprise context*, which includes all the organization inputs used to architect a solution architecture, including business context and organization policies. These artifacts are normally created before the solution architecture, but sometimes they don't exist and the project is responsible for their development. You may have to fill in these details, which will add additional effort to the project.

Below that, we have the *requirements*, *architecture* and *operations* sections that demonstrate the left to right development of the architecture. The *requirements* section includes the artifacts for gathering the functional and non-functional requirements for the solution. The *architecture* section includes the artifacts for the top-down decomposition of the solution architecture, starting with the architecture overview and system context. The *operations* section may be the last on this picture, but it's no less important and contains artifacts developed from the requirements and architecture parts of the framework.

At the bottom left is the *governance* section, including the artifacts used to support the overall development of the architecture and used at all stages of architecture development.

Finally, on the bottom right is the *assurance* section, which includes all the activities necessary to give us confidence in the design and implementation of the security controls, and these activities continue into Day-2 operations.

This is a starting point, and now we need to elaborate the framework.

Artifact Dependency Diagram

The framework in Figure 1-4 shows an *artifact dependency diagram* with the documents, diagrams, and tables created using techniques contained within this book. In the following chapters, we will walk through the creation of the artifacts using this diagram as a roadmap.

The number of artifacts may look overwhelming, but the artifacts can be individual diagrams and tables rather than a big document. It also has artifacts containing code, such as a deployable architecture. Use the artifacts and techniques as tools, depending on the project's specific requirements.

Diagram Format

The original diagrams we produced have been redrawn for consistency and to support publishing requirements. If you want to see selected original diagrams, they are hosted on the companion website (*https://securityarchitecture.cloud*) for the book.

It's likely that, as an architect, you will come across these artifacts, with varying levels of input depending on your role. As we discussed earlier, the application or infrastructure architect will own some of these artifacts, and you may add content to them. In other cases, you will own them. If someone doesn't own them, it's most likely that you do. When it comes to operations artifacts, you may not create the artifacts, but you are responsible for ensuring their delivery.

It's also not necessary to use every one of the artifacts, and the time spent on each one should be just enough to convey the architecturally important features of a system. For instance, when validating the effectiveness of control mechanisms, you don't have to consider every single transaction flow that could occur within the system. Instead, you should look for a representative collection of architecturally significant transaction flows that enable you to review all major paths through the system at least once.

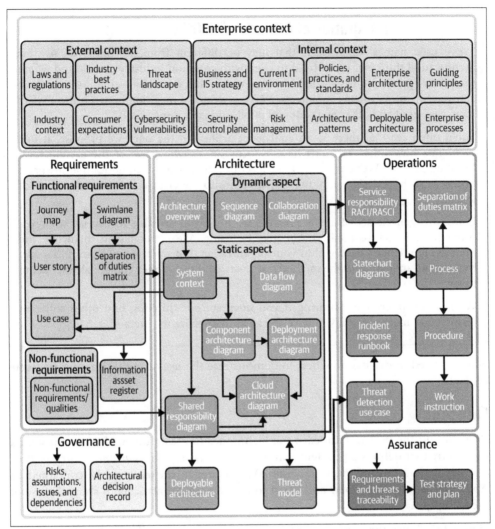

Figure 1-4. Artifact dependency diagram; see the original diagram (https://oreil.ly/ SAHC)

Create documentation appropriate to the context of the project and the sensitivity of the data the system is processing. There will be a need to create significant documentation for an application subject to regulations to give assurance to internal risk management and external auditors. An organization that's less tolerant of risk may require the identification of an extended list of threats and countermeasures.

Integration of Artifacts with Other Methods

We've used names for artifacts that may be different from the ones you use for architectural thinking. We've tried to align with common industry names, and where there isn't agreement, we've tried to assign names that would be recognizable to most software or infrastructure architects. We've provided a mapping between the artifact names we used and other methods and publications in Appendix B.

You'll often see that there is no equivalent artifact to the ones we propose. It just highlights how other methods have a focus on specific parts of the architectural thinking process. We've tried to create a set of artifacts and techniques that integrate practices such as design thinking and stretch into the critical operational aspects of security.

Using this generic set of artifact names, we hope you are able to overlay whatever software architecture method you may be using. We're not trying to dictate the underlying methods used within your organization, but we hope you can find a way to integrate and enhance the methods, artifacts, and techniques you are already using today.

We have an interest in knowing if you integrate our thinking into other software architecture methods or if you have any ideas to improve the method.

Now we need to discuss how best to demonstrate the use of the techniques to create artifacts.

Case Study

We've found the best way to learn the techniques to create the artifacts is through a case study that defines a problem with some *business context, current IT architecture*, and an *architecture overview diagram*. We reference the case study contained in Appendix A in each chapter and use it to create example artifacts to show the use of the technique.

Figure 1-5 shows the artifacts contained within the case study. It provides an overall business context to the project, through a discussion of the need to deliver a system to charge polluting vehicles for entry into the city. It describes the current IT architecture including the organizations that will need to integrate with the system, such as Clean Air Pay that needs RabbitMQ integration. If this was a project for an organization with many existing applications, there would be many more constraints on the solution.

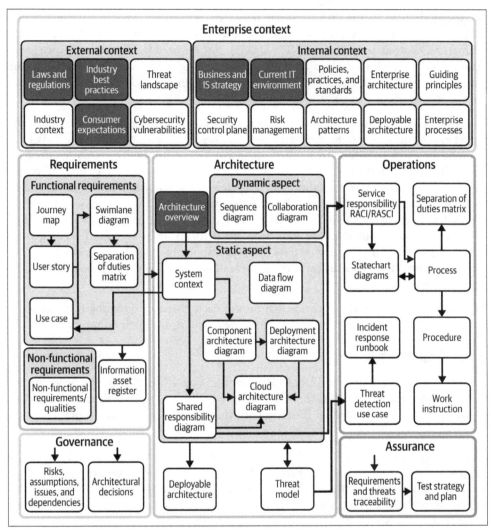

Figure 1-5. Case study artifact dependency diagram

As the system is processing personal data, the prevailing data privacy legislation will guide the required controls. The application needs to meet the Payment Card Industry Data Security Standard (PCI DSS) (*https://oreil.ly/kRIvM*) as it processes payments. The case study says little about the existing security policies but does talk about using the NIST Cybersecurity Framework (*https://oreil.ly/4P4yS*) as a practice the project needs to apply to the system.

The case study provides an *architecture overview diagram* to show the overall system. Don't expect the diagram to show all external actors for the system, and you may have to identify extra information from the description or implied systems to integrate with. This is the first diagram the project is likely to give you, or you need to create it yourself. It's a diagram that shows an overview of the solution, but it's not expected to be in a standard format and will be a diagram that anyone can understand from a non-technical perspective. In the case study diagram, we have components joined together by lines, but it could just be a block diagram of capabilities in groups without lines showing control or data flow. It's also likely to evolve over time, so keep an eye on changes to this diagram from the lead architect, as the updates may change your solution.

We will use an artifact dependency diagram in each chapter, to highlight the artifacts we're discussing. Let's walk through each of the chapters and their contents.

Book Organization

As discussed before, the book has chapters organized broadly in the order of the development process to construct a solution architecture with security included. Figure 1-6 shows the solution lifecycle with the boxes Plan, Design, Build, and Run representing the phases.

These solution lifecycle phases all feed the security architecture at the bottom of the diagram. The Govern, Identify, Protect, Detect, Respond, and Recover blocks align with the six functions in the NIST Cybersecurity Framework (*https://oreil.ly/NuxnB*), which we will discuss in Chapter 2, together with the security domains we've defined for an enterprise security architecture.

We'll now take you through the different parts of the book that align to the solution lifecycle phases in Figure 1-6. Each part contains one or more chapters.

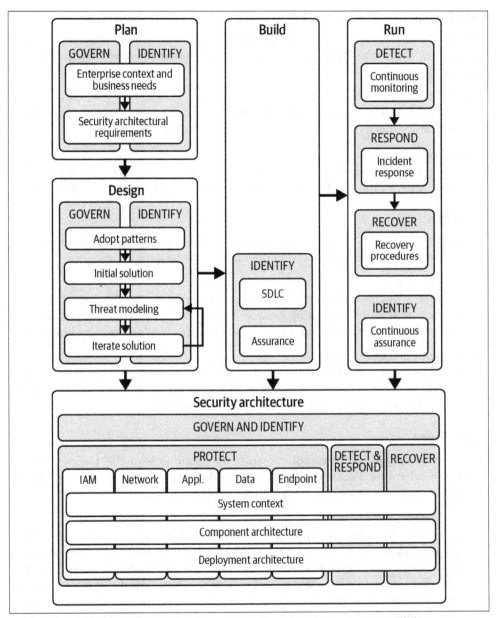

Figure 1-6. Architectural thinking for security framework; see the original diagram (https://oreil.ly/SAHC)

Part I. Concepts

We start the book with two chapters discussing the security and architecture concepts used within the book. These chapters provide a foundation before we get into the stages of the solution lifecycle:

Introduction
> Chapter 1 will give you some background to architecture, security architecture, and the approach this book uses to walk through the method.

Architecture Concepts
> Chapter 2 discusses where architectural thinking fits into the design and development lifecycle, and the difference between enterprise and solution architecture.

Part II. Plan

We continue with the *Plan* phase in Figure 1-6, where we discuss obtaining requirements from the enterprise context and then requirements definition:

Enterprise Context
> Chapter 3 discusses the information that's external to the development of the solution architecture including *business context, current IT environment, laws and regulations, policies and standards, enterprise architecture,* and *guiding principles.*

Requirements and Constraints
> Chapter 4 discusses the gathering of requirements, starting with external laws, regulations, and industry standards. It then goes on to discuss documenting the *functional* and *non-functional* requirements for a system.

Part III. Design

Now that we've gathered the requirements, we continue with the *Design* phase in Figure 1-6, where we discuss the design of the solution architecture, starting with the functional components and moving on to the deployed architecture:

System Context
> Chapter 5 discusses the core architectural thinking technique for protecting sensitive assets by focusing the boundary of the system, on where the data flows, where it's stored, and where it's processed. An architect uses the *system context* diagram to define the boundaries of the system and the external actors triggering data flows through interactions with the system. The chapter continues by describing the documentation of an *information asset register* and the classification of the data to identify the types of controls depending on data sensitivity.

Application Security
> Chapter 6 discusses the development of a functional architecture for an application or workload through documenting a *component architecture diagram*. It

continues by starting with threat modeling at a high level for the application components.

Shared Responsibilities
Chapter 7 will discuss the deployment of application subsystems onto technology platforms and document the *shared responsibilities* for a set of hybrid cloud platforms.

Infrastructure Security
Chapter 8 continues elaboration of the solution by deploying the functional components onto infrastructure and ensuring data flows use zero trust principles for protection. A *deployment architecture diagram* or *cloud architecture diagram* provides the documentation for a hybrid cloud infrastructure architecture. The architecture diagrams will then have the threat modeling repeated.

Architecture Patterns and Decisions
Chapter 9 looks at how you can accelerate architectural thinking by using *architecture patterns* and *deployable architectures*. The chapter will then introduce the use of *architectural decision records*.

Part IV. Build

Once we've designed a solution architecture, we continue with the *Build* phase in Figure 1-6 by considering the development lifecycle:

Secure Development and Assurance
Chapter 10 looks at the development lifecycle and how architectural thinking for security integrates into it, including *Agile* development and the role of a *security champion*. We then look at the role of the *risk, issue, assumption*, and *dependency* log during the design and development lifecycle.

Part V. Run

Finally, we need the system to remain secure after it's live, so we discuss the operational aspects of the system as shown in the *Run* phase in Figure 1-6:

Security Operations
Chapter 11 looks at elaborating the roles and responsibilities identified with the shared responsibility diagram into a Responsible, Accountable, Consulted, and Informed (RACI) table. The responsibilities are then documented through the *processes, procedures*, and *work instructions* needed to secure the system. We then continue with the documentation of the detection of threats and response to incidents through a *threat detection use case* and *incident response runbook*.

Part VI. Close

And the final chapter includes some closing thoughts:

Closing Thoughts

Chapter 12 concludes the book with some thoughts on best practices when architecting security into a solution architecture.

Architectural thinking is the decomposition of a solution through an iterative process into more and more detail. Let's discuss how we will do that.

Solution Architecture Decomposition

Throughout the book, we break down the solution architecture of the information system into layers, as shown in Figure 1-7. We start at the top layer by using a system context diagram to describe the system's boundary and how it connects to external human and system actors. In Chapter 5, we will talk more about this.

We will then look at the functional components of the application, or workload, that are inside the system boundary. We will describe how they interact with each other and start to examine the threats to the application. In Chapter 6, we will examine this in more detail.

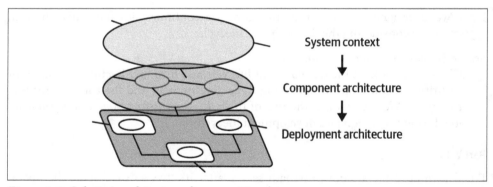

Figure 1-7. Solution architecture decomposition layers

On the bottom layer, we will examine the deployment of the functional components of the application onto the infrastructure and apply zero trust architecture practices. In Chapter 8, we will explore this layer in more detail.

Other architecture models may introduce additional layers, but we've tried to make it simple so you can apply the techniques to different architecture methods. However, it's likely that you will decompose each layer from a logical to a physical (or prescriptive) perspective. We give an example of that decomposition in Chapter 5. As another example, look at the container, component, and code diagram decomposition in the C4 Model (*https://c4model.com*).

We continue with a discussion of the steps involved in architectural thinking and decomposition.

Method Techniques

In each of the following chapters, you will find at least one architectural thinking technique discussed.

We split the techniques into two types:

Enterprise
> The techniques discussed apply to enterprise architecture and don't use the case study.

Case study
> The techniques discussed use the case study in Appendix A to demonstrate how to apply the techniques.

Table 1-2 lists the techniques and their type discussed in each chapter.

Table 1-2. Techniques by chapter

Chapter	Technique type	Technique
Chapter 2, "Architecture Concepts"	Enterprise	Enterprise security architecture
Chapter 3, "Enterprise Context"	Enterprise	All artifacts from the enterprise context group
Chapter 4, "Requirements and Constraints"	Case study	Use case Journey map User stories Swimlane diagram Separation of duties matrix Non-functional requirements Requirements traceability matrix
Chapter 5, "System Context"	Case study	System context diagram Information asset register
Chapter 6, "Application Security"	Case study	Data flow diagram Component architecture diagram Sequence diagram Collaboration diagram Threat model
Chapter 7, "Shared Responsibilities"	Case study	Shared responsibility diagram
Chapter 8, "Infrastructure Security"	Case study	Deployment architecture diagram Cloud architecture diagram
Chapter 9, "Architecture Patterns and Decisions"	Case study	Architecture patterns Deployable architecture Architectural decision record
Chapter 10, "Secure Development and Assurance"	Case study	Risks, assumptions, issues, and dependencies (RAID) log Test strategy and plan

Chapter	Technique type	Technique
Chapter 11, "Security Operations"	Case study	Shared responsibilities RACI Process (swimlane diagram) Statechart diagram Procedures Work instructions Separation of duties matrix Threat detection use case Incident response runbook Threat traceability matrix

Order of the Techniques

The order of the techniques throughout the book uses the same order we teach students for the MSc degree module in the UK. We designed the order to build up the architecture step by step. The documentation of the architectural decision records and RAID artifacts is something that should happen from the start of the architectural thinking process, but it makes more sense to discuss it after the completion of some architectural thinking.

In many chapters, we offer a QA checklist or extra detail on the steps you should perform to help deliver quality artifacts.

At the end of each chapter there is an Exercises section with multiple choice questions. The answers can be found in Appendix C. Further, summative questions with answers can be found on the companion website (*https://securityarchitecture.cloud*).

Let's close this chapter with some final thoughts.

Summary

We started by discussing four foundational techniques for designing security into systems and how it's a problem when they're not integrated together, creating a disjointed approach to integrating security into an information system. We believe there is a need to integrate the techniques to create a robust security architecture method to overlay existing information system and software architecture methods.

We went on to discuss the different types of architects that will use the method. We believe that all types of information system architects need to be able to design the security of an information system. A security architect is there to support other architects and develop architecture for security services. Think about your role as a consultant, architect, or engineer and how architectural thinking for security will fit within your current projects.

The final section discussed the structure of the book, with the artifact dependency diagram helping frame the journey through the architectural thinking for secure design method. The chapter contained a summary of later chapters, and the techniques used to create the artifacts. You might want to create a copy of the artifact dependency diagram to pin on your wall and use as a prompt in your project.

In Chapter 2, we will take some time to reflect on where architectural thinking fits into the development lifecycle. We often see a jump from design thinking to software engineering without architectural thinking, causing problems with major architectural changes needed at a later stage. We will also talk about the difference between enterprise and solution architecture, as this can often get confused. These topics will help give context to the following chapter, where we start on the journey through the artifact dependency diagram.

Further Reading

While we discuss a comprehensive method for architecting security into an information system, an understanding of other topics such as cloud security, software architecture, cybersecurity architecture, and enterprise security architecture will be beneficial.

Rather than hiding this at the end of the book, you may wish to consult some of these other books and online sources while you read our discussion of architectural thinking for secure design.

For cloud security technology that spans multiple cloud service providers, a good starting point is *Practical Cloud Security* (O'Reilly) by Chris Dotson. There are plenty of other sources online and in books that focus on specific cloud service providers.

For cybersecurity solution architecture, we suggest reading *Practical Cybersecurity Architecture* (*https://oreil.ly/89v5Z*) (Packt Publishing) by Ed Moyle and Diana Kelley.

If you would like to understand more about software architecture methods, we suggest three other sources. *Practical Software Architecture* (*https://oreil.ly/l8bfs*) (IBM Press) by Tilak Mitra discusses a method used widely across IBM with a focus on on-premises architecture for enterprise systems. For software architecture with an engineering approach, we suggest reading *Fundamentals of Software Architecture* (O'Reilly) by Mark Richards and Neal Ford. We also mention in several places the C4 Model (*https://c4model.com*) by Simon Brown, which provides a simple approach to visualizing software architecture.

For enterprise and solution architecture, *Enterprise Security Architecture (https:// oreil.ly/yukDV)* (CRC Press) by John Sherwood, Andrew Clark, and David Lynas describes the six-layer security architecture known as Sherwood Applied Business Security Architecture (SABSA). It's referenced in other places, including The Open Group. From The Open Group, there is the *Open Enterprise Security Architecture (O-ESA) (https://oreil.ly/umwhA)* that has a framework for enterprise security architecture.

Throughout the book, we will suggest additional reading.

Exercises

1. Which of the following are the foundational security techniques used in the method described in this book? Select all that apply.

   a. Secure by design with threat modeling

   b. Zero trust architecture

   c. Confidential computing

   d. Compliance management

   e. Data-centric security

2. What are the characteristics of secure by design? Select all that apply.

   a. It includes threat modeling.

   b. It precedes architectural thinking.

   c. It is targeted at the design of technology products.

   d. It scales to design a system of systems.

3. What are characteristics of zero trust architecture? Select all that apply.

   a. "Never trust, always verify."

   b. It's only about network security.

   c. Identity is the new perimeter.

   d. It's a product or solution.

4. Which one of these architect roles is specifically used in an Agile or DevOps development environment?

   a. Enterprise security architect

   b. Application architect

   c. Security champion

   d. Advisory security architect

5. Which of the artifact sections supports the overall development of the architecture during all stages of development?

   a. Requirements

   b. Architecture

   c. Operations

   d. Governance

   e. Assurance

6. The artifact dependency diagram contains which of the following types of artifacts? Select all that apply.

   a. Diagrams

   b. Event logs

   c. Automation

   d. Tables

7. Which of the following statements is correct?

   a. Solution architecture decomposition includes enterprise architecture, component architecture, and deployment architecture.

   b. Solution architecture decomposition includes architecture overview, component architecture, and deployment architecture.

   c. Solution architecture decomposition includes system context, component architecture, and deployment architecture.

   d. Solution architecture decomposition includes system context, component architecture, and data flow diagram.

CHAPTER 2

Architecture Concepts

Before we get into the method of integrating security and compliance into a security architecture, we're going to discuss two topics that offer some context to architectural thinking.

First we'll discuss the integration of architectural thinking into the design, build, and operation lifecycle of a system. There seems to be a trend to focus on *design thinking* and go straight to building or coding a system without considering *architectural thinking*. This often leads to a serious gap in the design of an information system that needs to support production workloads.

Second, you need to understand the difference between *enterprise architecture* and *solution architecture*. These two types of architectural thinking can be misunderstood, and the value of having both is sometimes not recognized. We will explore the value each of these types of architecture brings to designing a secure and compliant system.

We then follow up with a deep dive into *zero trust architecture*, including the NIST Core Zero Trust Logical Components. We continue with a discussion on how zero trust integrates with other security practices for use in architecting security. We then provide some guidance on solutions that support the implementation of zero trust.

We will go on to discuss a technique for the development of an enterprise security architecture.

Let's start with the first topic: understanding where architectural thinking fits into the design and development lifecycle.

From Design Thinking to Compliance

Before getting into security architecture, it's important to understand where architectural thinking fits in the design, build, and operation of an information system's lifecycle. First read the following sidebar as an example of the problems that can occur without architectural thinking.

A Proof of Concept or a Minimum Viable Product?

Someone comes up with a new idea for an application, and they suggest building a proof of concept (PoC) to prove the principles of the solution. The PoC gets the go-ahead, and work starts to develop the solution through design thinking and Agile working practices. Someone then says, "This should be a minimum viable product (MVP) so we can announce it at the conference next month."

What's the problem with this? A PoC demonstrates the basic functionality, but that doesn't mean the application will be secure, resilient, scalable, etc. Architectural thinking enables the system to support production workloads and may be missing between the design thinking and engineering of the system. The architect hasn't ensured that the system meets the required architectural characteristics for a production service, and the completion of testing hasn't confirmed production readiness.

So what could happen? The service may be well-received by new users right away, but it becomes overwhelmed. The operations team struggles to scale the service because it wasn't designed to scale, but they get it under control (for now).

External threat agents are then paying attention to the service and have decided to test the security of the system that's not fully patched or locked down. They gain access and start to extract sensitive information, but the organization running the system doesn't know this because there is no threat monitoring.

Someone urgently brought in a contract database administrator without conducting any background checks, and now this person has privileged access to all the sensitive data. There is no bastion host or threat monitoring in place, so this administrator could extract all the data without anyone knowing about it.

Six months later, the hackers release the data, and customers leave the service for a more secure platform while looking for recompense for their data loss.

Many of these problems have occurred before because a PoC became an MVP without the necessary architectural thinking.

So how should architectural thinking fit into the design of a system? We will examine how design thinking, architectural thinking, engineering, operations, and compliance integrate together as an end-to-end design process, as shown in Figure 2-1.

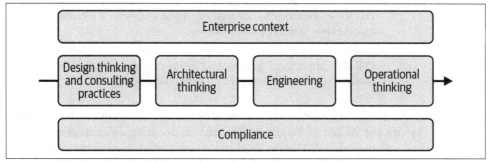

Figure 2-1. From design thinking to compliance

Let's continue this section by working through the diagram from left to right in our discussion.

Design Thinking and Consulting Practices

Over time there have been a number of consulting methods that gather business requirements for developing applications. They're a mix of generic practices used in many different contexts but there are others specific to the business problem. Many organizations currently use *design thinking* as a human centered and iterative approach to problem-solving that emphasizes empathy, experimentation, and iteration. Depending on the source, the origin of the method is either Larry Leifer, the founding director of the Stanford Center for Design Research (*https://oreil.ly/_q4ri*), or David Kelley from the global innovation agency IDEO (*https://www.ideou.com*).

Whatever the source, Stanford d.school (*https://oreil.ly/G0SVC*) suggests that design thinking is composed of five stages:

1. *Empathize*: Understand users' physical and emotional needs, and pain points.
2. *Define*: Define the core problem to solve.
3. *Ideate*: Generate many ideas to create prototypes.
4. *Prototype*: Iteratively generate prototype solutions.
5. *Test*: Obtain feedback from real users and the prototype solutions.

Learning Design Thinking

You can learn more about design thinking from:

- Books, such as *Design Thinking for Tech* (*https://oreil.ly/ OLDOB*) (Pearson) by George W. Anderson, which includes an overview of the popular methods
- Online courses, including Coursera (*https://oreil.ly/AIkXE*), O'Reilly (*https://oreil.ly/TimuA*), The Open University (*https:// oreil.ly/fF62j*), and Udemy (*https://oreil.ly/SzsOM*).

While design thinking focuses on the functional aspects of fulfilling customer needs, it doesn't explore the design of requirements such as security, compliance, scalability, resilience, and operability. Design thinking doesn't offer a systematic approach to architectural characteristics or non-functional requirements of an information system.[1]

We've seen projects jump from design thinking to the coding of an application without thinking about how the architecture of the application and infrastructure supports the successful delivery of a production business process. The result is a redesign and rebuild of an application when the application doesn't scale, isn't secure, and doesn't support the availability requirements of the business processes.

Design thinking needs to work with additional design processes to deliver a complete and effective information system. This is where *architectural thinking* comes in at the next stage.

Transitioning to Architectural Thinking

If you're wondering where design thinking turns into architectural thinking, Grady Booch, said it succinctly (*https://oreil.ly/HvBjx*) on X (formerly Twitter) in 2021:

> All architecture is design, but not all design is architecture.
>
> Architecture represents the set of significant design decisions that shape the form and the function of a system, where significant is measured by cost of change.

For example, in design thinking, we might suggest that before a user accesses a system, they need to complete identification and authentication with the functionality built into the user interface. We could then add the requirement that the system needs to support 500,000 users logging in using multi-factor authentication over a 15 minute period at the start of the business day.[2] This peak capacity requirement will

---

1 There is a debate about what these characteristics should be called. This will be discussed in Chapter 4.

2 We've deliberately used a scalability requirement for a security service. We see that it's often forgotten that security services have architecture characteristics that aren't just about security.

require significant architectural decisions and architectural thinking for the solution to deliver those requirements.

As discussed earlier there is difference between a proof of concept (PoC) and a minimum viable product (MVP). With a PoC, design will focus on the proof of functionality using test data and often not include architectural characteristics such as performance, scalability, resilience, security, and compliance. An MVP is the first implementation of a solution with minimum capacity but designed to scale to meet future growth and meet minimum production architectural characteristics for processing production data, including security and compliance.

This implies that the delivery of a PoC with design thinking using an Agile approach, without deep architectural thinking, is insufficient for production services. A PoC may involve making some architectural decisions, but not many to enable support for production workloads. With an MVP, the solution needs deep architectural thinking through clearly documented architecture, architectural decisions, and formal testing to support production workloads.

An MVP Without Architectural Thinking

If you come across an MVP without architectural thinking to support performance, scalability, security, and compliance, remember that this is in reality a PoC. By calling the project an MVP, the stakeholders may have the wrong expectations set, with the idea that the MVP can go straight into production. The whole solution may need rearchitecting to support production characteristics and the project might need to be restarted.

Let's discuss further about architecture, architectural thinking, and the role of an architect.

The architecture of an information system, or collection of systems, consists of functional components deployed on infrastructure while making significant decisions about the architecture design. This is *information system architecture* or simply *architecture*, and encompasses principles, relationships, processes, and standards that form the system's overall structure and operation.

Information System Architecture

We've used the term *information system architecture* rather than *IT architecture* given that the system described is about processing information using processes, people, and technology. It's not just about IT.

The aim of information system architecture is to match technology to business needs, ensuring the technology is flexible, scalable, secure, resilient, and efficient in supporting the organization's objectives. An information system architecture defines the boundaries, interfaces, and connections between different components to ensure their seamless collaboration in line with the organization's overarching IT strategy.

Architectural thinking is a methodical approach or process to construct an information system architecture through problem-solving and decision-making. It begins by examining the overall context of the system and establishing a set of functional and non-functional requirements. You should consider the functional components of the application, including their interactions, before deployment on infrastructure designed for architecture characteristics like adaptability, scalability, security, resilience, and efficiency. In terms of security, the process entails identifying threats, then implementing countermeasures and threat detection to manage risks to the processing of the information assets. The architectural thinking process should ensure alignment with the organization's overall business and information strategies.

The individual who applies a systematic approach to architectural thinking to create an information system architecture is an *architect*. Meanwhile, a security architect is a person who takes a security-focused viewpoint when engaging in the practice of architectural thinking.

There may be an overlap between an architect performing architectural thinking and a consultant performing design thinking. A consultant normally focuses on the business requirements, including the design of the organizational and process aspects of an information system and doesn't get into the technical or architectural aspects. However, the consultant will perform some architectural thinking activities. As an example, a consultant may make the architectural decision that the application is to be cloud native using a containerized platform.

An Architect or a Consultant?

We've come across the view that a security solution is either delivered by an architect or a consultant. In reality, many projects need both the skills of a consultant to understand the business requirements and the skills of an architect to design the technical solution. A *consulting architect* may have a blend of the right skills and experience, but asking a consultant to architect a solution architecture without the appropriate skills and experience increases the risk of project failure and an incomplete security solution.

Transitioning to Engineering

When does architectural thinking become engineering? In *The Art of Systems Architecting* (*https://oreil.ly/ElaJl*) (Routledge), Mark W. Maier and Eberhardt Rechtin introduce the distinction between architecting and engineering, where "Engineering aims for technical optimization, architecting for client satisfaction. Engineering is more of a science, and architecting more of an art." In other words, the engineering translates the architecture of a system into a realizable implementation of the information system.

Maier and Rechtin expand on this by saying:

> Architecting deals largely with unmeasurables using non-quantitative tools
> based on practical lessons learned; that is, architecting is an inductive process.
> Engineering deals almost entirely with measurables using analytical tools derived
> from mathematics and the hard sciences; that is engineering is a deductive process.

Engineering is a process that designs, builds, and improves information systems by applying scientific, mathematical, and practical knowledge. In this case, measurables are the specific configuration, scripts, code, or physical hardware that's used to construct an information system. That's the role of a software or hardware engineer. Software or information system engineering is just one of many disciplines with the overarching goal of developing practical solutions to real-world problems.

There are different roles in the engineering of an information system, including those of a software engineer for software development or a system reliability engineer (SRE), who will be programming to achieve high levels of operational reliability.

There may be an overlap between an architect performing some engineering activities and an engineer performing architectural thinking activities. As an example, a security architect may specify the individual firewall rules for deployment to a firewall to secure the data flowing through a system, which is more aligned with an engineering activity.

Operational Thinking

Operational thinking for security is critical to ensure the system continues to run securely and rapidly handle threats. It's a way of thinking that focuses on the practical, day-to-day operations of managing and running an information system.

Operational thinking requires understanding and putting into action the processes, procedures, and support systems needed for information systems to work effectively. By adopting an operational mindset, organizations can enforce security on an ongoing basis.

Sometimes, we see security operations overlooked in the delivery of an application with no capability to manage security. An adaptation is then required for the application to support the required security operations, with a project overrun and the associated cost impact.

As a security architect, inclusion of the architecture for security operations at the start of the design process is essential to ensuring effective security. Many operational processes require operational infrastructure that may require changes in the fundamental architecture and the implementation of the application.

For example, the interception of an encrypted session between a client and a server requires inspection of network traffic for malicious content and the leakage of confidential information. Aside from the additional network components required to examine traffic, there is a change in the application architecture alongside the need for a team to administer this new security service.

We will discuss the identification of the security services as a part of enterprise architecture later in this chapter and the security operations responsibilities and processes in Chapter 11. There is also the approach where development is integrated with operations through a model called DevOps that we will discuss in Chapter 10.

Now that we've reached the end of the lifecycle, let's discuss the *enterprise context* that influences the design and *compliance* that ensures the effectiveness of security.

Enterprise Context

Figure 2-1 shows the *enterprise context* influencing the whole lifecycle, which consists of internal and external factors that influence every stage from design thinking to operational thinking. Factors external to an organization include legal and regulatory frameworks and industry best practices. Internal policies, standards, processes, and procedures used in developing the security architecture will incorporate mandated security controls and guidance for delivery across the organization.

We will discuss the external and internal factors that influence architectural thinking in Chapter 3.

Compliance

Figure 2-1 shows *compliance* supporting the whole lifecycle, which ensures the design, build, and operation of the information system meet the relevant laws, regulations, policies, guidance, and procedures. The starting point is to define a baseline set of requirements, starting with external factors and then internal factors. We will discuss this further in Chapter 3.

Once you understand the baseline set of control requirements, it's important to demonstrate compliance by considering the requirements at each stage of design, development, and deployment. We do this by tracing requirements through each stage of the design and development with an artifact like a traceability matrix. We will discuss this further in Chapter 4.

There is a risk of ongoing development processes, operational processes, or a threat actor changing the configuration of the system components. To prevent unauthorized changes, this requires continuous compliance checks of the system configuration and other assurance processes, such as penetration testing. Assurance processes offer confidence in the secure operation of workloads. We will talk more about assurance processes and how they support demonstrating compliance in Chapter 10.

Waterfall to Agile Delivery

The transition by organizations from traditional waterfall to Agile delivery represents a significant shift in the delivery of information systems. The waterfall approach to information system development requires the completion of each stage before proceeding to the next. The model assumes the definition of requirements is at the start and then frozen before development begins.

In contrast, the Agile approach is iterative and incremental, with development taking place in short cycles known as *sprints*. Agile teams prioritize close collaboration with customers and stakeholders, seeking frequent feedback to ensure that the software they're developing meets their needs. The Agile model emphasizes flexibility and adaptability, allowing for easier change.

The need to deal with rapidly changing business and technological environments, a desire for earlier time to market through an MVP, and higher customer satisfaction were the driving forces behind the switch from waterfall to Agile delivery. Agile has grown in popularity in recent years with the move to cloud, with many organizations adopting it as their preferred development method.

Speed of Agile Development

Agile development of an application doesn't necessarily deliver the full function quicker than a waterfall development. It's there to deliver function incrementally, bring better stakeholder alignment, and reduce the risk of delivering a solution that doesn't meet the needs of the stakeholders.

However it can create two camps: those who believe in waterfall and those who believe in Agile. However, both waterfall and Agile have different benefits and drawbacks, and the approach chosen depends on the specific needs and constraints of a given project or organization.

In practice, a project may use both approaches, with waterfall for the development of a secure, scalable, and resilient infrastructure architecture to support multiple applications. With many applications and workloads using the same infrastructure, architectural decisions have a greater impact requiring more careful architectural thinking. The development of the application may then use an Agile approach.

Security Architecture in Agile

For the effective implementation of security, in addition to design thinking, a combination of architectural thinking, engineering, and operations is crucial. While some might associate architectural thinking with voluminous documentation from traditional waterfall delivery, the architectural thinking process is still required during Agile delivery.

With Agile delivery, architectural thinking must focus on "just enough" and "just-in-time" documentation that's iterative and integrated to support the Agile delivery process. This book approaches these needs through the creation of individual architectural artifacts rather than large documents to meet the needs of an Agile delivery environment.

A further discussion of Agile development processes and roles is in Chapter 10.

Continuous Architecture

The use of individual artifacts created just in time, rather than a heavy deliverable-based approach, aligns with a *continuous architecture* approach to architectural thinking. Murat Erder, Pierre Pureur, and Eoin Woods have documented an approach that integrates architectural thinking practices into Agile development practices in *Continuous Architecture in Practice* (*https://oreil.ly/Syw0N*) (Addison-Wesley).

They propose that continuous architecture follows these six principles:

Principle 1
Architect products; evolve from projects to products.[3]

Principle 2
Focus on quality attributes, not on functional requirements.[4]

Principle 3
Delay design decisions until they are absolutely necessary.

---

3 We will continue to use projects rather than products, even though secure by design starts with a product. However, we're focusing on architectural thinking for secure design, where a project manages the integration of a system containing many products or where a program manages the integration of a system of systems.

4 We discuss quality attributes as non-functional requirements in Chapter 4.

Principle 4
> Architect for change—leverage the "power of small."

Principle 5
> Architect for build, test, deploy, and operate.[5]

Principle 6
> Model the organization of your teams after the design of the system you are working on.

If you are applying the artifacts and techniques discussed in this book in an Agile working environment, we suggest you apply the principles and practices they have documented.

Let's go on to discuss enterprise architecture and solution architecture.

Enterprise and Solution Architecture

There are different types of architecture descriptions, and each serves a different purpose with different techniques and outputs. This book is primarily about *solution architecture* (SA), which provides a description of the architecture for the design and implementation of an information system that supports the delivery of specific business or technology processes. However, *enterprise architecture* is also an important part of the architectural thinking process.

Enterprise Architecture

An organization needs a methodical approach to ensure the continual alignment of business objectives and goals with their information systems and technology. An *enterprise architecture* (EA) is there to optimize the implementation of information systems through consistency and best practices to improve the effectiveness of delivery for an organization.

The most widely known enterprise architecture methodology and framework is the TOGAF® Standard (*https://oreil.ly/xLT3o*) from The Open Group (*https://www.open group.org*). The Open Group Architecture Framework (TOGAF) is a framework for developing an enterprise architecture. Organizations use it as a structured development method to design, plan, implement, and manage their enterprise architecture. It's a great foundation for enterprise architecture as it's vendor neutral and under continuous improvement.

---

5 The artifact diagram included artifacts and architectural thinking for all these stages of the development lifecycle.

The Open Group uses a definition for enterprise architecture from Gartner (*https://oreil.ly/AAARg*):

> The process of translating business vision and strategy into effective enterprise change by creating, communicating, and improving the key principles and models that describe the enterprise's future state and enable its evolution.

An enterprise architecture provides guidance when developing a solution architecture. It gives an overall holistic view with architectural building blocks and associated descriptions, guiding principles, and best practices for following across the different projects while creating solution architectures.

We can use architecture building blocks (ABBs) to describe generic characteristics or functionality as a part of an enterprise architecture for a defined problem space, such as a whole organization, line of business, or major program. An EA can also use the ABBs to describe how they relate internally or externally, but they don't try to describe the implementation of a specific information system.

The ABBs could also be high-level business processes or proposed generic IT components. We must also not forget that an information system is a blend of people, processes, and technology. The ABBs can reflect this by describing them as *services*.

The Enterprise Continuum

In the TOGAF standard, there is an "Enterprise Continuum" chapter (*https://oreil.ly/d2Cpj*). It describes the process of keeping enterprise architectures, building blocks, models, and solutions up to date and what their interdependencies are. Patterns could be either assets in the Architecture Continuum, or in the Solutions Continuum.

We will see later in this chapter that an enterprise architecture diagram can be particularly useful in categorizing, communicating, and describing security services.

Solution Architecture

A *solution architecture* describes the architecture of a specific solution for infrastructure, application, or workload. It will document the enterprise context, business and IT requirements, the functionality of the workload, and the deployment of the functionality onto deployed infrastructure. In other words, a solution architecture describes the solving of a business problem in terms of an information system consisting of people, processes, and technology. It will describe how specific technologies and products deliver the system's capabilities.

This book, including the artifacts and techniques, is about describing the security and compliance aspects of a solution architecture. The solution architecture may also describe the architecture for a security capability or service. We develop a solution architecture to describe the solution for a specific business problem or the supporting infrastructure on which to host workloads. It includes both a conceptual and a lower-level prescribed or physical view of the architecture.

Policies, practices, and processes created at the enterprise or organization level will serve as the foundation for a solution architecture's security. Their development will take place by incorporating external laws, regulations, and industry standards in accordance with the organization's risk tolerance. They will be the foundation of compliance activities for the organization, but they won't be sufficiently specific to enable consistency of implementation across the organization. An enterprise architecture, architecture patterns, and enterprise processes are likely to serve as a guide for ensuring consistency in the implementation of security controls. We'll discuss the external and internal contexts that influence architectural thinking further in Chapter 3.

Now let's take a deeper dive into zero trust architecture, following on from what we discussed in Chapter 1.

Zero Trust Architecture

We started with an overview of zero trust architecture concepts and principles and will continue with a deeper discussion of the core logical components of a zero trust architecture, which will provide further context on the subject.

We previously discussed zero trust principles, but they don't help us understand the practices we should use as part of architectural thinking. We'll therefore continue with a discussion on how the principles translate into the practices and highlight where in the book we apply the practices.

Core Architecture Components

During many security architecture conversations around zero trust, a discussion on the access model from the publication NIST SP 800-207 Zero Trust Architecture (*https://oreil.ly/GP8bk*) will arise. It defines the zero trust tenets and provides a basic diagram to describe the basic relationship between components and their interactions. Figure 2-2 comes from the original diagram in NIST SP 800-207.

The diagram has a subject (human actor or user) using a system to access an enterprise resource (data or functional component). Between the subject and resources, a policy enforcement point (PEP) acts as a proxy determining what resource the subject can access. The PEP uses the policy decision point (PDP) to make those decisions.

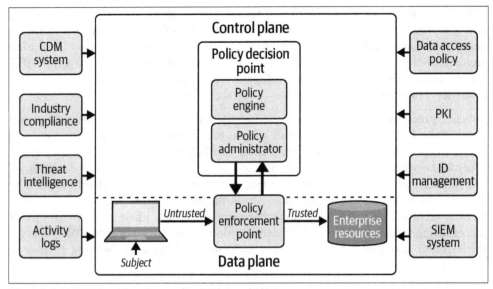

Figure 2-2. NIST core zero trust logical components

A more detailed breakdown of the key elements follows:

Subject
> The subject can be a human actor, system actor, or functional component that's looking to gain access to an enterprise resource, such as data.

Enterprise resource
> This is a resource under the control of your organization, such as data, a device, or functional component.

Policy enforcement point (PEP)
> The PEP provides inline access control between the subject and the enterprise resource managing the connection. The PEP will forward every access request to the PDP for evaluation, and the PEP will enforce the decision returned by the PDP. In reality, the PEP (and the PDP) often run on the same system as the enterprise resource for performance reasons. There are multiple types of configurations possible.

Policy decision point (PDP)
> The PDP contains two components. The first component is the policy engine (PE), which makes access decisions based on two data elements. First, it requires policies that define who gets access to what kind of resource and under what conditions. The second element is the contextual data needed by the access decision rules. As you can see in the diagram, there is a wide range of diverse

data sources that could provide contextual data. The second component is the policy administrator that manages communication with the PEPs.

Adaptive-Based Access Control

This conceptual framework model isn't new to people familiar with adaptive-based access control solutions like the ones based on the XACML standard (*https://oreil.ly/tz6Zr*), though there are some differences. The addition of the policy administrator differs from the XACML standard. It's also sometimes called context-based restrictions or access control.

Control and data plane

The PEP manages the traffic in the data plane, the network path carrying the application data. The communication between the PEP and the PDP is through the control plane, which is a restricted component that's separate from the data plane.

Data sources

The components on the left and right represent possible data sources of contextual information for the PE (all the arrows should point to the PDP as they represent the flow of contextual information to the PE). The contextual information could be about the subject who is requesting access, the device, the network path, or the system hosting the data. A few terms that need expanding include:

- The continuous diagnostics and mitigations (CDM) system monitors the state of devices and applications and should apply patches/fixes as needed.

- The security information and event management (SIEM) system detects potential threats and vulnerabilities.

This conceptual architecture is there to support the "never trust, always verify" principle and is applicable to those use cases where PEPs (and the related PDPs) can make use of contextual data to make access decisions.

Zero Trust for Access Control in Cloud Native Applications

NIST published an addition to the FIPS 800-207 document (*https://oreil.ly/1IgqN*) in early 2024. Quote from the NIST webpage: "The objective of this publication is to provide guidance for realizing an architecture that can enforce granular application-level policies while meeting the runtime requirements of ZTA for multi-cloud and hybrid environments."

Now that we've described the conceptual zero trust architecture from NIST, we'll discuss the translation of the zero trust principles into practices for use throughout the following chapters.

Architectural Thinking Integration

Zero trust principles are easy to understand but sometimes hard to implement. As you read in Chapter 1, there are multiple definitions and interpretations for the zero trust practices to implement. We touched on zero trust architecture, but as it's a complex area that relates to much of the architectural thinking process, we want to show you how it integrates into the method described throughout this book.

Zero trust is normally defined by a set of principles, tenets, or simply a way of thinking. Zero trust isn't an end-to-end method, and it needs integration with other architectural thinking techniques for the development of a comprehensive security solution. We've done this by converting the set of principles in Table 1-1 into a set of practices, listed in Table 2-1, that you can apply during your architectural thinking.

Table 2-1. Zero trust principles to practices mapping

Principles	Practices
Data-centric security	Identity, data, and transaction identification
Never trust, always verify	Continuous authentication
	Adaptive access control
	Least privilege
	Microsegmentation
Data protection everywhere	Encryption in transit, at rest, and in use
Assume breach	Threat detection and response

The method described in the book distributes zero trust architectural thinking throughout with a systematic way of identifying the resources and the security practices involved in zero trust architecture. For this reason, you won't find one single section on zero trust architectural thinking within this book, and so we will help direct you to the places where we integrate the practices into the method.

Let's explore each of these practices and discuss them in further detail.

Identity, data, and transaction identification

There needs to be a systematic way of considering all resources for the transportation and storage of the data. Without understanding the resources, we don't know what and where we need to protect the data assets. We do this by identifying the actors, data, and transaction flows through the system.

The identification starts with the creation of a *system context* diagram to identify users, devices, and services that are external to the system, as discussed in Chapter 5. The process continues through understanding the transaction flows and the threats to the data, traveling through the functional components discussed in Chapter 6. The process repeats with the flows through the deployed components on the infrastructure covered in Chapter 8.

Continuous authentication

In traditional identity and access management (IAM) solutions, a subject (human or system) will identify and authenticate with the session and it will stay open until the session is inactive or there is a requirement to re-authenticate after many weeks. However, how do we know that the session created two days ago is from the same person or system?

Authentication isn't only required at the start of a user or system session but also continuously during the lifetime of the session, also known as *continuous authentication*. If contextual information changes during the active session, then the system re-evaluates the access policies, and the outcome could be the termination of the active session.

Continuous authentication may include checking behavioral patterns such as typing speed, biometric authentication such as fingerprint scans, device authentication such as the security compliance of a device, and contextual information such as time of day or location. Detection of threats is possible by using the alerts from the continuous authentication mechanism when authentication fails.

We consider the use of continuous authentication as a part of the threat modeling analysis for the transaction flows through the system in Chapter 8.

There isn't yet widespread implementation of this practice, but it's often implemented with adaptive access control that shares these mechanisms.

Adaptive access control

Adaptive access control provides access based on the context of the subject accessing the enterprise resources. The access could increase or decrease depending on the context in which the user is accessing the system. For example, accessing from an office space may offer increased permissions over accessing remotely.

Behavioral patterns may alter the level of access depending on information, such as normal login times. Risk-based decisions may enable higher levels of access if using a trusted device and other contextual information, such as the location of the device. Adaptive access control should contain real-time access control components, like a PEP or the access logic built in, and should make use of the maximum possible information from the available contextual data.

Once a system makes a decision on the level of access, the capability may use a combination of access control approaches such as role-based access control, attribute-based access control and risk-based access control.

In many systems, the technical capability doesn't currently exist to perform adaptive access control and the impact on performance would make it undesirable. At the time of writing, the focus has been on zero trust solutions at the network edge using zero trust network access (ZTNA), which we will discuss further later on.

However, on cloud platforms, system-to-service, system-to-system, and service-to-service communication uses fine-grain access control and is starting to use adaptive-based access control with strong authentication for the boundaries of network segments and cloud services. We expect this to evolve into full zero trust capabilities for every network segment and cloud service connection.

We consider the use of adaptive access control as a part of the threat modeling analysis for the transaction flows through the system in Chapter 8.

Least privilege

Least privilege is a principle and practice that says a user or system should receive the minimum permissions to complete the activities they need to perform. As well as only having minimum access, a subject should have no access by default, and for sensitive processes, there should be the enforcement of separation of duties. Fine-grain access controls are available for the implementation of least privilege through role-based access control, attribute-based access control, and risk-based access control.

At the application layer, identity governance and administration solutions must ensure that employees don't have more entitlements and roles than they need to perform their job. This is especially difficult as privilege creep occurs when an employee has legacy entitlements from their past roles where revocation of privileges hasn't taken place.

In Chapter 4, we start examining the required privileges through the documentation of the functional requirements using a swimlane diagram and a separation of duties matrix.

In Chapter 8, we discuss the need to authorize sessions with least privilege between application components, services, and devices. Authorization takes place in real time through decisions based on the context of the requester. At the network level, the implementation of least privilege is also through microsegmentation to restrict the resources and services the workload has access to.

Multiple Policy Enforcement Points

It's suggested in the NIST model that a PEP provides a centralized policy decision to evaluate authorizations in real time. In reality, there will be multiple policy enforcement points, and they won't always be on the boundary of a system, as shown in ZTNA. For example, a cloud platform will have its own PEP that may be separate from the network and application PEPs.

In Chapter 11, we continue with a discussion on the use of a RACI matrix, process (swimlane diagram), procedure, and work instructions to help define least privilege requirements for security operations.

Microsegmentation

In the past, we split data centers into network segments containing hundreds of devices, but today we use microsegmentation, where compute resources are in small isolated segments to reduce lateral movement on a network. We discuss this further in Chapter 8.

Encryption in transit, at rest, and in use

Encryption of data in transit and at rest is an essential mechanism to protect sensitive data from disclosure, particularly on a cloud platform where you aren't in control of cloud operations. Encryption of data at rest needs to effectively prevent privileged users from having access to the most sensitive data. We will discuss this further in Chapter 8.

Threat detection and response

Assume breach means that the security design for a system should assume the compromise of the surrounding components on the same network and see them as hostile systems instead of trusted neighbors. This assumption is also true for all other systems with whom a system establishes a network connection. With this practice, the focus shifts to security monitoring to detect possible anomalies in all security domains.

During the threat modeling process, in Chapters 6 and 8, we discuss the identification of potential threats and any abnormal behavior. We can then use the identified threats for threat detection and incident response, as we discuss in Chapter 11.

Zero Trust Solutions

There are typical zero trust-based solutions that could enable you to realize the zero trust principles. It's beyond the scope of this book to do a deep dive on zero trust-based solutions, as they're rapidly evolving, but we'll give a summary here. Table 2-2 shows potential security solutions for the zero trust principles in the security domain.

Table 2-2. Examples of zero trust-based solutions

Zero trust principle	IAM	Data	Application	Endpoint	Network
Never trust, always verify	• Just-in-time access • Privileged access management • Continuous authentication • Adaptive access control	• Digital rights management • Adaptive access control	• Adaptive access control • Allowed processes list	• Trusted computing base • Privileged access management	• Adaptive access control • Microsegmentation • Dynamic network access control • Zero trust network access
Data protection everywhere		• mTLS • Certificate manager • Key manager & HSM	• mTLS • Certificate manager • Key manager & HSM	• mTLS • Certificate manager • Key manager & HSM	• IPSec
Assume breach	• User & entity behavior analytics	• Data loss prevention	• Endpoint detection & response	• Endpoint detection & response • File integrity monitoring	• Network detection & response

Although this table isn't a comprehensive overview, it gives you a general idea of the kinds of zero trust-based solutions you can choose from to achieve the result that the zero trust principles require.

Now let's discuss a technique for the development of an enterprise security architecture. With this technique, we're not using the case study.

Technique: Enterprise Security Architecture

Experience has shown that a lack of a standard security taxonomy, or organization of security capabilities, can create confusion across an organization. There are many different security processes that need organizing, and there is a need for a standard approach to decomposition from top-level security domains to the deployed services.

Security Processes or Services?

Before we go on to describe the enterprise architecture, let's explain why we prefer to use the term *service* rather than *process* to describe a security capability. Many organizations refer to a capability as a *process* to correspond with control process owners. A section of a control framework, such as access control or network security, has a process owner assigned to it. There may be a second level of process ownership within that section of a control framework. However, we prefer to refer not to a process but to a *service* because:

- Security capabilities consist of technology, processes, and people—not just processes. Security capabilities need a service design to ensure quality of delivery.
- Security capabilities often deliver requirements from multiple sections of a control framework—making process alignment based on control framework sections inappropriate.

For example, site-to-site virtual private network (VPN) isn't a *process*, it's a technology service that's administered by an operations team using processes. It needs quality of service as it needs to be available 24×7, and if it fails, it needs a Recovery Time Objective (RTO) of near zero as it supports the availability of the service. It also needs to meet control requirements from identity management, access control, and network security. Using a process to represent what is a service is insufficient.

A security service is also the representation used in *Enterprise Security Architecture* (*https://oreil.ly/w30wj*) (CRC Press) by John Sherwood, Andrew Clark, and David Lynas and in The Open Group (*https://www.opengroup.org*) document "Integrating Risk and Security within a TOGAF® Enterprise Architecture" (*https://oreil.ly/4d4jc*).

Enterprise Architecture Decomposition

We need a systematic and consistent approach for decomposition from a high-level set of groups that we will call *domains*. Figure 2-3 starts with domains that we decompose into categories that then decompose into security services.

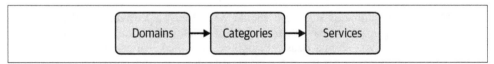

Figure 2-3. Enterprise architecture decomposition

Miller's Law

Miller's Law suggests that an average human can hold in short-term memory 7±2 objects. At each layer in the model, we've tried to create groupings of less than seven items. It's designed to be simple to understand but also complete so we can describe all security capabilities or services within it.

We will now go on to explain each of these stages of decomposition.

Security domains

Many organizations use enterprise architecture diagrams to sell a product or solution set, so they often leave them incomplete, otherwise it will show gaps in their solution. We need domains that classify a complete set of security services. So we've defined six security domains that should be familiar to you already. The selection of the set of six domains, as shown in Figure 2-4, came from merging many different enterprise security architectures from around the industry. We then assigned every security service we could find from different enterprise security architectures or models into one of the six domains.

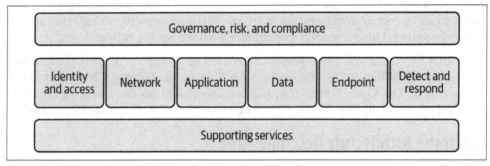

Figure 2-4. Enterprise security architecture domains

Opinionated Security Domains

The domains suggested should work for you as well, but often organizations have their own set of opinionated security domains that you should consider adopting. Just make sure the domains cover all types of control capabilities as a starting point. Using a single enterprise architecture with consistent decomposition is the key benefit to your organization.

The granting of access to an application for processing data has defined the order of the security domains. Reading the domains left to right, an end user will use *Identity and Access* before gaining access to an application. This gives access to a *Network* that controls access to an *Application* that processes *Data* that resides on an *Endpoint*. Services that *Detect and Respond* to threats are responsible for protecting the entire application. In effect, the order of the domains shows a process or transaction flow.

The domain at the top reflects the need for governance, risk, and compliance processes to operate the security services residing within the domains. The domain at the bottom provides supporting services, such as change management or capacity management, to effectively operate a security service.

NIST Cybersecurity Framework

You may be thinking, "What about the NIST Cybersecurity Framework (*https:// oreil.ly/6Kq9N*) with the Govern, Identify, Protect, Detect, Respond, and Recover functions organized by cybersecurity outcomes?"

The framework focuses on the full range of both technical and non-technical controls, whereas we've focused on the technical capabilities for architectural thinking. You will also find that the majority of the capabilities map to the Protect function, which doesn't give a simple decomposition for an enterprise architecture. Figure 2-5 shows a broad mapping between the NIST functions and the security domains we've defined.

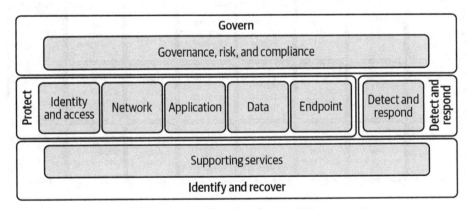

Figure 2-5. Functions to domains mapping

We could use both the NIST Cybersecurity Framework functions and the enterprise architecture domains but this will just make things confusing with two different representations.

We can now further decompose these security domains into categories.

Security categories

We then decompose the security domains into five categories for each domain, as shown in Figure 2-6. We could have created different numbers of categories for each domain, but we wanted to make the decomposition easier to remember with a fixed five categories for each domain.

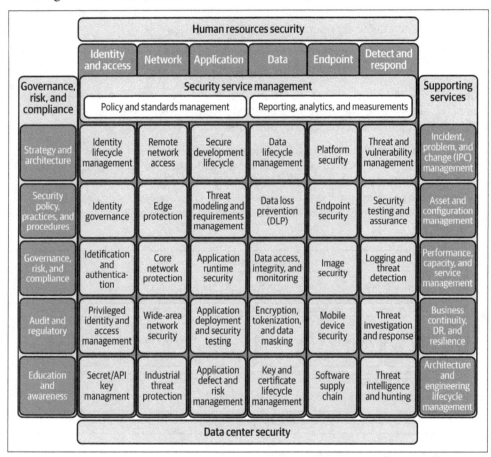

Figure 2-6. Enterprise security architecture domains; see the original diagram (https:// oreil.ly/SAHC)

The diagram becomes useful as a *heat map* to show what's relevant to your specific context. For example, you could shade the diagram to show what security services are relevant to the solution architecture you are designing. You could add colors to represent the compliance status of the service, such as red, amber, and green, which enables a focus on the areas of interest.

Decomposition Alignment

At this level of decomposition, the categories your organization uses are likely to be different but similar to those shown in Figure 2-6. The important thing to keep in mind is that an organization with a standard enterprise security architecture will have better alignment across different projects.

Security Service Management

We highlighted *security service management* in Figure 2-6 as separate from any other service management activities because it contains two important categories required for the effective enforcement of security controls.

This becomes particularly important when the resources requiring security are across many different technology platforms and are using microsegmentation. This creates large numbers, potentially millions, of access control list rules together with the security configuration of resources. This needs policy-based security configuration where resources are matched to a policy, not individual configuration items. Centralized *policy and standards management* becomes extremely important.

Once the policies and standards are in place, there needs to be independent reporting to ensure the enforcement of the policies and standards, and to drive behavior. Security services need to meet service levels to support applications. Centralized *reporting, analytics, and measurements* become essential for confidence in the security of your systems.

Next, we move on to decomposition into security services.

Security services

As we're limited in space, we then decompose some categories into security services, as shown in Figure 2-7. As an example, *identity lifecycle management* decomposes into four security services. They decompose down to a level you can implement primarily as a single technical component. The *joiners, movers, leavers (JML)* service is probably implemented within the HR system. The *create, modify and delete ID* service is probably part of an identity management system and will use the JML service. An *application access request* may be part of an identity management system or some other system. It will need a bit of discussion to get this right, but how services are already delivered will have a strong influence.

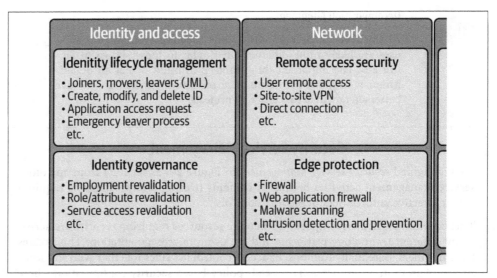

Figure 2-7. Security process or service decomposition

Modularity

We've given simple guidance on selecting the grouping of security services. If you want to get into more of a software engineering approach to modularity, we suggest you look at using cohesion, coupling, and connascence in Chapter 3 of *Fundamentals of Software Architecture* (*https://oreil.ly/-kjjt*).

Documenting an enterprise security architecture provides the organization with a standard security taxonomy with domains, categories, and services. But how else could we use the enterprise security architecture?

Security Services Responsibilities

Different teams and organizations can handle the delivery of security services. The enterprise architecture also provides a way of describing the team or organization that owns delivery of the services.

In Figure 2-8 we've split the services into three layers showing the organization or team delivering the services. The diagram shows that the cloud platform, infrastructure operations, and security operations provide different security services.

We've only shown some examples of security services, but there will be many more for your organization. If externally managed security services organizations are providing some services, there might be additional layers of responsibilities. What other additional security services could you add to this diagram for your organization?

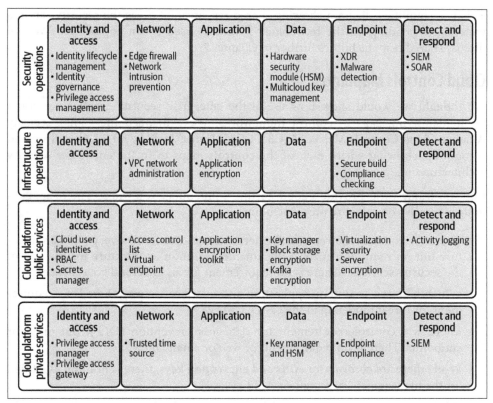

	Identity and access	Network	Application	Data	Endpoint	Detect and respond
Security operations	• Identity lifecycle management • Identity governance • Privilege access management	• Edge firewall • Network intrusion prevention		• Hardware security module (HSM) • Multicloud key management	• XDR • Malware detection	• SIEM • SOAR
Infrastructure operations		• VPC network administration	• Application encryption		• Secure build • Compliance checking	
Cloud platform public services	• Cloud user identities • RBAC • Secrets manager	• Access control list • Virtual endpoint	• Application encryption toolkit	• Key manager • Block storage encryption • Kafka encryption	• Virtualization security • Server encryption	• Activity logging
Cloud platform private services	• Privilege access manager • Privilege access gateway	• Trusted time source		• Key manager and HSM	• Endpoint compliance	• SIEM

Figure 2-8. Security services responsibility layers

With some services, there is a split between operation and administration. For example, the cloud service provider will operate the virtual private cloud (VPC) networking of the cloud platforms and make it available for the infrastructure operations team to configure and administer the cloud networking. Understanding this administration interface will define the responsibilities of the infrastructure operations team.

We've also split the cloud platform services into those that are publicly exposed and those that are private. Consumers of the cloud service will use the public services, and the private services will support the secure operation of those public services.

The solution architecture team can use this diagram to comprehend the distribution of duties within an organization and decide who they should consult with when designing the solution. We've found that documenting such a diagram reduces the need for each project to spend effort discovering the split of responsibilities and improves the effectiveness of security services for the organization.

This is a simplified diagram showing shared responsibilities, as the security services will vary depending on the technology platforms used by an application. We will discuss shared responsibilities further in Chapter 7.

Cloud Controls Mapping

We thought we would show how useful the enterprise security architecture could be at identifying gaps in control frameworks. We've mapped the Cloud Security Alliance Cloud Controls Matrix v4 (CSA CCM) (*https://oreil.ly/TjY9s*), used for cloud computing, showing where each of the controls maps to in the enterprise security architecture in Figure 2-9.[6]

Industry frameworks provide a good starting point, but as you will see, there are gaps in the controls you might require, including:

- There are control requirements for network and disaster recovery (DR) architecture but no requirement for a documented solution architecture for the rest of the security services.[7] There is no requirement for architectural governance.
- While there is a section on application and interface security, there is no requirement for threat modeling in the CSA CCM.
- There is a control requirement for data loss prevention (DLP), but only for endpoints. There is no requirement for web or email DLP.
- While there are controls for APIs and encryption keys, there is nothing identified for the management of secrets or API keys.
- While there is a requirement for logging commands, there is no explicit requirement for a bastion or jump host with the ability to video record login sessions.
- There are no control requirements for some ABBs, such as image security and remote network access.

This is a good example of why frameworks should provide guidance but not the final set of controls. Develop controls based on the legal and regulatory requirements, your assessment of the threat landscape, and the risk tolerance of your organization.

Let's move on. We've discussed how you should use services rather than processes, but how should you describe a security service?

---

6 It's a rough mapping, where it's likely you would come up with a different mapping with some more work.

7 It's one of our frustrations that there are many references to "secure by design" but little about the need to have a documented solution architecture as a part of that design.

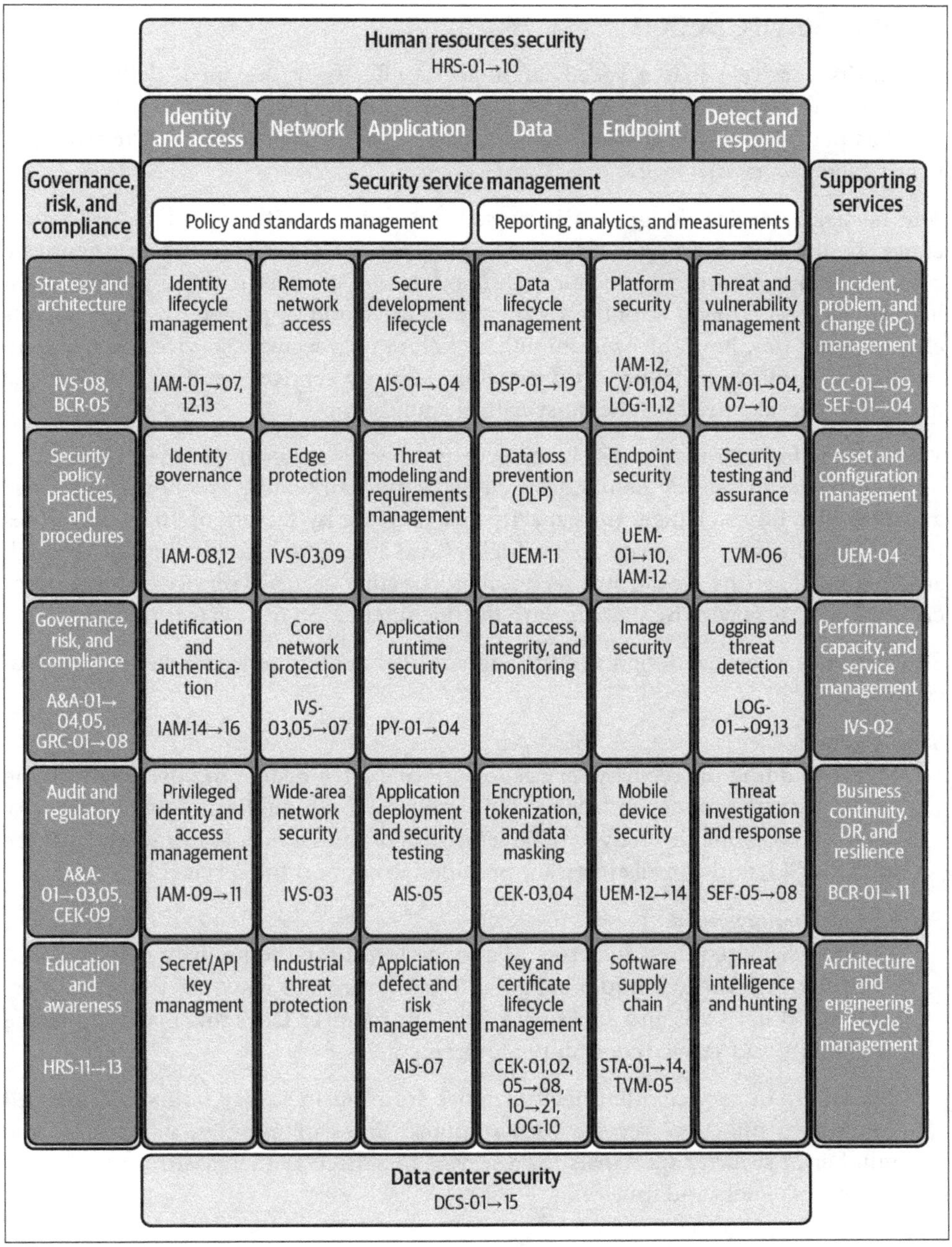

Figure 2-9. CSA CCM mapping on enterprise security architecture

Human resources security
HRS-01→10

Security service management
Policy and standards management | Reporting, analytics, and measurements

Governance, risk, and compliance	Identity and access	Network	Application	Data	Endpoint	Detect and respond	Supporting services
Strategy and architecture IVS-08, BCR-05	Identity lifecycle management IAM-01→07, 12,13	Remote network access	Secure development lifecycle AIS-01→04	Data lifecycle management DSP-01→19	Platform security IAM-12, ICV-01,04, LOG-11,12	Threat and vulnerability management TVM-01→04, 07→10	Incident, problem, and change (IPC) management CCC-01→09, SEF-01→04
Security policy, practices, and procedures	Identity governance IAM-08,12	Edge protection IVS-03,09	Threat modeling and requirements management	Data loss prevention (DLP) UEM-11	Endpoint security UEM-01→10, IAM-12	Security testing and assurance TVM-06	Asset and configuration management UEM-04
Governance, risk, and compliance A&A-01→04,05, GRC-01→08	Idetification and authentica-tion IAM-14→16	Core network protection IVS-03,05→07	Application runtime security IPY-01→04	Data access, integrity, and monitoring	Image security	Logging and threat detection LOG-01→09,13	Performance, capacity, and service management IVS-02
Audit and regulatory A&A-01→03,05, CEK-09	Privileged identity and access management IAM-09→11	Wide-area network security IVS-03	Application deployment and security testing AIS-05	Encryption, tokenization, and data masking CEK-03,04	Mobile device security UEM-12→14	Threat investigation and response SEF-05→08	Business continuity, DR, and resilience BCR-01→11
Education and awareness HRS-11→13	Secret/API key managment	Industrial threat protection	Applciation defect and risk management AIS-07	Key and certificate lifecycle management CEK-01,02, 05→08, 10→21, LOG-10	Software supply chain STA-01→14, TVM-05	Threat intelligence and hunting	Architecture and engineering lifecycle management

Data center security
DCS-01→15

Security Service Design

A security service needs a specification to be effectively designed, delivered, and operated. It's not just there to meet a set of security requirements; it's a service that has performance, resilience, support, and other architectural characteristics. It's what's called a *service design*.

The need for service design has increased dramatically with the advent of hybrid cloud. In the past, we might have used passwords or other secrets to authenticate communication between application components. A change in those secrets might happen every 12 or 24 months (if at all). With cloud applications, these secrets change every day, hour, or even minute. A failure of a security service can cause an immediate application failure, and therefore security services need security service quality to meet the needs of the most critical application.

We've seen this come as a shock to security operations teams as they struggle to respond to the increasing demands of cloud native workloads. The hours of service and response times change, the capacity can increase by factors of 10 or 100 times today, and the service needs to be highly available and recover rapidly through automation. For this reason, we recommend treating security services as any other critical business service by starting with the documentation of a service design.

So what does a service design need to include? Let's continue with a list of topics to consider:[8]

Service catalog
> Start by adding the security service to a service catalog, defining the details of the service, status, and dependencies. This applies to both public and private security services. Describe the delivery characteristics of the service. For example, is there an API, CLI, and console interface provided to support the service?

Service level management
> Define what's required in terms of service levels for the security service. Who will provide level 1, 2, and 3 support? What hours and response times will they operate? What skills and experience will staff require? Does this match up to the availability and service continuity requirements?

> The hours of service often need to move from business day hours with on call support to full 24×7 service with response times of minutes, not hours. The number of security specialists for a service may need to increase from two to six to cover sickness and time off.

---

8 We left security and compliance management out of this list as it's the core of the architectural thinking for security method we're discussing.

The delivery of support for security services needs to use the same service management processes used by other critical business services. A security operations team must not become an island and re-create existing service management processes.

Service performance and capacity

There is a need to scale the security services to meet the demands of the business. We've seen existing security services not scale to meet the needs of cloud native services. It needs careful thought and planning as transaction rates increase and the hourly, daily, weekly, and monthly profiles of transaction rates vary.

Although a security operations team may wish to make things simple by hosting security services using an on-premises control plane, the increased latency and reduced capacity of stretching services may not support new types of workload.

The security services will need integration with the performance management services to monitor and alert for immediate service issues, including support for short-, medium-, and long-term planning.

Service availability

A security service needs to meet availability targets in support of the availability targets for the workloads it supports. Establishment of service level objectives (SLOs) enables the development of the architecture for the service.

Consider the hours of service and what level of downtime is acceptable for the service. The availability characteristics of the workloads and the impact of loss of the service influence the availability characteristics. Consider if you can have downtime for updates of the service such as security patches. In Chapter 5, we discuss creating a data classification scheme for availability, and based on the classification, we can assign a set of availability and continuity requirements.

Service continuity

Service continuity considers what happens when (not if) the service has an outage. What's the recovery time objective (RTO) and recovery point objective (RPO) needed to meet the availability characteristics of the service? Like availability, use a data classification scheme to define the service continuity requirements.

The security service is likely to require instant failover within local data centers or availability zones. But what happens when there is a regional failure? How quickly must the security service recover in a remote location to support the workloads?

An application may require recovery within 30 minutes, but to do that, it may need 5 minutes of recovery time with no loss of data from a secrets manager service. With hybrid cloud computing, the security service architect needs a broad range of skills to understand the different storage and database architectures available.

In summary, a security capability is a service that requires consideration of service levels, performance, capacity, availability, and continuity in addition to security, risk, and compliance. Let's wrap up this chapter.

Summary

We started this chapter by understanding the role of architectural thinking in the development lifecycle. Being able to communicate its importance will equip you with the skills to fight your corner when it comes to including architectural thinking in a project. Included in the discussion was the difference between an MVP and a PoC, which will enable you to identify the danger signs when an MVP is in reality a PoC.

Remember that both consultants and architects, each with different skills and experience, have a critical role in projects. Consultants are there to discover and develop the business requirements to meet the needs of the stakeholders. They could be internal to an organization or brought in from an external professional services organization. An architect continues by expanding the non-functional requirements or architectural characteristics, then developing an architecture to meet those requirements for communication with those in engineering roles.

Throughout this book, we often refer to just an architect, and that's because security is the responsibility of all information systems architects, not just the security architect. A security architect is there to advise as a subject matter expert (SME) and focus on the architectural thinking for the security services.

It's important that your organization has a standard way to decompose and communicate the problem space for security. We discussed an enterprise security architecture and our approach to its construction, which should give you some ideas for your own. Ensure you think about security services, not just capabilities, when you are developing your own enterprise security architecture.

Now that we've discussed the role of architectural thinking in the development lifecycle and the use of an enterprise security architecture, the next chapter will continue by thinking about the external and internal sources of security requirements.

Exercises

1. What characteristics does design thinking have? Select all that apply.

   a. It uses experimentation.

   b. It is an iterative process.

   c. It focuses on non-functional requirements.

   d. It is an empathetic, human-centered process.

2. True or False: A team is starting the testing for the core business functionality of an application where testing the non-functional requirements is out of scope. After testing, the system is ready to be considered a minimum viable product (MVP).

   a. True

   b. False

3. What does Grady Booch say about architecture? Select all that apply.

   a. All architecture is design, but not all design is architecture.

   b. Design represents the set of significant decisions that shape the form and function of a system.

   c. The cost of implementation is a metric for important architecture decisions.

   d. Significant design decisions are measured by the cost of the requirement definition.

4. True or False: A consultant can design a resilient, scalable, available, adaptable, secure, and compliant system using architectural thinking.

   a. True

   b. False

5. True or false: Specifying firewall rules is an example of an architectural thinking activity.

   a. True

   b. False

6. True or false: Architectural thinking doesn't apply to DevOps, as there is no need to consider architectural characteristics.

   a. True

   b. False

7. An enterprise architecture has which of the following characteristics? Select all that apply.

    a. Provides alignment with business objectives and goals

    b. Is described using System Building Blocks (SBBs)

    c. Provides a holistic view of architecture for an organization

    d. Provides a vendor-specific architecture

8. A solution architecture has which of the following characteristics? Select all that apply.

    a. It solves a business problem using an information system.

    b. It only provides a conceptual view of a system.

    c. It describes how specific technologies deliver the system's capabilities.

    d. It's guided by architecture patterns, enterprise architecture, and enterprise processes.

9. Which of the following is true about the NIST Core Zero Trust Architecture?

    a. A Policy Enforcement Point (PEP) makes policy decisions based on the type of enterprise resource and the identity management policy.

    b. Enterprise resources include data, cloud resources, and administrators.

    c. A Policy Engine (PE) makes security decisions based on the kind of enterprise resource and the access policy.

    d. Administration of the security policies is part of the Policy Enforcement Administrator (PEA).

10. The term service should be used for security capabilities rather than alignment to a process or control framework because _____. Select all that apply.

    a. A service consists of technology, processes, and people.

    b. They need only control requirements to define the capabilities.

    c. Service design is required to ensure the quality of delivery.

    d. A service often delivers requirements from a single section of an industry control framework.

11. True or false: An industry control framework is a definitive source for specifying security control requirements.

    a. True

    b. False

PART II
Plan

The plan phase is where we discuss obtaining requirements from the enterprise context, covering both external and internal contexts. We elaborate on how we translate this into a requirements catalog documenting functional and non-functional requirements and how we establish requirement traceability.

CHAPTER 3

Enterprise Context

When starting to architect a solution, the architect starts to gather requirements external to the organization and internally as a part of enterprise governance. The requirements can often become inflexible constraints on the design, delivery, and operation of the infrastructure and application.

External factors such as laws and regulations include mandatory security, privacy, and compliance requirements for organizations to implement. Industry and professional organizations also offer best practices and standards for the design and operation of the information system.

Internally, there are many documents that govern the design and delivery of an information systems architecture, including security policies, practices, guiding principles, and an enterprise architecture. Their role is to support the consistent and effective enforcement of security controls and information systems across the organization.

For a comprehensive security architecture, a product, project, or program needs to consider both external and internal factors that guide the design and implementation of a solution architecture. This chapter will expand on many of these topics and show how the external and internal context can help support the delivery of effective security and compliance across an organization.

All the contextual information discussed in this chapter should ideally already exist at the top level of an organization to help you integrate security into a solution architecture. However, there may be gaps in the contextual information that will require filling in, and you may also need to assess how useful the contextual information is for the development of your architecture.

Chapter Artifacts

This chapter's main goal is to discuss the external and internal context of an organization and sources of information used to design security for a solution architecture. The artifact dependency diagram, shown in Figure 3-1, highlights, with white text in a black shaded box, the artifacts for discussion in this chapter. The *enterprise context* splits into two groups of artifacts labeled the *external context* and *internal context*.

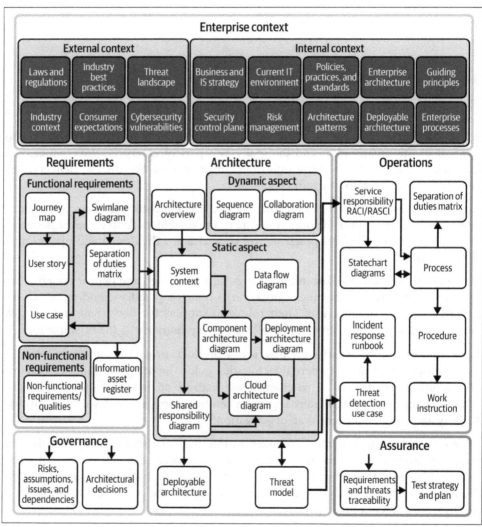

Figure 3-1. Enterprise context chapter artifacts

We're going to start with the *external context* and then follow that with the *internal context*.

External Context

There are many external influences that mandate or provide guidance for the design, delivery, and operation of security and compliance. This first major section will examine the external context by discussing the following topics:

- Laws and Regulations
- Industry or Expert Organization Best Practices
- Corporate Expectations
- Consumer Expectations
- Threat Landscape
- Cybersecurity Vulnerabilities

We will discuss each of these topics, including how they might impact your solution architecture and how you might use them during your architectural thinking, starting with laws and regulations.

Laws and Regulations

Governments and other organizations develop laws and regulations for security, privacy, and resilience to keep people, organizations, and society safe from possible risks, breaches, and weaknesses. They provide rules, guidelines, and protections to keep sensitive information private, safe, and available while information systems are processing it.

Laws are broad rules that are a legally binding and enforceable component of a country's legal system to ensure organizations and individuals meet certain standards. They provide protection through the legal system, and not complying can have serious repercussions such as fines, penalties, or even criminal sanctions. They differ from country to country and also have regional variations, such as those found in each state of the US.

In general, laws are stable and adapt slowly to changing social, economic, and technological conditions. Legislative bodies, such as parliaments or congresses, enact new laws and revise existing ones in response to new societal needs, advances in knowledge, and emerging challenges, such as critical infrastructure, cloud, and AI.

Laws often require regulatory organizations and governmental organizations to ensure adherence to particular guidelines or requirements. The regulatory bodies often play an important role in legal interpretation, implementation, enforcement, and adjudication. They develop regulations that are more detailed and provide specific, practical instructions and guidelines on how to comply with the laws. They typically address technical, operational, or administrative issues. Their creation often involves public input, stakeholder consultations, and industry expert opinions.

Laws and regulations that aren't made for security might have an impact on information security. For example, the Sarbanes Oxley Act (*https://sarbanes-oxley-act.com*) of 2002 in the US contains provisions for financial reporting, corporate governance, risk management, and auditing of public companies as a response to fraud and institutional failures. This resulted in increased information security obligations on organizations.

In general, the inclusion of laws and regulations about security, privacy, and resilience falls within the following five domains:

Data protection and privacy
> Data protection and privacy legislation exists to secure sensitive personal information while also protecting an individual's right to privacy. There are numerous data protection and privacy laws that specify how organizations must collect, use, store, and share personal information. These laws require organizations to acquire consent from individuals, implement security measures, and provide individuals with the ability to view, modify, and delete personal data.
>
> In the European Union, the General Data Protection Regulation (GDPR) (*https://gdpr.eu*) defines the control requirements. In the United States, each state is creating its own laws, creating a patchwork of different protections. At the time of this writing, the California Consumer Privacy Act (CCPA) (*https://oreil.ly/WZEv6*) is leading the way in setting standards for privacy in the US.
>
> Ensure you understand not only the laws for a country or region related to the storage of the data but also where access is coming from and where the data flows. If IT support or development originates from a remote country, export of the data will happen if the display of data takes place on the screen of the IT support personnel. This is a complex area, and getting legal advice is highly recommended to ensure the right legal agreements and controls are in place.

Breach notification
> Many jurisdictions have laws mandating organizations notify individuals and the proper authorities in the case of a data breach or security incident. These laws usually specify the timing, content, and method of notification. The goal is to promote transparency and provide affected individuals with the opportunity to act to protect themselves.
>
> The GDPR mandates breach notification to individuals within 72 hours of discovery. The CCPA doesn't give a specific time but does say a notification must take place as soon as possible without unreasonable delay.

Understand the breach notification requirements for the data processing jurisdictions and implement the appropriate technology, processes, and personnel to meet these needs.

Cybercrime and law enforcement

Cybercrime legislation is primarily concerned with criminalizing cybercrime activities such as hacking, unauthorized access, data theft, fraud, and other destructive acts. It creates legal frameworks for prosecuting offenders and determining the consequences. These regulations also make it easier for law enforcement authorities to collaborate in the fight against cybercrime threats.

In the United States, the Computer Fraud and Abuse Act (CFAA) (*https://oreil.ly/rSlSW*) is a federal law enacted in 1986 that criminalizes various forms of unauthorized access, computer fraud, and related activities. In Europe, the NIS2 Directive (*https://oreil.ly/umEbE*) includes guidelines on cross-border collaboration for information exchange and notification of cyber incidents.

These laws or regulations often result in the creation of national Computer Security Incident Response Team (CSIRT) organizations that support companies in responding to threats and investigating security incidents. Make sure it's clear how the incident management process of your organization integrates with national CSIRT organizations.

Critical infrastructure protection

Many countries have laws that support the protection of critical infrastructure, such as energy, transportation, healthcare, and finance, because they know how important it is to protect essential services. These laws often add additional security requirements, risk assessments, incident reporting requirements, and ways to share information to make critical systems more secure and reliable.

In Europe, the NIS2 Directive aims to enhance the security and resilience of critical infrastructure and digital services across the EU. In the US, for the electric power industry, the Department of Homeland Security has developed the Critical Infrastructure Protection (CIP) Standards. It provides cybersecurity requirements and measures to protect the security and resilience of the power grid.

Ensure you understand whether the classification of the system you are architecting could be critical national infrastructure and the resulting legislation that applies.

Operational resiliency

In recent years, operational resilience has emerged as a critical risk for financial institutions to manage. They must follow guidelines for protecting, detecting, containing, recovering from, and repairing incidents involving information systems. The publication of guidelines on how to report incidents, test operational resilience, and monitor third-party risk has heightened interest in this sector.

In Europe, the recent Digital Operational Resilience Act (DORA) has become a focus for financial services organizations and has created much debate on its application to cloud workloads.

Make sure you understand whether the system you are architecting has any operational resilience laws and regulations that might apply.

During our discussion of security, privacy, and resilience domains, we gave examples of laws, regulations, and standards that may apply. Ensure you understand what laws and regulations apply based on the location of data processing, transportation, and access.

Many laws and regulations provide guidance rather than specific controls, and it's up to the organization to interpret them based on its own risk tolerance before defining specific security controls to protect data and meet the needs of its business. The organization then adds additional controls to meet its risk appetite, as many laws and regulations only require a minimum baseline set of controls. For global organizations that want to deploy global security controls, this creates a challenge to show compliance with many laws and regulations.

The Chief Information Security Officer (CISO) and their team should have already incorporated these laws and regulations into the organization's policies, practices, and processes for architecting security for information systems.

As an architect, you normally don't need to do this work, but what if your organization doesn't have suitable policies, practices, and processes? You should then look at using industry guidelines, standards, and frameworks, as they will identify many of the controls you need. Further research may determine the need for additional legal and regulatory controls.

Following on from the laws and regulations there is a need for further in-depth guidance. This is where industry or expert organization best practices come in.

Industry or Expert Organization Best Practices

As we discussed previously, laws and regulations provide high-level guidance but aren't necessarily directly implementable by an organization. Organizations obtain further guidance from industry or expert organizations that issue further guidelines, standards, and other control documentation to help accelerate the definition of specific security controls. They're often developed through consensus and used to form a baseline for security controls within an organization.

In general, industry or expert best practices cover the following four areas:

Expert organization best practices

Expert organizations have created best practices based on industry consensus. One example is the Center for Internet Security (CIS) (*https://www.cisecurity.org*), which has created Critical Security Controls (*https://oreil.ly/0iZ1n*) to provide a prescriptive, prioritized, and simplified set of best practices for cybersecurity. The Cloud Security Alliance (CSA) (*https://oreil.ly/F7wQi*) has created a Cloud Controls Matrix (CCM) (*https://oreil.ly/vyZ-A*) for security in a cloud context. These control frameworks are applicable to most organizations and are a good starting point if you have no security controls framework or policy. They provide high-level requirements and broadly map to a set of security services but without detailed requirements, making them easy to use.

Expert organization standards or benchmarks

Other organizations have created standards that define the security configuration for specific software. The Center for Internet Security (*https://www.cisecurity.org*) (CIS) has created benchmarks (*https://oreil.ly/EPiIl*) for cloud providers, operating systems, server software, desktop software, DevSecOps tools, mobile devices, and multifunction print devices. NIST has a catalog of Security Technical Implementation Guides (STIGs) or benchmarks in the NIST National Checklist Program (*https://oreil.ly/xBjbc*) repository. Benchmark definitions may use the Security Content Automation Protocol (SCAP), which many tools support to check the compliance of software. As an architect, you need to build the system to support benchmarks and tooling to enable ongoing compliance.

National standards organizations

At a national level, the US National Institute of Standards and Technology (NIST) has created the Cybersecurity Framework (*https://oreil.ly/6Kq9N*), with "a set of activities to achieve specific cybersecurity *outcomes*, and references examples of guidance to achieve those outcomes." The core comprises four elements: functions, categories, subcategories, and informative references. In the new v2.0 framework, there are six functions that form the primary pillars of a successful and holistic cybersecurity program. The v2.0 release lists the core functions as:

Govern

The organization's cybersecurity risk management strategy, expectations, and policy are established, communicated, and monitored.

Identify

The organization's current cybersecurity risks are understood.

Protect

Safeguards to manage the organization's cybersecurity risks are used.

Detect

Possible cybersecurity attacks and compromises are found and analyzed.

Respond

Actions regarding a detected cybersecurity incident are taken.

Recover

Assets and operations affected by a cybersecurity incident are restored.

Many other countries, including Canada, the United Kingdom, Australia, Japan, and the EU, have embraced, referenced, or taken inspiration from the NIST Cybersecurity Framework.

The NIST Cybersecurity Framework is high-level and broadly maps to a set of security services without specific requirements. If you wish to have a more detailed list of control requirements, NIST SP800-53r5 Security and Privacy Controls for Information Systems and Organizations (*https://oreil.ly/pwGJ_*) provides a detailed catalog of control requirements with implementation guidance. It's also available using the Open Security Controls Assessment Language (OSCAL) (*https://oreil.ly/Zrm6c*) to automate compliance checking of controls.

Industry standards

Specific industries also develop security control frameworks and standards to which organizations must adhere. A good example is the Payment Card Industry Data Security Standard (PCI DSS) (*https://oreil.ly/lVV3-*) from the PCI Security Standards Council, which is a set of controls any organization involved in processing payments must comply with. More broadly, the examination of financial organizations in the US uses the Federal Financial Institutions Examination Council's (FFIEC) IT Examination Handbook (*https://oreil.ly/Rs-Is*).

ISO/IEC 27001 Information System Management System

Looking at this list, you may be thinking, "Where's ISO/IEC 27001? (*https://oreil.ly/KT4GT*)" We left this standard out because its focus is on an information security management system rather than a set of controls for a hybrid cloud architecture. ISO/IEC 27001 provides standards for the organization of a CISO team that will provide enterprise policies, practices, and procedures to guide an architect designing a solution architecture. More than likely, your organization and cloud service providers will need to comply, but that's not the focus of this book.

All these industry and expert standards can create confusion, as sometimes it's unclear where to start. If you are an architect who doesn't have a security policy or framework available in your organization, the standards from the CSA, CIS, and NIST are great places to start to form a catalog of requirements for your solution.

However, all standards are incomplete and they provide a minimum baseline that requires additional risk-based controls suitable for the protection of data for an organization and workload.

If you have multiple security frameworks and standards to comply with, you may have to merge these different control requirements into a single baseline set of control requirements for your project. For example, an organization may need to be compliant with the control requirements of the countries it does business in. A combined framework can support the consistent implementation of controls and ongoing compliance. We will talk later in this chapter about a service-based approach to doing this.

Even if an organization meets required legal and regulatory requirements, and uses industry standards, there may be an expectation for more confidence in the security and privacy controls.

Corporate Expectations

Organizations want to trade with partners that protect their data and the data of their customers. As a minimum, they expect organizations to meet standard control frameworks and standards for their industry, country, or state before they start adding their own control requirements.

Larger organizations use control frameworks and standards for their industry, but smaller organizations also have schemes to support consumer confidence. Schemes such as Cyber Essentials (*https://oreil.ly/5m3gk*) from the UK National Cyber Security Centre (NCSC) and Essential Eight (*https://oreil.ly/RDONO*) from the Australian Cyber Security Centre (ACSC) provide confidence in the security of services by enabling organizations to demonstrate the implementation of a core set of controls.

To show more extensive compliance, service providers will use external audits and certifications from independent organizations to demonstrate the depth of their controls. Compliance pages for the main cloud providers show a mix of global, regional, government, and industry programs; these providers include AWS (*https://oreil.ly/dXKVi*), Azure (*https://oreil.ly/AEj0u*), Google Cloud Platform (GCP) (*https://oreil.ly/XSSm9*) and IBM Cloud (*https://oreil.ly/k8Aue*).

As a security architect, a software as a service (SaaS) provider may need to meet different control frameworks and standards. The third-party risk from cloud service providers and their suppliers will be an important consideration in meeting legal and regulatory requirements. Compliance and audit reports provide some assurance, but often the security will depend on the way you architect the system to integrate cloud security services. There are also external factors, such as threats and vulnerabilities, that you will be less in control of but need to consider.

Unfortunately, these standards are proliferating, with organizations having to meet standards for every country in which they operate. Each has a slightly different set of controls and certifications, adding to the cost of doing business in each country.[1]

Consumer Expectations

Consumer or user expectations about the security and privacy of online applications can also shape the security and compliance of organizations. They expect the encryption of their data and the protection of their privacy. Some will avoid sites that don't have multi-factor authentication. Some consumers prefer using an online application with visible assurance that demonstrates the safeguarding of their security and privacy.

Demonstrating high levels of security contributes to increased trust in the service and the organization that supports it. Schemes like Cyber Essentials and Essential Eight are designed to improve the security of small businesses and the confidence of their customers in the effectiveness of the data protection implementation.

Threat Landscape

The external threat landscape will guide the choice of security controls for an information system. Many factors will come into play in assessing the threat to a specific organization, such as the industry of the organization, the country of hosting, the technology components used, and the level of exposure to the internet.

Performing research on the threat landscape can help you make better decisions on protection mechanisms that need to be in place. There are many government, industry, and expert reports available to review and identify the top threats to focus on. If you are in an industry using specialist technology, such as operational technology, ensure you review threat landscape reports specific to your industry.

The European Union Agency for Cybersecurity (ENISA) Threat Landscape (ETL) report for 2022 (*https://oreil.ly/bjgfN*) identified the top eight threat groupings, including ransomware, malware, social engineering, threats against data, threats against availability, disinformation and misinformation, and supply chain targeting. As an architect, review these threats from the latest reports and consider what control mechanisms are in place to protect your solution from these threats.

To understand more specific threats to your organization, threat research companies can search the dark web and threat actor internet sites for chatter specific to your

---

1 Even within a single trading bloc like the EU, each country has its own set of security controls that require compliance. The number of control frameworks is still expanding and is being used to protect countries' own local companies from suppliers outside their country. We can only hope control frameworks and certifications consolidate.

organization. For more prominent organizations or where information has a high value, this will be a useful step to understand any further steps needed to protect an information system.

We will discuss more about the threats and threat modeling in Chapter 6. Threats also come from vulnerabilities within the technology the system is using.

Cybersecurity Vulnerabilities

The technology components used in building an information system are highly likely to contain vulnerabilities for consideration in the design of a solution architecture. It may be as simple as ensuring patching of the software and firmware. However, it may require adaptation of the architecture to close vulnerabilities and provide defense in depth.[2] A useful source of software vulnerabilities for specific software is the MITRE Common Vulnerabilities and Exposures (CVE) database (*https://www.cve.org*).

It's important that the technology be rapidly patched to mitigate any zero-day vulnerabilities that may come to light during the operation of the system. An architect must identify the processes, technology, and operations team that will ensure the information system will remain secure. It may be that there is already an operations infrastructure to support patching of common technology components, but support isn't always available for patching all technologies, and this will become part of your solution architecture to close this gap.

Using a hybrid cloud architecture brings new threats from the complexity of using different technologies, the range of platforms, the differing service models, and the industry of the workloads. The technology architected on top of the cloud platform is under your control, and patching the cloud platform is the responsibility of the cloud service provider. However, it's not always clear, and it's important you understand what they patch and their impact on your architecture. You may not have control of their patching, and as a result, you may need to make your solution resilient to availability zone outages and automatic recovery after an update to the cloud platform.

Now that we've completed our discussion on the external context, let's continue with a discussion of the internal context.

Internal Context

There are many internal policies, standards, guidelines, and architecture documentation that guide the design, delivery, and operation of security and compliance. This section will examine the internal context by discussing the following topics:

---

2 See "Guiding Principles" on page 80 for a discussion.

- Business and Information Systems Strategy
- Current IT Environment and Security Control Plane
- Policies, Practices, and Standards
- Risk Management
- Enterprise Architecture
- Guiding Principles
- Architecture Patterns and Automation
- Enterprise Processes

We will discuss each of these topics, including how they might impact your solution architecture and how you might handle them during your architectural thinking. Let's start by discussing the influence of business and information systems strategy.

The Role of a Technical Leader

You may think some topics we discuss relate to a project manager and aren't in your remit. However, an architect is often *the* technical leader for a project and a subject matter expert. The role requires the identification of project technical activities and a close working relationship with the project manager to ensure inclusion in the project planning. Have a read of *The Software Architect Elevator* (*https://oreil.ly/DtnT7*) (O'Reilly) by Gregor Hohpe to understand the extended role of the architect to "join the dots" across the organization.

Business and Information Systems Strategy

The business and information systems strategy for the organization has an influence on the architecture of a solution. Read the annual report for your organization and you may find some strategy topics included. They may help support the case to implement security and compliance controls for the system.

Let's start with some business strategy areas to watch out for:

Vision and mission
The vision and mission set the overall aspirations of the organization and the purpose of the organization to enable delivery. For example, the organization may be targeting business-to-business rather than the consumer market. Does that change the external control framework you need to comply with?

Market analysis

A market analysis will look at the market for your organization, customer segments, and competitors. How does your organization compare to your competitors? Have they had a recent data breach? What could you learn from that? How could you increase clients' confidence that it won't happen to your organization?

Value proposition

The value proposition may identify how your organization wants to stand out. Is there something in the value proposition that you need to consider? For example, there may be an objective to be a "trusted" organization. How could security, privacy, and compliance help with this? Perhaps completing an external audit or obtaining a security certificate demonstrating the security of the system.

Strategic goals and initiatives

Are there specific projects in delivery that have an impact on your project? You may need to align with some ongoing projects, or a project may deliver a capability you need. Perhaps an update of the security policy is in progress? Or a new supplier compliance framework is in development that your managed security services supplier must comply with.

From an information systems (IS) strategy and enterprise architecture perspective, some areas to look out for include:

Alignment with business goals

An information systems strategy should start with the alignment of IS with the business strategy. This section of the IS strategy will contain some topics we discussed in business strategy but might give further insight on the implementation.

Technology vision

The technology vision may require the use of specific technologies or a transformation to a new technology platform that may require a change in dimensions for security services as the technology changes. For example, if the organization is moving from primarily monolithic applications using waterfall development techniques to a container-based architecture using Agile working practices, there is a need for a new architecture with a new set of security services.

Infrastructure and architecture

What existing security infrastructure exists, and are there any required architecture patterns for adoption? Are there enterprise processes, procedures, and standards for adoption by the security services?

IT operations and service management
> What processes for IT operations and service management will security services need to integrate with? Your organization is likely to require security projects to use the standard incident, problem, and change (IPC) processes.[3]

Data strategy
> More recently, the new role of Chief Data Officer (CDO) has been to oversee the processes and solutions that an organization uses to process data. You may need to take their guidance into account when including security in your solution architecture.

As an architect for a project, it's not just the specific requirements of the project that you need to take into consideration but also the other internal strategies and architecture that influence the project. Take time to understand the influences they bring.

Current IT Environment and Security Control Plane

It's unlikely you will have complete freedom to select the technology components, as the technology used within the current IT environment will guide and constrain the delivery of services. With security you'll need to ask yourself, where's the *security control plane*? In other words, where are all the security services and their management tooling hosted? The location for the hosting of the security services can have an impact on the running of the workloads or applications. Don't assume the current location of the security services is suitable for your project.

We've seen the hosting of security services in an on-premises data center, with communications stretched to each of the cloud platforms. When stretching services from on-premises to a cloud platform, what if there was a failure in the network between the control plane and the cloud platform? If the hosting of encryption keys is on premise, how long will it be before the workloads fail to operate? Does the architecture of the security services compromise the availability requirements for the workloads? Is an alternative architecture required? You need to balance the security controls with other risk aspects and the capability to deliver the workloads.

Another consideration is the latency between the control plane and the running workloads. If the security services are synchronous, is it going to slow the operation of the workload? If there is a unique encryption key for every transaction, what's the impact of a 10 ms latency versus a 2 ms latency with a cloud native security service? You may need to adapt the security services to meet workload needs.

---

3 If you are creating your own IPC processes for security operations, then we would suggest you reconsider. We've seen a security operations team bypass standard change review processes and impact all servers across the whole organization. They failed to perform a risk-based deployment approach by testing and performing staged deployments.

An alternative might be to have a distributed security control plane with resiliency or latency-sensitive security services hosted within the cloud platform and less critical or less frequently used components in an on-premises data center. Some organizations use the point of presence (PoP) or network location data center, connecting the on-premises data center with the cloud, to make the control plane independent of both the on-premises data centers and the cloud platforms. Another option would be a co-location data center near cloud data centers.

The security services may have a predefined location, but consider the architectural characteristics of the workloads consuming the security services to understand the potential risks.

Policies, Practices, and Standards

It's likely the CISO team from your organization has combined the external laws and regulations we discussed earlier with the culture, values, threat landscape, and risk tolerance of an organization to guide the development of policies, practices, and standards for security and compliance. An organization with a strong security culture is more likely to prioritize and invest in robust security controls, while others may resist the deployment of more costly and constraining controls.

To develop a solution architecture, you need to understand the policies, practices, and standards that will guide the deployment of security controls in the solution architecture you are designing. In our earlier discussions, we talked about the use of an enterprise architecture and the definition of security services. The security services will identify the integration points for your solution. The security guidelines and standards will guide the engineering aspects of solution delivery.

There is likely to be a controls checklist for the project, and you will need to complete a mapping demonstrating how you will deliver the controls. If you already have a set of predefined security services, a significant number of controls should already be predefined, and you will need to define how the services will integrate with your solution.

Don't just consider applying a baseline set of security policies, practices, and standards. You also need to consider risk-based security controls.

Risk Management

Risk management processes for an organization may require additional security controls for an information system. They may identify the organization-level threats and risks that systems need to mitigate based on the risk landscape. Review the organization's risk register for risks relevant to the information system architecture.

As well as suggesting additional controls, the risk management process may temporarily accept the risk of a security control not immediately applied to a system. Due to a dependency on another project to deliver a security service, there may be a delay in control implementation. It may also be that in the early stages of deployment, and the risk doesn't justify the cost of implementation.

Threat modeling enables the identification of risks specific to the solution architecture and there is a discussion of this is in Chapter 6.

Enterprise Architecture

The enterprise architecture (EA) of an organization enables the alignment of an organization's business objectives and goals with its IT infrastructure and resources. The practice provides a strategic perspective with longer-term guidance, enabling organizational alignment. There may be an overall enterprise architecture or an enterprise security architecture you need to consider in developing your solution architecture. We discussed the enterprise architecture and some techniques in "Enterprise and Solution Architecture" on page 39. Refresh your understanding and review how this might impact your design.

Guiding Principles

A set of guiding principles can inform the application of security to a solution architecture. They offer values and beliefs that act as a foundation for choosing what to do and how to do it. They provide a framework for an organization to make architectural decisions.

Typically, an organization will establish enterprise-level security guiding principles for projects when designing security for a solution architecture. These principles aid in directing the design and implementation of the architectural thought process for integrating security into solutions. The project may also add additional principles that are more specific to the context of the project.

Here are some security guiding principles that your organization may already use and can be a starting point if they don't already exist:

Defense in depth
> The principle of *defense in depth* refers to the practice of deploying multiple layers of security controls (defense) against potential threats or attacks within a given information system. Its purpose is to provide redundant levels of defense so that if a security control fails or exploitation of a vulnerability occurs, the system will continue to protect the information assets. The layers of defense encompass human, technical, physical, and process security controls. A multi-layered approach provides a more robust and resilient defense strategy.
>
> For example, the removal of malware occurs at multiple points using capabilities such as a firewall, an email gateway, a web gateway, and an endpoint. Typically, different capabilities come from different technology suppliers. If one supplier

offers a solution with a security flaw, another supplier may offer an effective technology that prevents a threat actor from exploiting the first flaw.

Least privilege

The principle of *least privilege* dictates that every component or user must have only the permissions or privileges necessary to carry out its intended function. There can be a tendency for the builders of systems to grant extensive privileges as a quick way to get information systems operational.

For example, the permissions for a toolchain may give it the right to administer all user IDs, which it doesn't need, which would give an unprivileged user the ability to create users and add new privileges for themselves.

Over time, in the management of a system, the assignment of temporary privileges or permissions for a change or temporary role may happen that aren't removed, resulting in permission creep. Routine reviews of permissions to detect permission creep ensure the enforcement of least privilege.

Minimize attack surface

The principle of *minimize attack surface* is the practice of minimizing an information system's potential points of vulnerability and attack. The number of potential entry points for an attacker to compromise a system serves as a measure of the attack surface. Reducing the attack surface can make an attack more difficult.

We can use a few essential techniques to reduce the attack surface:

Remove unused and vulnerable services and functionality

Disabling or, ideally, eliminating services that are insecure or unused can reduce the attack surface. For example, when you uninstall the FTP service from an operating system, it removes the possibility of an attacker using the service. Baseline security standards or benchmarks, as discussed in "Industry or Expert Organization Best Practices" on page 70, are a good starting point. You should use continuous compliance checks to verify that capabilities aren't reinstalled or re-enabled.

Regularly patch and update

Updating software with security patches and improving security functionality can reduce the number of vulnerabilities that attackers can exploit. You should use continuous compliance checks to verify that applied software updates aren't removed.

Network segmentation

Dividing the network into segments, or subnets, reduces the attack surface if an attacker gains access to one segment. It becomes more difficult to traverse from one component within a segment to another component within another segment. This technique started with simple three-tier network segments shared by multiple applications and progressed to microsegmentation, which we discuss later in this chapter and in Chapter 8.

Secure coding practices

Developers can avoid coding vulnerabilities when they develop software by following good coding practices. Software developers should use techniques such as input validation, session management, and cryptographic practices to reduce the attack surface. We will be talking more about this in Chapter 10.

Separation of duties[4]

The principle of *separation of duties* involves dividing privileged tasks between multiple individuals or roles to prevent conflicts of interest and unauthorized actions. We use the approach to reduce the risk of disclosing secrets, making errors, committing fraud, and engaging in malicious activities. A single individual shouldn't have full access to perform a business-critical process. The process should require multiple parties to complete its execution.

Here are some key use cases for using separation of duties:

Prevention of fraud

Using separation of duties reduces the potential for fraud. For example, the person who approves the request for a financial transaction shouldn't be the same person or someone in the same role as the person who initiated the transaction. It would therefore need collusion for an illegal financial transaction to take place.

Security controls compromise

Separation of duties is often used as a way of ensuring an individual can't compromise the security of a system. For example, the requester of access can't approve access to a system, or using multiple key holders in a key ceremony for the initialization of a hardware security module (HSM) ensures the secrecy of the master key.

Quality assurance

Having multiple people or roles in a transaction can improve the quality of the process. For example, in code development, the person who reviews and approves the check-in of code is separate from the person who developed and checked in the code.

---

4 We use separation rather than segregation as the latter has an association with racial discrimination and social injustice. The word separation is more neutral and less controversial.

We will be talking about the design of processes to enforce separation of duties in Chapter 4.

Zero trust

The principles of *zero trust* revolve around the idea of not automatically trusting any user, device, or system attempting to access a network or its resources. We've discussed this in Chapters 1 and 2 and will further discuss applying the practices in Chapters 6 and 8.

Microsegmentation

Microsegmentation is the practice of partitioning a network into smaller, more discrete zones using granular security policies and access controls. It recognizes that various application components have different security needs and risk profiles, rather than treating the entire network or an application layer as a single entity. Every layer of each application has its own network segment, rather than sharing layers between applications.

The principle ensures that security breaches or compromises in one segment don't automatically spread to other components by isolating the network segments. This containment helps lessen the impact of a security breach.

By default, network access controls restrict traffic, and we establish explicit rules to allow traffic only as needed. By ensuring that entities (users, devices, or applications) only have access to the resources necessary to perform their role, these access controls uphold the principle of least privilege.

We will be talking further about how to apply this principle to hybrid cloud infrastructure in Chapter 8.

Secure by default

Architects and engineers should prioritize security from the initial design and configuration through deployment by following the principle of *secure by default* in systems, software, and technologies. By default, the configuration of a system or piece of software should provide a high level of security without requiring the user or administrator to make additional modifications or settings.

The goal of *secure by default* is to reduce the risk from potential vulnerabilities by ensuring that a system's or software's default configuration complies with security best practices and implements strong security measures. Even if users aren't actively aware of or involved in the security configuration process, the system or software helps to protect them and their data by providing a secure default state.

We will be talking more about security in development in Chapter 10.

Secure by design

The principle of *secure by design* is an approach to designing and developing information systems, software products, or services with a strong focus on integrating security measures from the start of the design process. The principle aims to embed security as an integral part of system design rather than treat it as an afterthought or add-on feature.

This principle is often associated with threat modeling and secure engineering practices during software development. The method we discuss in this book is about a set of techniques and artifacts that extend this principle into an integrated architectural thinking method for the integration of complex systems.

KISS

The KISS principle stands for *keep it simple, stupid*. According to this principle, most systems perform better when they're kept simple rather than made complex. Therefore, architects should prioritize simplicity as a primary goal and strive to avoid complexity whenever possible.

We often see the incorporation of more and more controls in security, where managing integration becomes increasingly complex. It creates a greater risk of misconfiguration and limited resources with the skills to operate the security services 24×7. Using a smaller number of controls and operating them more effectively may be a better strategy.

Always keep KISS in mind. Ask yourself: If I add this new control, will I add more risk to the solution than the control mitigates?

Open design

The principle of *open design* refers to an approach that promotes transparency, collaboration, and the sharing of the security solution for external review. It's the opposite of security by obscurity, where the security of the system relies on hiding the design and implementation.

Experience has shown that enabling a wider review of a solution has enabled the identification of weaknesses or vulnerabilities. This has been especially valuable in the cryptography community, where algorithms are open to review across the wider community to identify potential weaknesses.

Making design information, blueprints, specifications, and other design components openly available to a larger community is a key component of open design. It promotes the involvement of many stakeholders and enables group feedback and advancement. It doesn't mean you need to publish it on the internet, but make sure you get a wide ranging review of the solution.

We've now discussed a set of security guiding principles at the organizational or enterprise level. It will be your role to add context to each principle and apply them to the solution you're working on. Projects may also define guiding principles specific to their project. We will discuss this further in Chapter 9.

Architecture Patterns and Automation

Solution architectures in an organization that follow guiding principles and industry best practices are similar to each other. They will have consistent controls implemented for securing data and enabling easier integration between applications. For these reasons, often the organization will create a set of architecture patterns for reuse across the enterprise to accelerate the development of an effective security solution.

Architecture patterns can also have corresponding automation to enable rapid deployment of solutions. In our artifact dependency diagram, we use the artifact *Deployable Architecture* to represent the automation of an architecture pattern. We will expand on architecture patterns and deployable architectures in Chapter 9.

Enterprise Processes

Policies, guidelines, and practices provide useful guidance for static controls, but for describing a sequence of activities, tasks, and workflows, there is a need for *enterprise processes*. Processes define the order of activities performed, the roles that need to perform the activities, control points to perform checks, and activities recorded for an audit trail.

ISO 9001:2015 Quality Management Principle 4 (*https://oreil.ly/Xxt6r*) defines an approach by considering an organization as a set of activities described through processes, procedures, and work instructions. A process defines the activities performed and why. You can apply processes to a broad range of different contexts, as they don't define how you will complete the activities or the individual steps in performing the activities. A large enterprise will write them to be independent of technology, enabling application in a broad range of contexts and ensuring they don't change even if the technology does.

Organizations use enterprise processes because they provide quality delivery with consistency, efficiency, reduced cost, reduced interruptions, and improved risk management. They ensure processes, with the associated procedures and work instructions, include the appropriate control points and audit events to ensure compliance with the policies of the organization. The definition of security processes should ideally be organization-wide, with procedures and work instructions to implement the processes defined within a line of business.

In your development of security for a solution architecture, ensure you have a good understanding of enterprise processes and procedures you may need to comply with. We will discuss processes, procedures, and work instructions further in Chapter 11.

Summary

During this chapter, we discussed the importance of examining the external and internal context for your organization when designing security for a solution architecture. With the internal context, you may find much of the information missing. You may need to develop the missing content and make assumptions to enable the development of a solution architecture, including security and compliance.

Earlier in the chapter, we discussed the secure by design principle. Often, the impression given is that the design of an information system only needs secure by design thinking, even for the most complex of mission-critical systems, whereas architectural thinking is also needed.

For example, secure by design guidance, such as the joint Security by Design guidance (*https://oreil.ly/DgFlB*), is more applicable to individual engineering at the level of compute, network, or storage components. However, it doesn't guide the architecture design for the integration of the different components together when integrating a complex system.

The following chapters will discuss a series of techniques and artifacts that will enable architectural thinking for secure design in the development of a hybrid cloud workload. We will continue the discussion with the documentation of requirements that will form the foundation of the ongoing architectural thinking.

Exercises

1. What are the characteristics of laws and regulations? Select all that apply.

   a. Provide a minimum baseline

   b. Always apply globally

   c. Provide guidance

   d. Vary depending on location

2. Which of the following frameworks provides a detailed catalog of security control requirements?

   a. Center for Internet Security (CIS) Critical Security Controls (CSC)

   b. Cloud Security Alliance (CSA) Cloud Controls Matrix (CCM)

   c. NIST Cybersecurity Framework

   d. NIST SP 800-53 Security and Privacy Controls for Information Systems and Organizations

3. What should a business strategy contain that may influence the application of security? Select all that apply.

   a. Vision and mission

   b. Technology vision

   c. Value proposition

   d. Data strategy

4. Where could I locate the security control plane if I wanted it independent of the data centers hosting the workload or application? Select all that apply.

   a. In a cloud data center

   b. In a network point of presence (PoP) data center

   c. In an on-premises data center

   d. In a co-location data center

5. What are the key use cases for separation of duties? Select all that apply.

   a. Prevention of fraud

   b. Security control compromise

   c. Separation of assurance

   d. Quality assurance

6. What's the security principle that delivers a high level of security configuration without requiring additional modifications or settings?

    a. Secure by design

    b. Zero trust

    c. Secure by default

    d. Defense in depth

7. A security process has which of the following characteristics? Select all that apply.

    a. It defines how activities will be completed.

    b. It is independent of technology.

    c. It assigns activities to roles.

    d. It defines control points.

CHAPTER 4

Requirements and Constraints

Requirements for an information system give a specification or description of the functional capabilities a system should deliver, along with characteristics or qualities it should adopt. Mandatory external and internal demands placed on a system turn requirements into constraints.

People often use non-functional requirements, architectural characteristics, and qualities interchangeably. They all refer to the same sort of requirements that define the approach to system delivery. We will discuss this further later in this chapter.

Documentation of requirements happens in different forms, depending on the type of requirement and the types of development and delivery methods. In this chapter, we will discuss the different techniques and focus on those techniques that are most appropriate for the definition of security requirements.

Finally, we will look at how traceability of requirements through the documentation of the architecture, operational documentation, and testing is essential to providing confidence in the delivery and operation of the requirements.

Chapter Artifacts

This chapter's main goal is to discuss the definition and documentation of security requirements for a system. Figure 4-1 highlights, with white text in a black shaded box, across the top of the artifact dependency diagram the requirements and constraints that come from the external and internal context of the organization. In the requirements domain, we highlight artifacts for the definition of functional and non-functional requirements, with the requirements traceability matrix highlighted at the bottom right.

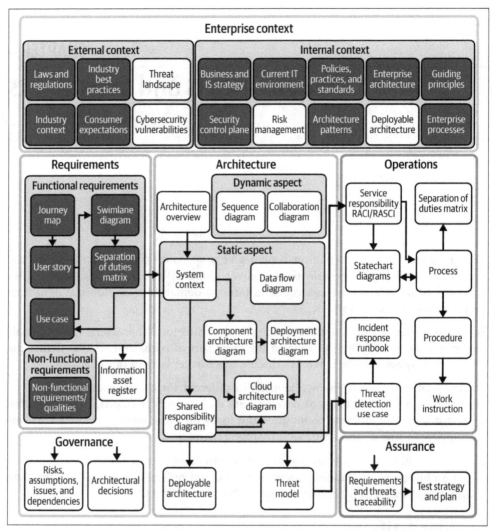

Figure 4-1. Requirements and constraints chapter artifact dependency diagram

We're going to start with a discussion on some concepts about requirements that will frame the discussion of the artifacts used to describe requirements.

Requirements Concepts

Requirements give a description of what an information system must deliver and offer guidance for the development of a solution architecture. They specify the functionality, architecture characteristics, and constraints of a system. Let's discuss this in a bit more detail.

Functional Requirements

Functional requirements describe *what* an information system is to deliver. In other words, they define the functional aspects of the information system as delivered by software. Functional requirements describe the sequence of activities, when they start and end, the inputs and outputs, and the behavior and processing of the data.

The second characteristic of functional requirements is that they describe the primary functionality provided by the system, such as placing an order for a product online. For security, this could be describing the sequence of steps for a customer to log into an online store but not the login sequence for the system administrator, which is a non-functional requirement. However, the techniques and artifacts used in describing the requirements can be the same for both.

Security can bring additional perspectives to consider when describing functional requirements. What are the decisions that affect the security of the system? How do we record activities to provide an audit trail? How do we monitor for activities that may be a threat to the system?

As an architect, you may be thinking that gathering requirements is the job of a business analyst or a security consultant. Even if someone else gathers those requirements, you will be accountable for the security architecture, and therefore you need to ensure that you receive complete and high-quality requirements.

When you have the complete context, you need to be able to challenge and modify non-security requirements, as they may have a negative impact on other characteristics of the system. Examples of this might be whether the application uses multifactor authentication for login and whether it's mandatory for authenticating certain transactions.

Non-Functional Requirements

Non-functional requirements describe *how* the information system should deliver the required functionality. They're often described as the *architecture characteristics* of the system and include security, privacy, scalability, availability, recoverability, usability, and many other characteristics.

You will find that many non-functional requirements apply to the overall system rather than specific parts of it. The non-functional requirement in Table 4-1 shows a requirement that applies to the whole system.

Table 4-1. System-wide non-functional requirement

ID	Requirement
NFR_SEC_AU_001	A change of all authentication credentials used in system-to-system communication MUST take place every 30 days.

Many non-functional requirements are included in control frameworks, security policies, and practices. You may end up with hundreds of these enterprise-wide, detailed requirements.

However, other non-functional requirements will be specific to the delivery of a capability in your solution architecture. The non-functional requirement in Table 4-2 shows a requirement that applies to a specific component of a system.

Table 4-2. Single capability non-functional requirement

ID	Requirement
NFR_SEC_FW_001	The edge firewall MUST support a peak application transaction rate of 1,000 active connections and 10 MB/sec outbound.

Characteristics, Qualities, or Non-Functional Requirements

Organizations use different terms to describe non-functional requirements, such as *architectural characteristics* or *quality properties.*

In Chapter 4 of *Fundamentals of Software Architecture*, Richards and Ford make the case for the use of the term *architectural characteristics* because the term non-functional requirements is self-denigrating. In other words, it could suggest that non-functional requirements aren't as important as functional requirements. This is far from the truth, as using non-functional requirements to describe the implementation of functional requirements is just as important.

ISO/IEC 25010:2023 on systems and software engineering (*https://oreil.ly/sfxga*) uses the term *product quality properties*, which consist of eight categories of characteristics:

- Functional suitability
- Performance efficiency
- Compatibility
- Usability
- Reliability

- Security
- Maintainability
- Portability

The security category contains subcharacteristics such as confidentiality, integrity, availability, non-repudiation, accountability, and authenticity. This should look like a familiar list to you. However, the eight categories they use are a small subset of what falls within the scope of non-functional requirements.

We're sticking with the term non-functional requirements, as architectural characteristics seems to imply that they're not requirements, and the qualities described by ISO 25010:2023 are just a small part of the scope of non-functional requirements. Just be aware that when you read different publications, they may refer to non-functional requirements using different terms.

Let's now discuss some categories of non-functional requirements (or architectural characteristics) that are important to architectural thinking for secure design:

Security

Security is normally expressed as the requirement to protect data from loss of confidentiality, integrity, and availability. You could say security is more of a family of architectural characteristics. From them, you can derive other requirements. Protection from loss of confidentiality requires identification and authentication to support accountability.

Many of these requirements come from policies, standards, and guidelines for the organization, but external industry standards specific to the application may add additional requirements. For example, an organization may require the use of at least transport layer security (TLS) 1.2, but the external standard requires TLS 1.3, which may then constrain the technology components used in the solution.

Collect the applicable policies, standards, and guidelines together at the start of a project and identify the control requirements that may cause you problems in terms of compliance. Add those to your list of risks or issues for management in your project. We will further discuss managing project risks and issues later in Chapter 10.

Privacy

With privacy enabled, an individual or group can protect themselves or information about themselves to control what information is publicly exposed. The domain of security, which encompasses concepts such as appropriate disclosure of information, somewhat interconnects with privacy.

As discussed in Chapter 3, privacy is important to consider for the protection of sensitive personal information. There may be laws or regulations, such as GDPR, that derived requirements will come from.

Scalability

Scalability is the ability of an information system to increase its compute, storage, and networking capacity. If the system doesn't scale, it can result in a loss of availability. It's an important consideration for an architect developing a solution for a security service. If a security service can't scale to meet the growth of customers, this could result in an outage of the overall system.

For example, the design of a privileged access management system may be for the infrequent retrieval of passwords when booting a server. The frequency greatly increases in a container environment and unless the service scales, it can cause a denial of service, impacting the availability of the service. You need to architect scalability from the start, together with ongoing planning from the security operations team. The inclusion of performance and capacity management becomes an important part of the solution for a privileged access management solution.

Availability

Availability focuses on keeping an information system available. With the move to cloud native applications that require continuous availability of security services, this becomes more important to the design of security services.

In the past, we might have rebooted an encrypted server every few months. The loss of a key management server would not have had an immediate impact and a reschedule of a server reboot could take place. In a container environment rebooted every few minutes or seconds, a key required for container startup becomes critical. There would be an immediate impact from the loss of a key manager.

For this reason, security services often need to have availability characteristics exceeding those of the applications they're supporting. You may need to consider keeping a security service available even after multiple failures of the infrastructure have occurred. The security operations team may need to move from on-call support with response times of hours to 24×7 support with response times of minutes.

Recoverability

Recoverability is the ability to recover data, services, and operations rapidly after a disruption to a service. We've discussed how critical security services become in the discussion on scalability and availability. It follows that recovery of the service is critical, especially due to the change in compute architecture to cloud native container applications.

In the recovery of a data center, security services will often need to be priority for recovery to enable the subsequent recovery of applications. Ensure backups are complete, data is synchronized, and recovery is regularly tested to guarantee you meet the needs of the dependent applications.

There are two key measurements for recovery: recovery point objective (RPO) and recovery time objective (RTO). RPO is the extent of the data loss when a failure occurs with an information system. Ideally, this is none, but when copying the data to a remote site with significant latency, the use of synchronous data replication may not be possible and asynchronous replication will result in data loss. Consider how you handle the data loss.

The RTO represents the time taken to recover from a failure. If the application has to recover within 30 minutes, the dependent security services may only have 10 minutes to recover, leaving 20 minutes for the application to recover. This may require the improvement of the availability characteristics to handle multiple component failures and increase the resilience of the security services.

Locking Your Keys in the Car

In the recovery of security services, you need to consider the recovery sequence. The retrieval of keys may not be possible unless storage has already completed decryption. For example, it could be that the reboot of the firewall can't take place as it enables communication with the HSM required to decrypt the boot disk of the firewall. If there isn't a different method to retrieve the keys, we can't resolve this circular dependency. This is the *keys locked in the car* scenario, where you can't open the car because of the keys locked inside. The same consideration needs to take place with secrets management and certificate management.

Usability

Usability is the ease with which a user or operator interacts with an information system. With security, it's particularly important because if the barrier to usability is too great, users will try to work around the security control placed in their way.

For example, the rules for reuse of a password have increased in sophistication over the years as users find a way to make it easy to remember their passwords. Another example is cumbersome identity verification processes that result in users providing false information to bypass the controls.

When adding security, think about whether it will promote behaviors that add additional vulnerabilities or bypass of controls.

Software Architecture Characteristics

We haven't tried to list all categories of non-functional requirements. Have a look in Chapter 4 of *Fundamentals of Software Architecture (https://oreil.ly/-kjjt)* for a more extensive discussion of architecture characteristics and the different categories of architecture characteristics (also known as non-functional requirements).

Security is often described as a non-functional requirement, but in reality, security is also specified through functional requirements. A login sequence for an application will require functionality to identify and authenticate the user before accessing the application. An example of a non-functional requirement associated with the functional requirement for the login of a user is in Table 4-3.

Table 4-3. Non-functional requirement

ID	Requirement
NFR_SEC_IA_001	The login sequence MUST take no more than 30 seconds to complete if 70% of the users start a login sequence between 8:30 a.m. and 9:30 a.m. on a business day.

It can get even more confusing because a security requirement can be both functional and non-functional, depending on the context. The key difference is that a functional requirement is about the *primary functionality* of the application, whereas non-functional requirements are about how the delivery of the functionality takes place.

For example, the requirement for identification and authentication of a customer is a functional requirement for the user interface of an online store, whereas the requirement for identification and authentication of all internal system-to-system connections is a non-functional requirement. With the first requirement, the system can't meet the primary system functionality without it, but with the second requirement, the system can meet all functional requirements with unauthenticated system-to-system connections.

Constraints

Many requirements become constraints on the solution architecture. Start with consideration of the external laws, regulations, and standards, as they become mandatory requirements for your solution. You will then consider these constraints through the normal requirements gathering process.

However, there are many other constraints created by the current IT environment and selected software components that may be less obvious and take work to discover. These include the following four important areas:

Software versions

Software version dependencies come from the underlying operating systems and middleware. You may get into a "deadly embrace" where your application software only supports an old unsupported library and an upgrade is impossible because the company that supplied the software no longer exists. This has the impact that the upgrade of all other software that depends on the unsupported library isn't possible. The security vulnerabilities will then increase over time and you may need to find additional security controls to mitigate the risk.

When you are architecting a system that has predefined software components, make sure the dependencies of all the software components line up in terms of their versions and dependent software components.

Security protocols

Even if supported versions of software components exist, the protocols may not align. For example, the TLS protocol, used for session-level encryption, has received upgrades to address newly identified vulnerabilities. Although your security standards may require TLS 1.3, the software may only support TLS v1.2 and lower. It could become even more difficult if interfacing software depreciates older protocols or ciphers and doesn't support TLS v1.2, so they can't integrate.

You will need to perform a check of the integration points to ensure the software protocols align. You may need to record risks for older protocols with vulnerabilities and mitigation put in place to prevent the exploitation of potential vulnerabilities. In this case, you may wrap the TLS in an Internet Protocol Security (IPsec) virtual private network (VPN) or encrypt the payload inside the TLS session.

API versions

With the use of REST APIs in many cloud services there is a need to version control for the development of new capabilities and vulnerability removal. The software integrating with the APIs needs updates to support new APIs as the depreciation of older APIs takes place. You have no choice but to make these changes as the change in versions isn't under your control.

If your security services rely on cloud APIs to implement security controls, ensure you have thought about the ongoing support for upgrading to new APIs. This consideration for ongoing support exists across all security services and is a significant risk that will need additional work during the development of your solution architecture.

Agent incompatibility

Security requires many different software agents for detecting threats, checking compliance, or performing configuration. Version incompatibilities may mean you can't install the agents on an older version of the operating system. This is an important consideration during your product selection.

Another challenge is the use of security appliances that can't support security agents, such as enterprise detection and response (EDR) agents. These security appliances then become a risk as monitoring for threats can't take place. Often, these appliances are just a version of Linux that would support the agents but the suppliers don't want to allow it for their support purposes. You may need to apply compensating controls.

As you can see from this discussion, there are many constraints that come out of the current IT environment and the software components selected as a part of the architectural thinking process. These investigations may result in new requirements or updates to the project risks, issues, assumptions, and dependencies that we will discuss managing in Chapter 9.

The next step is to consider how we might ensure the quality of the requirements we document.

Specifying Quality Requirements

We need to ensure that the definition of quality requirements is part of our architectural thinking process. One approach is to use the SMART framework. SMART refers to making requirements specific, measurable, attainable, relevant, and time-bound:[1]

Specific
Requirements must clearly specify the needs of the business. They must be clear, consistent, simple, unambiguous, and at an appropriate level of detail. A good starting point is to use the Five Ws: ask who, what, when, where, and why. They can help you define the problem more clearly so you can be more specific in your requirement definition.

Measurable
The construction of requirements must be such that it's possible to verify their implementation. Non-functional requirements often should be quantifiable and enable measurement of progress toward achievement. Ask yourself: Can you create a test for the requirement? Part of verification is through traceability of requirements, including testing, which we will discuss later in this chapter.

Attainable
The requirement should be technically feasible and be possible within the constraints of your solution architecture. Ask subject matter experts on the specific

---

1 There are many different definitions of what SMART stands for. We've chosen this definition because we believe it delivers the best quality security and compliance requirements.

technology solution to review the requirements. Check whether there has been successful delivery of the requirement before. If not, how sure are you that it's achievable? Perhaps record a risk or assumption in the project RAID log to track any concerns. We will discuss this artifact in Chapter 10.

Relevant[2]

Requirements must align with the overall business objectives and result in a valuable outcome. These requirements may pertain to the primary functionality or the security and compliance needs essential for conducting business. Be careful not to add security requirements that are outside the needs of the business or don't match the risk tolerance of the organization.

Time-bound[3]

The requirement should clearly specify when the capability is to be in place to ensure the alignment of the project team. Should the threat detection system be in place even for the start of the proof of concept, or can it wait until six months after the system has gone into production? The timescales may need a documented rationale through an architectural decision record. We will talk about how to document an architectural decision record in Chapter 9.

We've specified specific, measurable, and relevant criteria as a *must*, as all requirements should meet these criteria. Whereas attainable and time-bound criteria use *should*, as they can depend on the later definition of the overall dependencies, priorities, and risks of the overall project. Considering the requirements as a whole can enable a better assessment of these criteria.

Let's have a look at a couple of examples, starting with a poorly specified requirement in Table 4-4.

Table 4-4. Poorly specified requirement

ID	Requirement
REQ_1	An alert should immediately be raised with the relevant team for ransomware.

---

2 Sometimes the R in SMART is defined as *reasonable*. The criterion is to validate that the requirement has the appropriate resources to deliver the solution. We don't use that, as reasonable timescales are included in the time-bound criterion and then the overall requirement is tested for reasonableness as a part of prioritizing requirements.

3 Sometimes the T in SMART is *traceable*. Traceability of requirements through requirements specification, solution architecture, implementation, and testing is more related to ensuring the quality of requirements implementation than the quality of the written requirement itself. We will talk about the traceability of requirements later in this chapter.

It's not specific, as it doesn't specify who should raise the alert. How quick is immediate? We don't know who the "relevant team" is. What does "for ransomware" mean? It's not measurable because it's not specific enough. We have no idea whether it's attainable or relevant, as it's not well specified. Time isn't included. It fails to meet any of the quality criteria.

We've also demonstrated how not to label a requirement. Using the label REQ_1 doesn't give us an idea of what domain the requirement is from, and using 1 rather than 001 makes it difficult to sort.

Then we've created a well-specified requirement in Table 4-5.[4]

Table 4-5. Well-specified requirement

ID	Requirement
NFR_SEC_TD_001	The threat detection system MUST be in place before the system contains client data to issue an alert to the security operations center (SOC) within 15 minutes on the detection of event patterns that could indicate potential ransomware.

The requirement tells us the component that raises the alert and who will receive it. It's more specific in that it's about the detection of event patterns that could indicate potential ransomware. The patterns will be part of the detailed specification. It's time-bound by defining when threat detection needs to be in place. It's measurable, as within 15 minutes of detection, the alert needs raising. The requirement is relevant given its threat, which is a real risk to the organization.

How long it takes to detect the threat is difficult to specify, and defining additional requirements specifying the types of attack detection is an improvement. We can't tell whether it's attainable as we don't have the project context. It's a vast improvement over the first requirement.

You will notice the requirement has a complex sentence construction. Not every requirement will meet all these criteria, but they provide a quality checklist to see if you have missed documenting different aspects of a solution. The application of criteria may vary across different requirements. For example, the expression of the time-bound criterion may be in a single requirement that then applies to multiple requirements specifying the functionality.

We've also labeled the requirement in a better format. NFR stands for Non-Functional Requirement, SEC is for the group of security requirements, TD is for Threat Detection, and 001 is a sortable number.

Now that we have clear requirements, how could we prioritize them?

---

4 We're sure you could improve the requirement, given more context and time.

Prioritizing Requirements

We often end up with a long list of requirements for the solution architecture. While the implementation of some requirements is immediate, for others, the implementation priority can be within a specific time period.

For a minimum viable project (MVP), we *must* provide a username and password for identification and authentication and *could* offer multi-factor authentication if there is sufficient time. Another example is, with a small number of consumers of the service, we could decide that we *must* offer an RTO of 48 hours to start and *could* offer an RTO of 4 hours if we've had sufficient time to implement it.

One commonly used technique for prioritizing requirements is the MoSCoW method, where the capital letters represent:

Must have
> The project will implement the requirement. The completion of the project can't take place without the delivery of the requirements categorized as *Must*.

Should have
> The project will attempt to implement the requirement within the time given but may not have time to do so.

Could have
> The project could implement, but won't necessarily implement, the requirement. More than likely, the implementation of the requirement won't happen.

Would or Won't have[5]
> This could mean the project *would have* the requirement included if there was time, but it's not critical. An alternative is to sometimes specify a project *won't* implement a requirement. Perhaps because the requirement would introduce additional cost or complexity and needs to be explicitly excluded from a solution to ensure it doesn't get implemented.

Let's give some examples of prioritized requirements based on two sprints of a project, as shown in Table 4-6.

---

5 The authors prefer the use of *won't*, as any requirements that are not implemented based on lower priority are likely to be categorized as *Could have*. Sometimes you may need to specify that a requirement won't be implemented because you know someone who wants the requirement outside of the immediate project and you want to make it clear that the requirement must not be implemented.

Table 4-6. Prioritized requirements

Reference	Sprint 1	Sprint 2	Requirement
REQ_SEC_1	MUST	MUST	All users MUST be identified and authenticated before given access to the system.
REQ_SEC_2	SHOULD	MUST	All users MUST be authenticated using multi-factor authentication.
REQ_SEC_3	COULD	SHOULD	All users MUST be presented with a legal warning about unauthorized use of the system.

The table shows three requirements related to the identification and authentication of a user by a system with phased implementation. There must always be identification and authentication, with multi-factor authentication next and a legal notice coming later.

Now that we have a way of assessing the quality of requirements and a way of prioritizing them, let's move on to the specification of requirements, starting with functional requirements.

Specifying Functional Requirements

There are many different ways of specifying functional requirements. Writing functional requirements can be as simple as something the system will provide, such as in Table 4-7.

Table 4-7. Example use case description

ID	Requirement
FR_SEC_IA_001	The system will identify and authenticate a user using a username and password.

However, this doesn't describe the sequence of activities or the actors engaged in the activities. In this section, we're going to introduce a selection of different techniques, show the artifact, and discuss their use in the context of specifying functional requirements.

We will discuss the following techniques:

- Use cases
- Journey maps
- User stories
- Swimlane diagrams
- Separation of duties matrices

Use cases, a technique developed in the 1980s by Ivar Jacobson, who later codeveloped the Unified Modeling Language (UML), will be our starting point.

Use Cases

A *use case* is a description of system interactions by human and system actors. We will identify use cases as part of defining the system context diagram in Chapter 5. They need further description through the use of a UML use case diagram and use case descriptions.

We can use a UML use case diagram to visualize the behavior of a system with a box representing the system or subsystem boundary, people representing the human and system actors, and the use cases inside the box. We've taken a subset of the actors and use cases from the case study to show a use case diagram in Figure 4-2.

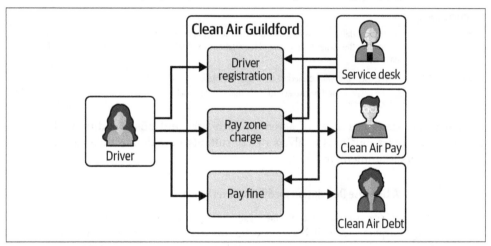

Figure 4-2. Case study UML use case diagram

The diagram shows the involvement of actors in each use case, but we need some more detail about the use case. We can document them either as an informal description or in a prescribed template, such as shown in Table 4-8.

Table 4-8. Case study use case description

Name of use case:	Driver registration
Description:	Register the driver details and the vehicles they own
Actors:	Driver
Preconditions:	1. The driver must not be registered already
Flow:	1. Register a username and password for the portal
	2. A validation email is sent to the driver
	3. The driver clicks on the link to validate the email
	4. The driver logs in again
	5. The driver registers name, address, and mobile phone
	6. The driver registers the vehicles that they own
	7. The driver registers a payment card to charge the fee
	8. Logout of the portal
Postconditions:	None
Exceptions	In step 1, if the driver has already registered the user interface will say "unable to register" and send an email to the owner telling them of the duplicate registration and guiding them to a reset of the password.
Requirements:	1. The username will be checked to check if it looks like an email address.
	2. The password will be checked to verify that it's not trivial.

Each use case describes a set of activities with pre- and post-conditions. For non-technical use cases, business analysts or consultants may define them for architects and developers to implement.

A Use Case Description for System Interaction

We've used a textual use case description, but we may also use sequence or collaboration diagrams to better describe the interaction between system actors and the system (or subsystem). We include a discussion of these artifacts in Chapter 6.

There are many security use cases for definition in every system, from the end-user application login to the reporting of a security incident. You must ensure the identification of the security-relevant actors and document their use cases.

Further UML Detail

For a more detailed description of use case diagrams, read Chapter 18 in the *Unified Modeling Language User Guide* (*https://oreil.ly/f-1aC*) (Addison-Wesley Professional) by Grady Booch, James Rumbaugh, and Ivar Jacobson.

As we discussed, use cases are interactions with a system. It becomes difficult to avoid considering a solution as part of the requirement definition. In Table 4-7, the requirement has already defined the need for a username and password. What about a passwordless system of identification and authentication? It would have been better to require multi-factor authentication as a quality and leave the solution to the architect.

As a result, in the past 20 years, there has been the development of techniques that focus on the end user. We're going to continue with a technique focused on the needs of a user, the definition of a journey map.

Journey Maps

We discussed design thinking in Chapter 2. The focus is on a human-centered approach to understanding personas (another term for actors) through their needs, pain points, and goals. One technique to better understand personas is to draw up a *journey map* to define their actions, thoughts, and feelings when engaging with a service or product. It's a more personal tool to place yourself in the position of a user or customer to understand their thoughts and emotions.

The journey map is normally created in a workshop using stickies on a wall to describe the phases, steps, feelings, and pain points. We've shown an example of a journey map in Figure 4-3 for the case study.

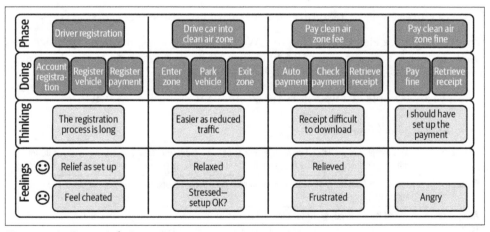

Figure 4-3. Case study journey map

A journey map is also called a user journey or scenario map with slight differences between different formats. We used the to-be scenario map format (*https://oreil.ly/ bp4lI*) from the IBM Enterprise Design Thinking method.

This technique is good for showing the end-to-end journey and getting into the head of the driver to understand their thoughts and feelings. However, a journey map doesn't offer enough detail to move into solution development and there is a need for an additional technique to decompose the problem. We'll now discuss using user stories for the next stage of development.

User Stories

In Agile development, functional requirements are often specified as a *user story*. It's a concept that comes from the eXtreme Programming methodology as a way to improve software quality and be more responsive to changing customer requirements. Users express their requirements and values through user stories. The users are those specified as human actors as a part of the system context diagram in Chapter 5 and as personas in design thinking. It provides a mechanism to communicate between the development team and the customer about the specification of the solution.

We develop user stories and put them into a catalog of stories called a *product backlog*. Based on priority, for each sprint or iteration, we move the user stories into the *sprint backlog*. The MoSCoW approach to prioritization, discussed earlier, is one way to decide which stories join the sprint backlog.

A user story is normally written in a three-part form:

As a `<role>` I want `<a feature/function>` so that I `<business reason/benefit>`.

This covers three elements of the five Ws for making a requirement specific: who, what, and why. Typically, you will add background information that provides context to the requirement and tests that determine its completion.

Let's give an example of a user story for a compliance report, as shown in Table 4-9.

Table 4-9. User story example

User story	As a compliance specialist, **I want** to be able to obtain a compliance report containing trend graphs for different perspectives **so that I** can identify the stakeholders I need to work with to close compliance gaps.
Context	This comes from the compliance team who have been doing this manually with spreadsheets and need it automated.
Acceptance tests	• Test it with trend reports for a line of business, application, technology platform, and country. • Test it with trend reports for weekly, monthly, quarterly, and yearly.

Not all users *want* to enter a username and password, and sometimes with security requirements, it's more appropriate to change the *I want* to *I'm required*, and then remove the *so that* clause. The core principle to remember is that the user story must be for a specific user role. Don't start a user story with "As a user"; a specific user needs identification.

We refer to larger user stories that may take more than one sprint as an *epic*. They often need further refinement into many user stories and are a sign that there is a need for further work to decompose the problem. As a result, some tooling defines an epic as a group of user stories rather than a large user story. It's worth agreeing on what an epic means within the team you are working with.

A *theme* is a collection of related user stories and epics organized into a group. For instance, a theme named "compliance reporting" could include stories and epics for each individual report.

Developers can easily forget about the users responsible for security and compliance when developing an application. This is why defining these actors (or users) is important in the system context diagram we will discuss in Chapter 5, as it's a good reminder that the users aren't just those for the primary business application. The overall information system also has to meet the needs of many other users, such as the "Compliance Team." In this case, we should consider that one of the primary functions of the application is to meet external regulatory requirements.

Further User Stories Detail

Further detail on applying user stories is in *User Stories Applied: For Agile Software Development* (*https://oreil.ly/0_OQs*) (Addison-Wesley Professional) by Mike Cohn.

At this point, we have a way of specifying the end-to-end user journey and functional requirements through user stories. We're missing a way of specifying the different users, how they interact, and describing the separation of duties. We therefore come back to a technique that has existed for much longer: a swimlane diagram.

Swimlane Diagrams

There are many different diagrams that describe a process flow or sequence of activities performed by an actor or user. There are flowcharts and UML activity diagrams that describe the steps in a process, but neither clearly shows roles without adding a table describing the sequence of activities.

Therefore, we use *swimlane diagrams* to describe the steps in a process, with each "swimlane" being a row or column representing the activities of an actor. The diagram enables you to show who performs what steps, the handover between actors, and decision points. The diagram can also show how to maintain separation of duties. Figure 4-4 shows an example of a swimlane diagram.

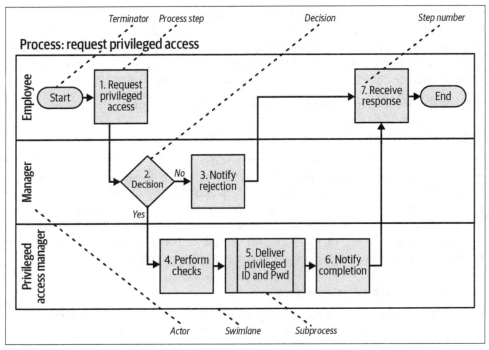

Figure 4-4. Swimlane diagram

We've used a simple set of diagram parts; you will find more complex diagrams, but you are likely to use these parts most of the time. Let's discuss the parts:

Actor
> These are the actors, personas, or users involved in the execution of the process. There can be both human and system actors as part of a system.

Swimlane
> A swimlane is a row or column holding the activities performed by an actor. They look like swimlanes in a swimming pool where swimmers stay within their own lane, which is where the name of the diagram comes from.

Terminator
> A terminator is the start or end of the described process.

Process step
> A process step is an activity performed by an actor.

Decision
> A decision occurs when someone makes a choice in the process. It's normally a two-way decision, like a yes/no or OK/not OK decision, but you could draw

the diagram with more than two options. Where there is a policy decision, the writing of an event record to a log will need to take place.

Subprocess

An individual process step may become too complex for a single diagram and a separate subprocess (or swimlane diagram) will describe the step in more detail.

Step numbers

This numbers the steps and is a useful way of referencing the steps in the process. It's a convention that swimlane diagrams should always go left-to-right or top-to-bottom, as they represent the execution of a process over time.

The swimlane diagram alone often doesn't provide sufficient description, so we require a text description in a table. Table 4-10 provides a short example with the first two steps from Figure 4-4 filled out.

Table 4-10. Swimlane diagram description

Activity	Actor	Title	Description
1.	Request privileged access	Employee	The employee starts by opening the web page for the IAM request tool and completes a request for privileged access. The request includes the ID required and a business justification for obtaining that level of access. This must be linked back to an incident, problem, or change ticket.
2.	Decision	Manager	The manager reviews the request from the employee and checks that there is sufficient justification for the access and that the requested permissions are appropriate to the activities.
n.	etc.	etc.	etc.

Note that the table includes the number of the activity, the actor, and the title, with the addition of a description. If you want to use a flowchart or UML activity diagram, this table can record the actors rather than using swimlanes.

For the next stage, we must ensure that an actor doesn't receive inappropriate rights to perform a process step. We do this with a separation of duties matrix.

Separation of Duties Matrices

In Chapter 3, we discussed separation of duties as an important guiding principle. There are many security-relevant processes where a user must not perform a combination of activities and they need to follow the separation of duties principle.

For example, a user requesting privileged user access shouldn't be able to approve their access or have the ability to issue their own privileged access. We use a separation of duties matrix to represent what they can and can't do. Figure 4-5 is an example for the swimlane diagram in Figure 4-4.

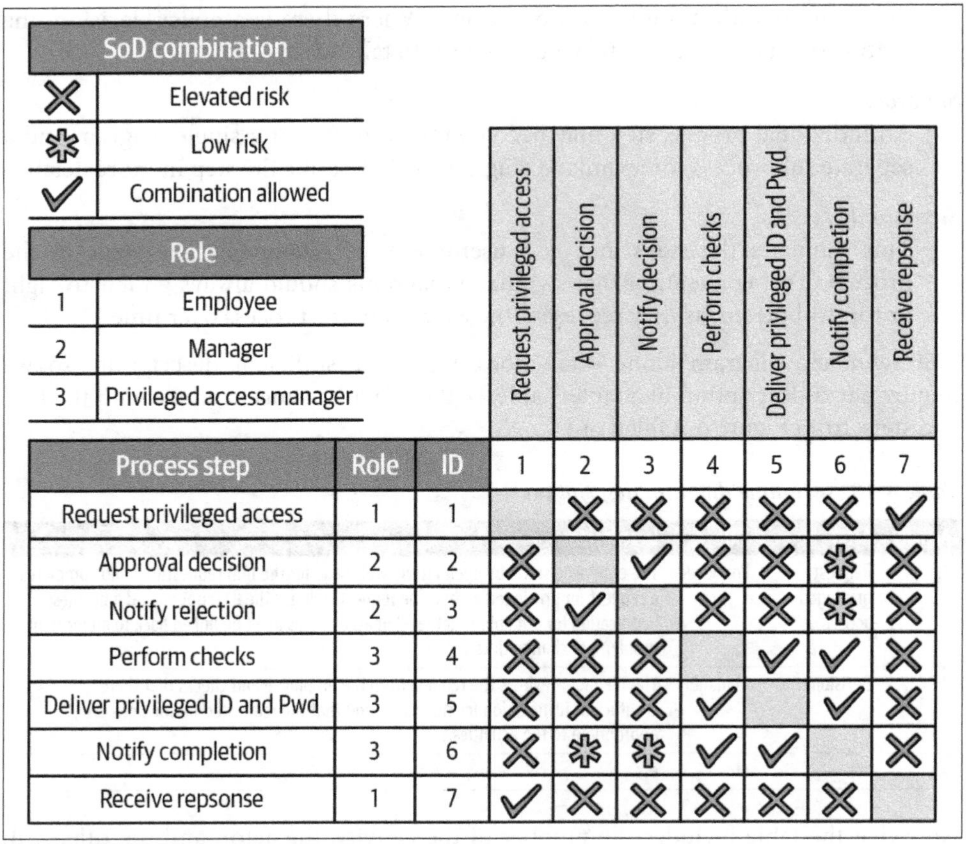

Figure 4-5. Separation of duties matrix

The parts of the diagram are:

Process step
> These are all the process steps in the swimlane diagram.

Role
> This is the number of the role, as shown by the key, that performs a process step.

ID
> The ID is the number of the process step used in the swimlane diagram. The ID is both vertical and horizontal on the matrix.

Risk matrix

In the center of the table is a 7×7 matrix showing what process steps a role can/cannot perform together. Where a combination of process steps is an elevated risk, an "X" marks a combination of activities that a role must not perform together. Where a "*" shows the combination is low risk, the role should avoid the combination. It's not a showstopper and the role could perform the combination if there was no other choice. A tick marks a combination of activities that can be performed by the same person.

So how do the functional requirements artifacts work with the case study we're using?

Case Study: Process Definition

We created a journey map for a driver in Figure 4-3, but this is too high-level and has no detail to provide functional requirements for the system. The first security-relevant activity on the journey map is driver account registration.

We've used a swimlane diagram to describe the driver account registration process as shown in Figure 4-6. We're using a vertical form of the diagram so we can display all the process steps on a portrait page without decomposing into additional swimlane diagrams.

In this example, there is a single human actor and two system actors. We've identified two technical components among the two system actors and started the architectural thinking process. We don't have multiple human actors, so we don't need a detailed separation of duties analysis.

The identity provider and email provider could be two different cloud services. We may have a requirement that the identity provider make all identity-related decisions and not the email provider. It could be that we've gained greater trust in the identity provider and don't want to spread the business logic for identity-related decisions across multiple services. An architectural decision record should document that only the identity provider will make these decisions. In this case, we can see in the swimlane diagram that the email provider only sends emails andcperforms business-logic decisions.

This is an example of a business process making security-impacting decisions. We don't have to create a swimlane diagram for every process. We suggest you document any process involved in making a security decision using a swimlane diagram to be clear about the sequence of activities and security decisions. We will show in Chapter 11 further details on process decomposition and how to document the writing of security events into an audit log.

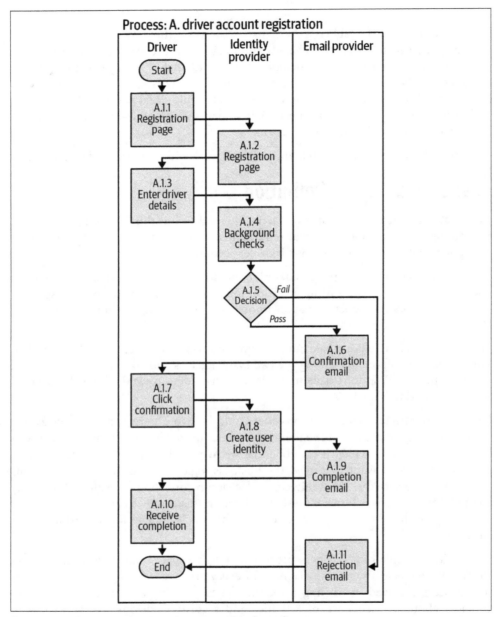

Figure 4-6. Driver account registration swimlane diagram

Now let's move on to the specification of non-functional requirements.

Specifying Non-Functional Requirements

We talked earlier about how non-functional requirements describe *how* the information system should deliver functionality. We then talked about some categories of non-functional requirements, how to measure their quality, and how to prioritize them. So where do these requirements come from, and what's the best way to record them?

Sources of Non-Functional Requirements

In Chapter 3, we talked about the external and internal sources for requirements. External laws, regulations, and industry or expert organization best practices enable an organization to develop its internal policies, standards, and guidelines. From these documents, an architect needs to extract the relevant non-functional requirements. These non-functional requirements are often constraints on your project, as they can reduce the choice of security solution. Figure 4-7 shows how the external, internal, and project contexts inform the solution architecture containing the security controls.

We discussed the external and internal context in Chapter 3. Once there is a project, we now have a project context that gives us additional requirements to work with, including the project objectives and scope. Resources, skills, tools, standards, budget, and timescale all have an influence on the solution we're considering.

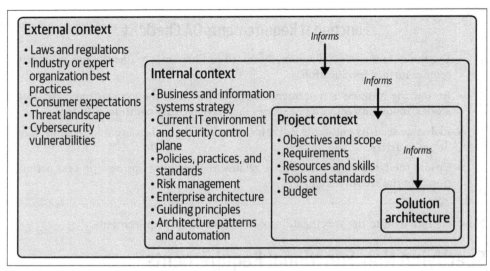

Figure 4-7. External, internal, and project context

The project context brings into consideration the project management triangle with the balancing of cost and time with scope, quality, and risk, as shown in Figure 4-8. However, the diagram shouldn't only focus on scope and quality but also consider balancing cost and time with qualities such as security, resilience, and availability.

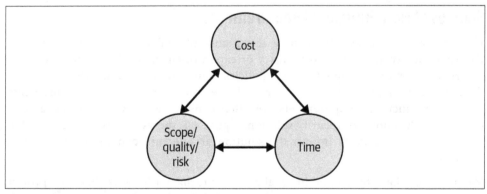

Figure 4-8. Project management triangle

This balance is something you need to consider when specifying requirements, as meeting all requirements may not be viable in terms of cost or time. You may need to look for alternative security controls that are lower-cost and have faster implementation.

Not all requirements are explicit, and so we derive implicit non-functional requirements from other sources, such as the applications or workloads the security services are securing. If an application has an RTO of eight hours, the security services may need to be available in a much shorter time in the event of a widely impacting outage. Or if an application needs to have 80% of the users log in within a short time, the security service supporting the application will need to scale to meet the needs of the application. This will result in a set of non-functional requirements for security related to availability and resilience.

Depending on the delivery of the security capabilities, you may not be in control of the security service functionality and architecture characteristics. They also become a constraint you need to work with.

Non-Functional Requirement Dependencies

You may be in control of the implementation of the security requirements through the project you control or you may have dependencies on security services delivered elsewhere. For security services delivered outside your project, you will need to assess whether those workloads can use the security services to meet the non-functional requirements of the project.

For example, if the application uses a specific technology, does the security service also support it? If not, will the workload need to change, or will you need to fill the gap? A good starting point is to obtain a list of key software components, their software versions, and the platforms they run on. The shared responsibility stack diagram we discuss in Chapter 7 helps with the analysis, as you can use it to think about the different layers of the solution for each platform.

Identifying Software Versions

In on-premises architectural thinking, the checking of software versions may have been later in the process. We've found this happens earlier in the process for hybrid cloud, with software versions requiring major changes to the architecture and operations.

For instance, the solution might require a software version or feature that the CSP doesn't support, resulting in the need to replace a cloud service with software on a virtual server. The cost is then likely to increase and the viability of the project may be in doubt. As a result, the project may decide to use an alternative service.

Even if the solution is already software rather than a service, it could be that you need to change the security software from one vendor to another. The earlier you perform a software version check, the less likely there will be the surprise of a major change in software components at a later stage.

You should work through each of the key software components, examining what security services need integration and assessing their compatibility. Some questions you might ask are:

- What are the operating systems, and are security tools like antivirus and endpoint detection and response (EDR) supported?

- Does the messaging tool require payload encryption inside the encrypted network session, and is there a security service to support it?

- Does the database need activity monitoring to detect misuse of the data by an employee or an external threat actor? Is there a supported solution?

There might be even more restrictions for cloud services regarding the services used in workloads, such as databases, and the security services, such as access control, that the cloud service provider is delivering.

Documenting Non-Functional Requirements

We've talked about where the non-functional requirements come from and the derivation of requirements from dependent technology. Earlier in this chapter, we also talked about deriving and creating quality requirements using SMART. We now need a list of requirements that we can use to demonstrate compliance with the policies and any other requirements that come from different sources. It would be simple if we could just have a single document with all the requirements listed, but that's not how it normally works.

We find the best way to approach this is to create a spreadsheet or table of all requirements and initially ignore the quality of the source requirements. Then categorize using the non-functional categories, and for security requirements, use the security domains as discussed in "Technique: Enterprise Security Architecture" on page 48. Then insert the original requirement with a reference to the source document, followed by the proposed solution and service owner of the requirement, as shown in Table 4-11.

Table 4-11. Control implementation mapping example

NFR	Domain	Category	Prio	Requirement	Ext. Ref.	Solution	Service owner
SEC	IAM	PAM_003	MUST	Rapid retrieval of privileged passwords is needed.	EXT_REF_nn	The hosting of the privileged access management (PAM) service will be on infrastructure components that are independent of the core infrastructure and will be available during a DDoS attack via a break glass remote VPN service.	Security operations manager

This gives you a format that's good if you have a single project, but if you are running a program with many projects or an organization with many projects, creating a list of requirements from all the different sources will add up to lots of duplicated effort. In this case, it's worth improving the quality of the requirements catalog. Let's review some techniques for improving the requirements.

Improving Requirement Specification

You may end up pulling requirements from different sources, resulting in a variety of different formats and qualities. If you review the control requirements from NIST SP 800-53r5 Security and Privacy Controls for Information Systems and Organizations (*https://oreil.ly/wMrey*), the requirements are policy, technology, and sector neutral, which many people would not understand, and there are parameters that need completing.

The requirements pulled together will often benefit from rewriting into a consistent set that people can understand without resulting in inconsistent interpretation. You are then able to use the high-quality requirements many times across projects or contexts.

We've developed a useful set of approaches for the derivation of a consistent and high-quality security requirements catalog for repeated use. Iteratively use each technique to derive the necessary requirements and use them in the order that best works for you.

While you are doing this, ensure you maintain a mapping between the new requirement and the original requirement. As you make changes, recheck the mapping back to the original requirement to ensure it still holds. If you reword, split, or merge requirements, they could come out of sync with the original requirements.

Let's start by sorting the requirements based on *domain* and then *category* to group related requirements. Then process the requirements in the following ways:

Reorder

Although you have sorted the requirements into groups of common types of requirements, often they only make sense in a certain sequence. For example, you may have two requirements: the first requiring authentication using multi-factor authentication, and the second requiring identification and authentication before a user accesses a system. These two requirements need swapping so that one can build on the next.

Split

You may find that you can split a requirement into multiple requirements. A requirement with "and" in the sentence is an indication of a requirement that you may need to split. For example, take the following requirement AC-2 a. from NIST SP 800-53r5. The first part is a documentation requirement, and the second part could be a requirement for a technical control enforced by tooling. Splitting the requirement into two requirements enables allocation to different teams for clear accountability, if needed:

> AC-2 a. Define and document the types of accounts allowed and specifically prohibited for use within the system.

Merge

Once you have reordered and decomposed, you may find two requirements that are effectively the same requirement. At this point, you may be able to merge them into a common requirement. Look for any subtle phrasing between the two requirements before you merge them and check back against any source requirements.

Recategorize

Sometimes a requirement may be mapped against the wrong category and need remapping. For example, NIST SP 800-53r5 states that many control families require the development of a policy, which is typically written independently of the team responsible for implementing the requirement.[6] You are likely to have a team that's accountable for all policy development. These requirements will need recategorization to a different *domain* and *category* for improved alignment with the accountable owner.

Subcategorize

You can end up with a long list of requirements that you have reordered, split, and merged. You may notice requirements come together into common themes. Grouping the requirements into further subcategories can make them easier to manage.

Dimensions

Requirements should be as neutral as possible so that, as the context and technology change, you can apply them to the appropriate scope without changing the requirements. However, there is a need for some context. For example, take the requirement SI-3 a. from NIST SP 800-53r5. It says to implement the code protection mechanism at system entry and exit. You could take this to mean only implementing a control on a server, but the implementation of this control is at many control boundaries:

> SI-3 a. Implement [Selection (one or more): signature based; non-signature based] malicious code protection mechanisms at system entry and exit points to detect and eradicate malicious code;

---

6 This is one example of why using accountability based on a control family within a control framework isn't effective. There are many other examples, but this is the most obvious example to use.

In the discussion for the control, it says, "System entry and exit points include firewalls, remote access servers, workstations, electronic mail servers, web servers, proxy servers, notebook computers, and mobile devices." This requirement needs these multiple dimensions to be explicitly documented with the requirement. Otherwise, people may misunderstand the expected scope.

As it applies to all requirements related to malicious code, we suggest you keep the dimensions of the requirement in a list independent of the requirement for referencing multiple requirements. As the dimensions change, you only need to update them once.

Parameterize

Requirement *SI-3 a.* that we used in the previous example has parameters that require filling out for the type of malicious code detection capability. As with the dimensions, we suggest you keep this list external to the requirement so you can apply the same parameters to more than one requirement if needed.

Non-align

The security industry creates lots of new terms for new capabilities and unfortunately, those terms can end up in requirements. For example, the term *smart protection*[7] used by multiple ISVs doesn't tell us what the requirement is. Is it AI-based brand protection or malware protection technology?

A requirement shouldn't lock any organization into a single product. You will need to spot these and replace them with a requirement that's not aligned with branded offerings. You may need to define your own terms and create a glossary to provide a description of the terms in the context of your organization.

Let's talk through an example to give you an idea of the improvements gained from improving the specification of a requirements catalog for use across projects.

Case Study: Specifying a Requirements Catalog

We discussed the specification of the functional requirements using a process flow and improving the quality of the requirements. In a project where the requirements aren't reused, justifying a significant effort to improve them is unlikely.

When there is a need to reuse the same set of requirements across multiple projects, improving their quality reduces the time spent discussing the meaning of poor-quality requirements. Furthermore, with requirements scattered across different security documents, it's difficult, without a single list to work through, to demonstrate compliance. In these cases, a single requirements catalog is valuable.

---

7 This has nothing to do with using the SMART approach to improving the quality of requirements.

Technical Design Authority or Architecture Board

We talk about the creation of documents for use across an organization for many projects. To do this, we need a Technical Design Authority (TDA) where technical leaders from across the organization, with varying skills and experience, come together to assess, advise, and agree on best practices. A requirements catalog is one of those artifacts they will agree to use across the whole organization. The TOGAF Standard (*https://oreil.ly/6Sjhr*) from The Open Group is a good starting point for understanding architecture governance and the roles and functions of an architecture board or TDA.

Identifying Security Requirements

The case study asks us to document the top 10 to 20 requirements for implementation as a part of the MVP. It's suggested we use the NIST Cybersecurity Framework (CSF) (*https://oreil.ly/W8asf*) as a starting point for the requirements. As an example, let's start to build the requirements for vulnerability management from the framework, as shown in Table 4-12.

Table 4-12. NIST CSF—vulnerability management

Function	Category	Subcategory	Information references
PROTECT (PR)	**Information Protection Processes and Procedures (PR.IP):** Security policies (that address purpose, scope, roles, responsibilities, management commitment, and coordination among organizational entities), processes, and procedures are maintained and used to manage protection of information systems and assets.	**PR.IP-12:** A vulnerability management plan is developed and implemented	CIS CSC 4, 18, 20 **COBIT 5** BAI03.10, DSS05.01, DSS05.02 **ISO/IEC 27001:2013** A.12.6.1, A.14.2.3, A.16.1.3, A.18.2.2, A.18.2.3 **NIST SP 800-53 Rev. 4** RA-3, RA-5, SI-2
DETECT (DE)	**Security Continuous Monitoring (DE.CM):** The information system and assets are monitored to identify cybersecurity events and verify the effectiveness of protective measures.	**DE.CM-8:** Vulnerability scans are performed	CIS CSC 4, 20 **COBIT 5** BAI03.10, DSS05.01 **ISA 62443-2-1:2009** 4.2.3.1, 4.2.3.7 **ISO/IEC 27001:2013** A.12.6.1 **NIST SP 800-53** Rev. 4 RA-5

Two subcategories within the NIST CSF, each serving different "functions," lead to the requirements. Organizations often integrate these requirements into a vulnerability management service. Note there isn't a one-to-one match between the security services and the NIST CSF functions, demonstrating you can't use the CSF functions to describe security services.

The subcategories define the "building blocks" of security in the NIST CSF but are insufficient as requirements, leaving many questions unanswered and open to interpretation. They're good for a high-level checklist but not for the specification of security requirements needed for a demonstration of compliance. For example, they say nothing about the *dimensions* we discussed previously. They have no *parameters* specifying the frequency of vulnerability scanning or the time required to remove a vulnerability.

Elaborating Security Requirements

Each of the subcategories has references to NIST SP 800-53r5, Security and Privacy Controls for Information Systems and Organizations (*https://oreil.ly/NNlaA*). It's a control catalog that provides a more comprehensive set of control requirements to work with.

In NIST SP 800-53r5, the first requirement for vulnerability monitoring and scanning is RA-5 (a), as shown in Table 4-13.

Table 4-13. NIST SP 800-53r5 vulnerability monitoring and scanning

ID	Requirement
RA-5 (a)	Monitor and scan for vulnerabilities in the system and hosted applications [Assignment: organization-defined frequency and/or randomly in accordance with organization-defined process] and when new vulnerabilities potentially affecting the system are identified and reported;

While it's more comprehensive, RA-5 (a) has many control requirements, dimensions, and parameters in the same sentence. Here is the list of what we found:

- A vulnerability scanning tool to identify vulnerabilities—DE.CM-8 in NIST CSF
- A vulnerability management process—PR.IP-12 in NIST CSF
- A parameter for the frequency of scanning according to policy
- A dimension for scanning "system and hosted applications"
- A new requirement for notifying the vulnerability management service when new intelligence has identified vulnerabilities or threats to vulnerabilities in the system.[8]

We can't leave RA-5 (a) as an integrated, multidimensional requirement to effectively demonstrate compliance and need to rewrite it into separate components.

---

8 This could be a new software vulnerability reported in the CVE (*https://www.cve.org*) database or a threat intelligence about the exploit of a vulnerability. Ideally, you should add a requirement for the automatic patching of a software product.

Rewriting Security Requirements

Integrating multiple requirements, parameters, and dimensions into one control requirement makes it difficult to assign accountability and measure compliance. Decomposing the RA-5 (a) control requirement into discrete requirements, dimensions, and parameters, as shown in Table 4-14, is the best way to rewrite it.

Table 4-14. Rewritten vulnerability management requirements

Topic	ID	Description	Control mapping
Control Requirements	VM-01	Define and implement threat and vulnerability management processes and procedures.	NIST SP 800-53 RA-5 (a) NIST CSF PR.IP-12
	VM-02	Vulnerability scanning MUST be performed at a frequency {VM-P-01,02,03,04} for the system component types {VM-D-01}.	NIST SP 800-53 RA-5 (a) NIST CSF DE.CM-8
	TIM-01	Notify the *Vulnerability Management* service of a potential system component vulnerability MUST be performed within {TIM-P-01}.	NIST SP 800-53 RA-5 (a)
Control Dimensions	VM-D-01	Networking components, servers (physical and virtual), containers, cloud platform, container platform, application	NIST SP 800-53 RA-5 (a)
Control Parameters	VM-P-01	no less than weekly	NIST SP 800-53 RA-5 (a)
	VM-P-02	after a significant system component change	NIST SP800-53 RA-5 (a)
	VM-P-03	within 24 hours after notification of potential system component vulnerability	NIST SP 800-53 RA-5 (a)
	VM-P-04	during penetration testing	NIST SP800-53 CA-8
	TIM-P-01	within 24 hours	NIST SP 800-53 RA-5 (a)
Key	VM = Vulnerability Management TIM = Threat Intelligence Monitoring {} = Parameter/Dimension Substitution		

We began by creating requirement VM-01 for processes and procedures, which is a fundamental requirement necessary for all services and requested in the RA-5 (a) assignment. Then RA-5 (a) requires a control requirement, VM-02, for vulnerability scanning and then a derived requirement, TIM-01, for the threat intelligence monitoring service to notify them of potential vulnerabilities. The TIM-01 control requirement, which isn't explicitly mentioned in any vulnerability management or threat intelligence requirements, critically determines the successful delivery of the VM-01 control requirement.

The dimensions or scope of the service are missing. RA-5 (a) talks about a "system and hosted applications," but that's incomplete and depends on the technology components used in the environment. When we read RA-5 (a), we might think we just need to perform a vulnerability scan of servers and applications, but this doesn't include the network, cloud platform, containers, and container platform vulnerabilities. Adding the dimension VM-D-01 improved the scope of vulnerability scanning.

Control Family/Domain Misalignment

You may have noticed the control families and domains in NIST CSF and SP 800-53 don't fully align with the resulting security requirements, dimensions, and parameters. We derived a new requirement for *Threat Intelligence Monitoring* and discovered a new requirement for *Vulnerability Management* related to penetration testing. The result is that you can't assign accountability for security processes and service delivery by simply allocating ownership of control families or domains to these frameworks.

The parameters for the service are missing. It doesn't define how often the scans need to run or how quickly the owners of the vulnerabilities need notification. What's the length of time for storing the vulnerability records? Many of these parameters could come from a policy, but if they aren't specified there, it's not clear when we've met the requirements. Adding the parameters VM-P-01, VM-P-02, VM-P-03, and TIM-P-01 has improved the understanding of the requirements.

We added a parameter VM-P-04 because we found the requirement CA-8 requires the ability to perform vulnerability scanning for penetration testing. This requirement needs documenting because it may change the number of supported human actors and require an increase in the capacity of the security service.

Non-Functional Requirements QA Checklist

- Consider all sources: external context, internal context, and project context.
- Identify dependent application and service components and use to determine the security integration requirements, including:
  - Software version dependencies
  - Workload-specific security requirements
  - Capacity requirements
- Assess the quality of each requirement using SMART
- Assess the priority of each requirement using MoSCoW
- Ensure requirement includes:
  - A label providing a unique identifier
  - A label identifying its source
  - Dimensions that define the scope
  - Parameters that define the variable aspects
- Try to balance the cost, scope/quality/risk, and time in requirement specification.

Up until now, we've discussed establishing a requirements catalog for a workload or application. But how can we use this catalog to make sure the implementation and operation of the security are in accordance with the requirements? We'll talk about that in the following section.

Requirements Traceability

Once we've documented the requirements and identified the solution, we need to ensure the documentation of the solution at both a logical and prescribed level, the completion of testing, and the availability of operational documentation. We do this by creating a mapping from the requirements to the specific documentation, as shown in Table 4-15.

Table 4-15. Requirements traceability matrix

ID	Requirement	HLD[a]	LLD[b]	Test plan	Documentation
SEC_IAM_PAM_003	The system response time at all stages of retrieval for a privileged credential MUST take less than 5 seconds to load a page even if the core systems infrastructure is under extreme load.	4.2 Privileged Access Management (PAM)	11.3 Privileged Access Management (PAM)	6.5 Unit Test 7.8 Integration Test 9.7 Resiliency Test	Ops Manual—5.6 Emergency Break Glass VPN Process

[a] High-level design
[b] Low-level design

The table has a column for each stage of the documentation for the solution architecture, including testing and operations. Your table may contain further columns for your project but these are the minimum we would expect.

We can then be more confident about the documented solution architecture and the implementation and operation of the capabilities to maintain security. We will talk more about the development of the design and operational artifacts in the design documentation within Chapters 6 and 8, the required testing in Chapter 10, and the operations documentation in Chapter 11.

Indexing Requirement References

We've given each requirement a unique identity code to use as a reference. A useful approach to validating the inclusion of all requirements in a design document is to include the ID within a sentence, such as [SEC_IAM_PAM_003], and then mark it as an entry for an index. You can then find where the design specification documented a requirement and ensure coverage of all requirements by reviewing the index for completeness.

Let's finish with a summary of this chapter.

Summary

Some authors have expressed the view that documenting requirements are no longer needed in an Agile working environment. I hope we've demonstrated the value of spending effort documenting both functional and non-functional processes. You can scale the level of documentation to meet the size of the organization and project. We've indicated how to do it for the largest of organizations and highlighted some ways to scale down the work for smaller projects.

Security requirements aren't just non-functional requirements but where they form the primary function of the system, they become functional requirements.

Functional requirements often follow an iterative process that can start with a journey map to identify user stories that may contain control decisions. User stories provide the next level of decomposition in an Agile environment, but for some processes, they're insufficient, and that's where the swimlane diagrams and separation of duties matrix help.

Non-functional requirements need a clear definition, and we talked about the various approaches to improving quality and prioritizing. We demonstrated the challenges when integrating control frameworks and project requirements through a set of improvements to the definition of requirements for the case study.

We've come to the end of discussing the documentation of requirements and constraints but not the end of using the requirements to define the security for a solution architecture. This should set you up for the following chapters, where we start with defining the boundaries of the system, the actors that interact with the system, and the data that requires protection.

Exercises

1. A functional requirement _____. Select all that apply.

   a. Describes the primary functionality of the solution

   b. Defines how the system should be delivered

   c. Defines what the system should deliver

   d. Doesn't define any security requirements

2. What terms are used for requirements that describe how the information system should deliver the required functionality? Select all that apply.

   a. Non-functional requirements

   b. Architectural characteristics

   c. Non-functional characteristics

   d. Product quality properties

3. Which of the following is true about requirements for security services?

   a. Applications should be recovered before security services during disaster recovery.

   b. Moving from client-server to container workloads doesn't require a change in security services.

   c. In moving to the cloud, there is no need to adjust the way security operations are delivered.

   d. The loss of availability of security services can have an almost immediate impact on workload availability.

4. What does "locking your keys in the car" refer to? Select all that apply.

   a. Your keys can get locked in your car accidentally if they are not detected by key proximity inside the car.

   b. The retrieval of keys may not be possible unless storage has already completed decryption.

   c. Encryption keys accidentally get locked inside a physical safe.

   d. The reboot of the firewall can't take place, as it enables communication with the hardware security module (HSM) required to decrypt the boot disk of the firewall.

5. What are the suggested qualities to look for in security requirements?

    a. Who, What, When, Where, and Why

    b. Must Have, Should Have, Could Have, and Won't Have

    c. Specific, Measurable, Attainable, Relevant, and Time-bound

    d. Traceable, Testable, and Timely

6. What is the best functional requirements definition technique for identifying end-user functional requirements? Select all that apply.

    a. Use cases

    b. A journey map

    c. Swimlane diagrams

    d. User stories

7. What is the best functional requirements definition technique for the formal definition of the sequence of security-enforcing activities taking place between different end users?

    a. Use cases

    b. Journey map

    c. Swimlane diagrams

    d. User stories

8. What factors does the project management triangle need to take into consideration when balancing scope, cost, and time? Select all that apply.

    a. Skills

    b. Quality

    c. Viability

    d. Risk

9. What are the primary reasons you perform a software version check early in the requirements process for hybrid cloud? Select all that apply.

    a. Version incompatibility may require a major architectural change.

    b. A cloud service may not support the prerequisite software version.

    c. The security information and event management (SIEM) solution may not have been tested to process that specific software version.

    d. The security product doesn't support any version of the operating system being used.

10. In the process of improving requirement specifications, what steps are used to consider the scope of requirements?

   a. Split

   b. Dimensions

   c. Merge

   d. Parameterize

PART III

Design

Now that we've gathered the requirements, we continue with the design phase, where we discuss the design of the solution architecture, starting with establishing the system context, identifying the information assets and their protection requirements. We establish the functional viewpoint via the component architecture and discuss the role of threat modeling in identifying risk-based security controls. Moving to the deployed architecture, we elaborate on the shared responsibility model in a cloud computing context and describe the approach to developing the infrastructure and cloud architecture based on zero trust principles. The role of architecture patterns and the importance of architectural decisions conclude this part.

CHAPTER 5

System Context

How often do you hear people say things like, "It's all about the data!"? When it comes to security, what matters is protecting the data from having its availability, integrity, and confidentiality compromised in any way. Unfortunately, a lot of the time, the emphasis shifts from protecting the data that an application is processing to protecting the infrastructure that stores and processes the data. This lack of awareness demonstrates the necessity of taking a data-centric approach to the design of security controls, where an architect considers how to safeguard data.

This chapter begins our exploration into the process of designing security for information systems by emphasizing that data protection is central to information security while the data is in transit, at rest, or in use. We explain the context for why security is about safeguarding important information assets, not just IT systems. We will look at how to categorize data assets based on asset classes and remind you that processing data creates new assets, including metadata. The classification of the data is then performed based on its sensitivity to loss of confidentiality, integrity, and availability.

By creating a system context diagram and then identifying the business transactions that will handle the data flowing in and out of the system, this will be the start of an information asset register listing the data flowing through the system. We then classify the data based on sensitivity, together with the legal and regulatory constraints that will apply. This helps design security controls that are appropriate to the data's sensitivity.

Chapter Artifacts

This chapter's main goal is to set the stage for the development of a broader architecture.

In each chapter, we will highlight, with white text in a black shaded box, the artifacts in the artifact dependency diagram, shown in Figure 5-1, to show the journey we're taking while architecting security into a system. The system context diagram and information asset register are two key artifacts created after examining the many different artifacts in the enterprise context. Ensure you record the key requirements and contextual information that influence the architecture. Record key assumptions made in the RAID log, as discussed later on in Chapter 10.

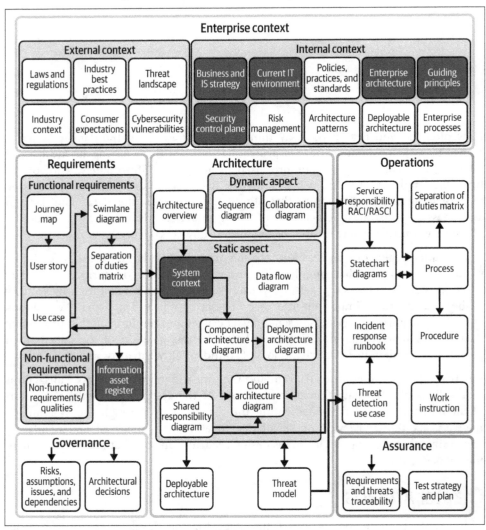

Figure 5-1. System context chapter artifacts

Case Study Context

As a reminder, to help reinforce the learning, the case study in Appendix A has information about the business context and current IT environment for this chapter.

We will continue this chapter with some context around data protection including a discussion on the value of data, the lifecycle of data that requires consideration, and the relationship with zero trust architecture.

Data Protection

Information security isn't primarily concerned with the implementation of various security capabilities. Rather, the purpose of information security is to protect the data of both the organization and its customers, which in turn protects those aspects of the organization that are valuable, such as its reputation and the firm's compliance with applicable laws and regulations.

By identifying the data flowing through the system boundary, classifying it based on sensitivity, and defining the required security controls based on policy, we can prioritize the protection of what truly matters to the business, with information security becoming a strategic advantage rather than a liability.

Let's have a discussion on some background concepts in data protection in the following subsections:

- Value of Data
- Data Security Lifecycle
- Metadata
- Zero Trust and Data Flows

This will help us understand the context of the techniques in this book.

Value of Data

The value of data to an organization is the key factor in determining the security controls requiring implementation.

The first step is to identify the data that's critical to the organization and use categories or asset classes that help identify the data that needs protection. The following is an example set of asset classes:

Crown jewels
> Data that represents the most valuable information assets for the organization, and if disclosed, modified, or made unavailable, it could cause the business to fail. This isn't just the original data but new data created from data processing.

Personal information (PI)
> Data related to a person or identifiable individual that isn't sensitive enough that its disclosure could cause irrevocable harm to the person. An example would be your name and address.

Sensitive personal information (SPI)
> Data concerning a person or identifiable individual that's so sensitive that its disclosure could cause irrevocable harm to the person. This includes information on racial or ethnic origin, sexual life, political opinions, criminal records, religious beliefs, trade union activities, and physical or mental health.

Financial information
> Data that relates to the financial records of a person or identifiable individual, including bank records, tax records, and accounting records.

If you don't have such a list of asset classes for an organization, you should create your own list for the solution you are architecting to enable clear communication of the data value within the project.

The common asset classes described in the NIST publication "NIST SP 800-160 Vol. 1 Engineering Trustworthy Secure Systems" (*https://oreil.ly/AhLi9*) may be another useful reference for you. It provides a list that's more focused on government systems but may give you ideas for the development of your own asset classes for your organization.

Data Security Lifecycle

As a system processes data, it goes through a lifecycle from creation to processing and, finally, destruction. By understanding the lifecycle of data in a system, we can understand where the data flows and its stages of processing in a system and identify the appropriate security controls at each stage of processing.

There are many examples of a data security lifecycle such as the lifecycle used in *Security Guidance for Critical Areas of Focus In Cloud Computing* (*https://oreil.ly/7m8nU*) produced by the Cloud Security Alliance (CSA). However, there is no consistent industry standard to describe a lifecycle, so we put together our own data security lifecycle model, in Figure 5-2, with eight stages to highlight important stages.

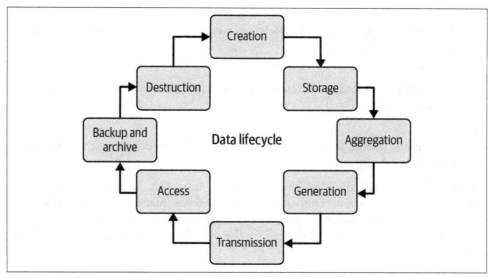

Figure 5-2. Data security lifecycle

Creation

The initial creation of data, such as when a user enters information into a form, or a sensor generates data.

Storage

Retention of data, either at rest or in processing, such as when disk storage or a database contains data.

Aggregation

The integration of data from multiple sources into a single data set. This is important as the aggregation may increase the sensitivity of the resulting information created.

Generation

The creation of new data through processing or analysis of existing data. Again, the resulting data may increase the sensitivity of the resulting information created.

Transmission

The movement of data from one location to another. An example is when the transport of data takes place over a public or private network. Also, keep in mind that even when in transit, at some point in the journey, storage of the data may take place.

Access
> The retrieval and use of data, such as when a user views a report, or a system performs a computation.

Backup and archive
> The medium and long-term retention of data for recovery, compliance, or historical purposes.

Destruction
> The removal of data from a system. An example is the deletion or secure erasure of data from storage.

Use the data lifecycle model to think about the transport, storage, and processing of data. Data needs security controls to protect it from unauthorized access, modification, or disclosure during *all* stages of the data lifecycle. The controls that need design and implementation will depend on the sensitivity of the data and the assigned classification.

Metadata

The processing of the data creates new data that records insights about the original data. The new data is metadata and provides information about the data, including:

Descriptive metadata
> Describes the content of the data by attaching labels such as title, artist, publisher.

Structural metadata
> Describes the organizational structure of a chapter in a book or track on a music album.

Technical metadata
> Describes the technical characteristics of the data such as the dimensions of a book or format of a video recording.

Administrative metadata
> Used to support activities for the administration of the data. This includes metadata such as the date of the last change to the record, the security classification of the data, or data for a digital rights management system.

It's important to remember that metadata is a valuable resource for giving insights, improving search capabilities, and assisting with the management of the data. For organizations that provide search capabilities or artificial intelligence (AI), this metadata may be the foundation of their business.

Metadata may represent an existential risk to the organization if data about the organization and its customers isn't effectively protected, resulting in the loss of sensitive information. It may be that this data is the "crown jewels" and more sensitive than the original data, requiring additional security controls beyond those of the original data.

Zero Trust and Data Flows

To implement a solution using zero trust principles, it's essential to examine data flows, as zero trust is the foundation for stringent controls to protect the data, together with ongoing security monitoring to detect unauthorized access to sensitive data.

To reduce or eliminate implicit trust, every device, service, and user attempting to access a resource must first authenticate and authorize access to the system in a zero trust solution. We've found that one of the consequences of the "assume breach" principle is that the security controls should be as close as possible to the data, as the assumption is that other systems are potentially breached.

By examining data flows, an architect can better understand how users and devices behave within their networks, and spot unusual activity that might point to a security threat. This can reduce the risk that an attacker can cause harm by enabling security teams to monitor data flows to detect threats, spot potential weaknesses, and take proactive measures to fix them before they're exploited.

Working with organizations, we've found that organizations are able to reduce the number of zero trust solutions by thinking holistically across multiple business processes. Incorporating the data classification approach we discussed earlier helps guide the extent of the security controls applied to a system. Both strategies can result in reduced implementation costs, improved speed of delivery, and reduced ongoing support issues.

Overall, looking at data flows is an important part of a zero trust architecture because it lets architects identify effective security controls and make sure the data flows are always monitored for threats.

Let's continue this chapter with understanding the interactions at the boundary of the system that will transport data in and out of the system. From this boundary we're able to define the scope of the system and start to identify the data requiring protection.

System Context Diagram

We've discussed the importance of understanding the sensitivity of the data. A transaction flow through a system transports data that's then processed and stored.

When architecting a system, we start by identifying the boundary of the system and how transactions flow across that boundary. Human or system actors trigger these transaction flows.

We showed an architecture decomposition diagram in Figure 1-6. The first layer is the system context diagram, where we describe the system boundary and provide the top layer of the architecture decomposition, as shown in Figure 5-3. At this stage, we're considering a system that human and system actors interact with, while keeping its internal mechanisms hidden.

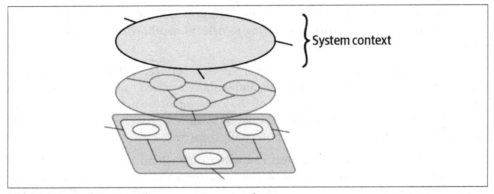

Figure 5-3. Architecture decomposition—top layer

Originating in the 1960s, the *system context* (*https://oreil.ly/PI6JO*) diagram is a widely used technique in systems engineering and documented in the "International Council on Systems Engineering (INCOSE) Systems Engineering Body of Knowledge (SEBok)" (*https://www.sebokwiki.org*). It's considered one of the first steps in an architectural thinking process, and it's described in publications such as *Practical Software Architecture* (*https://oreil.ly/OoV7b*) (IBM Press) by Tilak Mitra and C4 Model (*https://c4model.com*) by Simon Brown.

We will examine the next two layers of the architecture in Chapters 6 and 8.

Use cases or user stories describe the activities performed by the actors that trigger data flows in and out of the system, as we discussed in Chapter 4.

Before we start diving into the details, let's look at who the owner of the system context diagram would be.

System and Security Architect Roles

Application and infrastructure architects use the system context diagram to visually describe the interaction between a solution and its surrounding environment. They use it to specify a system's boundaries, the actors engaging with it, and the use cases for interaction. They then take a look at the use cases-driven transaction flows through the system.

For security, we take this idea a step further by identifying the data flowing through these transaction flows. This lets architects start making an information asset inventory for the system. To help find zero trust technology solutions, identify the known interface types, such as an API, HTTPS, or MQTT. Then, based on the data classification, identify the right security controls. In later chapters, we'll look at the processing of the data within the system.

In situations where a security architect is collaborating with an application architect to design an application, the security architect may augment the application architect's artifacts with additional security-related information. However, if the security architect is solely responsible for the solution architecture, they will need to carry out all the analysis. For instance, if the security architect is accountable for creating a security service like an identity and access management system, they will have complete responsibility for the solution architecture.

Now we can continue discussing the concepts.

System Context Concepts

A system context diagram is important when creating a solution architecture because it provides a high-level view of the system, including the external actors and systems with which it interacts. It helps define the boundaries of the system and clarifies the scope of the architecture work.

By understanding the external context of the system, architects can identify the relevant use cases and data flows for consideration in designing the solution. It also helps to identify any constraints or limitations imposed by the current IT environment for consideration. Identification of potential security threats and other risks associated with the external actor interactions can take place.

Overall, the system context diagram is a crucial tool for creating a solution architecture that meets the business requirements and aligns with the overall IT strategy of the organization.

Let's start with a simple example of a system context diagram to demonstrate the concepts used for the creation of the diagram. Figure 5-4 shows a simple system context diagram for an online store with some actors missing, and as we go through the discussion, you will identify that there are many updates needed.

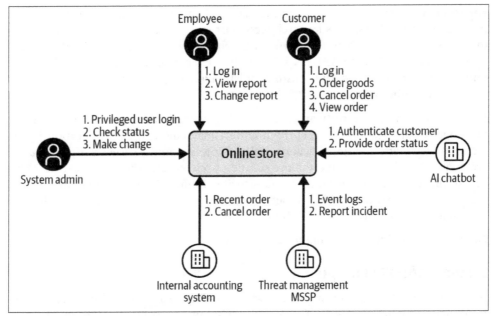

Figure 5-4. Example system context

The diagram in Figure 5-4 has the following attributes:

Human actor

Human actors in a system context diagram refer to individuals or groups of people that interact with the system through a set of processes or use cases where data flows in and out of the system. This includes people both internal and external to the organization that owns the system. An organization's internal staff may include accounting, developers, IT support staff, cybersecurity personnel, customers, internal compliance, and any other people or groups who interact with a system. Identify actors by roles rather than individuals.

In the diagram, we've included the role "Employee," but this isn't specific enough to identify the role of the employee. A role such as "Sales Administrator" could be an alternative. The "System Admin" role is more specific, but there may be many types of administrative roles, and the role may require further decomposition.

System actor

System actors in a system context diagram refer to information technology (IT), operational technology (OT), and Internet of Things (IoT) systems that are external to the system. They are integrated with the system through a set of transactions, or use cases, where data flows in and out of the system. System actors might include payment providers, externally managed security services, or logistics systems. In the example in Figure 5-4 we have a threat management managed security service provider (MSSP) integrated into the system.

When we say "external," we mean external to the system and not external to the organization. External systems include those that belong to another department and aren't part of the project's system design. In this case, this includes the internal accounting system.

 Generally speaking, a system actor subject to a different security policy from the main system shouldn't be present in the system. If the system has its own policy, it's likely that it's a SaaS service where the security governance is through a contractual relationship with the organization. However, since it's subject to a contract with a third party, such as a SWIFT (*https://www.swift.com*) payment gateway, it's possible that an internal system actor will have to abide by a different policy. SWIFT requires the implementation of specific controls as a condition of connection.

It's also important not to get too detailed, but sometimes, you may find this gets too complex when the diagram shows all the human and system actors. For one project, we created two system context diagrams, one for human actors and one for system actors.

Use case

For each actor, there is a set of use cases listed that will trigger a transaction flow that transports and processes data. The transaction flow enables you to identify the kinds of data flowing to and from the system. We discussed the definition of use cases or user stories in Chapter 4.

We will give further examples and discuss the construction of a system context as we go through this chapter, but if you want to learn more about creating a system context diagram, you may find "Chapter 4: The System Context" in *Practical Software Architecture* (*https://oreil.ly/TanKz*) useful.

Technical Design Diagram Notation

A big part of an architect's work is communicating complex topics, not only in words but also in drawings and diagrams. As with all communication, it's important to agree on the language so that all parties can communicate in a format that's clearly understood. This is again valid for words, but equally relevant for design diagrams. A common design language eases the understanding of what the viewer of the diagram sees.

We have a situation where each CSP proposes a notation for drawing cloud architecture diagrams that's branded and implementation-specific, using color, which can make them difficult to work with. We like to work with diagrams that are CSP-independent and can support a hybrid cloud architecture.

We've chosen a technical design notation that's independent of CSPs and supports IBM's Unified Method Framework for IBM Architects. The IBM Design Language site (*https://oreil.ly/EZXcj*) has a section on technical diagrams (*https://oreil.ly/Ts3s4*).

Diagrams can have different levels of abstraction. A *logical* view shows a high-level representation of a system that is not representative of the actual implementation. Previously, architects would refer to a physical view of a system, but with the advent of virtualization and containers, we now refer to a diagram as a *prescribed* view.

In this book, we use a subset of the technical design notation as outlined in Figure 5-5.[1] The notation has been adapted for the page size of a printed book and publishing consistency. Selected original diagrams can be found on the book's companion website (*https://securityarchitecture.cloud*).

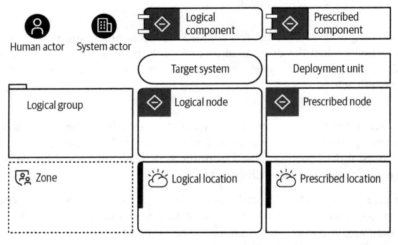

Figure 5-5. Technical design diagram notation; see the original diagram (https://oreil.ly/SAHC)

---

1 It's fine if your organization uses a different notation, but it's important that you use the same notation for all diagrams to encourage more effective communication.

We use the following basic elements in our diagrams:

Actor

We're illustrating actors as a circle. We distinguish between human actors and system actors who are interacting with the solution. We're introducing actors for the first time in Chapter 5.

Target system

The target system is the system we're designing, the system in the middle of the system context diagram.

Deployment unit

We illustrate deployment units as rectangles with square corners. They represent deployed instances of functionality on a node. For example, an application or a database. You might face a situation where you have many deployment units on one node. To prevent filling the diagram with many rectangles on one node, you can also list the deployment units as a text list directly on the node stencil, without a separate border.

Location

We're illustrating locations as a rectangle with a thick black marker in the top left corner. Rounded corners illustrate logical locations, while square corners illustrate prescribed locations. Locations can be geographical and organizational locations, which we first introduce in Chapter 8.

Component

We illustrate components as rectangles with two connectors and a framed symbol in the top left corner. Rounded corners illustrate logical components, while square corners illustrate prescribed components. Components represent the functionality of the solution and are introduced in Chapter 6.

Logical group

We illustrate a logical group as a rectangle with square corners and a marker in the top left corner. They logically group components, and in the very simplest form, those grouped components share similar non-functional requirements or other commonalities.

Nodes

To execute or run the functionality, we deploy (or place) functional components on a node. For instance, we can deploy a functional component as an executable program (deployment unit) onto a virtual server (node).

We illustrate nodes as rectangles with a framed symbol in the top left corner. Rounded corners illustrate logical nodes, while square corners illustrate prescribed nodes. Components are deployed via deployment units on nodes. Nodes are specified with the selected technology and size and can, for example, be virtual servers.

To simplify the diagrams and make more space on the page for printing of the book, we've chosen to draw prescribed nodes without a box for cloud services or resource instances.

Zone

To document a location with a common security policy and threats, use a network zone. We illustrate network zones as a frame with square corners and a dashed border. Components and nodes are placed within zones. Zones can span locations.

 We opted to use the IBM Cloud icons that were released in issue 3914 (*https://oreil.ly/qUgp1*) of the draw.io GitHub site that are clear when published in black and white. Just before publication date, the architecture icons were republished (*https://oreil.ly/sbgwf*) using colored boxes with icons too small to be used in a published book. We'll leave you to set the standard for the icons you use for your own diagrams.

To create a system context diagram, we need some context. Let's discuss it before applying it to the case study.

Business and IT Context

To develop the system context diagram, you need to understand the business context of the system and the existing IT environment that will impose constraints on your solution. The business objectives will determine the target solution architecture's business processes, which in turn will provide a foundation for identifying human and system actors for the system context. Meanwhile, the current IT environment will establish existing actors requiring integration into the system and, in certain situations, may restrict the solution's development.

In this book, we've provided a case study in Appendix A to provide information on the business context and current IT environment to demonstrate how to apply the information to the development of the artifacts. If you don't have this information for a project, it's likely the project is at an early stage, and working with the key stakeholders to develop a system context can help develop the business context.

We continue by applying the concepts to the development of a system context diagram using the case study in Appendix A.

Case Study: System Context Diagram

The first step to defining a system context is to identify the boundary of the system. It will define what functional components of a system are within the system and what human and system actors are external to the system.

We discussed the definition of human and system actors previously, and now we need to identify actors from the case study. In the case study, we have an architecture overview diagram to help, but you may not have that and must read some written text or listen to a description during an interview. The marked-up section from the case study highlights text with a solid box around potential system actors. We suggest that you mark-up the case study yourself, as shown in the sidebar that follows.

Marked-up Case Study to Identify System Actors

- For those vehicle owners who don't pay the fee at the end of the 48-hour period, a debt collection agency, Clean Air Debt, will receive information on the driver. They will send out letters notifying the vehicle owner of the fine and, after a period, pursue collection of the fine.

- The vehicle owners will be able to use their Google or Microsoft IDs to log in to the portal and register their car with the program so that, upon entering Guildford, the payments are automatically made.

- The scheme uses the Guildford Service SaaS application in a service center to respond to queries by phone and take payments.

- An AI chatbot, provided as a cloud service by the public cloud provider, will handle driver queries more rapidly without waiting for telephone support via the service center.

- Clean Threats, a threat management company, will manage all the security services from their Security Operations Center (SOC).

In Figure 5-6, the drawing of a system context shows a box in the middle and the actors arranged around the system. There are no components identified inside the box, as we're focusing on the boundary of the system. Elaboration of the components inside the box is discussed in Chapter 6.

Human actors use two types of person icons. The dark-shaded icon shows actors associated with the business process operation, and the light icon shows actors associated with the operations of the system. A building icon represents the system actors. We will talk more about the differences in Chapter 6.

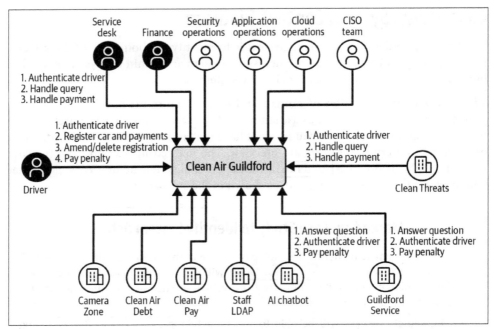

Figure 5-6. Case study system context; see the original diagram (https://oreil.ly/SAHC)

Icons for Actors

The different icons used to illustrate the different types of actors aren't prescribed as part of the method. Your organization may have its own style.

For some of the actors, we have shown some example use cases to show how events can trigger transaction flows through the system. Think about what use cases are missing and try to document them for the rest of the actors.

Let's discuss the identification of human actors.

Identifying Human Actors

To draw the system context diagram from the case study in Appendix A, it's necessary to identify all the human actors mentioned. The case study only mentions one human actor, but many more will be interacting with the system. Read the case study, identifying roles that might need access to the system.

The case study mentions there is a service desk, which will have employees that run the desk. In this case, the service desk employees are Clean Air Guildford employees and are human actors. For an outsourced service desk application, draw a system actor for a SaaS application named Guildford Service..

There will be distinct roles needed to operate the system that aren't explicitly mentioned in the case study. It's your responsibility to identify these different roles. For example, consider the Finance department, which needs to access financial capabilities related to payments. Add a human actor called Finance.

In this case, the Cloud Operations team is responsible for the infrastructure, the Application Operations team is responsible for the application, and the Security Operations team is responsible for the security. An outsourced team may change from a human actor to a system actor if their access is via a system rather than an interactive login. For example, system management activities may be automated within a service management portal hosted in the data center of the outsourced team. If their team is also using a jump host or bastion host for access, an icon for a human actor will be needed. You might need both icons to represent both paths to access the system.

Examine the Data Lifecycle

Think about the lifecycle of the data within the system. For example, data stored in the database may require backup, archive, and cyber-recovery capabilities. If so, will there be human or system actors needed to deal with cyber recovery, and will the system components need to be internal or external to the system? You could store this on a to-do list or perhaps as an issue in the RAID log that we will talk about in Chapter 10. The critical thing is that you must not lose sight of this required activity.

Have you noticed any human actors that are missing from the system context? We could imagine creating a user for the system requires some form of approval, perhaps from a line manager in each department. So, we suggest adding a new role, "Line Manager," just to make sure that the capabilities exist for that role.

We've talked about identifying many different actors, but you could end up identifying actors that have no impact on the architecture. For example, there will be many different human actors for an email system run as a SaaS application. While a manager and a generic employee may have different capabilities within the email system, the architecture doesn't change. You don't need to identify them all; perhaps a generic role like "Email User" would be appropriate.

Let's continue with discussing the identification of system actors.

Identifying System Actors

While architecting the IT systems, you should start by focusing on the functional components and not the underlying technology implementation. Once you have identified the functional components, split the components into two groups: those that are internal and those that are external *to the system*.

After identifying the functional components, it's important to determine whether your organization owns and operates them. If your organization has no control over the design of the application, the service provider controls the cloud account, or the security policy in place isn't your own organization's policy, then it's likely that the component is an external actor to the system being designed. This means that for an external system, you would need a contract as an agreement for what security controls need to be implemented by the supplier or what controls the supplier requires from the system you are designing.

It's also possible that other systems within an organization are external system actors rather than internal components, especially if the systems reside in different parts of the organization. In such cases, negotiating with the supplier of the other internal system may be necessary. For example, the case study may not have identified the accounting system but if it's an internal system not in the scope of the project, it should be an external system actor on the system context diagram. It may be that an internal agreement, such as a document of understanding (DoU), is needed to agree what security controls are required from both parties.

Interface Modification

An external system's interface may be incompatible with a system actor's, leaving a choice of which system needs modification. The decision over which interface needs changing—the external actor or the new system—may need an enterprise design authority decision.

Can you see a system actor that's missing? Have a look back at the architecture overview diagram in the case study in Appendix A. How are the drivers going to identify and authenticate with the application for the handling of payments? You might have noticed already that integration with the identity providers from Google and Microsoft is missing.

Would you suggest that a system actor is really a component within the system we're designing from the case study? In this case, we have an actor that's a PaaS service within the public cloud platform hosting the application and doesn't already exist as a fully customized service. The AI chatbot should probably be a component inside the system, as it will need training as a part of the project.

Overall, to make the right diagram, you need to do a thorough analysis of all the human and system actors mentioned in the case study. You also need to think about who owns and runs the functional components, along with the internal and external actors connected to the system.

Now let's bring this information together by documenting the system context diagram.

Documenting the System Context

While diagrams may be sufficient for some projects, others require a more comprehensive description. The actors, along with their respective descriptions and interfaces, are listed in Table 5-1. Initially, the interfaces may not be fully understood, but the table will later have additional detail added.

Table 5-1. Actors and interfaces table

Actor	Description	Interface
Driver	Driver of the vehicle entering and leaving the clean air zone	A TLS[a] 1.2 session to the Clean Air Guildford web application. A second interface is telephony to make calls to the Clean Air Guildford service desk.
Service desk	Employees of Clean Air Guildford who use the application to support the drivers of the vehicles	A TLS 1.2 session to the Clean Air Guildford web application. A second interface is telephony to receive calls from the drivers.
Camera zone	Organization managing the cameras providing Automatic Number Plate Recognition (ANPR)	Provides a REST API to retrieve camera data within a TLS 1.3 session over a dedicated private network link.
...	...	...

[a] Transport layer security (TLS) session-level encryption requires at least 1.2, and preferably 1.3, as known vulnerabilities exist in earlier implementations.

Note that there are two interfaces for the driver and service desk, with both a web and telephony interface. Think about all the different interfaces—email and SMS messaging may be additions.

We've provided a checklist to help you review the quality and potential follow-on activities for the development of a system context diagram.

System Context QA Checklist

- Consider all the human actors that could interact with the system, including company employees and third parties contracted to provide a service. In this example, there is the CISO team, but there might be a separate compliance or audit team as well.

- Decompose the human actors to a level at which an identified role has associated use cases or user stories. In this example, there is a finance role where enforcement of separation of duties may require multiple roles.

- Consider the decomposition of a human actor based on location, such as one role for an office worker and one for a remote worker, to consider the different transaction flows.

- Identify the system actors that interface with the system. In this system, there is no email gateway or text messaging service. In systems that transport a physical item, there will be some sort of logistics or delivery service needed.

- Identify where the system actors are all outside your control and will need agreements in place to interface with the system.

- Consider timed or batch events that could trigger transaction flows. These flows may process different data and travel along a path not considered by just looking at external events.

System Interface Implementation Perspective

The system context we described is conceptual, but there is a way of using the same sort of diagram to think about the actual implementation of the system. Let's have a look at how it can help with describing the integration.

Use a variation of the system context diagram to describe the data flows for specific network connections and define the network security controls. We're skipping ahead into implementation detail, but if you are a software engineer developing a software appliance, this may be the form of system context you want to work with.

In the example in Figure 5-7, a single box shows connectivity to and from the system that's used to describe the data flows on specific network ports. The diagram shows those connections that flow separately on the public and private network interfaces of the software system. Network connections that come out of the top of the diagram show those that use the public network interface, with those out of the bottom showing the private network. The ICMP connectivity out of the side requires connectivity to exist for both the private and public networks.

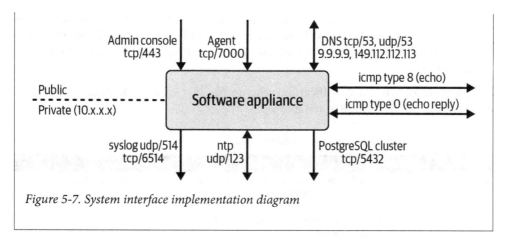

Figure 5-7. System interface implementation diagram

Now that we've completed a system context diagram, the next step is to record the identified data and classify it according to its sensitivity in an information asset register. From this, we can determine the security controls required according to the data classification.

Information Asset Register

An information asset register is an important part of creating a solution architecture because it helps identify and classify the data that's transported, processed, and stored in the system. By identifying and classifying the data, it becomes possible to determine the appropriate security measures needed to protect it.

In addition, an information asset register can help ensure the handling of data is in compliance with legal and regulatory requirements. For example, if the data processed includes personally identifiable information, then the information asset register can help ensure that it's handled in compliance with data privacy laws and regulations.

Overall, the information asset register provides a comprehensive understanding of the information assets within the system and allows for a more effective and targeted approach to securing and managing those assets.

Before we get into recording an information asset register, let's discuss the data classification used to identify the controls required for data with different sensitivities.

Data Classification

When it comes to data security, organizations must take the necessary steps to classify data based on its sensitivity to guide the controls used to protect it. This classification is typically based on the CIA triad of confidentiality, integrity, and availability.

The potential impact of data disclosure defines the confidentiality classification. A typical classification scheme will generally start with publicly available data and progress to the most sensitive data within an organization, with the greatest potential impact if lost.

An example of what a classification scheme for loss of confidentiality within an organization might include is in Table 5-2.

Table 5-2. Classification scheme for confidentiality

Category	Description	Control guidance
Public	Information that's available to the public and the loss of which would not have an impact on the organization or its customers. An example of this would be any content that's published on a public website on the internet.	Security controls aren't required.
Internal	Information that's available to all employees but not published on a public website. An example of this might be the menu in the restaurant or information on the process to request a new laptop. Disclosure would not have a significant impact, but it shouldn't be publicly available.	The hosting of the data must be within the internal network of a company and not require identification or authentication for accountability.[a]
Confidential	Information that could be damaging to the organization but not in contravention of laws or regulations. An example might include draft product information before formal release or internal product roadmaps.	The data requires the identification and authentication of an individual for individual accountability and controlled access based on a specific role. You must encrypt all data in transit and at rest.
Highly confidential	Information that if disclosed could be seriously damaging to the organization and its customers, including legal and regulatory consequences. An example may include sensitive personal information about customers that could result in a financial penalty due to a breach of data protection laws and seriously damage the reputation of the company.	In addition to previous controls, the data requires wrapping or encryption of the individual columns in a database so that even privileged administrators aren't able to view the data.

[a] In this example, there is an assumption there is a control boundary to the organization and zero trust has not been adopted for internal networks.

Note that the final column in the table provides some ideas for the different controls to apply to the data depending on classification. You might come up with a longer list of different security controls.

While data classification for loss of integrity isn't as common as other forms of classification, it's no less important. A loss of integrity can have serious consequences, such as a financial transaction altered without the knowledge of the participants or an AI model that is changed to force an incorrect decision to be made.

An example of what a classification scheme for loss of integrity within an organization might include is in Table 5-3.

Table 5-3. Classification scheme for integrity

Category	Description	Control guidance
Low risk	Data that has had its integrity compromised and has a minimal impact on the organization. This might include public information or non-critical historical data. For example, this would include yesterday's menu for the restaurant or a poster for a free yoga class.	
Moderate risk	Data that has had its integrity compromised and has a moderate impact on the organization. This might include a customer's telephone number or tomorrow's restaurant menu.	This data should include simple controls such as checking that the telephone number is valid or that the menu items are part of a standard set of items.
High risk	Data that has had its integrity compromised and has a significant impact on the organization. Examples include sensitive personal information about customers, legal documents, or trade secrets.	The data must have a hash to detect modification.
Critical risk	Data that has had its integrity compromised and has a critical impact on the organization. Examples include data that's vital for the operation of the organization, such as financial transactions, medical records, or personal identification numbers.	This data must be cryptographically signed to ensure detection of modification, even by privileged administrators.

In today's hybrid cloud world, ensuring the availability of business processes is a critical aspect of cybersecurity. The responsibility for this risk often falls on a resiliency team, but it's important to remember that some controls, such as DDoS protection, fall under the remit of a security team.

A classification scheme for the availability of business processes within an organization should consider various factors, including the required uptime, recovery time, and acceptable data loss. An example of what such a scheme might include is in Table 5-4.

Table 5-4. Classification scheme for availability

Category	Description	Control guidance
Category A	Business processes that have a critical impact on the operation of the organization if they become unavailable. They're normally considered mission-critical processes. Examples might include payment systems, air traffic control, or nuclear power plant control systems.	These services require annual availability of 99.999% with a recovery time objective (RTO) of 0 and recovery point objective (RPO) of near 0 with no loss of data.
Category B	Business processes that have a high impact on the operation of the organization if they become unavailable. Examples might include warehouse inventory management systems or overnight batch processes.	These services require annual availability of 99.99% with an RTO of 2 hours and RPO of near 0 with no loss of data.

Category	Description	Control guidance
Category C	Business processes that have a moderate impact on the operation of the organization if they become unavailable. Examples might include customer service databases or weekly financial process execution.	These services require annual availability of 99.9% with an RTO of 48 hours and RPO of 2 hours.
Category D	Business processes that have a low impact on the operation of the organization if they become unavailable. Examples might include an employee recognition application or employee support system.	These services require annual availability of 99% with an RTO of 72 hours and RPO of 24 hours.

The importance of availability in security services has grown with the need for tighter integration and end-to-end automation with instant response times. In the past, a password change might have occurred every 90 days, where the loss of an identity and access management application would not have had an immediate impact. However, as applications move to use cloud native services, credentials may change every few minutes with each authentication, making the loss of security services an instant and potentially severe issue, requiring a higher level of resilience than the applications they support.

When architecting security, it's crucial to understand the different availability requirements for various systems and services. As security architects, we must be aware of key concepts such as percentage availability, recovery time objective (RTO), and recovery point objective (RPO).

Percentage availability, also known as "nines availability," refers to the percentage of time a service or system must be operational and available to users over a year. For example, 99% availability means that a service or system can be down for a maximum of 87.6 hours per year. Table 5-5 shows the various levels of availability and the number of unavailable minutes.

Table 5-5. Availability bands

Availability	Unavailable for less than
99%	87.6 hours
99.9%	8.76 hours
99.99%	52.45 minutes
99.999%	5.26 minutes

RTO, on the other hand, is the maximum amount of time a business process can be down before it starts to have an impact on the organization. It's the time required for an organization to recover its systems and restore normal operations.

RPO is the maximum amount of data loss that an organization can tolerate. After an incident, the organization must recover its data to this point to minimize the impact on its operations.

As we delve deeper into the topic of infrastructure security, we'll explore these concepts in more detail and how they impact the design of secure systems. You might also like to look at other schemes for categorization of data including NIST FIPS 199 Standards for Security Categorization of Federal Information and Information Systems (*https://oreil.ly/GszLe*).

For now, let's continue with documenting the actors, the use cases, and the data.

Actor Use Case and Data

As a next step, one approach is to identify the actors and their respective use cases with associated data requirements. This practice enables a better understanding of the data types involved by aligning them with the respective actors and use cases. Table 5-6 shows an example of the use cases for the Driver actor and the data processed.

Table 5-6. Actor use cases and data mapping

Actor	Use cases	Data type processed
Driver	Authenticate driver	Identification and authentication info
	Register vehicle and payments	Contact details Vehicle details Payment details
	Amend/delete registration	Contact details Vehicle details Payment details
	Pay penalty	Contact details Payment details
...	...	...

After identifying the data types associated with the use cases, the next step is to create an information asset inventory for the application. This inventory lists all the data types and their associated confidentiality classifications, as well as any additional categorization for data that may fall within data privacy legislation and PCI DSS.

Table 5-7 provides an example of an information asset inventory with the confidentiality classification provided earlier in Table 5-2. We haven't included availability classification, as that's focused on process availability, or integrity classification, as that will be focused on the individual transactions we should consider later.

Table 5-7. Information asset inventory

Data type	Data field	Confidentiality classification	Legal and regulatory
Identification and authentication information	Username	Confidential	PI
	Password	Highly confidential	PI
Contact details	Name	Confidential	PI
	Address	Confidential	PI
	Phone Number	Confidential	PI
Payment details	Car number plate	Confidential	
	Car manufacturer	Confidential	
	Car model	Confidential	
	Color	Confidential	
	Age of vehicle	Confidential	
Payment details	Card name	Confidential	PI & PCI DSS
	Credit card number	Confidential	PCI DSS
	Expiry date	Confidential	PCI DSS
	Security code	Highly confidential	PCI DSS
	Billing address	Confidential	PI & PCI DSS
Payment transaction	Payment log event	Confidential	PCI DSS

In Table 5-7, PI is personal information and PCI DSS is the Payment Card Industry Data Security Standard. The last row of the table contains data derived from the processing of payment transactions within the system.

From the classification of the data, we can then derive new requirements for the solution and identify-specific security controls needed to meet legal and regulatory requirements. Data that's in transit, at rest, and in processing needs the specification of security control requirements.

We've provided a checklist to help you review the quality of the information asset register stage of the architectural thinking process.

Information Asset QA Checklist

- Identify data involved in each of the use cases for each human and system actor.
- Add data triggered via a timed event or derived from transaction processing.
- Classify the data based on the classification scheme of the organization and identify data that needs additional legal and regulatory controls.

Let's close this chapter with a few thoughts about our experiences and tips for using the techniques.

Summary

You may think the development of a system context is easy and you don't need to spend much time on it. Our experience has shown that without discussing, documenting, and communicating this simple diagram, major misunderstandings can result within a project. There will be different ideas about the scope of the project that may cause problems later on if not resolved early on.

The diagram may also have external integration points or human actors missing. It may miss how the management components of the system will integrate, requiring additional IT and non-IT actors to interact with the system. Identification of additional actors is likely to happen through reviews of the diagram with a broad range of team members.

If you are a security architect developing a solution for a security service, you will develop the system context. If you are a security architect assisting an application architect, then you won't own the system context diagram, but you will be providing supplementary information. It may be that you need to ask for the addition of use cases or user stories after reviews with key stakeholders.

When it comes to the information asset register, the security architect is more likely to own the artifact. If the application architect has no security architect to help, then they need to own the artifact. Like the system context diagram, you may think it's unnecessary, but again, it's important for communication and alignment across the team. For example, recording that the system is going to process payment data and will require compliance with PCI DSS makes it a tracked requirement for the project. Otherwise, it could get ignored until later in the project, causing changes in the solution and resulting in delays.

Iterate with New Requirements

You should now understand the context of the system and have an idea of the types of data processed. The artifacts created during the first stage of the architectural thinking process will need updating to reflect new requirements identified and new architectural decisions made. As you continue through the following chapters, you will also come back to record new actors, data, and use cases.

If you can't complete the artifacts because information is missing, insert placeholders and record them in the risks, assumptions, issues, and dependencies (RAID) log. For example, you could record an issue for missing information or record an assumption for validation. We will discuss the use of the RAID log in Chapter 10.

Communication, Communication, Communication

You may have noticed we talked about communication. Communication is the primary purpose of documenting the artifacts to ensure a project team is fully aligned. Don't let what you write become a document hidden in a folder that's not read. Spend time briefing the project team and wider stakeholders to gain their agreement. A second purpose is to communicate the architecture to operations and follow-on project teams after you have moved on to another project. It enables them to understand the solution and your thinking.

Now that we've looked at the boundary of the system and the external interactions from actors, we will next look inside the system. The next chapter is going to discuss the functional components of an application or workload and how they interact.

Exercises

1. You are architecting the security for a health insurance system that collects data about physical and mental health. What category of information is being collected?

   a. Crown jewels

   b. Personal information (PI)

   c. Sensitive personal information (SPI)

   d. Financial information

2. What steps in the data lifecycle could increase the sensitivity of the resulting information being protected? Select all that apply.

   a. Creation

   b. Aggregation

   c. Generation

   d. Transmission

3. What does a system context diagram describe? Select all that apply.

   a. The system boundary

   b. Human and system actors

   c. System functionality

   d. Data flows

4. What type of human actor might be part of a system context diagram for an online store? Select all that apply.

   a. Cloud data center security guard

   b. Database administrator

   c. Finance system

   d. Service desk agent

5. What type of system actor might be part of a system context diagram for an online store? Select all that apply.

   a. A parcel logistics system

   b. An HR system

   c. A card payment system

   d. An AI chatbot platform as a service (PaaS)

6. True or False: An employee accessing the system within office space and an employee accessing the system using Internet remote access should be treated as two separate human actors.

    a. True

    b. False

7. A secrets manager service serves applications updated secrets every few minutes 24×7. It supports high-impact business processes, but they aren't mission-critical and don't need cross-regional resilience. What should be the availability classification for the secrets manager service?

    a. Category A

    b. Category B

    c. Category C

    d. Category D

CHAPTER 6

Application Security

In the prior chapters, we talked about external elements that can influence and drive required security controls, which form a baseline of security measures that our system needs to take into consideration. To strike a balance between the cost of security measures and the actual business value, i.e., decreasing the risk to the organization, we need to complement or change those baseline security measures with measures that address specific risks that the exposed system faces. This will allow us to bring the cost of security measures in line with the actual business benefit. Because of this, we need to investigate the inner workings of the system to comprehend its functioning.

In our role as security architects, we're working closely with architects from other domains to comprehend, construct, expand, and customize the system. The security architecture evolves alongside the overall system architecture as it develops throughout the course of the system's lifetime, turning into an iterative process. To begin the architectural thought process, we must first establish the system's functional building blocks. In the first part of this chapter, we will decompose the system to understand its functional building blocks, trust boundaries, data flows, and interactions. In the second phase, we will examine the exposure of the system to threats, the inherent vulnerabilities of the current system architecture, and the risks this poses to the organization. This will assist us in identifying and prioritizing countermeasures for the identified risks.

Chapter Artifacts

The component architecture artifact shown in Figure 6-1, with its dynamic variations in the form of an interaction diagram and a collaboration diagram, is the main artifact used to decompose the architecture into functional building blocks. These diagrams are typically created by other domain architects, unless you are developing a full security architecture yourself, but we require them for the development of the security architecture. If other architects haven't developed them, the security architect must step in and develop them with feedback from those who understand the system functionally.

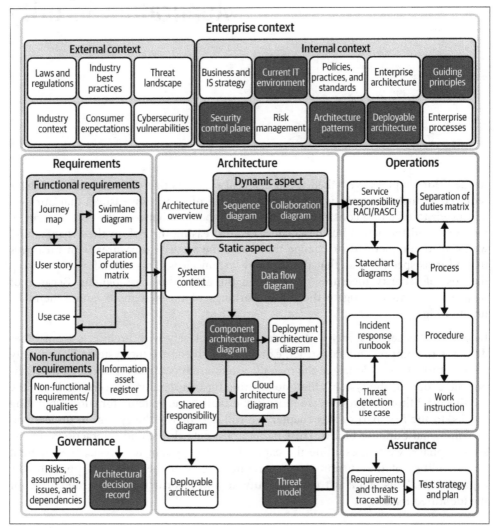

Figure 6-1. Application security chapter artifacts

The data flow diagram complements the component architecture artifacts from a data perspective and is an important input to the threat model artifact, which is the main artifact of this chapter and documents threat actors, threats, assets, and countermeasures.

Functional Viewpoint

The system context diagram helped us to describe the external connections and interactions, and with that, the boundaries and scope of the system we're securing. We're now looking inside the system boundary to understand and document the functionality of the system, as shown in Figure 6-2.

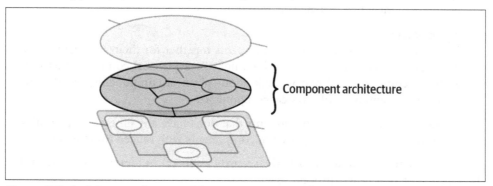

Figure 6-2. Architecture decomposition—component architecture

We describe the functionality of a system through the composition of components and document the same in the component architecture. Within the software domain, we define a component as an encapsulated part of a software system with a well-defined interface that provides access to its services.

Components aren't restricted to application components; they can also be technical components, system software components, hardware components, SaaS components, infrastructure as code (IaC) components, etc.

Component Decomposition

Components can also consist of additional components, such as Server → Pods → Containers → Knative Functions.

In Chapter 8, we will discuss how we can place those components on nodes or resource instances, which represent the infrastructure or the operational view, and how we can document it in the deployment architecture.

Component Architecture

The component architecture is an abstraction of the system architecture that omits most of the design complexities in order to present an overview of the functioning of the system.

The component architecture aids in the definition of the system's structure, component types, and recurring interactions and dependencies between sets of components.

We can break down the component architectures into two levels:

The logical level
Specifies the components, responsibilities, and qualities required to deliver technology and meet product-neutral requirements.

The deployed level
Describes how to assemble the components together for them to meet the previously established specifications. This might be a physical component as well as a virtual component. When we talk about physical components, we also mean virtual representations of physical components.

A subsystem is a collection of components that don't have any inherent capabilities or interfaces. It's just a way to group a set of components with related functionality.

The component architecture assists the security architect in identifying the data that the solution or system will process:

- Data in transit
- Data at rest
- Data generated by processing transactions (data in use)
- Confidential data
- Sensitive data
- Classified or highly sensitive data
- "Crown jewels"—often considered business-critical data or highly sensitive data

We can identify components based on their responsibilities in achieving the intended system behavior. Component interfaces represent a service agreement that outlines component duties and data access through the interfaces.

We will now look at what different forms of visualization we can use to document a component architecture and how these different forms provide the security architect with relevant information. For many of the diagrams in this section we're using simplified versions of diagrams defined in UML (*https://oreil.ly/894La*) as a basis. Use the diagrams aligned to what your organization uses. We've documented a mapping showing the equivalent diagrams for different methods in Appendix B.

Component Architecture Diagram

Based on the UML component diagram (*https://oreil.ly/KDHS4*), the component architecture diagram (static model) displays the dependencies and relationships between static components. Figure 6-3 illustrates a simplified version of the logical component architecture.

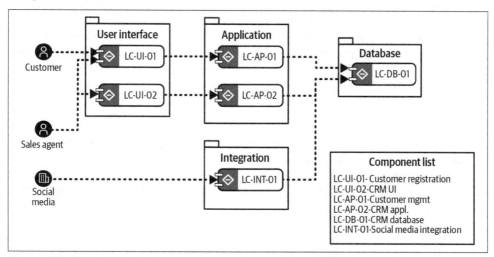

Figure 6-3. Example logical component architecture (simplified)

In many practical situations, a simplified version of the UML notation is sufficient to gain the relevant insights for the security architect. We use the following diagram elements:

Component name

We use rounded rectangles with the component names to depict the actual components.

Subsystem

To illustrate subsystems, we draw rectangles around components with the subsystems' names. Lines and arrows between components specify the relationship between two or more components. The direction of the arrow specifies the direction of the interaction between the components. In the example in Figure 6-3, the sales agent actor is using the customer registration user interface.

Actors

The actors in the component architecture should match up with the actors in the system context diagram.

The component architecture diagram is one of the most used diagrams outlining the components of a system.

Sequence Diagram

A sequence diagram, on the other hand, shows the dynamic interactions between individual components and how these components collaborate to realize a given scenario. Sequence diagrams are mainly used for architecturally significant use cases, and we document them using a UML sequence diagram (*https://oreil.ly/z475G*). Sequence diagrams are especially useful when it's important to understand the order and timing of the execution of methods and when data is flowing from one component to another.

Figure 6-4 illustrates an example of a sequence diagram. The example diagram depicts a typical login routine for a website that uses an authentication provider such as Microsoft or Google. The user enters the website's address into the browser and forwarding of the user takes place to the authentication provider, who subsequently redirects back to the web app, which validates the authentication and displays the protected resource.

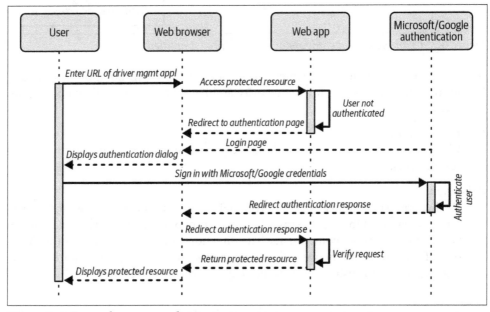

Figure 6-4. Example sequence diagram

We use the following key diagram elements:

Lifeline elements
Boxes at the top of the diagram represent actors and components relevant to the diagram.

Activation bars

Activation bars visualize the period of active processing of a method. In the example in Figure 6-4, the activation bar for the user visualizes the period from when the user enters the URL into the web browser until it displays the protected resource.

Messages

Messages represent the interaction between the actors and components. Arrows between the lifelines represent messages. A full line represents the call, and a dotted line represents the reply message, if applicable. Return messages are optional in the diagram; their usage depends on the level of required detail.

Self-messages

Self-messages illustrate that a return message depends on a method execution before that return message. In the example in Figure 6-4, the *authenticate user* self-message with the Microsoft/Google authentication illustrates that the user first needs authentication with Microsoft/Google before the return of the redirection response.

We draw messages from the top to the bottom and, with that, document the timely sequence of the interactions.

Collaboration Diagram

A collaboration diagram is a different way of looking at the dynamic relationships of components to describe how a system collaborates. Instead of showing the flow of information, the collaboration diagram depicts the components residing in the overall architecture of the system represented by the UML collaboration diagram. Figure 6-5 illustrates an example of a component collaboration diagram.

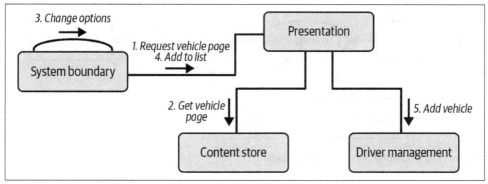

Figure 6-5. Example collaboration diagram

We use the following key diagram elements:

Component name
> We depict the actual components as rectangles with the component names.

Links
> Links represent a relationship between the components represented by solid lines.

Arrows
> Arrows between the components represent messages. The associated numbers indicate the order of the message flow.

Sequence diagrams and collaboration diagrams express similar information but visualize this in different ways. Collaboration diagrams are especially useful for illustrating simpler interactions between a small number of objects and may be a better representation for a business stakeholder. If the number of objects and interactions increases, the diagram becomes increasingly hard to read. A sequence diagram might then be a better choice.

Data Flow Diagram

The previous diagrams concentrated on the system's decomposition into functional components and how those components interact with one another. Another important aspect to consider is how data flows, where it's processed, and where it's stored, because data is what we're concerned about. The data flow diagram (DFD) is a graphical representation of the data flow within a system or process. It depicts how data moves from one component or entity to another within a system, emphasizing inputs, outputs, processes, and data storage. Figure 6-6 illustrates an example of a data flow diagram.

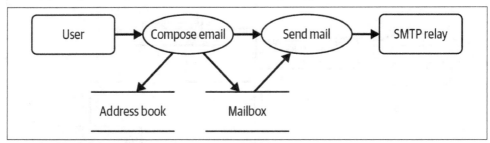

Figure 6-6. Example data flow diagram

A data flow diagram typically includes the following elements:

Processes
> Processes are activities or operations within the system that manipulate or transform data. These operations can take the form of computations, alterations to data, or anything else that's carried out inside the system. An ellipse represents processes.

Data flows
> Data flows show the movement of data between system components or processes. They depict the paths along which data flows from a source to a destination. They're represented as an arrow pointing in the direction of data movement. Keep in mind that the arrows are unidirectional. This is especially important during threat modeling, where you want to understand what data is flowing in what direction.

Data stores
> Data stores are repositories or storage locations for data within the system, for example, databases, files, or any other form of persistent data storage. They're drawn in the shape of a rectangle with parallel lines.

External entities
> External entities are entities that interact with the system from outside of it. They can be users, other systems, or any other external data source or destination. They're visualized as a box.

Because they depict the processing and sharing of data within a system, data flow diagrams are helpful tools in system analysis and design. They help in identifying potential bottlenecks, comprehending dependencies, and assessing information flow, all of which are necessary for evaluating system functionality, recognizing possible risks, and developing efficient processes.

Component Architectural Thinking Process

Now that we understand several ways of visualizing a component architecture in order to acquire meaningful information from it, we must understand how we actually construct the component architecture. We develop a component architecture in three stages, increasing the level of detail as we go:

Plan: What are we building?
> Determine the key components that comprise the system. We strongly encouraged you to use applicable architecture patterns, reference architectures, and reusable assets during this process to speed up the process and improve the quality of the solution. More on this in Chapter 9. After identifying the major components, divide them into subsystems and components, and then assign

functional responsibilities. Structure the components to ensure loose coupling, high cohesion, and other desirable properties.

Design: How will it work?
Now that we know what components exist in the system, we must define their interfaces, the data that's transferred, pre- and post-conditions, and interaction sequences.

Deploy: How do we build it?
We describe the realization of the components in this final stage of the modeling process. We must outline the implementation strategy and identify internal and third-party products, packages, and solutions. This is the stage at which you will make important architectural decisions. We describe the significance of architectural patterns and decisions in Chapter 9.

We continue by applying the concepts to the development of a component architecture using the case study in Appendix A.

Case Study: Component Architecture

To begin the definition of a component architecture, we start by looking at the system context diagram (Figure 6-7) that we developed earlier to identify the actors that we need to consider. Every actor somehow interacts with our system, so they need one or another type of interface, be it a web UI or an API.

We have three types of actors in our system:

Functional human actors (illustrated as solid user icons)
Those actors will need a user interface to interact with the system.

Operational human actors (illustrated as outlined user icons)
Until we've established the operational view of the solution, we wait to include those actors in the decomposition of the system.

System actors (illustrated as building icons)
Those actors require integration capability to either receive incoming functional calls or establish outgoing functional calls.

The case study doesn't provide enough information to determine if the Clean Threats actor is a human or a system actor. It might be a human actor, such as SOC analysts accessing a SIEM or security, orchestration, automation, and response (SOAR) capability that's part of our system, or it can be a system actor when the SIEM or SOAR capability isn't part of our system. This is an item that we need to clarify with relevant stakeholders when we architect the operational solution. We could add this as an issue to resolve in the RAID log we will discuss in Chapter 10.

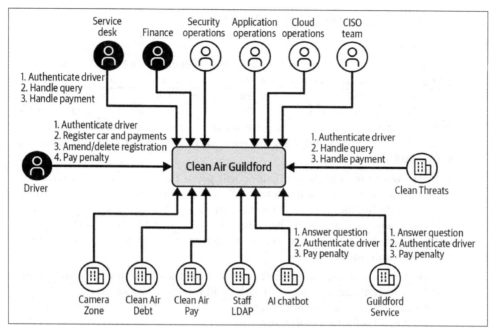

Figure 6-7. Case study system context diagram

Let's have a look at the case study to understand what functional building blocks our system requires. We've highlighted those parts of the case study that provide us with information about the components and interfaces. A solid border highlights databases, a dotted border highlights system integration; and a dashed border highlights user interfaces. Have a read through the marked-up case study.

Marked-Up Case Study

The project has already started to build the new hybrid cloud solution, with the core application hosted using PostgreSQL on a public cloud platform.

- With the Clean Air application containing:
  - Systems of engagement using Open Liberty running on OpenShift at the center
  - Cached and state data stored in MongoDB and Redis cloud databases
- Connected to on-premises systems
  - A payments gateway connecting to Clean Air Pay using Apache Kafka Streams

— Integration into a debt facility using RabbitMQ

- The installation of Automatic Number Plate Recognition (ANPR) cameras has taken place on the roads leading into the clean air zone. Camera Zone reads the number plates of vehicles and sends information to Clean Air Guildford (CAG). CAG checks the type of vehicle in the Driver and Vehicle Licensing Agency's (DVLA) database. Camera Zone provides an outsourced service for the running of the ANPR cameras and does the same service for other clean air schemes, police, and security services.

- Vehicle owners with higher emissions will pay a £10 fee to enter the clean air zone during peak hours of 07:00 to 19:00 Monday through Saturday. Within 48 hours of entering the clean air zone, they must pay this fee via a payment portal that the scheme will provide. They have selected Clean Air Pay as their payment provider. As this is a payment service, the design of the application must include PCI DSS requirements.

- For those vehicle owners who don't pay the fee at the end of the 48-hour period, a debt collection agency, Clean Air Debt, will receive information on the driver. They will send out letters notifying the vehicle owner of the fine and, after a period, pursue collection of the fine.

- The vehicle owners will be able to use their Google or Microsoft IDs to log in to the portal and register their car with the program so that, upon entering Guildford, the payments are automatically made.

- The scheme uses the Guildford Service SaaS application in a service center to respond to queries by phone and take payments.

- An AI chatbot, provided as a cloud service by the public cloud provider, will handle driver queries more rapidly without waiting for telephone support via the service center.

The program manager has no security solution but has identified one high-level security requirement:

IAM_001 Integrate single sign-on by using the Staff LDAP Directory as an Identity Provider for staff.

With the markup of the case study, we can now create a list of the functional building blocks of the system.

As you can see in Table 6-1, we've made a number of assumptions where the information wasn't provided in the first place. We need to document these assumptions in the RAID log so that we can validate them at a later point in time. We will introduce the RAID log in Chapter 10.

Table 6-1. Identified functional building blocks

Type	Purpose	Technology	Component
Databases [solid border]	Main database	PostgreSQL	LC-DB-01
	Cache, state data	MongoDB	LC-DB-02
	Cache, state data	Redis DB	LC-DB-03
Integrations [dotted border]	CAG → Clean Air Pay	Kafka streams	LC-INT-01
	CAG → Clean Air Debt	RabbitMQ	LC-INT-04
	Camera Zone → CAG	Not defined—we assume REST API	LC-INT-03
	CAG → DVLA	Not defined—we assume REST API	LC-INT-05
	CAG → Google/Microsoft	OAuth 2.0, OpenID	LC-UI-02
	AI chatbot → CAG	Not defined—we assume REST API	LC-INT-02
	CAG → Staff LDAP Directory	SAML 2.0, OpenID Connect, OAuth 2.0, and WS-Federation	LC-UI-01
User interfaces [dashed border]	Driver and car registration	Not defined—we assume web portal	LC-UI-02
	Payment portal	Not defined—we assume web portal	LC-UI-02
Application components	Driver management	Red Hat OpenShift	LC-AP-01
	Vehicle management	Red Hat OpenShift	LC-AP-02
	Payment management	Red Hat OpenShift	LC-AP-03

Another observation that illustrates the iterative process we're in is that we've identified actors that we hadn't identified in our initial version of the system context: the DVLA for vehicle verification and Google or Microsoft ID for driver authentication. Did you also recognize that the case study highlights the Guildford Service SaaS application for the service desk? We've also included that in our system context diagram. Though we assume that the only technical integration used in our system is that Guildford Service SaaS is using Staff Lightweight Directory Access Protocol (LDAP) for single sign-on for the service desk users. That means that we also need a user interface for the service desk users as well as the finance users, which we also identified when we developed the system context. We're also making the first architectural decisions, when we assume REST APIs and the authentication protocol for some integrations. In Chapter 9 we will discuss the significance of the decision and how we document the decision in architectural decision records.

Based on this information, we can now draw the initial version of the component architecture for our system in Figure 6-8.

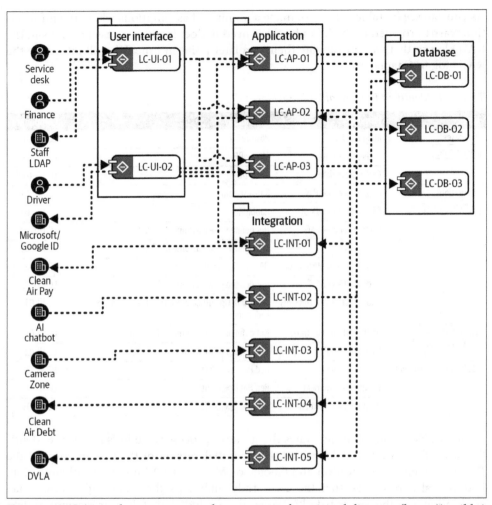

Figure 6-8. Case study component architecture; see the original diagram (https://oreil.ly/ SAHC)

This component architecture forms the basis for the next step, when we're going to model threats and countermeasures for our system.

As mentioned earlier, we've not yet considered the operational actors in our component architecture, as they mainly represent non-functional aspects of the solution. Once we've developed the deployment architecture of our system, we might need to adapt the component architecture.

In the checklist, we provide you with important considerations to remember when you develop the component architecture.

> ## Component Architecture QA Checklist
>
> - Make sure that you represent all functional actors in the component architecture and understand what interface they use to interact with the functional components.
>
> - Verify that you have defined components to satisfy all identified functional requirements.
>
> - Verify that you have identified all interfaces between the components and that you understand whether the interface is passing or receiving the respective data. Is the data that you identified during the development of the system context diagram flowing correctly through the functional components?
>
> - Because you don't know everything yet, you've made several assumptions throughout the process. Make sure you have documented those assumptions in the RAID log.
>
> - Application architects who develop the component architecture will have to think about many more details, which aren't that relevant for what we, as security architects, are using the component architecture for. For example:
>
>   — Verify that you partitioned the components in a way that allows the development work to be divided between developers.
>
>   — Verify that you loosely couple the components to allow for independent development work.

With the techniques of component architecture at hand, we will now use this information as a basis for building a threat model.

Security Concepts

Before we dive into threat modeling, we want to recap some fundamental security concepts and relationships by extending the definitions from Common Criteria (CC) ISO/IEC 15408-1:2022 (*https://oreil.ly/qVEkC*), as illustrated in Figure 6-9.

We're considering information assets for storage, processing, and transmission by IT systems and how they meet the requirements defined by the information's owners. Owners can realize the intended value of the information by performing processes on it.

Owners of information demand the preservation of confidentiality, integrity, and availability, and the reduction of risks to an acceptable level. Additional controls or countermeasures are necessary to achieve this, with countermeasures mitigating the vulnerabilities that threat actors might exploit.

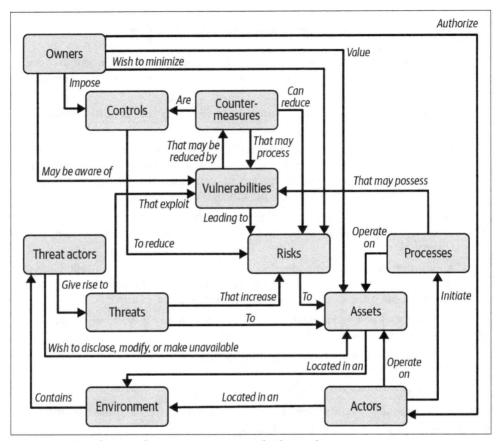

Figure 6-9. Fundamental security concepts and relationships

Let's illustrate these fundamental concepts with an example:

> We assume our solution has a SQL injection *vulnerability*, a weakness or flaw that allows an attacker (threat actor) to inject malicious SQL code into a query. The *threat actor* poses a *threat* or danger of unauthorized access to data (the *assets*) or unauthorized manipulation of data assets through an exploit of the vulnerability. The vulnerability leads to a *risk*, and the fact that the threat can exploit the vulnerability increases the overall risk to the organization. The location of assets in the *environment* determines the risk from threat actors, the exposure to threats, and the *processes* that authorized *actors* use to operate on the assets. Implementing *countermeasures*, such as input validation and the use of parameterized queries, can lower the risk by ensuring that the application treats inputs as data rather than executable code.

For a more in-depth discussion of information risk management concepts, we suggest you read *Information Risk Management* (*https://oreil.ly/PAdF_*) (BCS) by David Sutton.

Now that we've established the core security language and linkages, we're ready to dive into threat modeling.

Threat Modeling

We saw in "Component Architecture" on page 163 how we can compose and decompose a system into functional building blocks to meet its functional requirements. Functional requirements are typically well specified because they define the primary reason for the system's existence. As you saw in Chapter 4, security requirements derive from external rules, internal policies and standards, and, most importantly, the actual threats exposing a system. So, basically, we need to figure out how to breach the system to identify countermeasures to detect, correct, and prevent threats.

Threat modeling is a process to identify those threats to the system, the associated risks, and the correct controls to produce effective countermeasures.

Threat modeling is the cornerstone of application security and the secure by design discipline. When done correctly, threat models can help teams identify and mitigate issues early in the solution lifecycle. Threat models also help feed downstream security processes like assurance processes (for example, QA testing, code scanning, and penetration testing) as well as threat detection use cases, as illustrated in Figure 6-1.

There is a fundamental difficulty in developing threat models, as you never know when you have reached the end. The level of creativity, expertise, and time available limits the number of threats you are able to identify. There are many different threat modeling techniques available that require different levels of expertise and effort with varying numbers of layers. In Table 6-2, we're listing some of the various techniques, which you can apply individually or combined.

Table 6-2. Threat modeling techniques

Level of expertise	Threat model layers	Rooted in		
		Systems engineering	System analysis	Process engineering
High	<ul><li>CVE (*https://www.cve.org*)</li><li>CWE (*https://cwe.mitre.org*)</li><li>Security controls</li><li>Persona non-grata (*https://oreil.ly/rJj29*)</li><li>MITRE ATT&CK framework</li></ul>	TARA (*https://oreil.ly/O62UY*)	<ul><li>PASTA (*https://oreil.ly/IHhz4*)</li><li>Attack Trees (*https://oreil.ly/iVaJn*)</li></ul>	
Medium	<ul><li>Application components</li><li>Infrastructure components</li><li>Data flows</li><li>Threat actors</li><li>Threat vectors</li></ul>	Trike (*https://www.octotrike.org*)	OWASP Application Threat Modeling (*https://oreil.ly/TGq-V*)	Microsoft Threat Modeling Tool (*https://oreil.ly/dtEMP*)

Level of expertise	Threat model layers	Rooted in	
Low	• Boundaries/zones of control • Assets • Threats • Threat actors • Controls/countermeasures	STRIDE (*https://oreil.ly/AYsl0*)	VAST (*https://oreil.ly/7W1Fk*)

Our objective is to introduce threat modeling as a technique and explain how this technique fits into the overall security architectural thinking process. You can find more information and deeper insights into the topic in books like *Threat Modeling: Designing for Security* (*https://oreil.ly/dNLnk*) and *Threat Modeling* (*https://oreil.ly/PB1O5*) (O'Reilly) by Izar Tarandach and Matthew J. Coles.

We're describing here a common approach for threat modeling that allows you to apply different threat modeling techniques depending on the type of system you are assessing and the level of expertise of the people involved in the threat modeling process. Our description and the case study example assume a low level of expertise in threat modeling.

For this approach, it's required to have a visual of the solution design. A commonly used artifact is a component architecture, which we've looked at in the previous section. Another option is to use a data flow diagram as a starting point. The described steps are valid for both types of diagrams. We recommend selecting key use cases and following the associated data through the solution.

For simple architectures, we can use tags within the visual to mark the elements of the threat model. For more complex architectures, it's good practice to use threat modeling tools to support this process.

Documenting the Threat Modeling Process

For each step in the threat modeling process, we're providing recommendations in the form of documentation activities on how to depict and document the information that we identified in the respective step. With each step, you will add a layer of information to the threat modeling diagram. Figure 6-13 shows the final version of that diagram assembling all steps.

We will now go through six steps to develop the threat model. In each step, we will add a layer of information to the threat model diagram. To structure and focus your efforts it's also good practice to work through different use cases of your solution and perform the following steps per use case. We identified a number of use cases when we developed the system context diagram, and starting from there, you can trace the data flow through the system.

Identify Boundaries

Boundaries are demarcations that separate one entity from another and where data flows from one entity to another. That can, for example, be between deployment components, between processes, between an application and a file system, between an actor and an interface, between technology boundaries as described in Chapter 7, security policies, etc. These boundaries represent the attack surface of the system, and many threats will cluster around these boundaries. The trust boundaries are a point of security enforcement where you place firewalls, enforce authentication, terminate encryption, etc.

It's therefore important to know where the trust boundaries are within the architecture (system, solution, product, etc.).

Often, a combination of the component architecture and the deployment architecture, which we're introducing in Chapter 8, will provide the most comprehensive basis to identify and draw the trust boundaries.

In the example in Figure 6-10, we've drawn trust boundaries into the diagram as dashed lines around the network boundaries internet and public cloud as well as system boundaries of the Kubernetes cluster and the database.

Identify the Trust Boundaries

To document the identified boundaries on the component diagram, complete the following documentation activity:

- Draw in trust boundaries as dashed boxes into the diagram.

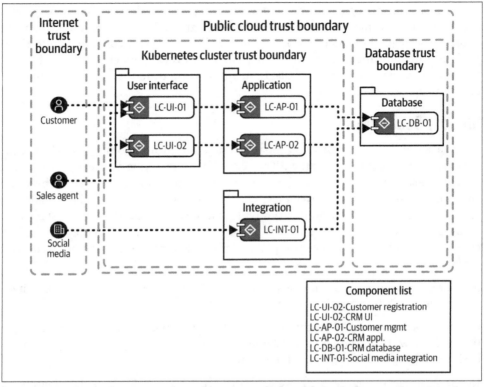

Figure 6-10. Example component architecture with trust boundaries; see the original diagram (https://oreil.ly/SAHC)

Identify Assets

We need to understand what assets we need to protect in the system. In Chapter 5, we identified different types of data our system is transferring, processing, and storing. We now need to identify the location of the assets in the system.

Storage of data takes place in different locations: data stores, credential stores, third-party tools, solutions, and software.

Document the Assets

To document the identified assets on the component diagram, complete the following documentation activities:

- Draw a numbered, colored label $\boxed{A01}$ on the components where the storage of assets takes place. See Figure 6-13 for an example.
- Document the type and volume of assets identified.

Identify Threat Actors

Now that we know where the assets are and what threats they're exposed to within the system, we need to understand who the threat actors are. Information about the threat actors helps us understand the likelihood of the exploitation of a threat by threat actors in relation to the location of the threat in the system.

On a high level, we can distinguish between the following categories of threat actors:

External threat actors
    External threat actors are external to the organization:

    External authorized malicious actors
        Individuals with legitimate access and malicious intent.

    External unauthorized malicious actors
        Individuals without legitimate access and with malicious intent. This can also be further broken down into nation-state-sponsored, activists, criminal organizations, etc.

Internal threat actors
    Internal threat actors are internal to the organization. This can be an employee, a contractor, etc.; someone who has legitimate insights about the organization:

    Internal unauthorized malicious actors
        Individuals without legitimate access and with malicious intent

    Internal authorized, "honest but curious" actors
        Individuals with legitimate access to the data, just not all the data

    Inadvertent actors
        Individuals who inadvertently compromise security through careless actions or a lack of awareness

Document the Threat Actors

To document the identified threat actors on the component diagram, complete the following documentation activities:

- Draw the numbered, colored label $\boxed{\text{TA01}}$ on the logical
  boundaries identified in step Identify Boundaries.
- Document the types of threat actors.

We recommend finding a classification of threat actors that's most relevant for your
organization. This is relevant for drawing the right conclusions and easing communication within your organization.

Identify Threats

You can apply different, complementary techniques to identify threats. When you
perform manual threat modeling, you can start with high-level threats informed by
the OWASP Top Ten (*https://oreil.ly/ok4VB*).

For a more structured approach to developing threats and mitigation techniques,
we recommend methods like STRIDE or attack trees. We're briefly describing these
methods in the following sections. For a more exhaustive description we recommend
books like *Threat Modeling: Designing for Security* (*https://oreil.ly/dNLnk*).

STRIDE

STRIDE is a threat modeling method that assists in the identification and categorization of potential threats in software systems. The STRIDE approach was developed in
1999 by Loren Kohnfelder and Praerit Garg at Microsoft. It offers a systematic way
to identify and mitigate security risks. Each letter of the word STRIDE represents a
different category of threats:

Spoofing
    Spoofing threats are those in which an attacker impersonates another user, entity,
    or system to gain unauthorized access or deceive the system.

Tampering
    Tampering threats entail unauthorized changes or modifications to data, code,
    or system components. Attackers may modify data, implant malicious code, or
    change system settings.

Repudiation
    Repudiation threats occur when an attacker performs an action and then denies
    performing it. Modifying logs, interfering with audit trails, or fabricating records
    are examples of such activities.

Information disclosure

This category comprises threats in which sensitive or secret information is inadvertently or maliciously given to unauthorized parties. It can happen due to vulnerabilities that expose data during transmission, storage, or processing.

Denial of service

Denial of service (DoS) threats try to disrupt or prevent the normal operation of a system or service. Attackers may flood the system with requests, drain system resources, or exploit vulnerabilities to cause system failures or outages.

Elevation of privilege

Elevation of privilege threats include attackers gaining illegal access or privileges within a system. They may use vulnerabilities to increase their privileges, circumvent access controls, or do operations that exceed their authorized degree of access.

The purpose of a STRIDE analysis is to identify potential threats within each category for the specific system under consideration. This entails examining the system's components, relationships, and capabilities to determine how each threat category might materialize. Just to emphasize, the goal isn't the categorization of threats, but the identification of them. The STRIDE categories are a way to brainstorm threats. Microsoft developed a card game Elevation of Privilege (EoP) (*https://www.micro soft.com/en-gb/download/details.aspx?id=20303*) to support the creative process of identifying threats. This game helps teams to think about how to *break* the solution.

Attack trees

Attack trees are graphical models used to represent and analyze potential attack paths and scenarios in a system. They provide a structured way to understand the steps an attacker might take to exploit vulnerabilities and achieve specific goals.

Attack trees serve as a visual representation and analysis tool for understanding the potential attack vectors and sequences an adversary may follow. They help in prioritizing security measures, identifying vulnerabilities, and designing effective defenses. Figure 6-11 illustrates an attack tree based on a simple non-IT goal to break into a house to illustrate the concept. Out of the diagram, we can derive controls; for example, storage of the key shouldn't be under the doormat, and installation of an alarm should take place to detect a break-in.

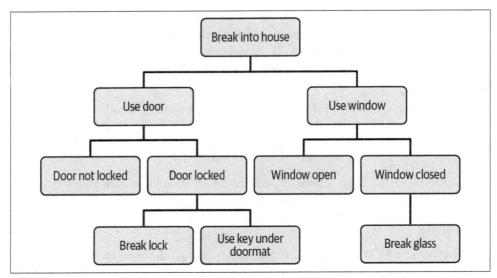

Figure 6-11. Example attack tree

Here's how attack trees work:

Goal-oriented
Attack trees start with a specific attacker's goal, such as gaining unauthorized access to a system, stealing sensitive data, or disrupting a service. The top node of the attack tree represents this primary goal.

Decomposition
We break down the primary goal into subgoals or attack steps, forming a tree-like structure. Each subgoal represents a specific objective that an attacker needs to accomplish to progress toward the primary goal.

Attack techniques
For each subgoal, we identify different attack techniques or methods. These techniques describe the specific actions an attacker may take to achieve the subgoal. Attack techniques can include exploiting vulnerabilities, social engineering, brute-force attacks, or any other means of compromising the system.

Leaf nodes
The attack tree branches continue until they reach the leaf nodes, which represent the lowest-level attack steps. These steps are typically simple and concrete actions that an attacker can perform, such as executing a specific command, bypassing an authentication mechanism, or exploiting a vulnerability.

Dependencies

Attack trees can include dependencies between different attack steps. These dependencies represent the conditions or prerequisites needed for a successful attack. Dependencies can include factors like prior access, knowledge, or the successful completion of another attack step.

Probability and impact

Attack trees can incorporate probability and impact assessments for each attack step or subgoal. This involves assigning values or probabilities to estimate the likelihood of success or failure for each step, as well as evaluating the potential impact if the step is successful.

Analysis and mitigation

Attack trees enable the analysis of attack paths and provide insights into the critical attack steps and potential vulnerabilities in a system. This analysis helps us identify areas where we can apply security controls, countermeasures, or mitigation strategies to disrupt or prevent the attack paths.

The MITRE ATT&CK framework (*https://attack.mitre.org*) provides a framework for a more low-level threat analysis as well as for the identification of mitigation approaches. We recommend you leverage threat modeling tools that feed information from MITRE, NIST, and CERT databases and allow a more comprehensive way of documenting the different elements of a threat model.

Document the Threats

To document the identified threats on the component diagram, complete the following documentation activities:

- Draw a numbered, colored label $\boxed{T01}$ to the components or connections where you have identified the respective threat.
- Document the type of threat.

LINDDUN

The previously mentioned techniques don't specifically address privacy-related issues. The LINDDUN Privacy Threat Modeling Framework (*https://linddun.org*) developed by privacy experts at KU Leuven closes that gap. LINDDUN provides a systematic approach to reason about privacy concerns structured in seven privacy threat types that make up the word LINDDUN:

Linking

Linking data items or user actions may have unintended privacy consequences, even if it does not reveal one's identity.

Identifying

Many systems require the identification of data subjects; identifying threats arise when leaks, deduction, or inference reveal the identity, even if it is not intentional or desired.

Nonrepudiation

Being able to assign a claim, i.e. knowing, doing, or saying something, to a specific person. This results in the loss of plausible deniability, as seen with a whistleblower who may face prosecution.

Detecting

Observing someone and determining their level of involvement. Detecting threats does not require the ability to read the actual data; simply knowing that it exists is enough to infer more (sensitive) information.

Data disclosure

Excessive collection, storage, processing, or sharing of personal data. Data disclosure threats are situations in which the disclosure of personal data to, within, and from the system is considered problematic.

Unawareness and unintervenability

Inadequate information, involvement, or empowerment of individuals in the processing of their personal data.

Noncompliance

The system deviates from best practices in security and data management, as well as standards and legislation, resulting in incomplete risk management. The emphasis is on the organizational and operational management context within which a system or service operates.

The authors of LINDDUN have developed methods for a lean and a more exhaustive approach to the topic. The method is equally supported by a card game, like STRIDE is. The card game helps to facilitate brainstorming sessions. This concludes the approaches to identifying threats; as a next step, we need to consider what we can do about them.

Identify Controls

Now that we have a good understanding of the threats to which the system is vulnerable, we must define the controls that will most effectively mitigate the identified threats. There are three types of security controls: detective, preventive, and corrective. Each category focuses on a different aspect of security and aims to mitigate risks in distinct ways. Here are the definitions of each type of control:

Detective security controls

Detective controls identify and detect security incidents, anomalies, or violations that have already occurred within a system or network. They help in discovering and investigating security breaches or unauthorized activities. Detective controls include:

Intrusion detection systems (IDS)

These systems monitor network traffic, looking for patterns or signatures that indicate potential security breaches or malicious activity.

Security information and event management (SIEM)

SIEM systems collect and analyze logs and events from various sources to identify potential security incidents and provide real-time alerts.

Log monitoring and analysis

Regularly reviewing logs and analyzing them can help detect unauthorized access attempts, system changes, or suspicious activities.

Security audits and assessments

Periodic assessments and audits of systems, networks, and applications can identify vulnerabilities, weaknesses, or noncompliance with security policies.

Continuous compliance

Continuous compliance refers to the ongoing process of monitoring an organization's information technology assets to ensure that they're in compliance with defined security standards.

Preventive security controls

Preventive controls are proactive measures implemented to reduce the likelihood of security incidents or breaches. They focus on preventing threats from occurring or gaining access to sensitive information. Preventive controls include:

Access control systems

These controls enforce authentication and authorization mechanisms, ensuring that only authorized users can access systems, data, or resources.

Firewalls

Firewalls act as a barrier between internal and external networks, filtering network traffic and blocking unauthorized access attempts.

Antivirus and anti-malware software

These tools scan for and prevent the execution of malicious software, viruses, or other forms of malware.

Security awareness training

Educating employees or users about security best practices and policies helps prevent social engineering attacks and improves overall security posture.

Software development proactive controls

OWASP has defined a list of the top 10 security techniques in the OWASP Proactive Controls (*https://oreil.ly/wtsnX*), which should be included in every software development project.

Corrective security controls

Corrective controls are measures taken after the identification of a security incident or breach. They aim to mitigate the impact, recover from the incident, and restore normal operations. Corrective controls include:

Incident response plans

These plans specify the actions and procedures that organizations must take in the event of a security incident to ensure a coordinated and effective response.

Backup and disaster recovery

Regularly backing up data and having a well-defined disaster recovery plan helps recover from incidents and minimize data loss.

Patch management

Applying security patches and updates to systems and software helps address vulnerabilities and protect against known exploits.

Forensic analysis

Conducting forensic analysis and investigation helps determine the cause, extent, and impact of a security incident and gathers evidence for legal purposes.

By combining detective, preventive, and corrective security controls, organizations can establish a comprehensive and layered security approach that safeguards assets and mitigates risks effectively.

How Many Controls Are Enough?

You can now ask, *How many detective, preventive, and corrective controls do I need?* When deciding on the controls and the type of controls, you need to keep the goal in mind. The objective of security architecture is to reduce the risk that the organization faces to a level that is acceptable. Preventive controls have, in many cases, the biggest effect as they stop bad things from happening, but they usually come with the highest cost. Detective controls are the second choice, as they help to decrease the time to respond to an incident and, with that, the impact on the organization. And the last resort are corrective controls.

You might face situations where the cost of the protective control outweighs the benefit, and a detective control might be the better choice. Imagine an industrial company that needs to secure their OT environment. Installing security updates might require

---

service windows where the production systems need to be shut down by the company; this makes this operation extremely expensive. With frequent security updates, this would become a commercially unviable process. The decision might therefore be to focus more on detective controls to quickly identify malicious activities, which then enables fast response actions. In the next section, we will look into how we prioritize controls in a structured way.

For the identification of relevant and effective controls, established reference frameworks can be useful, for example:

- Enterprise security architecture as described in Chapter 2
- Reference architectures as described in Chapter 3
- MITRE ATT&CK framework (*https://attack.mitre.org*)
- Common Attack Pattern Enumeration and Classification (CAPEC) (*https://capec.mitre.org/*)
- The 18 CIS Critical Security Controls (*https://oreil.ly/0R-y2*)

We determined the location of the assets as well as the placement of threat actors and threats. In the end, we want to ensure the confidentiality, integrity, and availability of the assets. The assets don't only exist at rest in our solution but also in motion from one component to another. This is important for us to consider not only when we identify threats but also when we identify effective controls.

As we mentioned earlier, this threat modeling process can be based on either a component architecture diagram or a data flow diagram. In Figure 6-12, we've visualized an example flow of customer information [A02] from the customer through the user interface on the webserver and the application on the application server to the database. Threat [T02] is about missing transport layer encryption. As customer information is critical for this example solution, we decided for control [C03] link encryption consistently throughout the whole flow.

The arrows in the diagram visualize the direction of the respective data flows. For the visualization of a whole solution with many different types of data, this might become difficult to read; therefore, we started to look at key use cases. You can also create different data flow diagrams for different use cases and assemble the collective controls in a layered component architecture diagram, which we will continue with.

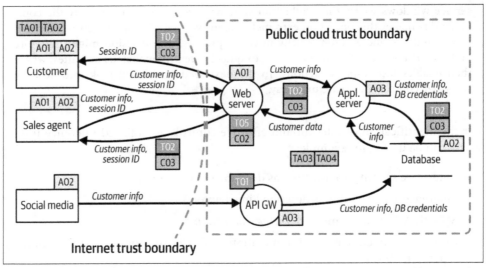

Figure 6-12. Data flow considerations; see the original diagram (https://oreil.ly/SAHC)

Document the Controls

To document the identified controls on the component diagram, complete the following documentation activities:

- Draw the numbered, colored label C01 next to where you previously labeled threats. This indicates that the control is addressing the respective threat.
- Document the control.

As you can see in Figure 6-13, adding all the information from the last five steps into one diagram as layers provides a very good overview and eases communication.

With each step of the iterative process we just went through, we were adding one layer of information to the diagram. Many diagramming tools support layers. It's a good idea to create a layer for each step. By doing so, you can quickly adapt the diagram to different audiences depending on the message you want to convey.

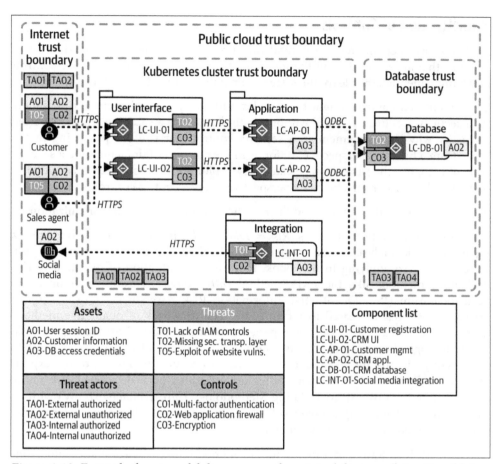

Figure 6-13. Example threat model diagram; see the original diagram (https://oreil.ly/ SAHC)

Prioritization of Controls

With the last step in the threat modeling process, we've now identified a list of controls that are mitigating all the identified threats in the system. If those controls aren't implemented, they leave the system vulnerable to the identified threat.

Some identified controls might be complex and costly to implement and maintain. As a security architect, you will without doubt come into a situation where you need to justify why the investment in a security control that you are proposing makes sense from a business perspective. If, for example, the cost of implementing a security control is higher than the damage caused by exploiting the associated threat, then it doesn't make sense from a business perspective to invest in this control.

That means we need to understand the risk the threat is posing to the organization.

The common definition of risk is: *Risk = Likelihood x Impact*. Within cybersecurity, qualitative risk analysis is the most commonly used approach to evaluating risk, which we're also applying in this book. However, the adoption of quantitative risk evaluation methods like the FAIR method (*https://oreil.ly/DosKe*) or Information Security Forum (ISF) Quantitative Information Risk Assessment (QIRA) (*https://oreil.ly/6O44x*) has increased in recent years. The drawback of qualitative methods is that there is bias based on the experience of the individual evaluating the risk. While it might be easier to identify the impact category of a risk, it's difficult to consistently identify the likelihood of a threat. To reduce the impact of the experiences of individuals, OWASP and other organizations have developed risk rating methods like the OWASP Risk Rating Methodology (*https://oreil.ly/61exW*) with its associated calculator (*https://oreil.ly/t948_*). Using this method removes a lot of bias and produces good enough, reproducible results.

The OWASP Risk Rating Method divides likelihood into threat agent and vulnerability factors, and impact into technical and business impact factors. We can influence all factors except the threat agent factor through the chosen risk treatment action. Threat agents are external factors outside of our area of influence.

Risk treatment approaches, also referred to as risk response strategies, are methods or strategies that organizations may implement to address identified risks and mitigate the potential impact of those risks. There are typically four common risk treatment approaches:

Avoidance
> The avoidance strategy involves eliminating or avoiding the risk altogether by changing business practices or avoiding certain activities or situations that pose a significant risk. This approach is suitable when the potential risk outweighs the benefits and the organization chooses not to engage in the activity or use the resource associated with the risk.

Mitigation

> Risk mitigation focuses on reducing the likelihood or impact of a risk. This approach involves implementing measures or controls to minimize the probability of the risk occurring or to decrease the potential consequences. Mitigation strategies may include implementing security controls, conducting regular backups, applying software patches, and enforcing policies and procedures.

Transfer

> Risk transfer involves shifting the responsibility for managing the risk to a third party. This is often done through insurance policies or contracts, where the organization transfers the financial burden or liability associated with the risk to another party. By transferring the risk, the organization mitigates the potential financial impact of the risk, should it materialize.

Acceptance

> Sometimes, organizations may choose to accept certain risks when they're deemed acceptable or when the cost of implementing further risk mitigation measures outweighs the potential impact. Acceptance can be passive, with no specific actions taken to address the risk, or active, with the organization acknowledging the risk but establishing contingency plans or mitigation measures to minimize the impact if the risk occurs.

It's important to note that the choice of risk treatment approach depends on various factors, including the organization's risk appetite, available resources, legal and regulatory requirements, and the potential impact of the risk. A comprehensive risk management approach typically involves a combination of these strategies, tailored to the specific risks and context of the organization.

Documenting the risk treatment approach in a risk register, like the one in Figure 6-14, allows one to understand the risk before (inherent risk) and after applying the identified controls (residual risk). It also aids in determining which risk factors the control addresses. In many cases the risk can't be completely eliminated, it remains a residual risk. It's important for organizations to assess and manage residual risks to ensure that they're at an acceptable level and don't pose a significant threat to achieving objectives. Organizations may choose to accept certain residual risks if they're deemed low enough and the cost of further mitigation outweighs the potential impact of the risk. Alternatively, organizations may implement additional mitigation measures to further reduce residual risks if they're deemed too high.

Threat target (asset)	Attack technique/ threat	Threat actor	STRIDE	Inherent risk			Risk mitigation			Residual risk		
				Likelihood	Impact	Overall risk	Preventive	Detective	Corrective	Likelihood	Impact	Overall risk

Figure 6-14. Risk register

A risk matrix can help visualize the impact of the risk treatment actions. The risk management approach of the organization usually provides risk categories and definitions for impact and likelihood, as well as acceptable risk. In case this isn't available, we can use the risk matrix as outlined in Figure 6-15, with the acceptable risk indicated as the bold black line.

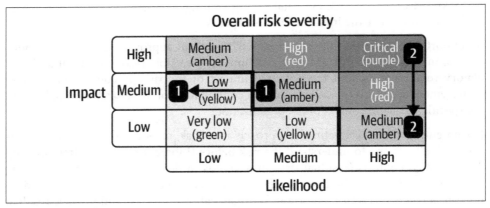

Figure 6-15. Risk matrix

The residual risk should ideally be below the acceptable risk for the organization. Arrows on individual risk items indicate how the risk treatment approach addressed likelihood and impact, as well as whether the approach resulted in a risk that was lower than the organization's acceptable risk.

Threat Modeling Tools

In the previous sections, we went through the key steps of developing a threat model in a manual way. This is good to develop a *quick* threat overview of the system and to develop response use cases which we will look further into in Chapter 11. Though it's also obvious that the more complex the system is and the deeper you go into the level of detail in the model, the more difficult it is to document and maintain the model in a manual way. That's where threat modeling tools that offer structured frameworks, automation, and visualization capabilities can improve this process. Using threat modeling tools has multiple benefits, such as:

- A *structured approach* will help you systematically identify potential threats, vulnerabilities, and security risks. Threat modeling tools will lead you through this process. This ensures you don't forget about any important security features of your system.

- Threat modeling tools enforce a *consistent approach* for risk assessment and threat identification throughout the organization, so that the threat modeler is less likely to miss threats as a result of human error or inconsistent method use.

- Many tools *automate* the creation of threat models, the detection of potential threats, and the evaluation of related risks. They primarily help in detecting *low hanging fruit* threats. This expedites the procedure and provides a more thorough threat modeling exercise so that the security architect can focus on the identification of more complex threats and abuse cases.

- Tools for threat modeling frequently offer *visual representations* of the system's architecture, data flow, and potential threats. These visualizations facilitate communication and make it easier for stakeholders to understand the security posture of the system.

- Facilitating *collaboration* between team members, including security experts, developers, architects, and business stakeholders, is a tool for threat modeling, making it possible to assess security risks from a multidisciplinary perspective.

- The *documentation* that's produced by threat modeling tools can help explain security risks to various stakeholders, such as developers, testers, and management. This documentation is useful for tracking the gradual reduction of identified threats.

- Numerous tools offer ways to classify or *prioritize risks* for the identified threats. This assists the team in concentrating on fixing the most important vulnerabilities first.

- Some threat modeling tools can *integrate with DevOps and development workflows*, making it simpler to include security considerations in the software development lifecycle.

- Tools for threat modeling frequently encourage the use of premade templates, industry standards, and security patterns. *Standardizing* the threat modeling process across projects encourages the reuse of tested threat models.

- Manual threat modeling can be laborious as systems become more complex. Particularly for large-scale systems, tools assist in managing complexity and enable more effective threat analysis and risk assessment with increased *scalability*.

- Threat modeling tools are useful in sectors with stringent security and compliance standards and *regulatory requirements* to demonstrate the systematic evaluation and reduction of security risks.

There are open source as well as commercial threat modeling tools on the market, for example:

- Open source
  — OWASP Threat Dragon (*https://oreil.ly/Q5pLh*)
  — OWASP pytm (*https://oreil.ly/5fm46*)
- Commercial
  — Microsoft Threat Modeling Tool (*https://oreil.ly/qme5s*) (no cost)
  — IriusRisk (*https://www.iriusrisk.com*) (licensed)
  — ThreatModeler (*https://threatmodeler.com*) (licensed)

Overall, threat modeling tools streamline the process of identifying and addressing security risks, driving the security of software applications and systems in a more efficient, consistent, and effective manner.

Now that we've gone through the process of developing a threat model, we will apply the methods and techniques to our case study in the following section.

Case Study: Threat Model

As we've not yet developed the deployment architecture of the system, which we will introduce in Chapter 8, we also cannot yet identify all trust boundaries. With the knowledge that we've gained, we can identify the internet, the public cloud environment, the OpenShift platform, and the databases as obvious trust boundaries because they represent system boundaries.

We developed an initial information asset register in Chapter 5. We're now identifying in the threat model the location of those assets:

- A01—Contact details
- A02—Vehicle details
- A03—Payment detail

- A04—Identification and authentication information
- A05—Payment transaction

All four types of threat actors are present in our solution, and we can place them on the model:

- TA01—External authorized
- TA02—External unauthorized
- TA03—Internal authorized
- TA04—Internal unauthorized

We use the STRIDE model to identify threats and mitigating controls. The list in Table 6-3 isn't comprehensive and should just illustrate the concept.

Table 6-3. Case study STRIDE threats and controls

STRIDE category	Threat	Control
Spoofing	T01—Attackers utilize local credentials to access the service by performing CSRF or other attacks on the users' browsers.	C01—Prevent local credential setup (preventive).
Tampering	T02—Malicious user has direct access to a database through a management interface.	C02—Implement separation of duties and the least privilege principle when assigning administrative privileges (preventive).
Repudiation	T03—Not able to verify who created a transaction during payment.	C03—Ensure all transactions are authenticated (preventive).
Information disclosure	T04—An attacker gains access to sensitive data through a man-in-the-middle attack. T05—An attacker exploits a vulnerability by performing a mass data exfiltration of the database.	C04—Utilize modern encryption protocols (Consider TLS1.3 and PFS ciphers) (preventive). C05.1—Detect mass exfiltration of database (detective). C05.2—Implement separation of duties and the least privilege principle for application components authorized to query the database (preventive).
Denial of service	T06—Attackers perform a denial of service toward the service, preventing legitimate users from consuming the service.	C06—Configure appropriate public cloud-provided DDoS protection (protective).
Elevation of privileges	T07—An attacker exploits features that should be reserved for privileged users.	C07—Implement the least privilege design principle and design privileges for users (protective).

We can now represent the specified boundaries, assets, threats, threat actors, and controls in the threat model diagram in Figure 6-16.

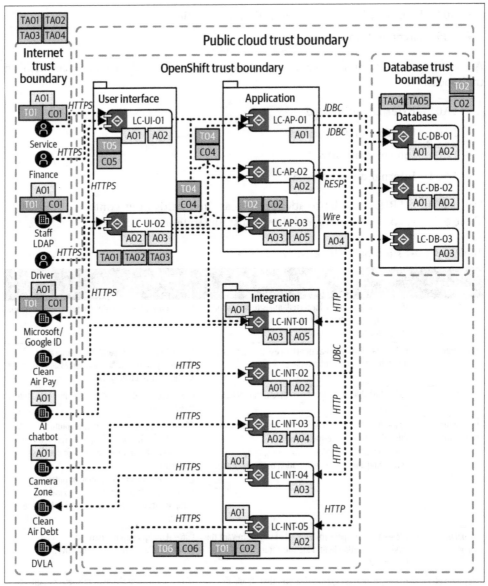

Figure 6-16. Case study threat model; see the original diagram (https://oreil.ly/SAHC)

The risk assessment demonstrated for the denial-of-service threat, T06, that external unauthorized threat actors can perform the attack.

Applying the OWASP Risk Rating Methodology, we get an overall high-severity risk rating, as shown in Table 6-4.

Table 6-4. Case study: Risk evaluation before applying controls

Likelihood factors		Impact factors	
Threat agent factors	**Vulnerability factors**	**Technical impact factors**	**Business impact factors**
Skill Level *5—Advanced computer user*	Ease of discovery *9—Automated tools available*	Loss of confidentiality *0—N/A*	Financial damage *7—Significant effect on annual profit*
Motive *4—Possible reward*	Ease of exploit *9—Automated tools available*	Loss of integrity *0—N/A*	Reputation damage *5—Loss of goodwill*
Opportunity *7—Some access or resource required*	Awareness *9—Public knowledge*	Loss of availability *7—Extensive primary services interrupted*	Noncompliance *0—N/A*
Size *9—Anonymous internet user*	Intrusion detection *9—Not logged*	Loss of accountability *7—Possibly traceable*	Privacy violation *0—N/A*
Threat agent factor HIGH	**Vulnerability factor** HIGH	**Technical impact factor** MEDIUM	**Business impact factor** MEDIUM
Likelihood factor—HIGH		**Impact factor—MEDIUM**	
Overall risk severity—HIGH			

If we do the same assessment with the recommended DDoS protection controls, we get a significantly lower risk rating (see Table 6-5). The DDoS protection control greatly reduces the technical and business impact as it diverts network traffic loads away from the business application and allows the normal interactions with the application. We can't address the threat agent factor, as this is outside of our control.

Table 6-5. Case study risk evaluation after applying controls (residual risk)

Likelihood factors		Impact factors	
Threat agent factors	**Vulnerability factors**	**Technical impact factors**	**Business impact factors**
Skill Level *5—Advanced computer user*	Ease of discovery *3—Difficult*	Loss of confidentiality *0—N/A*	Financial damage *0—N/A*
Motive *4—Possible reward*	Ease of exploit *3—Difficult*	Loss of integrity *0—N/A*	Reputation damage *0—N/A*
Opportunity *7—Some access or resource required*	Awareness *4—Hidden*	Loss of Availability *1—Minimal secondary services interrupted*	Noncompliance *0—N/A*
Size *9—Anonymous internet user*	Intrusion detection *9—Not logged*	Loss of accountability *7—Possibly traceable*	Privacy violation *0—N/A*
Threat agent factor HIGH	**Vulnerability factor** MEDIUM	**Technical impact factor** LOW	**Business impact factor** LOW
Likelihood factor—MEDIUM		**Impact factor—LOW**	
Overall risk severity—LOW			

DDoS protection addresses to some extent the vulnerability factor, but mainly the technical and business impact factors, leaving the organization at low risk, as illustrated in Figure 6-17.

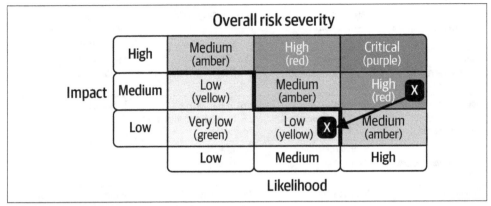

Figure 6-17. Case study risk matrix

We can now also add this risk into the risk register in Figure 6-18 where we document the original inherent risk as well as the controls that reduce the initial risk to the residual risk. In our example the residual risk is below the *acceptable risk* line and therefore acceptable to the organization. So we have achieved the objective of reducing the risk of a DDoS attack to an acceptable level by introducing preventive, detective, and corrective controls.

Threat target (asset)	Attack technique/ threat	Threat actor	STRIDE	Inherent risk			Risk mitigation			Residual risk		
				Likelihood	Impact	Overall risk	Preventive	Detective	Corrective	Likelihood	Impact	Overall risk
User interface	DDoS attack	External unauthorized	DoS	H	M	H	DDoS protection	Monitor network flow	DDoD protection	M	L	L

Figure 6-18. Case study risk register

In the following checklist, we've collected the key considerations that should help you develop a high-quality threat model.

Threat Model QA Checklist

- It's easy to identify the functional assets in a system. Also identify the metadata, logs, etc., which can contain data fragments of your functional assets.

- There are various methods available to identify threats. If you don't know where to start, use the OWASP Top 10 and try STRIDE. Make sure you don't overdo the threat model; you can easily lose yourself in detail. Start with a high-level view of key use cases and iterate through the different levels of detail over time, depending on the location of the critical assets.

- Verify that you have defined controls for all the threats you identified.

- Make sure that the identified controls reduce the likelihood and/or impact of the associated risk in the intended direction. If a control has no impact on either likelihood or impact, it basically has no effect at all.

Let's summarize what we went through in this chapter.

Summary

With the conclusion of this chapter, we've complemented security controls coming from external and internal regulations, policies, and standards with threat- and risk-based security controls that we developed after analyzing the functional layer of our system. The threat model is essential to this analysis.

In order to develop the threat model, we discussed how we can compose or decompose the functionality of the system with components in a component architecture and how different forms of component architecture diagrams can help to visualize static and dynamic views of the architecture.

We then discussed how we can develop a threat model using various techniques with the purpose of identifying those security controls that reduce the organization's risk.

A key thing to remember is that the threat model not only defines preventive controls but also detective and corrective controls. We will discuss in Chapter 11 how we use those controls as input to threat detection use cases for continuous security monitoring.

Remember, the threat model is a living artifact where you will need to update the initial version with every change or modification to the system, be it a functionally or non-functionally related change or modification.

While this chapter focused on the functional layer of the system, in Chapter 7, we're taking the first step toward a deployable architecture by discussing important aspects that come with a hybrid cloud strategy.

Exercises

1. Which of the following are objectives of documenting component architecture? Select all that apply.

   a. Provide detailed specifications of the components of the solution, such as product names, versions, and IP addresses

   b. Decompose the solution into functional building blocks

   c. Provide an abstraction of the system architecture, omitting many of the complexities

   d. Illustrate non-functional properties of the solution architecture

2. When is the threat modeling process complete? Select all that apply.

   a. Threat modeling should be done in iterations, increasing the level of detail with each iteration.

   b. After a one-hour workshop with relevant stakeholders.

   c. It's never complete.

   d. When the last element of the spoofing, tampering, repudiation, information disclosure, denial of service, and elevation of privilege (STRIDE) model is completed.

3. What are the key outcomes of a developed threat model? Select all that apply.

   a. Security controls which mitigate identified threats

   b. A solution architecture without vulnerabilities

   c. Security controls which reduce the risk to the organization

   d. Input to threat detection use cases

4. When do you need to develop or update a threat model? Select all that apply.

   a. When you change one line of code.

   b. When the solution architecture is initially developed.

   c. Every time there is a significant change to the solution.

   d. Before the solution goes into production.

5. How do you justify the importance of identified security controls?

   a. Security controls are important by default.

   b. Complete a risk assessment to identify those security controls that reduce the risk to an acceptable level.

   c. Security controls that address risks with a very high impact have the highest importance.

   d. Critical security risks must be addressed first.

6. How do you identify controls at the most relevant places in the solution architecture?

   a. Every component requires at least one security control.

   b. Every component which stores data requires security controls.

   c. Follow the data flows through the system and assess every trust boundary for threats, identifying relevant controls.

   d. Focus on those components with an incoming connection.

CHAPTER 7

Shared Responsibilities

In the past, an application or workload might have resided on just one or two technology platforms. The data might have resided in a relational database on a mainframe and the application server on a mid-range server. With the move to a hybrid cloud strategy by many organizations, the complexity has increased with the freedom to use on-premises, many different cloud providers, cloud service models, technology platforms, and cloud native compute options.

The simplified perimeter view with a hard boundary depicted in the system context diagram in Figure 5-6 from Chapter 5 is no longer enough. When using zero trust principles, there is no security boundary due to the removal of internal implicit trust, and identity becomes the new perimeter. With the workload hosted on many different technology platforms, we need a way of visually describing these different platforms that makes it easy to discuss and communicate the different options.

Each technology platform can have a different set of shared responsibilities in a hybrid cloud environment. The organization handling the data retains accountability even though the cloud service providers have the responsibility for securing the platform. Without a clear set of responsibilities, there won't be an owner to provide security to the cloud platform. We need a clear way of representing these shared responsibilities that enables decomposition down to detailed roles and responsibilities.

Each platform also has different security policies and practices that apply, making it complex to ensure security and compliance for the different platforms. The added complexity also makes it more difficult to architect security to secure sensitive workloads. We need a systematic way of analyzing the security controls that apply.

Before we discuss the approach to describing shared responsibilities, it's important to understand the different cloud computing terminology to effectively use the techniques and artifacts described in this chapter. We therefore start by reviewing cloud computing benefits, cloud service models, cloud computing platforms, shared responsibilities, landing zones, and hybrid cloud. It also shows how the role of an architect has changed with the many new challenges.

The second part of the chapter delves into techniques and shared responsibility artifacts to describe technology platforms, shared responsibilities, and landing zones. The artifacts help facilitate conversations about ownership of security in a hybrid cloud environment where there are multiple landing zones and platforms.

You can use the techniques discussed in this chapter when you build a new application or migrate an existing application to the cloud. In both cases, they enable a common understanding of the proposed compute platforms, the ownership of the shared responsibilities, and the security policies that apply to each layer of a compute platform. Let's continue by reviewing the artifacts we're working with in this chapter.

Chapter Artifacts

This chapter's main goal is to define a systematic way of defining shared responsibilities, including security, for a hybrid cloud infrastructure.

Figure 7-1 highlights, with white text in a black shaded box, the shared responsibility diagram artifact and many artifacts from the enterprise context used in the discussion within this chapter. The large number of enterprise context artifacts shows there will be a collection of information from a wide range of internal and external sources.

Enterprise Context

As a reminder, to help reinforce learning, the case study in Appendix A has information about the enterprise context for the worked examples in this chapter.

We're going to start with essential cloud computing concepts that will enable a discussion of the shared responsibility diagram and techniques later in the chapter.

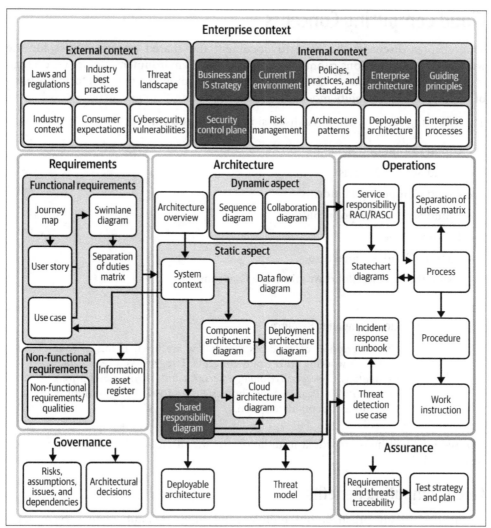

Figure 7-1. Shared responsibilities chapter artifacts

Cloud Computing Concepts

This chapter discusses the need to document the shared responsibilities for the workloads or applications running in a hybrid cloud environment. Before we do that, it's important to be clear on the cloud computing terminology that will form the basis of the shared responsibility model discussed later in the chapter.

The following sections contain a discussion of key cloud concepts:

- Cloud Computing Benefits
- Cloud Service Models
- Cloud Computing Platforms
- Cloud Security Responsibilities
- Landing Zones
- Hybrid Cloud Architecture
- Using the Hybrid Cloud Architecture Diagram

Cloud Computing Resources

The description of concepts that follow are brief. If this is your first time working with cloud concepts, I suggest you read *Cloud Computing: Concepts, Technology, Security and Architecture* (*https://oreil.ly/GE4ii*) (Pearson) by Thomas Erl and Eric Barcelo Monroy for a more in-depth description.

The sections will help provide a foundation for the discussion on describing shared responsibilities.

Cloud Computing Benefits

In the past, many organizations built a computing capability with servers, local storage, and networking in data centers to provide infrastructure for applications and workloads. However, this infrastructure involved the purchase of underutilized hardware and didn't offer the rapid elasticity needed for their business workloads.

Cloud computing started with the delivery of computing services via the internet, which enabled users to remotely access and use compute, network, storage, and cloud services. Many organizations have adopted this approach to hosting applications as it offers many benefits, including:

On-demand self-service

Provisioning of cloud resources happens on-demand via a console, command-line interface, or APIs. There is no need to purchase hardware or software because it's included in the cloud service fees.

With on-demand services, architects need to think more about the provision of virtual services, the different processing models available, and the need to automate the deployment of services through infrastructure as code (IaC).

Rapid elasticity

Rapid provisioning of compute, storage, and networking resources for workloads comes from a pool of cloud resources. It enables businesses to support peak events like Black Friday sales.

For an architect, the design of a cloud platform with rapid elasticity needs to optimize the use of resources by scaling up and down rapidly and efficiently. This means they need to understand the processing models and automation, such as infrastructure as code (IaC) that enable this elasticity.

Consumption-based pricing

Costs are only incurred for the resources used, as opposed to all the resources in a traditional data center. For workloads that make use of rapid elasticity and shared resources, this can result in lower overall costs. However, if you commit large amounts of compute and storage resources over extended periods, an on-premises platform may be more cost-effective.

For an architect, this becomes a critical quality attribute requiring an awareness of the operational capabilities of the cloud services that may influence the architecture. The cost of securing the services, monitoring performance, planning for capacity, and tracking costs will be a core part of any cloud computing solution for an architect.

Resource pooling

The sharing of the cloud platform's resources is among many consumers, allowing for pooling of resources and lower costs.

For an architect, they need to be aware of the risks of using shared resources and balance the benefits with operational risks. Often, there are varying options to use dedicated resources that reduce this risk and give the user more control over security and compliance. Shared services may require additional controls, such as encryption of sensitive data.

Resiliency

The use of three availability zones within a region and multiple regions provides levels of resilience that traditional pairs of data centers with disaster recovery models don't. Three availability zones enable the deployment of 150% of capacity instead of using the 200% capacity model in a dual data center model.

For an architect, this new data center model requires the architecting (or re-architecting) of workloads for high availability, fault tolerance, disaster recovery, and cyber recovery.

Security
> The use of security built in to the cloud platform and cloud has enabled the deployment of a more robust set of controls to protect workloads. It also includes a broader set of controls in the platform's ongoing operations.

For an architect, the increased risk from using shared services has placed a greater focus on adopting best practices for security design and implementation. Security services must meet the resilience levels of the workloads they support. Organizations and regulators are looking for greater control transparency and compliance levels through assurance activities.

Architect Responsibility

We've used the term "architect" rather than "security architect" when describing the advantages and the impact on architectural thinking. The lead architect for the solution is responsible for security; it's not "someone else's problem." Unless they're the lead architect for a security service, a security architect's role is to assist in designing the security controls (or security application).

Cloud Service Models

Cloud platforms can remove many of the responsibilities of operating a traditional on-premises data center. The shared responsibilities vary depending on the service model:

Infrastructure as a service (IaaS)
> IaaS offers cloud services for infrastructure components, including compute, networking, and storage capabilities. Dedicated physical devices or virtual instances running on shared resources may offer these capabilities.

> These capabilities form the foundation of all cloud services, leaving the consumer to provision and operate all other capabilities running on the cloud infrastructure. These responsibilities include provisioning the operating systems, setting up the different environments to develop, test, and run an application, and securing all workloads.

Platform as a service (PaaS)

PaaS builds on the infrastructure by running services operated and secured by the cloud service provider. These services include middleware and database capabilities, eliminating the need for a consumer to hire specialists to run this software. It also includes packaged environments that enable the development, testing, and lifecycle management of applications.

With PaaS, the cloud service provider manages a large portion of the provisioning, operation, and security of a service, while the consumer performs the configuration. While it eliminates a significant portion of security responsibilities for the consumer, it does not eliminate them entirely.

Software as a service (SaaS)

SaaS provides a fully managed application that integrates individual cloud services without exposing them to the consumer. The consumer does not need to understand the implementation details, but they will still have some responsibility for configuring the application's security.

Figure 7-2 depicts the responsibilities for the cloud service models through a series of functional layers, shaded to indicate the respective responsibilities. In our example, the cloud service provider owns the layers with light shading and black text, while the consumer owns the layers with dark shading and white text.

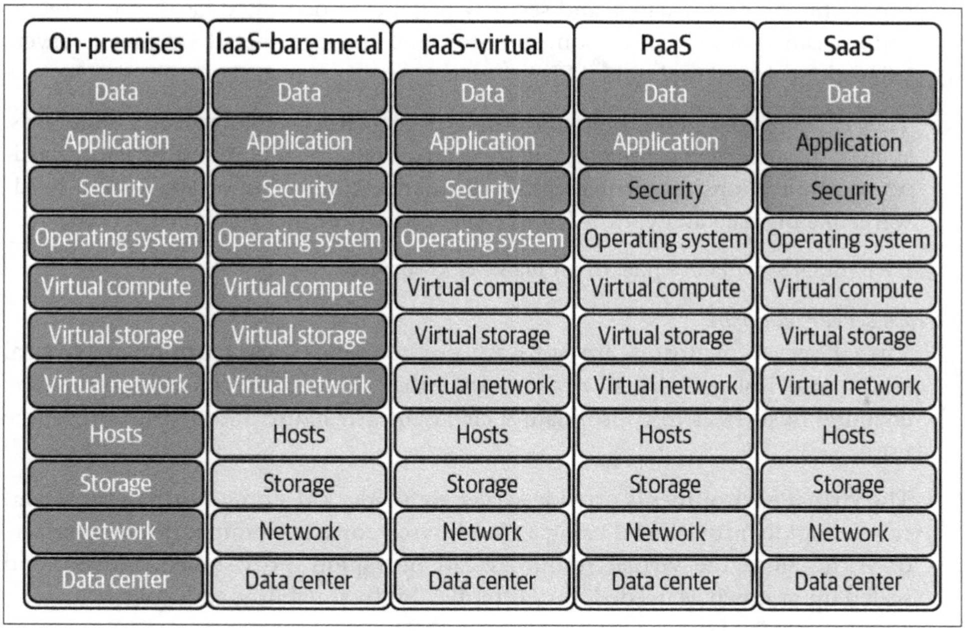

On-premises	IaaS-bare metal	IaaS-virtual	PaaS	SaaS
Data	Data	Data	Data	Data
Application	Application	Application	Application	Application
Security	Security	Security	Security	Security
Operating system	Operating system	Operating system	Operating system	Operating system
Virtual compute	Virtual compute	Virtual compute	Virtual compute	Virtual compute
Virtual storage	Virtual storage	Virtual storage	Virtual storage	Virtual storage
Virtual network	Virtual network	Virtual network	Virtual network	Virtual network
Hosts	Hosts	Hosts	Hosts	Hosts
Storage	Storage	Storage	Storage	Storage
Network	Network	Network	Network	Network
Data center	Data center	Data center	Data center	Data center

Figure 7-2. Cloud shared responsibility model

In some cases, there is a sharing of responsibilities, such as security, in the PaaS service model. It's important to note that responsibilities can change based on the technology in use. For instance, the cloud service provider fully manages the virtual private cloud (VPC) architecture in the IaaS-virtual service model, requiring significantly less support from the consumer. However, the IaaS-bare metal service using OpenStack requires the consumer to operate the OpenStack software provisioned by the cloud service provider.

Cloud Computing Platforms

We discussed a high-level model for cloud services, but we can further decompose it into different cloud computing platforms. A cloud platform is a type of cloud computing service that offers programmers the infrastructure and tools they need to create, launch, and manage cloud-based applications. In addition to tools for developing, deploying, and managing applications, a cloud platform typically offers services like computing, storage, databases, networking, security, and safety.

The cloud computing platforms that a cloud service provider often includes are:

Bare metal servers

Bare metal servers provide dedicated hardware resources to a single user or customer, combining the flexibility and scalability of cloud computing while providing the performance and security benefits of dedicated hardware. Organizations can remotely provision, monitor, and manage their bare metal servers using cloud-based tools and APIs.

They're employed in sectors with stringent regulatory or compliance standards, such as finance or healthcare, where security requires dedicated physical hardware. Applications requiring high-performance computing or specialized hardware, like big data analytics, AI, and research, can use the bare metal servers.

Bare metal servers are part of an IaaS cloud service.

Virtual server platform

Virtual server platforms are software environments that partition a physical server into isolated virtual environments that cloud platform users can share, enabling businesses to consolidate their IT infrastructure and optimize resource use.

The virtual environments provide server, network, and storage virtualization and can be rapidly provisioned using a cloud-based console, command-line interface, or APIs. Since the virtual resources can be rapidly provisioned, moved, and scaled up or down as needed, they offer flexibility, scalability, and agility.

The server virtualization technologies for virtual server platforms include VMware, Microsoft Hyper-V, Kernel-based Virtual Machine (KVM), and Citrix XenServer. The needs and requirements of the organization define the choice of technology, with each technology having its own set of features, capabilities, and management tools. Cloud service providers use these different technologies to provide their virtual server platforms.

A virtual server platform is part of an IaaS cloud service.

Container platform

A container platform provides tools and services to create, deploy, scale, and manage containerized applications. Developers can package applications with their dependencies into portable, lightweight units that can operate consistently across various environments using containers, a type of workload virtualization.

Container platforms usually come with a container orchestration system like Kubernetes that makes it easy to deploy, scale, and manage containers. Container platforms may also have extra features like automated builds, CI/CD pipelines, container image registries, monitoring and logging tools, and security and compliance controls.

Popular container platforms include Kubernetes, Docker Swarm, Red Hat Open-Shift (which includes Kubernetes), Amazon Elastic Container Service (ECS), Amazon Elastic Kubernetes Service (EKS), IBM Cloud Kubernetes Service (IKS), and Google Kubernetes Engine (GKE).

A container platform is a PaaS cloud service.

Serverless platform

Serverless platforms are cloud computing platforms where programmers create and deploy functions or applications as compact, independent units of code in response to particular events. Developers can concentrate on writing and deploying code without having to worry about managing servers or infrastructure because the cloud provider manages the infrastructure and automatically allocates and provisions compute resources as needed.

As a result, they're frequently more cost-effective than traditional server-based computing or a container platform. Cloud service providers typically charge for the actual execution time of a function or application component.

AWS Lambda, Azure Functions, IBM Code Engine, Red Hat OpenShift Serverless, and Google Cloud Functions are a few examples of well-known serverless platforms.

A serverless platform is a PaaS cloud service.

Understanding the cloud computing platforms used is important, as applications often host across these different platforms. Each has different characteristics that result in different architectural decisions for an architect and shared responsibilities for security.

Cloud Security Responsibilities

On cloud platforms, who is responsible for security depends on how much help the cloud service provider provides as a part of the service. As we've already discussed, cloud computing platforms offer different levels of service depending on their capabilities. This is particularly true for security capabilities, as shown in Figure 7-3.

At the low end of security support, the security of a bare metal server is mainly in the hands of the consumer of the cloud service. Whereas, with a serverless platform, much of the security is in the hands of the cloud service provider.

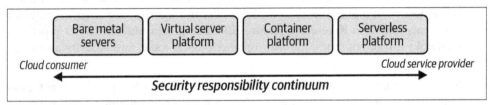

Figure 7-3. Security responsibility continuum

Even with SaaS applications, there is still security administration needed to configure the platform to meet the requirements of the organization. For this reason, we suggest you describe the running of the cloud platform as "security operations" and the maintenance of the configuration as "security administration." A discussion of the cloud shared responsibility model is later in the chapter.

Landing Zones

A cloud computing platform gives you the building blocks and tools you need to create and deploy applications, but it still needs more work before it can host production workloads. A *landing zone*, sometimes called a *cloud foundation*, is a collection of best practices, guidelines, and automation used to design, deploy, and administer a well-architected and secure cloud environment. Effectively, it's a package of different design elements for accelerating and ensuring consistent use of cloud resources.

The package enables an organization to use the cloud platforms and resources consistently. This serves as the foundation for cloud governance and management. The package can contain the following elements:

Principles

Principles guide the decision-making process for the deployment of the solution to a landing zone. They cover topics like resilience, performance, reliability, sustainability, operations, security, and compliance. We discuss principles in depth in Chapter 3.

Policies

Policies define the rules that an organization follows. This isn't just security and compliance; it might also include other topics that impact the delivery of workloads on the cloud, including social media, data privacy, and marketing.

Practices

Practices suggest the most effective and proven approach to architecting, building, and operating a cloud environment. They cover topics like resilience, performance, reliability, sustainability, operations, security, and compliance.

Processes and procedures

Processes and processes ensure consistency of operations across an organization. Definitions of processes are at the level of an organization, with procedures defining and implementing the processes customized for a specific environment. Further detail on processes, procedures, and work instructions is in Chapter 11.

Enterprise pattern

An enterprise pattern describes organization of the cloud for an enterprise with many different lines of business, workloads, and projects. The topics include cloud account management, identity and access management, network hubs and spokes, scalability guidelines, and resilience guidelines. This guidance enables an organization to support thousands of applications within the cloud.

Architecture patterns

An architecture pattern is a best practice for the construction of types of workloads or single workloads of a particular type. Cloud service providers often offer their own libraries of architecture patterns that organizations should customize and publish internally for their own use to ensure consistency. They cover specific architectures such as event-driven applications or specific industry solutions.

Practical Cloud Security (O'Reilly) by Chris Dotson and *Hybrid Cloud Security Patterns* (*https://oreil.ly/Id9yQ*) (Packt Publishing) by Sreekanth Iyer offer example security patterns for adoption by an organization.

Resiliency patterns

To deliver the desired resiliency for workloads, resiliency patterns show how to achieve the required service levels. They're critical to ensuring the continued availability of security services that will need to meet high levels of resilience.

Cloud service providers and solution providers offer recommended patterns for an organization to follow to achieve high levels of resilience.

Deployment automation

It's good to have documented architectures and practices to follow, but it's even better if these architectures have automation to deploy them. Cloud service providers are now providing customizable automation to enable rapid deployment of different architectures aligned to best practices. Deployment automation uses IaC including solutions such as Jenkins (*https://www.jenkins.io*), Tekton (*https://tekton.dev*), and Terraform (*https://www.terraform.io*) for building deployment pipelines.

Together, a landing zone for a cloud computing platform makes up a cloud solution. A landing zone can help make sure that cloud deployments are safe, legal, and well-architected.

Cloud service providers, including AWS (*https://oreil.ly/xCDGJ*), Azure (*https://oreil.ly/mkWLL*), Google Cloud (*https://oreil.ly/YS0rj*), and IBM Cloud (*https://oreil.ly/paALD*), offer their own perspective on good architectural thinking practices in a *well-architected framework*.

Hybrid Cloud Architecture

A hybrid cloud architecture unifies on-premises data centers with multiple public and private cloud environments into a single integrated cloud infrastructure. In this model, businesses can combine cloud platforms from multiple public cloud providers with their own internal private cloud infrastructure to meet their specific requirements. For simplicity, we will refer ongoing to hybrid cloud, but this will also imply the use of a multicloud architecture.

The main goal of a hybrid cloud strategy is to give you the freedom to use the best computing environment for each workload, cut costs, and take advantage of the unique features and capabilities of each cloud platform. To take advantage of public cloud scalability and cost-effectiveness, an organization might decide to use a public cloud platform for some workloads while using a private cloud environment in an on-premises data center for sensitive data that needs stronger levels of security and compliance.

Public Cloud, Lower Cost?

Using a public cloud platform to host workloads doesn't always lower costs; it may work better for use cases where workloads need to be flexible enough to handle burst workloads or for the deployment of temporary testing infrastructures. Other workloads may benefit from specialized on-premises infrastructure or a co-location data center with data that can't use a public cloud infrastructure.

Conversely, an on-premises private cloud environment may not have stronger security because the organization doesn't have the necessary skills to support security operations that run 24×7×365. This could make the public cloud a better choice.

In a hybrid cloud environment, deployment and management across the different IaaS and PaaS platforms often take place. Using a single common cloud computing platform, like Red Hat OpenShift (*https://oreil.ly/yanZY*) for container workloads or VMware (*https://www.vmware.com*) for virtual servers, can make it easier to move workloads between different cloud service providers.

The diagram in Figure 7-4 shows multiple cloud platforms that are both on-premises and in two public cloud service providers, each containing two cloud platforms. Red Hat OpenShift promotes the idea of a common cloud platform that supports workload portability across public and private clouds.[1]

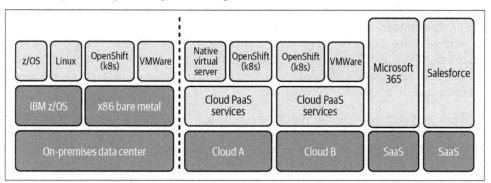

Figure 7-4. Hybrid cloud architecture diagram

---

1 Others argue that using the full cloud native capabilities provided by a CSP is a better approach to getting the greatest value, even if it is a proprietary platform.

The on-premises data center may continue hosting an application on IBM z/OS because it's not easy to migrate the workload off that platform. It may be the better location anyway, as the platform has significantly better resilience and may be more cost-effective as well.

We've included Office 365 and Salesforce on the right, as they can integrate into the workloads running on the public and private cloud.

This flexibility provides many benefits, but maintaining a hybrid cloud environment, on the other hand, can be more difficult and requiring specialized skills and experience. Balancing the added complexity is necessary when considering the benefits of a hybrid cloud strategy.

An architect must carefully plan to build and operate landing zones to ensure a hybrid cloud strategy is secure, compliant, and cost-effective for organizations. Each of these landing zones is likely to have a different set of shared responsibilities.

Using the Hybrid Cloud Architecture Diagram

Once you create the system context diagram, you should define the hybrid cloud architecture diagram in Figure 7-4, based on the information you have so far. Additional requirements and constraints influence the development of the diagram.

Often, when we start the architectural thinking process, we know the computing platforms because the application owner has a predefined architecture. In this case, it's useful to validate what's known in terms of the architecture layers and the responsibilities, as this may change the architected solution. For example, VMware vSphere requires a different set of operational skills than a cloud native virtual private cloud platform. If you are working on a cloud platform, the database provided as a PaaS service may be a specific technology or version, introducing constraints on the target architecture.

If it's a new application, starting to document the target architecture will enable agreement on the target computing platforms and define the environmental constraints the application will have to handle. For example, if we identify that we'll be using a cloud Multi-Zone Region (MZR), we now know the low-latency synchronous disk replication we can use on premises won't be available in the cloud, and this may change the characteristics of the application.

Think Operations from the Beginning

An organization was having a discussion about modernizing an application for hosting on a public cloud infrastructure. The solution architecture was complete, including the operational tooling needed for ongoing operations of the application. At this point, they decided to look at who would be performing the system integration and running the operations.

Has this happened to you? A rearchitected solution resulted as the shared responsibilities changed for the operations team. The operational tooling selected for operations wasn't supported by the organization providing the operations service. Drive early discussions using the shared responsibility diagram.

We now move on to a discussion of how to describe the shared responsibilities between the cloud service provider and the cloud consumer for each of the platforms described in the hybrid cloud architecture model.

Shared Responsibilities Model

The ideas we've talked about so far are the foundation for describing how each computing platform shares responsibilities. Each layer of a computing platform has its own set of shared responsibilities and has a different set of layers depending on the technology.

Describing shared responsibilities is important when creating a solution architecture as it helps to identify and allocate responsibilities for different aspects of the system to the various parties involved in its development, deployment, and maintenance. This includes not just technical responsibilities, but also non-technical responsibilities related to compliance, risk management, and other business considerations.

By discussing and documenting these shared responsibilities, it ensures that all parties understand their roles and obligations, and it reduces the risk of gaps or overlaps in responsibility that could lead to confusion or errors. This is especially important in complex systems, such as hybrid cloud, involving many platforms with multiple stakeholders that change over the lifecycle of the system.

So how can we clearly describe shared responsibilities for hybrid cloud?

Shared Responsibilities Stack Diagram

Let's start by applying the concepts in Figures 7-2 and 7-4 by creating what we will call a *shared responsibilities stack* diagram in Figure 7-5.

We will talk through the concepts and the techniques needed to develop this style of diagram. On the left the layers are labeled and we will start to describe them starting from the bottom:

Location

This shows where the primary, secondary, and disaster recovery (DR) locations are for both on-premises and cloud locations. In this diagram, there are just primary and secondary locations for the two on-premises data centers.

When a workload migrates to the cloud, you can upgrade the resiliency to support three availability zones within a Multi-Zone Region (MZR) and designate a second MZR as a DR location.

This brings new benefits in terms of resilience, but to deliver that, there is a new challenge with the distance between locations, as they introduce latency and bandwidth constraints for network communication that can have an impact on security services.

Name of platform

Different kinds of computing platforms use different kinds of technology and have different capabilities to handle different workloads. The name highlights the different platforms. All the blocks above this row in the diagram are services hosted on or in support of the named technology platform.

Physical location

Definition of shared responsibilities starts with the physical location. They're normally either on-premises data centers or cloud data centers.

The appropriate organization is responsible for operating the physical security of on-premises data centers in accordance with its security requirements. A co-location data center provider or an outsourcer may sometimes manage this on behalf of the organization.

With the cloud data centers, they will follow the security requirements of the cloud service provider. The CSP won't normally allow physical access to a cloud data center to protect all clients. The rationale being that if they let one client in, they would have to let hundreds of clients in to review physical security, resulting in additional risk and cost to every client.

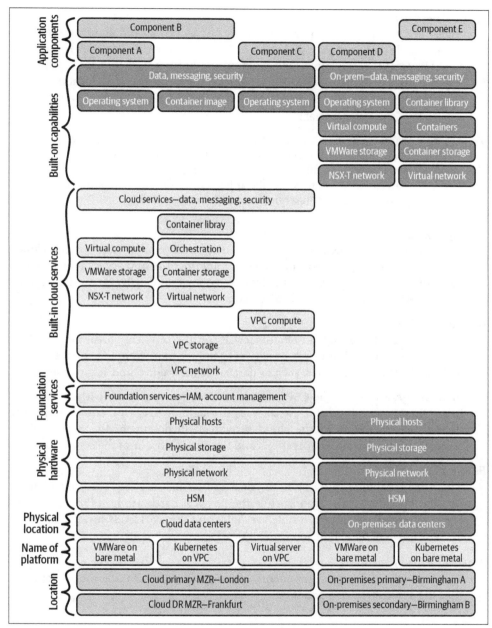

Figure 7-5. Hybrid cloud shared responsibilities stack diagram

Physical hardware

These are the physical compute, storage, networking, and hardware security modules (HSMs) used to support the delivery of the virtual services running on top. The CSP is responsible for providing the hardware in the cloud, while the organization owning the workload provides it for an on-premises location.

 Compressed Diagram

You could draw a compressed version of Figure 7-5. We separated out the built-in cloud services and the built-on capabilities into two layers to highlight the difference in responsibilities. If you have access to color to show the differences, you can compress and overlap the built-in services and built-on capabilities.

Foundation services

The cloud service provider needs a set of foundational services for the cloud's operation, including account management and identity and access management. All cloud services use these services to control the delivery of the services through APIs, a CLI, and a web-based console.

Built-in cloud services

The CSP runs these built-in cloud services on the physical hardware. It will be a mix of IaaS capabilities such as network, storage, and compute services. There will also be PaaS capabilities, such as databases, messaging, and security services.

With all these services, the CSP provides the service operations with an interface to configure and administer the services through an API, CLI, and console. The online documentation of the cloud provider will document the details of the separation between cloud operations and the administrator of the service.

Built-on capabilities

These are capabilities built on to physical and virtual services. The built-in cloud services host this in the cloud, while the physical hardware hosts this on premises. The organization responsible for delivering the workloads installs, operates, and administers these built-on capabilities.

Application components

These are the different components of an application. One or more platforms host the application components.

Considering different sets of responsibilities enables us to separate and consider the shared responsibilities of each compute platform. The responsibilities for running VMware vSphere on bare metal are very different from those for running Red Hat OpenShift on a virtual private cloud.

Each of the computing platforms may be further decomposed into separate computing platforms based on the configuration, software versions, or operational teams supporting the services or capabilities. For example, Red Hat OpenShift 3.11 may serve as the foundation for the first generation of a Kubernetes platform, while Red Hat OpenShift 4.10 with different DevSecOps operations teams may serve as the foundation for the second generation. Or perhaps a team hosted one version on bare metal and another team hosted the second version on a virtual private cloud.

So how does this impact the security policy that applies? All services in on-premises locations shown on the right of Figure 7-5 are normally the responsibility of the organization owning the workloads and will operate according to the policies and practices of that organization. Sometimes, they may outsource or outtask the services to an outsourcing or professional services organization to operate.

With the cloud services on the left side of the diagram, the cloud service provider and the organization responsible for the application workload will share responsibilities. The CSP has sole ownership of the responsibilities at the bottom of the diagram, and as you move up, you start to share those responsibilities with other parties until the organization in charge of the workloads has full ownership.

Diagrams are a useful tool to discuss shared responsibilities, but they don't have sufficient detail. We will go on to discuss using tables to delve deeper into the shared responsibilities.

Cloud Service Provider Responsibilities

Once you know the layers of the target computing platform, you can further describe the shared responsibilities of the CSP and the consumer of the cloud services. Figure 7-6 shows a table describing the level of service delivered at each layer.

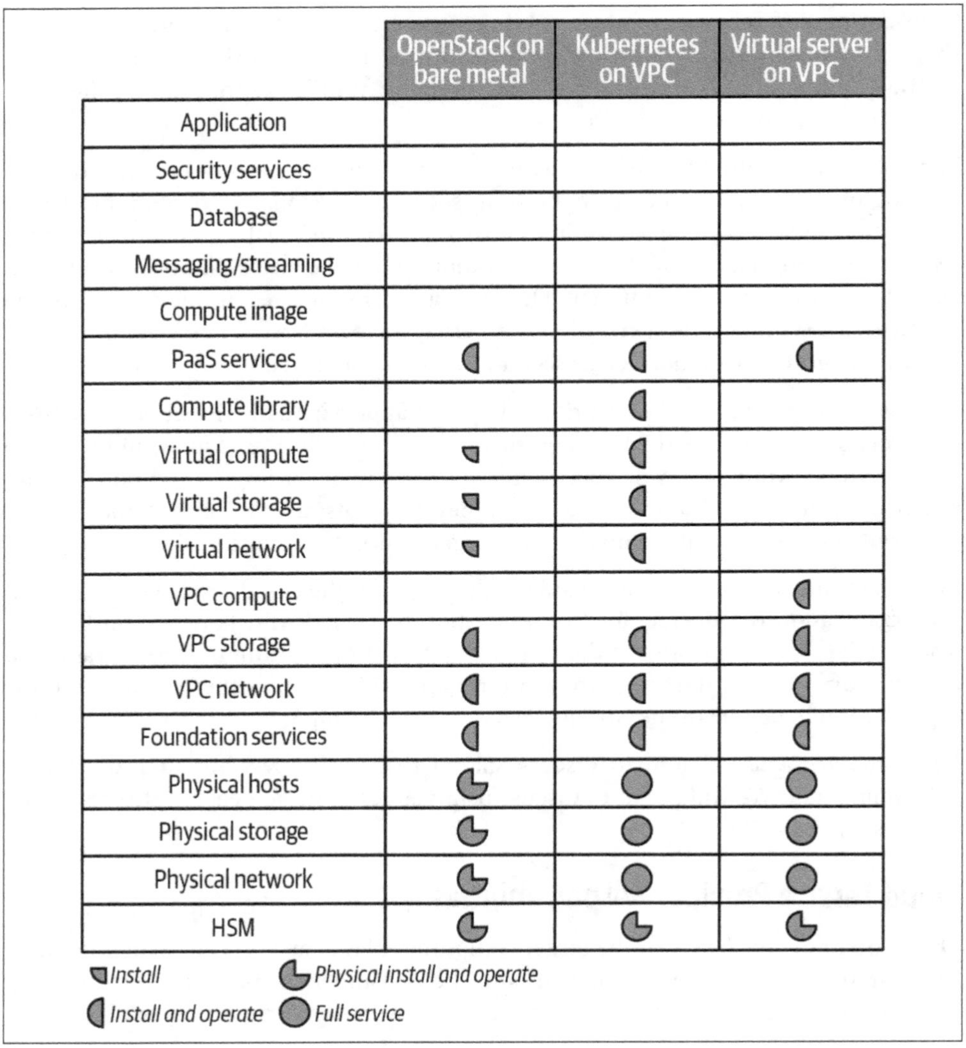

	OpenStack on bare metal	Kubernetes on VPC	Virtual server on VPC
Application			
Security services			
Database			
Messaging/streaming			
Compute image			
PaaS services	◖	◖	◖
Compute library		◖	
Virtual compute	◸	◖	
Virtual storage	◸	◖	
Virtual network	◸	◖	
VPC compute			◖
VPC storage	◖	◖	◖
VPC network	◖	◖	◖
Foundation services	◖	◖	◖
Physical hosts	◕	●	●
Physical storage	◕	●	●
Physical network	◕	●	●
HSM	◕	◕	◕

◸ Install   ◕ Physical install and operate

◖ Install and operate   ● Full service

Figure 7-6. CSP shared responsibilities table

The table shows the proportion of responsibilities that the CSP fulfills, resulting in the consumer having the rest of the responsibilities. We created our own definitions, which you may wish to change to meet your needs, and they are as follows:

Install

The responsibility is simply the installation of the capability, and all other responsibilities reside with the consumer. In the CSP shared responsibilities table, installation of the OpenStack software is with minimal configuration and all other operations are down to the consumer.

Install and operate

The responsibility is both the installation and underlying operation of the service, with ongoing administration down to the consumer. In the CSP shared responsibilities table, the CSP will install and operate the VPC networking, but the configuration and ongoing administration are the responsibility of the consumer. This is typical of most cloud services.

Physical install and operate

The CSP performs the installation and operation of the physical hardware, but the consumer still has some control over the hardware. This includes bare metal servers.

Full service

This is for components that are completely hidden from the consumers and they have no control over the service.

It's clear that the consumer of cloud services still has a significant amount of work to perform. For the OpenStack on VPC bare metal platform, the CSP offers bare metal servers (physical hosts) for the service consumer to configure. The OpenStack infrastructure may have an initial automated deployment, and from then on, the CSP hands over the operation to the user of the cloud services.

You may also wish to allocate responsibilities to more than one team. We continue discussing how to do that.

Cloud User Responsibilities

The consumer of the cloud service requires a breakdown of the shared responsibilities. There may be multiple teams involved in the delivery, and the responsibilities may change during the route to live (design, delivery, and run) for the delivery of the application workload. In Figure 7-7, there is a table showing responsibilities as they change for just the OpenStack on bare metal platform.

We've split the responsibilities into two categories using the terms "operations" and "administration." Operations is what the CSP configures or administers through its own operations teams. For example, a cloud service provider provides the ability to configure the security of the VPC network through the operations teams.

We then assigned responsibilities to the system integrator's team that designed and built the solution, followed by the outsourced operation teams that took over for the operation of the solution. In this example, both the systems integrator's administration team and the outsourced operation teams can configure the VPC network. There will need to be processes to govern the configuration to ensure control of the changes.

O = Operations or service provider A = Administrator or integrator	OpenStack on VPC bare metal														
	Design					Build					Run				
	Cloud provider	System integrator	System operations	Security operations	App. integrator and operations	Cloud provider	System integrator	System operations	Security operations	App. integrator and operations	Cloud provider	System integrator	System operations	Security operations	App. integrator and operations
Application					O/A					O/A					O/A
Security services				O/A					O/A					O/A	
Database		O/A			A		O/A			A			O/A		A
Messaging/streaming		O/A			A		O/A			A			O/A		A
Compute image		O/A					O/A						O/A		
PaaS services	O	A			A	O	A			A	O		A		A
Compute library	O	A				O	A				O		A		
Virtual compute	O	A				O	A				O		A		
Virtual storage	O	A				O	A				O		A		
Virtual network	O	A				O	A				O		A		
VPC compute	O	A				O	A				O		A		
VPC storage	O	A				O	A				O		A		
VPC network	O	A				O	A				O		A		
Foundation services	O	A		A		O	A		A		O		A	A	
Physical hosts	O	A				O	A				O		A		
Physical storage	O	A				O	A				O		A		
Physical network	O	A				O	A				O		A		
HSM	O	A				O	A				O		A		

Figure 7-7. Route-to-live shared responsibilities table

The system integrator team performs the design and build, and the system operations team performs the system run, as shown in Figure 7-7 through the shaded cells in the table. These teams may be two different teams within the user's organization or two different third-party organizations.

Figures 7-6 and 7-7 split out a single layer in Figure 7-5 into separate layers of security services, database, and messaging/streaming. The layers suggested in the diagrams and tables are examples, and you are likely to come up with a different set of layers after discussions within your own team.

Figure 7-7 shows responsibilities for one platform, and it requires a table for each computing platform, both on cloud and on premises. For example, replace "Design," "Build," and "Run" with cloud platforms from Figure 7-6.

But how does this inform what security policy applies? Let's continue with a discussion on that.

Cloud Security Policy Responsibility

The consumer who uses the service is *accountable* for the security of the data, no matter where it's stored—on premises or in the public cloud. However, the cloud service provider is *responsible* for the security of the cloud platform "below the line" from the users of the service. In other words, the security controls hidden from the consumer of the cloud will use the policies and practices of the CSP to secure the cloud platform.

The user of the cloud needs assurance about the effective implementation of the security controls. CSPs provide a commitment to protecting users' data, perform their own compliance activities, and then engage organizations to perform independent reviews and audits.

Often, people who use cloud services will map their control framework to the services and controls that the CSP provides. The CSP doesn't deliver everything in the control framework, and the consumer of the cloud platform may need to build additional security capabilities to run, either on the cloud or on premises, to fill those control gaps. There may be the option to integrate third-party services provided as a SaaS offering by other suppliers.

The CSP exposes some security controls to enable the user of the cloud service to configure the cloud service to meet their specific needs. This is the administrative role that the cloud consumer needs to perform using the API, CLI, or web console.

Any security measures that don't fall "below the line" must adhere to the application workload owner's security policy. You can delegate the responsibility for providing these security measures to one or more internal or external suppliers. Even though those suppliers will have responsibility for the delivery of security, the owner of the application workload will still have the accountability to ensure the delivery of controls.

 Have you seen a news headline where a specific cloud provider exposed object storage to the public internet? By default, nobody has access to object storage. It's not the cloud provider who exposed the object storage but the organization that set the storage to be public. Increasingly, cloud providers are having to add layers of controls to prevent and detect these mistakes.

You may need to set up additional agreements to ensure clarity about the security practices the suppliers need to follow. Use the diagrams and tables discussed in this chapter in discussions to ensure all parties are clear through documented responsibilities and agreements. Internally, this may be a document of understanding (DoU) or, externally, a contract. We discuss the use of a RACI, processes, and procedures to further define shared responsibilities in Chapter 11.

Let's continue by applying the techniques to the case study.

Case Study: Shared Responsibility Model

Review the case study in Appendix A and the information provided that can describe the shared responsibilities. We suggest you start by reading through the text of the case study and marking in different colors the different platforms you identify. In "Marked-Up Case Study to Identify Platforms" on page 228, you will see items marked up in two types of markup. The dashed box is for platform types, and the solid box is for the different development environments.

Marked-Up Case Study to Identify Platforms

The local authority has hired Clean Air Guildford to design, construct, and manage a system to charge polluting car drivers to enter the city. Cameras will monitor cars entering the city to detect the number plate on the car. To enter the city, the car drivers will need to pay a charge within 48 hours or receive a fine.

The project has already started to build the new hybrid cloud solution, with the core application hosted using PostgreSQL on a public cloud platform. As a security architect, you have received a request to urgently develop a security solution for the system.

The project deployment approach agreed upon between the CIO, Business Sponsors, and the Project Executive (PE) leading the integration is as follows:

- Start with a development environment using Red Hat OpenShift to build a cloud native container application using DevOps practices on a public cloud platform.
- Then build a full route to live with preproduction and production environments in the public cloud.
- With the Clean Air Application containing:
  - Systems of engagement using Open Liberty running on OpenShift at the center

Let's use the marked-up case study to document the components of the shared responsibilities, starting with PaaS services.

Identifying PaaS Services

Look for the dashed box that identifies the different platform types. The case study talks about PostgreSQL but is silent as to whether this will be a PaaS service or if it's a database run on a virtual server or within a container on the OpenShift platform. If it's not run as a PaaS service, it would require Clean Air Guildford to have the skills to manage the database. One of the key benefits of using cloud is that you don't need to have the skills to run a database as a service; the CSP can do that for you. So we will assume this will be a PaaS service run by the CSP. Additionally, you may notice that Open Liberty runs on OpenShift, so we assume a container hosts the database.

By reviewing the rest of the case study, we can identify further PaaS services:

- PostgreSQL
- MongoDB
- Redis
- Kafka
- RabbitMQ

Now we will move on to identifying SaaS services.

Identifying SaaS Services

Using the architecture overview diagram and description in the case study, we can further identify integrated SaaS services used by the core application:

- Camera Zone provides the Automatic Number Plate Recognition (ANPR) system.
- Clean Air Pay provides the payment infrastructure.

- Clean Air Debt provides debt collection.
- Guildford Service provides the service center.
- Clean Threats provides threat detection and response services.

With each of the identified services, Clean Air Guildford will have the opportunity to negotiate contracts and potentially require additional security controls and assurance activities, such as an independent third-party audit. There are other services, such as identity providers and directories, where you have no opportunity to change the contractual agreements and will have to trust the service provider. Listed following are these sets of services:

- Microsoft identity provider for customer identification
- Google identity provider for customer identification
- Staff LDAP Directory for employee identification
- Disclosure and Barring Service for employee vetting (note this isn't on the architecture overview diagram, but it's contained in the text)

Next, we will return to the core workload and identify the compute platforms.

Identifying the Compute Platforms

We can see that SaaS will provide virtually all components, and the Red Hat Open-Shift container platform is the only platform identified within the core Clean Air Platform system. In more complex solutions, there will be multiple application components that originate from different sources or suppliers, such as independent software vendors (ISVs). Identify the dependent technology platforms for each of the application components.

Then look to optimize the number of platforms used by looking for the sharing of platform instances. If different components of the application use the same type of technology platform, look to merge onto the same instance of the platform. For example, an application of two components using containers could run on the same instance of Red Hat OpenShift. However, if an ISV is managing an application component, to enable the ISV to commit to service level agreements (SLAs), a dedicated instance of Red Hat OpenShift would be a requirement implying a different security policy may apply. Resilience and scalability requirements may then add to the solution by requiring multiple instances.

We will need different environments to bring the application to a production service. Let's identify the environments in the case study.

Identifying Environments

An environment is an instance of a platform used for a specific purpose. For example, environments may include development, testing, preproduction staging, and production. The environments may have specific security policies applied to them. For example, development and test environments must not contain production data that may contain sensitive personal information. Also, administrators with access to production data must not have access to manage development environments.

Let's look at the case study to see what it tells us. The [solid box] identifies the different environments on the route to live. It has specified a preproduction environment for final integration testing but is silent on testing before that. Therefore, we can assume there should have been a test environment specified. Therefore, we have four environments:

- Development
- Test
- Preproduction
- Production

You will use the list of environments when you get to Chapter 8.

Let's continue with documenting what we've discovered from the case study.

Documenting a Shared Responsibilities Stack Diagram

So how can we draw a shared responsibilities stack diagram to represent this?

In Figure 7-8, we've drawn a shared responsibilities model for Clean Air Guildford based on the information contained in the case study in Appendix A and the component architecture diagram in Figure 6-16. The CSP's services are those with responsibility blocks in light gray shading with black text. The components run by Clean Air Guildford's IT operations team are those with dark gray shading and white text in the responsibility blocks at the top.

You will see we've added a stack for the PaaS services from the same cloud service provider as the compute platform. The dotted line around the left two stacks shows the scope of the system context diagram.

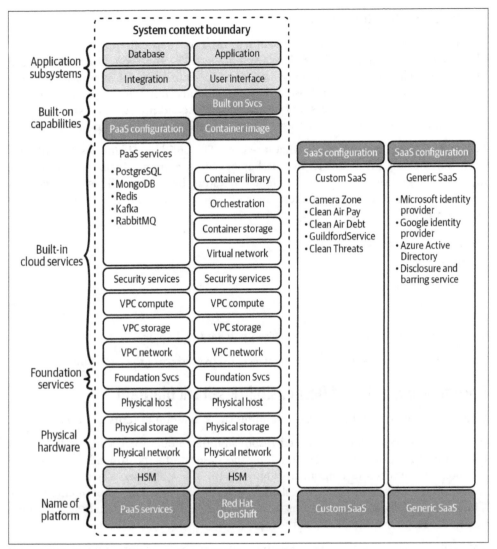

Figure 7-8. Case study shared responsibilities stack diagram

Adapt the Format

You will see the formatting of the shared responsibilities stack is different from Figure 7-5. There is an overall format for these diagrams, but not all will be the same, as they may need to show different aspects of shared responsibilities in a diagram. Adapt the format to meet your needs and best communicate shared responsibilities.

At the top, in lighter gray with white text, are the application subsystems. If you refer back to Figure 6-16, you will see the component architecture diagram has four subsystems. The hosting of the application and user interface subsystems is on Red Hat OpenShift, with the database and integration subsystems as PaaS services.

We didn't create an individual stack for each PaaS or SaaS service but for each category of services to highlight the type of contractual agreement that will need to be in place. Each contractual agreement may have a different set of controls and different ways of demonstrating compliance. For the SaaS services, some are negotiable, and others are contracts where you must accept the terms and conditions set. Depending on the provider, you can negotiate the shared responsibilities stack of the *Custom SaaS*.

A cloud service provider runs the responsibility blocks in light gray with black text, and these services require configuration. For example, with PostgreSQL, the consumer of the service needs to configure the access controls for security and storage for backup. We've therefore added a block for PaaS and SaaS configuration in the built-on category, as it will need skilled resources provided by Clean Air Guildford to configure these services, including security.

Management of Cloud Infrastructure

We often speak to teams where they think there is no requirement for infrastructure operations for cloud computing, and therefore there is no allocation of skilled and experienced resources to tasks like network and security configuration. The outcome is that security vulnerabilities result, and so this diagram provides a way of having a discussion to identify an owner to secure the services.

We've made a lot of assumptions because the case study is unclear, and this is typical of many projects. You start with some unclear specifications, make assumptions, and then validate them with the other members of the project and stakeholders. Add your assumptions to a RAID log to ensure you don't miss validating those assumptions. A more in-depth discussion of a RAID log is in Chapter 10.

We've provided a checklist to help you review the quality of the shared responsibilities model stage of the architectural thinking process.

Shared Responsibilities QA Checklist

- Determine the proposed cloud computing platforms that the application workload will use.
- Identify the SaaS platforms used outside of the application to identify the transport and storage of sensitive business data.

- Record the shared responsibilities of the cloud platform, infrastructure management, security operations, and application management for each identified platform. This serves as a guide for the security policy that applies to each stack.

- Identify the main application components, the infrastructure platforms, and their locations.

- Determine the precise locations each infrastructure platforms will occupy to comprehend the connectivity and data locality restrictions that go along with them. Don't forget primary, secondary and DR locations.

Let's continue with a few topics to think about.

Summary

This chapter has talked about three different ways to break down shared responsibility, but you might think that's not enough. You would be correct in thinking that the suggested diagram and tables are just the beginning. We discuss further in Chapter 11 the follow-on steps to decompose the responsibilities into a detailed set of responsibilities using a Responsible, Accountable, Consulted, and Informed (RACI) table for inserting into a contract or document of understanding (DoU).

While many cloud service providers talk about the shared responsibilities of the cloud, there is little discussion of the shared responsibilities required for the workload that the cloud runs. We've seen many projects not deal with shared responsibilities because it can be a difficult subject to agree on, and others where it's just ignored. Don't avoid agreeing on shared responsibilities.

Documenting shared responsibilities is an iterative process that requires discussions with many stakeholders and members of the project. The responsibilities will change over time as the shape of the project changes. Feel comfortable with that change, as it's the natural evolution of a project, and you have something documented rather than incorrect project assumptions that will have a later impact on the security design.

We now have a defined scope for the system with the system context diagram, defined the subsystems and components for the workload or application, and documented the target platforms for the workload with a high-level draft of shared responsibilities. It's now time to discuss the design of the infrastructure security in the next chapter.

Exercises

1. What are seen as key benefits of cloud computing? Select all that apply.

   a. On-demand self-service

   b. Rapid elasticity

   c. Infrastructure as code (IaC)

   d. Resource pooling

2. True or false: Software as a service (SaaS) doesn't require the cloud consumer to manage security.

   a. True

   b. False

3. What security management responsibilities does a cloud service provider always assume for infrastructure as a service (IaaS), platform as a service (PaaS), and software as a service (SaaS)? Select all that apply.

   a. Storage subsystem security

   b. Server operating system security

   c. Network device security

   d. Data center physical security

4. What elements does a landing zone package contain? Select all that apply.

   a. An enterprise pattern

   b. Architecture patterns

   c. Resiliency patterns

   d. Principles

5. True or false: Public cloud always costs less than using an on-premises data center.

   a. True

   b. False

6. True or false: A hybrid cloud architecture includes one or more cloud services and on-premises data centers.

   a. True

   b. False

7. What characteristics does a hybrid cloud environment have? Select all that apply.

    a. Varying shared responsibilities

    b. Multiple security operations teams

    c. A common security policy

    d. Built-in security services

8. True or false: Security services will be provided for the cloud platform, and they need to be administered by the consumer to secure the workloads.

    a. True

    b. False

9. How can you ensure that all parties within an organization understand their shared responsibilities? Select all that apply.

    a. Define a security policy.

    b. Define a document of understanding (DoU).

    c. Draw a shared responsibility diagram or table.

    d. Define processes and procedures.

CHAPTER 8

Infrastructure Security

These days, the term "IT infrastructure" has a different meaning than fifteen years ago. At that time, most of the infrastructure had the goal of running both applications on physical or virtualized systems hosted in on-premises data centers. In a hybrid cloud context, the infrastructure is a mixture of on-premises installed systems with different types of cloud service models using different cloud computing platforms.

Another evolution also took place with industrial control systems (ICS) and operational technology (OT), resulting in a tighter integration between the IT and OT worlds. Together, these different technologies extended the scope of IT infrastructure.

Operational Technology

Operational technology is hardware and software used for monitoring and controlling industrial equipment, assets, processes, and events. In the past, OT devices weren't connected to the IT environment but these days the systems monitoring and controlling these OT devices are integrated with the IT environment. A similar situation is taking place with Internet of Things (IoT) devices connected to the internet. The IoT devices are sometimes part of an OT environment, sometimes just an extension to the IT environment (e.g., wearables as an extension to end-user devices).

The logical consequence of these evolutions at the infrastructure level is that security had to evolve as well to cope with new threats. So, in this chapter, we refer to the term "infrastructure security" as the sum of all security measures applied to the IT components under the control of your organization that host functional application or workload components. That could be, for example, how you should perform security-relevant configuration on out-of-the-box installations. So even on a SaaS solution, you can configure settings that are important from a security point of view, but you don't manage or control the underlying systems or infrastructure.

We will use the term "security architect" throughout the chapter; you might recall that in Chapter 1 we summed up the possible security architect roles. The types of security architects needed during the infrastructure design are: a solution security architect, a product security architect, or a consulting security architect. Depending on the type of project and its scope, there may be an involvement of all these roles. Hence, we use the generic term security architect to represent these roles.

In this chapter, we'll start by giving an overview of a *deployment architecture diagram*, its security aspects, and the steps needed to construct it. This design activity isn't only about the technical architecture of the solution; it's also one of the design steps where you, as a security architect, will use the *zero trust principles* to drive the outcome of the design. So to get you going, we'll explain the zero trust principles, a possible approach to implementing zero trust, and provide some examples.

An important foundational element of IT and OT architectures is network design, and it also has a significant impact on security design as it's still the first layer of defense for many organizations. Network segmentation still plays a crucial role in the layer of defense even when the zero trust principles reduce the role of the location on the network as part of access management. These days, organizations typically deploy new solutions in a hybrid cloud context, so in addition to the deployment architecture diagram you will also need a specific *cloud architecture diagram*.

Chapter Artifacts

You'll learn through the chapter how to create several artifacts as part of infrastructure security design. You will use a *deployment architecture diagram* to describe the deployment of the functional components onto compute nodes and services in a hybrid cloud. As a security architect, you may not be the owner of this artifact, unless it concerns the design of a security-specific solution. Yet the security architect should play a highly active role in this design activity, as you must add all the required security controls to the design. You will have to do this analysis from the network layer up to the application layer and position the specific security components where needed. If the solution is a cloud only solution, then a *cloud architecture diagram* should be enough.

Beside these two static views, it could also be useful to document the dynamic interaction between the solution components. As you learned in Chapter 6 you can create *sequence diagrams* and *collaboration diagrams* to document the interaction between actors. You could use these types of diagrams both for functional design and for security design aspects. For example, the authentication process for applications is often documented within a sequence diagram to show the exact order of the different steps and the kinds of interactions between the actors.

The artifacts required as input for this design activity are *enterprise context, architecture patterns,* and *guiding principles.* In a cloud context, common architecture patterns are available on the websites of the cloud service providers (CSPs). These best practices will help you build your solution securely. Additionally, your organization could create or update patterns for the selected solution and store these patterns in a dedicated repository. This continuous improvement also applies to another important artifact, namely guiding principles. The zero trust principles are part of the general guiding principles and define the outcome of the design. If there aren't any organization-wide guiding principles, then you may need to document guiding principles for your project and perhaps trigger later an initiative for adoption by your organization.

Lastly, a document that you will often update during infrastructure security design is *architectural decision records.* As a security architect, you'll have to document each architectural decision made in relation to the security solution components and validate them with the stakeholders. You'll learn more about architectural decisions in Chapter 9. We've highlighted each of the artifacts for this chapter in Figure 8-1.

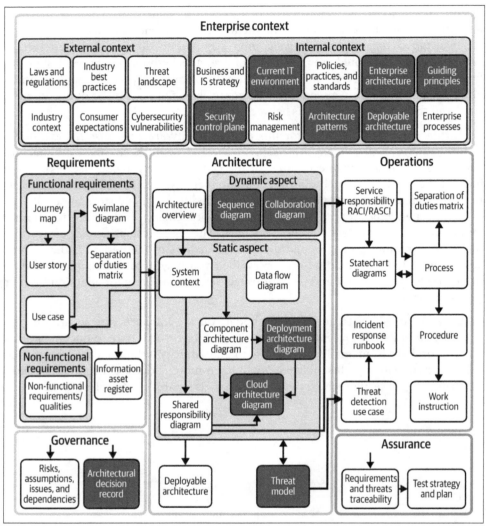

Figure 8-1. Infrastructure security chapter artifacts

Let's move on to discuss some basic concepts for the design of infrastructure security.

Deployment Viewpoint

In Chapter 6, you learned how architects create a component architecture diagram to identify the functional building blocks of a solution. We explained how you could use the architecture to perform a first high-level threat modeling exercise. The next step is to define the technical or infrastructure architecture, during which you will define where to deploy each functional component and on which type of node. A node describes the infrastructure device or cloud service where the functional components will be hosted. Figure 8-2 shows we've progressed to the bottom of our architecture decomposition.

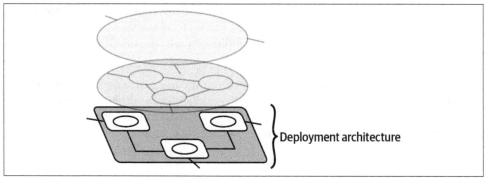

Figure 8-2. Architecture decomposition—deployment architecture

The deployment architecture activity is the last design step before you can initiate the solution-building activities. The solution-building activity itself could result in new additional insights, like not-yet-known technology constraints, that might lead to an adaptation of the detailed design, including the related security aspects. When you have completed the deployment architecture activity, you should have sufficient information to continue with the implementation of the solution. As you progress through each stage of the architectural thinking process and into implementation, you will increasingly fill in more detail.

Operational or Deployment Architecture

Different architecture methods use different terms for what we call a deployment architecture. Some use the term operational model or architecture but this can get confused with the need for a solution that supports the system operations or operational aspect of the infrastructure. For this reason, we decided to use the term "deployment architecture," which describes the action of deploying functional components onto infrastructure. The term "deployment diagram" is also used in the C4 model (*https://oreil.ly/s4BUe*).

Let's use an example application to bring this stage of architectural thinking to life.

An application has a subsystem that performs the processing of a credit card payment. The subsystem contains three functional components to perform the processing. We now need to decide how to implement these functional components. We could place the components on the same compute platform or split them across multiple compute platforms. We could decide whether to implement them using virtual servers, containers, or serverless functions. We say that placing the component onto the chosen compute infrastructure is "deployment" of the functionality.

We then make further decisions about the location of the compute, storage, and networking that define the architecture. We do that by thinking about transaction flows through a set of infrastructure nodes for each of the use cases we identified in the system context diagram and the components we identified in the component architecture diagram.

Once we've met the functional requirements from the use cases, we can then consider non-functional requirements such as security, availability, and performance. We will work through architectural decisions such as the redundancy of the "nodes" and services we may need to add for security or security operations.

We need a diagram to describe the deployment architecture.

Deployment Architecture

There are different diagrams that we can use to describe a deployment architecture. Cloud service providers each have their own notation for describing their own cloud resources. However, we also need a technology-agnostic approach to describing a hybrid cloud environment where we have on-premises data centers and multiple cloud providers.

Nodes and Resources

We talked about using the technology-agnostic term "node" to describe the compute platform. In a cloud context, we refer to "nodes" as resource instances.

In a hybrid cloud solution, you'll need the following artifacts:

Deployment architecture diagram (DAD)
> This diagram will be part of the infrastructure design document, or detailed design. You should document the infrastructure elements in an integrated format that's cloud-agnostic for both on-premises and cloud environments.

Cloud architecture diagram (CAD)
> Cloud service providers have their own specific way to design cloud-based solutions on their platforms, and so they also have specific infrastructure elements with a corresponding symbol set. This diagram will define the CSP elements needed, the placement, the connectivity requirements, and the metadata needed for the deployment of the cloud components.

You could draw the deployment architecture diagram first as a logical diagram in a technology-agnostic way, without sizing specifications. This conceptual diagram has its purpose in a high-level design document. For the solution's build and deployment, you'll need a more detailed design with the specified technology and key sizing attributes. Such a diagram and related configuration data are part of the detailed design document.

Let's continue by discussing a deployment architecture diagram in more depth.

Deployment Architecture Diagram

We use a deployment architecture diagram to describe the nodes used for the deployment of the functional components contained in a component architecture diagram. The diagram can describe both on-premises and public cloud locations.

In Figure 8-3, there is an example diagram containing different infrastructure elements. For both on-premises and public clouds, use a dashed rectangle to represent the network zones. The icons on black backgrounds represent the nodes with information on the selected technology and size indication. To simplify the diagram, cloud services are icons without boxes; they're still nodes, but without the box. The dashed arrows illustrate connectivity paths between the nodes. For an extended description of the notation, refer to "Technical Design Diagram Notation" on page 141.

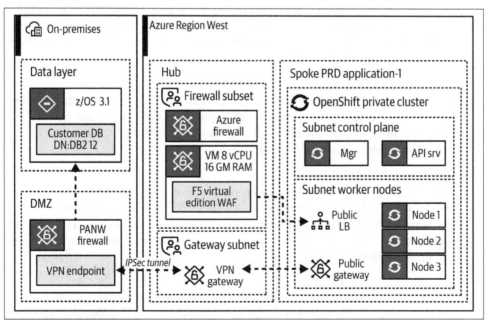

Figure 8-3. Example deployment architecture diagram

C4 Model Format

In a deployment architecture like the C4 model, the software application is a rectangle in the hosting infrastructure node.

Let's go deeper by discussing further the elements of a deployment architecture diagram:

Infrastructure node location

The exact location of the nodes or infrastructure elements is key for a security architecture. Already, with the analysis and creation of the system context, you've started to position solution components and actors. A location could be physical (a city) or logical (a VPC in a cloud instance).

In the deployment architecture diagram, the location isn't only a driving factor in how your diagram will look; for the security design, it will also help to determine what kind of extra security controls you need. The possible threats to a node could be different based on its location. Beside that, you'll also learn that in a zero trust-based approach, location on the network is no longer the only criteria to allow network connectivity. In a zero trust view, every network, internal or external, is a "hostile" environment.

The location could also be relevant for compliance with regulations if there are data residency requirements. Lastly, even if systems are in the same physical location, that doesn't mean there is network connectivity possible between them. So network connectivity will be the next design aspect of your diagram.

Network segmentation approach

For each physical or logical location, you have to define how you should segment the network traffic. How many network segments do you need, and how do you group the infrastructure elements on the same segment? We will elaborate on this topic in more detail later in the chapter.

Infrastructure node description

If it concerns a virtual machine in an on-premises location, a physical network appliance, or a PaaS database server, all these different types of infrastructure elements do have sizing attributes and configuration attributes. The diagram should indicate the most relevant ones, and the accompanying document should contain more detailed information.

Network connectivity requirements

Once you have concluded the network segmentation design, you should double-check the network connectivity requirements between the nodes that reside in different segments. You can do this by returning to your system context and tracing through the transaction flow through the system of each use case for each actor. This analysis might result in an update to the network design or the reallocation of the nodes to a different network segment.

Technology choices per node type

The technology selection per type of infrastructure element is another key activity during design. The choice will result in possibilities, but also constraints that you have to consider. Possibly, you might choose different technologies for nodes of the same type. A concrete example is the deployment of a web application firewall (WAF). You could use a WAF appliance or a managed security service hosted on the internet by a CSP or managed service.

Enterprise Technology Selection

A centralized enterprise architecture or security team often selects technology products and services for an organization, conducting due diligence to evaluate the proposed functionality and support. There are many security products that may meet policy requirements, but they may not meet the resiliency requirements of the business application, or the supplier doesn't have the resources to respond to urgent support issues.

A project team will likely receive a mandate to use and align their solution with the chosen enterprise products and services. However, the project will also need to perform its own due diligence on the product's suitability to meet the overall solution requirements. For instance, a mandated technology could potentially introduce unacceptable additional risks or fail to support the specific business technology under consideration. In that case, there may be a need for an alternative product, but the due diligence required may have an impact on the time and cost of the project.

Depending on the type of cloud delivery model, the effort for the definition of a deployment architecture diagram will vary depending on whether the selected solution is a third-party SaaS or if it concerns an application deployed in your own data center. Where you are using physical or bare metal servers, you should define the security controls for all components, starting from the physical server up to the application layer. When you select SaaS or function as a service (FaaS) components as part of the solution, there is still architecture work to perform, especially security design work. For these types of cloud services, you should consider data protection, identity and access management, and the protection of the API used for application integration.

Now that we've considered the different parts of the deployment architecture diagram, let's expand on the documentation that should accompany the diagram.

Deployment Architecture and Supporting Documentation

The type and quantity of documents required for the deployment architecture will depend on the solution itself and the project's overall needs. We suggest you complete or update the following content during the development of your deployment architecture:

Deployment architecture diagram
   This diagram visualizes the mapping of the functional components into the infrastructure components. This mapping could be a one-to-one mapping or a one-to-many mapping.

Detailed node description
   In the diagram, you won't be able to capture all the information that you need to implement the solution. So in a detailed design document, you should record detailed information for each node in the diagram. The detailed information will be attributes like the version of the software components on the node or network details.

Implementation approach
   The solution you're building could be a green field solution, an extension of an existing application, or possibly the replacement of a complete solution. In all scenarios, you need to document your implementation approach to ensure a smooth transition from the current state to the next version. For larger projects that could require intermediate steps from the current state to the target solution.

Security controls implementation
   During the previous solution steps, there wasn't much focus yet on the implementation of the required security controls. For some of them, you can count on existing shared services like anti-malware; for others, you might have to design specific solutions.

Requirement traceability
   An important aspect of a solution is requirement traceability. How can you ensure you haven't forgotten a key requirement? In the infrastructure design, the focus will be on the non-functional requirements, including the security requirements related to compliance, general cyber risk mitigation, and the mitigation actions resulting from the threat modeling. See Chapter 4 for further discussion on requirements traceability.

Test plan and test cases
   For each requirement, you should define one or more test cases. The outcome of the test will provide increased confidence that the implemented solution addresses the requirements. In the test plan, you will document how and when

you will perform the different types of tests. See Chapter 10 for more information on developing a test strategy and plan.

Network design

The level of detail for the network design will vary per type of landing zone. In this design, you need to define the required network connectivity, including the related bandwidth, maximum allowed latency, type of network protocols, and so forth.

Storage design

In a data center context, the storage design should be an integral part of the overall solution, and as a security architect, you'll immediately look after the protection of the data at rest and the access control model for storage.

Systems operations and service management

Once the deployed solution is up and running (it's "live"), the service management and systems operations teams will monitor the deployed application and supporting infrastructure. To keep the service running, they will respond to incidents, problems, and changes. Organizations are automating this type of activity more and more thanks to cloud and AI-based functionality.

Security operations

When you take a high-level view of security-related operational activities, you could state that there are at least three types of security operations. The first one is threat management. This is everything related to the detection of anomalies and triggering security incident processes. The second type is security infrastructure-specific. It includes activities like the secure configuration of the infrastructure components and applications, the detection of possible deviations from the secure configuration standards, or the detection of vulnerabilities and their remediation. The third one is everything related to identity and access management. Every day, the identity and access management (IAM) operations team will make changes to the access entitlements of end users and entitlements for a given role.

Similar to systems management operations, here, more and more security tools perform these activities in an automated way. See Chapter 11 for more detail on defining a solution for the management of security services.

Convergence of Network and Security Operations

You may have noticed that we haven't listed network-specific operations, even though the network operations team is essential to the overall security approach. You could think of the management of firewalls, network crypto devices, internet proxies, and security devices as either part of the networking or security teams. The exact organization of security and network teams depends on the company's size and type. We regularly see the first steps of convergence taking place at the operational level between the network and security operations.

Architectural decision records

As the architectural thinking progresses, document all decisions in an architectural decision record and share them with those working on the solution. We'll talk more about this in Chapter 9.

We've talked a lot about the deployment architecture diagram and the associated documentation; let's continue with the process of architecting infrastructure security.

Architecting Infrastructure Security

The foundation for designing security for infrastructure is the deployment architecture diagram, and we need a systematic way of including security. Figure 8-4 illustrates the overall architectural thinking process flow to infuse security into the deployment architecture.

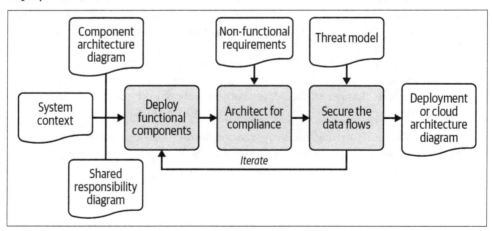

Figure 8-4. Architecting infrastructure security process flow

Let's talk through the three steps in the architectural thinking process.

Deploy functional components

Now we bring together all the previous architectural thinking to create a deployment architecture for hybrid cloud. We start to identify the placement of the functional components on the technology platforms identified in the shared responsibility diagram. Where possible, components will use PaaS services from the cloud platform to remove the need to manage the services. Based on the technology strategy, you will select the appropriate compute platforms for each functional component. The system context will then identify the interfaces to add to the deployment architecture.

We use a component architecture diagram, such as Figure 6-8, to identify the logical technical components (nodes) without selecting a specific product or technology yet. Once you have identified all the nodes, you need to place them in the right location. Location is both a geographical location and a network location. Latency, data sovereignty, and resiliency requirements will help you decide on a geographic location. The network location, latency, and network segmentation requirements will guide you in the network design. Defining the network location will raise questions about establishing network connectivity between the locations and ensuring communication security. Later in this chapter, we will discuss the topic of network segmentation in more detail.

Architect for compliance

Next, we start to bring in the non-functional requirements (NFRs), including security, to refine the deployment architecture. Meeting these requirements often requires demonstrating compliance, as they originate from a security policy or control framework.[1] The requirements are often easily mapped to standard security capabilities.

Integration with existing operational capabilities and the reuse of existing security services often fulfill these security capabilities. There is normally no need to build new services and this might include security-related operations like threat monitoring, vulnerability management, access management, and others. So the first step is to identify what existing services can support the requirements and adjust the deployment architecture to include points of integration.

Many organizations have security standards and practices documented that you will need to adopt. That could be a specific solution building block, a complete pattern, or even better, a security service that's already operational. In case you need to add a new security capability, you should also evaluate if this security capability is specific to the solution you are building or whether it could support other applications in the future as well. You may then need to work with your security operations team to create a standard pattern or service.

---

1 Remember that security requirements are NFRs unless they specify the primary functionality of the application.

There will be a broad set of security requirement statements that impact the majority of the solution components. A good example of such a requirement is the secure configuration (also known as hardening) of the infrastructure components. Other security requirements could be specific to a particular process or only applicable to a limited number of elements. For example, data from the R&D department stored in the cloud might need a data encryption solution based on a Bring Your Own Key (BYOK) key management scheme.

If you can't find existing services, review the enterprise security architecture from Chapter 2 to help you identify missing security services. Add these services to the deployment architecture and record an issue in the RAID log we will discuss in Chapter 10.

Some requirements, such as those related to availability and scalability, may conflict with security and require changes in the architecture of the security solution. If they're identified late, they can have a major impact on the solution cost and the viability of the solution. Many workloads require support for challenging service levels and rely on the high availability of security services, such as a privileged access management solution. You'll need to consider these requirements early on in the design process and find the right balance between sometimes conflicting requirements. At the same time, the chosen architecture could also be a good solution to address other requirements, like scalability.[2]

 Availability Service Level Objectives

In Chapter 5, we introduced the classification for the availability of business processes and how to define the service level objectives for availability, RTO, and RPO.

Now that we've met the key security requirements for compliance, we need to come back to thinking about securing the data. We'll consider it in two parts: the workload or application and the underlying infrastructure.

Secure the data flows

It's not only compliance with regulations or project-specific needs that will define security requirements. These requirements don't identify specific controls related to the risk to data in transit, at rest, or in processing. We need to think about the data or transaction flows through the system to identify the security controls to apply.

We need to return to the start of the architectural thinking process by taking each of the use cases from the system context diagram and tracing each of the data

---

2 It might be simpler to use a PaaS or SaaS service than design and run your own bespoke security service.

flows through the system to identify threats. You should have done this first while developing the component architecture diagram in Chapter 6. If you didn't complete threat modeling as part of your earlier design activities, now is a good time to do it. It will help you determine whether the current infrastructure design has material security flaws.

We're going to think about it from four perspectives: human or system actor to compute node, compute node to compute node, compute node to cloud service, and cloud service to cloud service. We show these four foundational types of flow in Figure 8-5.

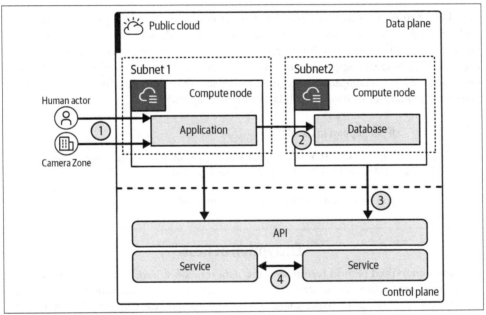

Figure 8-5. Communication paths for zero trust use cases; see the original diagram (https://oreil.ly/SAHC)

This continues using the first zero trust practice we identified, *identity, data, and transaction identification*. The diagram shows the flow, marked as ①, where an external human or system actor initiates a transaction or data flow with a compute node that may be implemented via a server or container. This transaction continues, marked as ②, with an interaction between two nodes. The node then uses a cloud service, marked as ③, and that may cause an interaction between cloud services, marked as ④. For many cloud service to cloud service transactions, they're not in your control as the CSP provides them, but for other services, you may have control and require the correct configuration.

We're going to discuss each of these flows in turn to make it clear what artifacts we will use in the technique and what you need to consider. We'll leave the added complexity of additional zero trust practices for a further iteration in this chapter after we've discussed these core principles.

1. Human or system actor to compute node.   External human and system actors will initiate transactions that transport data to a compute node. The system context diagram, as we discussed in Chapter 5, will document each of the use cases that initiate these transaction flows. This could be through a user interface or through system communication such as APIs and messaging.

One key requirement to meet zero trust practices is to encrypt all sessions in transit with mutual authentication. You should use a session-based encryption technology, such as TLS, with mutual authentication for communication *between functional components*. Where legacy applications don't support TLS, you will need to use link-based encryption *between compute nodes*, such as IPSec. We're going to discuss how to apply zero trust principles in more depth later in this chapter.

IPSec Support in Cloud

TLS uses a TCP-based protocol as a transport. IPSec uses other protocols for key management, such as IKE, and the CSP may not support the protocol. Validate support with your cloud provider, as you may need to look for an alternative solution.

Encryption at Rest

As each encrypted session terminates, the data may be stored, and at that point, you need to consider how to secure the data when written to storage. While most service providers now use a provider-managed key to encrypt data at rest, this may not protect the data from service provider employees.

Your organization should control the encryption key you use to encrypt the data, and this key should be specific to the data you're storing. We refer to this type of key management as Bring Your Own Key (BYOK). There are many different variations of key management, including those that offer control over your own hardware security module (HSM).

Processing of extremely sensitive data may occur using confidential computing (*https://oreil.ly/Uo9CG*) in a secure enclave where encrypted data is processed. As this is a rapidly developing area of technology, we won't delve into it. Just make sure that you consider how to protect data while it's at rest and processing.

These flows then continue through the system.

---

2. Compute node to compute node. Processing takes place on a compute node and that initiates a transaction (and data) flow to another compute node. In this case, we have an application calling a database running as software on top of the cloud platform. The transaction flow needs mutual authentication and session-level encryption to secure the flow, as we discussed previously.

At either end of the flow, we have compute nodes that store data in file or block storage. CSPs provide device-level encryption using an encryption key specific to your storage; it's designed to prevent disclosure of the data if threat actors steal the physical storage devices or when the reallocation of storage to another cloud user takes place. It doesn't protect data from privileged users who have access to the system and could disclose the data. Consider if you need additional levels of encryption to protect against the threat of disclosure by privileged users.

Some solutions, such as storage, database, or messaging products, may provide internal encryption at rest to protect data from privileged users, but the writing of an unencrypted or obscured key to disk may be open to brute force attacks. You'll need to investigate the key protection mechanism used for data encryption and look for products that retrieve keys from a key manager and HSM.

Architecturally Significant Transaction Flows

There is no need to examine every type of transaction flow through the deployment architecture diagram. Pick those flows that have a significant effect on the architectural decisions and aren't repeats of other flows already considered. This reduces repetitive architectural thinking.

Consider what transaction flows aren't triggered by system or human actors. There may be other events that trigger a transaction flow, including incidents, errors, or timed batch transactions. Consider the architecturally significant flows triggered through system events.

Additionally, consider the transaction flows that threat actors might generate in their attempts to compromise the system. For example, consider whether an SSH session occurring between devices that should never occur could be a significant flow for examination.

Data flows through a system aren't only started by use cases linked to human actors. Initiation of data flows can take place through components triggering events through errors or timed events. For example, a security alert may trigger the passing of an event record from a running workload to a threat management system. The tracing of the data flow through the system identifies threats and any additional security controls. Another example is a batch event triggered at a specific time or date. Add these as use cases to your list of transaction (and data) flows to review.

These compute nodes then use cloud services.

3. Compute node to cloud service.   Each compute node will use at least one and often many IaaS and platform services, such as storage and key management. They may also use PaaS services such as databases and messaging. Communication normally takes place over mutually authenticated encrypted TLS sessions with the cloud service using protected APIs with identity and access management controls. The APIs may also use private endpoints restricted to communication within a local network.

Some cloud services don't only use APIs. For example, storage can use iSCSI or NFS, which may not always provide encryption in transit. This means you need to validate these underlying data flows to secure your data effectively. This isn't just for cloud services; there are many software solutions that manage storage, including virtual storage and backup solutions. It may be a matter of configuring the security, but in others, effective encryption doesn't exist.

We also need to consider that services communicate with each other.

4. Cloud service to cloud service.   Cloud services need to communicate between themselves. Within a service, there is a need to share data for resilience within an MZR and across regions. To maintain the security of the data, the same encryption in transit principles we've discussed for the other communication paths apply. You'll need to assess the security of the data communication mechanism to ensure effective security controls are in place.

Securing Cloud Services

The same principles apply to the development of cloud services, with the services run on a compute node, such as a Kubernetes-managed container, and communication taking place at another compute node. The cloud service will still have a system context, component architecture, and deployment architecture. It's the responsibility of the cloud service architect to understand the security of the communication and storage, as they will require effective configuration to secure the data.

We then move on to the final stage of the architecting infrastructure process from Figure 8-4.

Iterate architectural thinking

You'll need to perform this three-step process every time you make an update to the solution architecture. The changes you make could include the deployment of new functional components, the inclusion of additional compliance requirements, and identification of new threats when threat modeling is repeated.

Managing Production Change

Once the workload is in production, there will be many changes, and each requested change will need an impact assessment to determine the required depth of design review. You may need to recheck compliance and update the threat modeling for changed data flows. The outcome may be significant changes in the threat landscape and then you should review the in-place security operations and plan for the adaptations.

There should be a process to add new threat monitoring use cases and detection rules. Another possible example is vulnerability management. When projects deploy new types of nodes, both infrastructure and application nodes, you will have to adapt the vulnerability scan rules and define node-specific remediation actions. We will discuss the definition of processes and threat management in Chapter 11.

As you may have noticed during the discussion on architectural thinking, you must make a number of architectural decisions. It's key that you document architectural decision records as you go along. We'll discuss documenting architectural decision records in Chapter 9.

Before we discuss the application of the techniques to the case study, we'll first explore the network segmentation practice in more detail.

Network Segmentation

The reality today is that the "corporate network" is a fragmented collection of diverse networks. The data, applications, and end users are no longer located in one place but are widely distributed between your own data centers, office networks, IaaS solutions, SaaS solutions, etc., and the change of their location is more dynamic than ever before. At the same moment, the applications, which are part of a minimum viable company, require high availability and, thus, redundant network connectivity.

In the following subsections, we'll take a closer look at concepts related to network segmentation in a hybrid cloud context. Even though slogans like "the perimeter is gone" or "the internet is your corporate network" fill our inboxes, there is still some work left for the security architect when shaping the network (security) design, including network segmentation.

Public cloud network segmentation

When your organization is making use of public cloud IaaS and PaaS services, you'll have to configure network segments to manage traffic between the compute nodes, cloud services, and external networks. The public cloud provides a significant benefit by providing its own software-defined networking (SDN) capabilities to support a network segmentation model. A consumer doesn't need to worry about physical networking devices, as the SDN provides a programmable overlay network that can hide the underlying implementation.

Each CSP has a similar network segmentation model but each has its own names for the networking resources, with a slightly different implementation for each of the network security building blocks. All decompose the network into different segments with the ability to apply network security access control lists (ACLs) based on source and destination network addresses for specific ports. Network boundaries, service interfaces, and compute resources can have ACLs applied. An ACL for a virtual machine's network interface provides you with a subset of capabilities provided by a host-based firewall. A host-based firewall can apply to the processes within the host.

CSPs are also starting to use context-based access controls that support zero trust principles. These controls use contextual information to constantly evaluate the security of the network connection, such as a restriction on the time of day or the location of the source connection.

You should always make use of the out-of-the-box capabilities for controlling virtual network security, as the cloud platform embeds integration with other security services such as identity and access management. We'll explore further the different network security building blocks later in this chapter when we discuss drawing the cloud architecture diagram.

Microsegmentation

It's no longer sufficient to protect an application by just separating the user interface, application, and database with a firewall. Once malware or an attacker lands on a node in a specific network segment, network access to all other systems in the same segment may be a default. Microsegmentation is one of the zero trust practices that solves this by creating application "bubbles," where policies control both the traffic within the bubble as well as the incoming and outgoing traffic.

When lateral movement by malware in your public cloud network is a huge concern, then consider adding microsegmentation capabilities on top of the cloud SDN capabilities. You can overlay cloud native SDN security using an abstraction layer independent of the CSP. Third-party microsegmentation solutions analyze the network traffic and suggest new policies based on the traffic flow, whereas cloud native segmentation features won't currently provide that kind of insight.

The overlay network security can also provide policy-driven security to reduce management overhead by having a single place to manage a policy change for all instances of the same type of application. These solutions can support different CSPs and on-premises platforms, providing the capability to hide the differences between the networking security models through a common security model.

Network edge protection

There is usually still a need to separate internet traffic from corporate traffic. At most organizations, this perimeter between "internal network" and "external network = internet" still exists, and a firewall is managing the North-South traffic flowing in and out of an organization.

In the cloud, you're likely to also need a virtual firewall on the boundary between the internet and other networks. Depending on the type of exposed interface (web user interface, API, etc.), you will need a "NextGen" firewall that may include support for a web application firewall for layer 7 network traffic and API protection, allowing you to inspect the traffic and better protect the exposed applications. However, the web application firewall capabilities of a "NextGen" firewall may not be as comprehensive as those of a dedicated standalone web application firewall (WAF).

Between data centers and cloud instances, depending on the scenario, there could be a site-to-site VPN with an extra firewall at both ends for additional traffic inspection and packet filtering. Alternatively, SD-WAN connectivity could also provide such security measures.

Architecture patterns

How you combine these different network security capabilities together is important, and there exist architecture patterns based on security best practices. Traditionally, we've used architecture patterns like the three-tier application. In such an approach, the presentation, application, and data layers are in different network segments protected by firewalls to establish the boundaries of the network segments and block direct access between the layers.

Within the cloud, the three-tier model has evolved into an n-tier model with many different layers providing defense in depth and preventing attackers from moving laterally between cloud resources.

Another pattern is the hub-and-spoke model, which reduces complexity and shares security services between workloads by routing all north-south traffic in and out of the cloud through a shared network hub.

These are just three examples. We'll be discussing more about architecture patterns in an enterprise context in Chapter 9. Let's move on by applying the techniques and artifacts we've discussed to the case study.

Case Study: Deployment Architecture Diagram

Looking at the Clean Air Guildford case study, we have enough to start the first draft of the deployment architecture diagram. As we're moving to the deployed solution, the correct positioning of all the components is crucial. The system context diagram, shared responsibility diagram, and the component architecture diagram can help you determine the correct location. You need to define the different network connections between the Clean Air Guildford (CAG) application and the other components.

As part of the infrastructure design, we listed a number of architectural decisions you need to consider:

Table 8-1. Clean Air Guildford high-level decisions

ID	Decision	Rationale	Implication
AD01	Consume middleware components as a PaaS.	In the cloud, there is the choice of deploying the middleware components either as software run on a compute node or as a PaaS service. The project will select PaaS services by default, unless there are specific capabilities unavailable from the CSP. It may be that the only way of delivering the capability is by installing, configuring, and operating the middleware component on a compute node for management by the operations team for the organization.	• PaaS services should be available to the CAG application components and have to support the requirements. • The PaaS services used by the components for payments need to have a PCI DSS Attestation of Compliance (AOC).
AD02	Use hub-and-spoke architecture for the network topology.	A hub-and-spoke architecture allows the centralization of the security controls for controlling the ingress and egress traffic at the Transit VPC.	• The hub and each spoke network use the cloud native VPC services. • The hub will host security components similar to the DMZ of a data center.
AD03	One spoke VPC required per application.	To facilitate the deployment through CI/CD pipelines, we will set up a pipeline of dedicated VPCs per application for each stage of the deployment. This should avoid possible conflicting access for the DevOps teams.	• The cloud operations team will need to define an approach to automate the assignment of the entitlements for the DevOps teams.

Long Form Architectural Decision Record

The examples of architectural decisions we've listed are in short form, and for more complex decisions, we might list different options with an extended rationale. We will discuss a longer form of an architectural decision record in Chapter 9.

We're going to start by reviewing the functional components we identified when developing the component architecture diagram in Table 6-1. The shared responsibility diagram, in Figure 7-8, will guide the deployment of the functional components together with any architectural decisions made about placement. We'll identify the relevant compute, storage, and PaaS services required to host the Clean Air Guildford application and summarize the mapping in Table 8-2. We've used AD01 to use PaaS services wherever possible.

Table 8-2. Deploying functional building blocks

Type	Purpose	Technology	Component	Deployment Type
Databases	Main database	PostgreSQL	LC-DB-01	PaaS
	Cache, state data	MongoDB	LC-DB-02	PaaS
	Cache, state data	Redis DB	LC-DB-03	PaaS
Integrations	CAG → Clean Air Pay	Kafka Streams	LC-INT-01	PaaS
	CAG → Clean Air Debt	RabbitMQ	LC-INT-04	PaaS
	Camera Zone → CAG	Not defined	LC-INT-03	REST API
	CAG → DVLA	Not defined	LC-INT-05	REST API
	CAG → Google/Microsoft	OAuth 2.0, OpenID	LC-UI-02	REST API
	AI Chatbot → CAG	Not defined	LC-INT-02	REST API
	CAG → Staff LDAP Directory	SAML 2.0, OpenID Connect, OAuth 2.0, and WS-Federation	LC-UI-01	PaaS
User interfaces	Driver and car registration	Not defined	LC-UI-02	Web portal
	Payment portal	Not defined	LC-UI-02	Web portal
Application components	Driver management	Red Hat OpenShift	LC-AP-01	Red Hat OpenShift
	Vehicle management	Red Hat OpenShift	LC-AP-02	Red Hat OpenShift
	Payment management	Red Hat OpenShift	LC-AP-03	Red Hat OpenShift

Deploying Across Many Compute Platforms

In this deployment exercise, we've used one compute platform but we've worked with solutions where deployment takes place across five or more different compute platforms. This is when the architectural thinking process of deploying components onto compute platforms using the shared responsibility diagram becomes important. It ensures everyone in a team is clear on what the compute solution is for the workload.

Before we move on to the full version of the deployment architecture diagram, let's use a cut-down version in Figure 8-6.

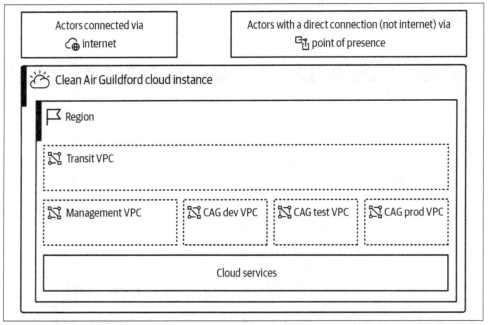

Figure 8-6. Deployment architecture diagram—two network segments; see the original diagram (https://oreil.ly/SAHC)

We'll start with the network segments within the *Clean Air Guildford cloud instance*. At the top, we have the transit VPC. This is a virtual network that's private to an organization and isn't open to any network traffic by default. All traffic in and out of the cloud and between other VPCs flows through the Transit VPC.

We have a *management VPC* that contains any compute hosts that manage resources on the other VPCs. Then there are three VPCs for the workload: *CAG dev VPC* for application development, *CAG test VPC* for testing, and *CAG prod VPC* for running the workload in production.

At the bottom, we have the collection of cloud services provided by the CSP. At the top, we have two ways in and out of the cloud platform. The first is the internet, which provides connectivity to human and system actors accessible via the internet. The second is the point of presence (PoP), which is the networking provider hosting private network connectivity to human and system actors.

We identified earlier in Table 6-1 the functional components and the technology required for each and then made architectural decisions on the potential technology platforms in Figure 7-8, resulting in Figure 8-7.[3] Figure 5-5, as we discussed, describes the technical diagram notation used in the diagram.

Let's describe the parts of the diagram by network segment:

Transit VPC

In the *transit VPC*, we have a *NextGen firewall* through which all traffic in and out of the cloud platform flows. On the left, we have a *VPN* termination point that could be a cloud service or a part of the NextGen firewall. Internet connectivity using VPNs terminates at this point. On the right, we have an *API gateway* that protects API access for the application. Just below the transit VPC is a *transit gateway* that joins the VPC's networks.

Management VPC

In the management VPC, we have a *bastion host* that provides support for remote administration. Administrators must first log in to this server before accessing any other resource in the cloud. The server automatically retrieves usernames and passwords from the *privileged access management* server for login to the hosted cloud resources. In this case, it's a software solution and not a cloud service. In the event of an investigation, the bastion host will record the activity of a remote administrator.

CAG VPCs

We have three workload VPCs for the Clean Air Guildford (CAG) application, with one for development, one for testing, and one for production. In each VPC, there is an instance of *Red Hat OpenShift* for running the application.

---

3 We selected IBM Cloud as a CSP because of our familiarity and the new icons that make architecture diagrams clearer, but the diagrams for other public cloud providers would be similar in format. We think the color icons that are used to promote different CSPs make architecture diagrams more difficult to read and work with.

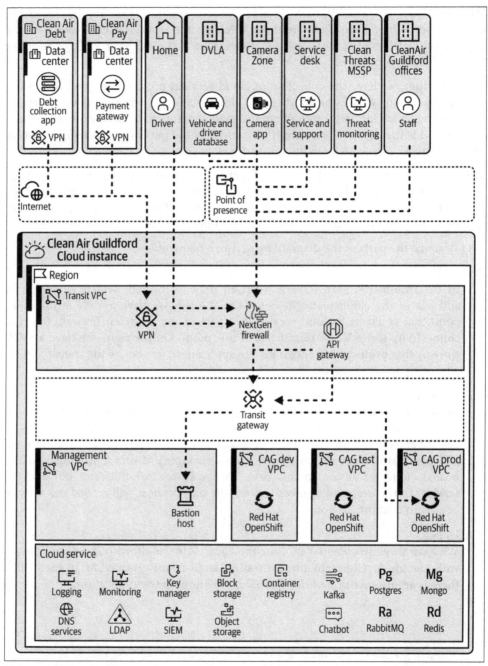

Figure 8-7. Deployment architecture diagram; see the original diagram (https://oreil.ly/ SAHC)

Platform services

On the left-hand side of the platform services, we've used the standard *logging, monitoring,* and *DNS services* provided by the CSP. The solution required an *LDAP* Directory for employees and so we've also used that as a cloud service rather than running our own software.

Moving toward the right from the left-hand side, you will see two security services: the *key manager* for encryption and the *SIEM* service for threat detection.

Moving across again to the middle, there is *block storage* and *object storage* that the compute nodes, hosted on the management and workload VPCs, will need.

Next, instead of running a container library in Red Hat OpenShift, we've used the *container registry* provided by the cloud provider, as it's more tightly integrated with the cloud platform.

Finally, on the right is the set of required PaaS services to run the application, including *Postgres* for a SQL database, *Mongo* for a no-SQL database, *RabbitMQ* for messaging, *Redis* as an in-memory database, *Kafka* for streaming, and *Chatbot* for the chatbot requirement.

The VPC network will have private endpoints for each of the cloud services, ensuring there is no public network connectivity. This removes the possibility of exposing the cloud services to the internet.

Internet connectivity

At the top left is the internet connectivity. The case study said the *debt collection app* and the *payment gateway* are available via the internet using a VPN connection to secure access. A third internet connection enables the drivers to access the portal for the administration of the drivers, vehicles, and payments.

Point of presence connectivity

At the top right is private connectivity through the point of presence (PoP). Third-party networking service providers typically manage the PoP, which enables connectivity to other networks. The data doesn't flow over the internet, and in this case, we didn't use a site-to-site VPN to protect the confidentiality of the data.[4]

---

4 You may be thinking we should use a VPN. You would be correct, but we wanted to make the point that a diagram will evolve over time.

As you put together the diagram, you will identify additional cloud services needed to support the application operations, and this diagram will evolve as you go through design iterations. Let's now move on to a further discussion on zero trust practices for the next iteration of the deployment architecture diagram.

Zero Trust-Based Security Infrastructure

Chapter 1 already introduced the zero trust principles and practices, and we reviewed zero trust architecture in Chapter 2. We'll now build on that with an overview of the most common zero trust architecture practices at the infrastructure layer and then continue with a discussion on how to use some zero trust practices in developing a deployment architecture diagram.

Network-Based Solutions

First, let's start by discussing two zero trust networking solutions: zero trust network access (ZTNA) and microsegmentation. ZTNA operates at the edge of the data center, and microsegmentation is internal to the data center.

Zero trust network access (ZTNA)
> ZTNA is typically used to control network traffic between an end user and an enterprise application. An enterprise application is an application that's only accessible to employees and possibly some partners of an organization. ZTNA is a brokered network connection that uses an encrypted micro-tunnel to connect a device to the system hosting the application. It only permits network connectivity to the port that has been explicitly defined by policies and blocks all other traffic. For a more complete description, read the definition of ZTNA from Gartner (*https://oreil.ly/itDc0*):
>
>> Zero trust network access (ZTNA) is a product or service that creates an identity- and context-based, logical access boundary around an application or set of applications. The applications are hidden from discovery, and access is restricted via a trust broker to a set of named entities. The broker verifies the identity, context and policy adherence of the specified participants before allowing access and prohibits lateral movement elsewhere in the network. This removes application assets from public visibility and significantly reduces the surface area for attack.[5]
>
> ZTNA is the most common implementation of the software-defined perimeter (SDP) pattern and allows organizations to define logical perimeters to protect private applications. While ZTNA could use both human and system actors, we see in practice that organizations select ZTNA primarily to manage end-user

---

[5] The authors had a debate as to whether we would see ZTNA at the level of application components (and not just an application) built into the cloud platform as default in the next few years. What do you think?

access. An important advantage of ZTNA is that it isolates the applications from the internet, thus reducing the attack surface of the organizations. The use cases where ZTNA comes into the picture are: replacement of remote access VPN, acceleration of cross-organization application access during a merger or acquisition, and multi-cloud access.

Ever Changing Network Perimeter

Be aware that the "perimeter" of your corporate network will become more and more dynamic, and for example, it might contain applications exposed to the internet through the public IP range of the cloud provider instead of your own public IP address range. So, besides managing access to the logical network perimeter, you should also monitor the external attack surface by performing automated external attack surface scanning to detect possible vulnerabilities from the outside.

Microsegmentation

Microsegmentation limits the communication between applications and related systems within one or more network zones. It restricts the network to the TCP/IP ports needed by the applications through explicitly defined policies, and it inhibits all other traffic. There are several approaches possible to microsegmentation, mostly by packet filters at the endpoint level or at the network level.

Both solutions share the characteristic that network communication is only possible if an explicit policy permits such connectivity. Figure 8-8 positions both solutions against a cloud hub and spoke network architecture. The ZTNA solutions will manage network access to enterprise applications independent of the location of the actors and the applications. ZTNA establishes a software-defined perimeter around a set of applications and manages access by end users. Microsegmentation focuses on system-to-system network connectivity. Even if computing nodes are on the same network segment, microsegmentation can manage all point-to-point network connections within that segment. There might be some overlapping use cases but, in general, we see that ZTNA provides a logical perimeter for frontend applications, and microsegmentation controls the communication between computing nodes themselves.

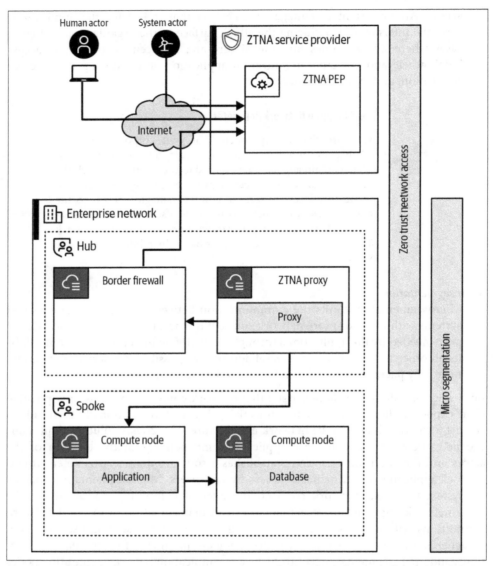

Figure 8-8. ZTNA versus microsegmentation; see the original diagram (https://oreil.ly/ SAHC)

A closer look at ZTNA implementation use cases shows us that the most recurring use case concerns the replacement of client-side VPN access for the remote work-force. Saying that, it's important to note that ZTNA-based solutions can provide the same type of protection to the workforce at the office too. Such a comprehensive approach ensures the enforcement of the same policies, independent of the location of the employee. There are three major differences between a VPN network connection and a ZTNA-based network connection:

The policy enforcement point (PEP) location
Most solutions put the VPN concentrator in the DMZ in front of the internal network. With ZTNA, the PEP is in a public cloud, which means that the PEP takes access decisions outside of the organization perimeter and thus even before establishing the network connection to the internal network.

The initiation of the network traffic
With VPN connectivity, the traffic is ingress; the flow is from outside to the inside network, whereas with ZTNA, the traffic is egress. The ZTNA proxy establishes an outgoing connection to the PEP. The net result is that the internal network no longer gets exposed to computers outside the perimeter. The PEP brokers the traffic from the user device to the ZTNA proxy (which, in turn, establishes the network connection to the system hosting the application frontend).

No more open network connectivity
With a remote access VPN, the user device typically has the same network connectivity as at the office, and most of the time that's quite open. Often, VPN implementations have policies that allow many types of network protocols, and from the VPN concentrator to the internal, there is no or little restriction on the destination IP addresses. A lot of organizations also use remote access VPNs, not only for their own employees but also for their business partners. It's clear that a remote access VPN for third parties brings an additional risk as the organization potentially exposes too much of its internal infrastructure to them.

With ZTNA, an administrator or the tool itself will define a policy for every type of network connectivity between the end-user device and the internal application. As a result, possible malware on the end-user device can no longer propagate to other systems using protocols like SSH, WinRM, or RDP.

Another advantage of ZTNA is that most vendors deliver the ZTNA solution as part of secure access service edge (SASE), which provides extra security controls at the policy enforcement point like traffic inspections, for example. This multifaceted security check at the PEP reduces traffic redirection to different types of security components.

Figure 8-9 clearly shows that with this type of ZTNA implementation, the ZTNA proxy initiates the network session from within the corporate network to the PEP of the ZTNA provider. When an end user establishes a connection with a PEP in the same ZTNA solution, the PEP brokers the network traffic via the ZTNA network components.

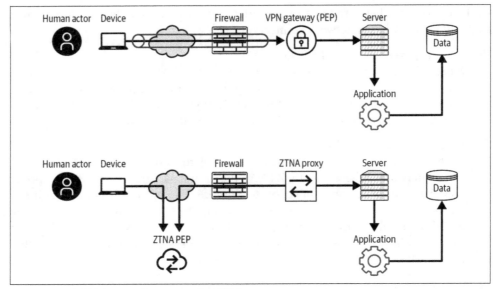

Figure 8-9. ZTNA as replacement for VPN

ZTNA Manages Network Access

Keep in mind that, strictly speaking, ZTNA manages network access, not application access. So ZTNA vendors typically also provide single sign-on (SSO) capabilities to authenticate the user at the application layer. If such a solution wasn't in place, then the end user would have to authenticate twice: first at the network layer (ZTNA), and once there is network connectivity, a second time at the application layer. Despite the SSO, you will continue to maintain the authorization at both levels. ZTNA controls access to the application, and the application will manage authorization within the application.

There are some even more fine-grain solutions for container-based applications that we should discuss.

Service Mesh Solutions

You'll notice that there are even more fine-grained zero trust-based solutions. When your organization develops container-based applications, they may use a service mesh for secure communication. There are several solutions, and some of them have a sidecar that acts as the PEP in front of the service. These sidecars will encrypt all the traffic on the data plane and will also authorize access. A well-known implementation of such a sidecar is the Envoy Proxy (*https://www.envoyproxy.io*), part of the Cloud Native Computing Foundation (CNCF).

We've talked about the network, but what about endpoints? Let's see how zero trust applies.

Endpoint-Based Solutions

Looking back at Table 2-2 with some zero trust based solutions, you'll see that for the endpoint domain, there are security solutions listed that are already in place, independent of zero trust based strategies. So the question is: how do these endpoint-based solutions contribute to the zero trust principles?

Never trust, always verify
> This applies first to the endpoint itself. Can you trust the device that connects to your network? This verification uses multiple assessment criteria. First, there is the security posture of the device itself. A solution can use a combination of device-specific attributes for the posture check, like:

> - Does it have a trusted platform module (TPM) chip?
> - Is the hard drive encrypted and does it store the keys in the TPM?
> - Is the endpoint managed by your organization?
> - Is it hardened in line with the security configuration specification from your organization?
> - Is the operating system (and other software) up to date (are the latest patches installed)?
> - Are there known severe vulnerabilities?

Assume breach
> Applying this principle to an endpoint is about the implementation of as many layers of defense as possible on the endpoint itself. It starts with protective controls like host-based firewalls, host-based intrusion prevention solutions, and access control. Additionally, there should be detective controls, ideally combined with a local response capability.

> Here, endpoint detection and response (EDR) solutions come into play. Even with all possible protective controls in place, the assume breach principle implies not only the compromise of surrounding systems but also the endpoint itself. Hence, a detection capability is key. First to initiate the necessary response actions to restore the endpoint to its original state, but also to detect issues with other solutions as contextual information. The EDR solution may deny other resources to the end user or application running on a compromised endpoint.

Also, there are even more dynamic measurements possible of the security posture based on EDR solutions. These security products calculate a risk score based on both static and dynamic data. For example, if there is detection at the endpoint of some suspicious behavior, the risk score will increase. Other zero trust based solutions, like ZTNA, take this risk score as extra contextual information for the evaluation of access policies. Denial of access to the network can take place if devices have a risk score that's too high.

Now that we've considered zero trust for endpoints, let's move on to consider how zero trust impacts identity and access management.

Identity and Access Management

Identity and access management (IAM) are capabilities you will need for each IT layer in the organization. So beside the infrastructure layer, IAM plays a key role for application and cloud security too. In the context of zero trust, it's clear that identity is a core element of many zero trust based solutions. All actors requiring access will require a unique identity and many resources will have an identity too. The verification of the identity is the recurring baseline for zero trust. An employee will only get access to an internal application after validation of their identity, including all contextual information. That might include historical data on both employee login times and locations.

Privileged access management (PAM) provides strict control over administrator-equivalent access to systems and applications. Applying zero trust to such types of solutions is mostly based on additional conditions before granting access. For example, before a system administrator can access a system via PAM, there should be a service ticket in the service management tool. Additionally, the granted access could have a limited duration. This is how least privilege reduces further the implicit permissions.

Lastly, the recent development of identity threat detection and response (ITDR) solutions is another layer in the IAM portfolio. In a hybrid cloud context with many more identities to manage and the rise of threats to identity tools themselves, there is a need for a detection capability similar to what EDR does for the endpoint. ITDR will be another key zero trust solution to maintain trustworthy identities and detect possible anomalies with them.

There is a lot of material available around zero trust. If you are considering using the zero trust principles to further improve the security maturity of your organization, take the time to read through the publications from NIST and others before diving into the product data sheets and brochures.

Focus on Identity and Access Management

In many organizations, a dedicated team outside the security archi-tects takes care of IAM solutions. We see IAM rather as another foundational security element, so together with network security, they realize most of the protective controls. Hence, independent of whether there is a separate IAM team or not, you should focus on IAM during design and build.

Architecting Zero Trust Practices

Now that you have had an overview of possible zero trust solutions, let's build on the architectural thinking approach we described in Figure 8-3 to see how zero trust principles and practices could drive the outcome of the solution design. The typical way to start with zero trust is to take a risk-driven approach and adopt the overall principle to implement zero trust-based solutions for the use cases where there is the highest impact on risk mitigation.

The zero trust implementation approach overlays the architectural thinking approach we discussed in Figure 8-4 and integrates with the threat modeling from Chapter 6. It also returns to the requirements and reflects any updates in the overall solution.

We suggest adding the following activities to the *Secure the Data Flows* process step in Figure 8-4:

Review and update threat modeling
> Return to the threat modeling you completed in Chapter 6 and perform an update of the STRIDE threats and controls identified in Table 6-3. This time, look at the data flow through the infrastructure and complete it for each use case, any internally triggered flows, and the four types of flows identified in Figure 8-5.

Integrate relevant zero trust practices
> Identify any zero trust practices for adding to the STRIDE threats and controls table. Update and add any relevant risk evaluations.

Add controls to requirements
> Take each of the identified controls and update the requirements, taking care to define requirements that can help identify the technical and process solutions needed to implement the controls.

Iterate the requirements mapping
> Take the requirements and identify their implementation by updating require-ments mappings that document their implementation.

Update architecture solution

Update architecture diagrams to reflect changes, starting with the system context diagram with any new actors. Update the deployment architecture diagrams as needed. If you have selected a ZTNA solution, there may be a need to create a standalone solution architecture to provide sufficient detail. It's likely to require consideration of non-functional requirements such as availability and performance.

Maintaining Architecture Documentation

One of the biggest challenges in the industry is maintaining architecture documentation. Undocumented system changes, without a re-assessment of system threats, can diminish the effectiveness of security. Requiring updates as a part of the incident, problem, and change processes will help, but that's not the whole answer. Perhaps AI will eventually help track, document, and assess the impact of changes. We leave you with this dilemma to think about as you bring architectural thinking for security into your organization.

Update operations solution

You might discover new security services that require management by a security operations team, like ZTNA. Use the techniques to update and develop new operations artifacts, including RACI, processes, procedures, and work instructions, as described in Chapter 11.

This approach should be holistic and isn't limited to the typical zero trust solutions mentioned before. Think about the overall zero trust principles and practices. The goal here is to mitigate the known risks to an acceptable level, and zero trust-based solutions are just one way to mitigate cyber risks.

Review the design or solution and try to find cases where connectivity or access would still rely on implicit trust. For example, system A has network connectivity to system B because both systems reside on the same VLAN or network zone (for example, the production environment), while these two systems don't require connectivity between them. While implicit trust situations are most common at the network layer, at other layers you may find such cases, be it at the operating system level or at the application level. You should try to remove implicit trust where possible; you can often do this without adding new technology.

Starting with Zero Trust

Applying zero trust to one solution is a good start, but it should be part of a larger strategy.

Zero trust-based solutions won't protect an organization against all the possible threats that it's facing. As a security architect, it's important that you understand the limitations of zero trust-based solutions. A good example is a software vulnerability in an internet-facing web application. That isn't something you will solve with adaptive access control or microsegmentation, just to name two common zero trust-based solutions.

Start with the applications with the highest risk. You won't have the budget or the time to apply zero trust to the full extent on all applications. Identify where a zero trust approach has the most impact on risk reduction.

To conclude, it's important to keep in mind that zero trust is a set of principles that drive the outcome of infrastructure design. Also, it's a journey, so don't expect that you can apply all the principles and practices to their full extent with the first release. Instead, it's important to have zero trust as a continuous approach for both the new projects and an improvement track for current operational solutions.

Now let's apply the zero trust techniques we've discussed to the case study.

Zero Trust-Based Security Infrastructure QA Checklist

- Ensure solution includes network-based solutions using ZTNA and microsegmentation.
- Review and ensure the inclusion of endpoint-based solutions.
- Review and ensure the inclusion of identity and access management solutions.
- Use the list of zero trust practices to review the deployment architecture diagram.

Case Study: Zero Trust

As a security architect, you should review the deployment architecture diagram and investigate where zero trust-based solutions could have a significant risk reduction. From the threat modeling exercise, you've learned that unauthorized privilege access is one of the identified risks. To mitigate the risk, you decided to take the following actions:

Implement a ZTNA solution
> There will be a ZTNA remote access SaaS service added for the Clear Air Guildford workforce and business partners, and the transit VPC will include a proxy to support access to the cloud platform. We've decided to use a SaaS service as they can provide a more flexible and available service than we could implement with software.

Add privileged access management (PAM)
> We've added a PAM solution to control all privileged access to the CAG systems and applications. We've decided to run as software on the management VPC as the software we require isn't available from the CSP.

Implementing a PAM solution is part of an iterative approach to architecting security, wherein you gradually add more capabilities to the solution. A possible step you could take to reach even higher maturity could be through the integration of the PAM solution with the service management solution. Starting from that moment, an administrator will only be able to check out a privileged account from the PAM system if there is an approved ticket in the service management solution. This just-in-time approach is a more granular access control for privileged access as it establishes a dependency between service management and administrative access to systems.

The deployment architecture diagram in Figure 8-10 highlights the additional security components with shading.

The changes included in the diagram are:

ZTNA service provider
> We've added a ZTNA provider as an extra third party. As a result, we also introduced a ZTNA proxy running on a compute node in the transit VPC. We have not identified whether this will be a virtual server or a container-based solution. The infrastructure deployment pipeline should deploy the ZTNA proxy in the different availability zones of the hub VPC so the component can satisfy high availability requirements (note that the availability zones aren't shown on this diagram).

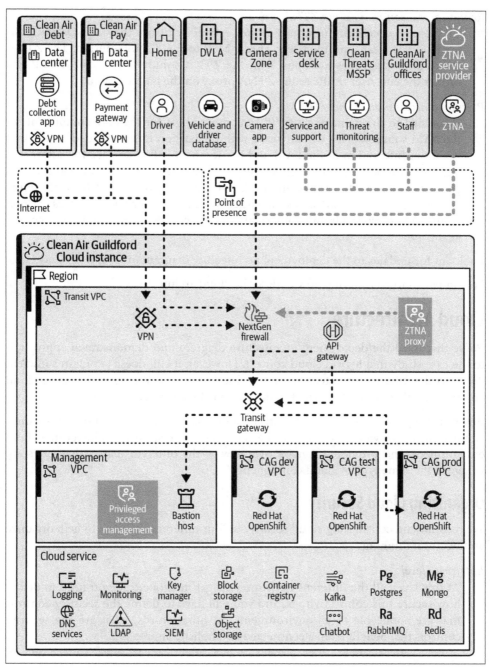

Figure 8-10. Zero trust based solutions added to the architecture; see the original diagram (https://oreil.ly/SAHC)

Remote access connections via ZTNA proxy

The remote access connections are now established from the CAG Office, Guilford Service Desk, and the Clear Threat MSP to the ZTNA solution. The ZTNA proxy also establishes a session with the ZTNA solution. The ZTNA PEP will broker the end-user traffic to the ZTNA proxy on the target system.

Privileged access management (PAM)

We added to the management VPC a compute host for the core components of the PAM solution. This will integrate with the bastion host we added on the first iteration. Integration of the PAM and bastion host will take place for automated login without knowledge of the privileged user credentials. CAG personnel and partners will have to request to check out a privileged account from the PAM system before they can access a target system with privileged access. Upon completion of their administrative activities, they have to check in to the account again.

Look out for updates to the deployment architecture diagram in Chapters 9 and 11.

Let's move on to considering how to describe cloud architecture.

Cloud Architecture

We've discussed the deployment architecture diagram and demonstrated applying it to the case study in a hybrid cloud context. However, it still doesn't contain sufficient detail to describe the architecture of the cloud platform. We normally use a cloud architecture diagram in the format of the chosen cloud service provider.

Before getting there, we'll first give an introduction to the topic of how to organize cloud security, provide an outline of the activities of the security architect in a cloud environment, and provide a concise overview of the different names that CSPs are using for the same type of cloud components.

Organizing Cloud Security

We recommend considering cloud security in four different domains to help organize architectural thinking:

Enterprise level

At this level, all the different environments get integrated, so you need to define how secure this connectivity is, and you will have to define the security controls that are applicable to all environments. In other words, what are the security controls that benefit from a centralized and holistic approach?

Before an organization can deploy applications in a cloud environment, the cloud operations team of your organization will prepare and configure the public cloud and define a governance model to manage it. Here are a few topics to consider at an enterprise level:

- Adding a (new) IaaS cloud instance to an existing IT environment requires an integration design and related security measures.

- Decide ow to set up the interconnectivity between different landing zones (both cloud and data centers), and also how to secure this network path.

- Provide guidance on the network segmentation approach required for the given cloud instance.

- Make and document the decisions about when you should deploy which security controls at the enterprise level and the specific controls for a given landing zone.

CSP/landing zone level

Each type of cloud environment or data center will require its own specific set of security controls. These are in addition to the earlier mentioned enterprise-wide security measures.

The second step in the cloud security design process will be the configuration of the cloud instance itself, if it's a total new instance. The onboarding of a cloud instance from a new CSP will result in a lot of design activities for the security architect. The discussion of a cloud security operating model in Chapter 10 will provide some further concepts. Let's give some examples in this context:

- The cloud comes with its own specific threats, so you should use a cloud security control framework to address these threats.

- Together with the other architects, you need to define how to configure the cloud resources in line with the security policies and make these pre-configured resources available for the DevOps teams.

- Identify if the cloud native security tools are sufficient or if you would need third-party technologies. A recurring topic in this area is security monitoring. While this is typically organized at the enterprise level, it might make sense to use specific security monitoring solutions per cloud provider and only consolidate alerts at the enterprise level.

- Review the operational processes to keep the applications and workloads secure in the cloud. An example could be the setup of privileged access management for the cloud instance. Use the artifacts and techniques from Chapter 11.

Application and CI/CD level

You need specific security controls throughout the application lifecycle (design, code development, testing, deployment, and run).

You can find the overall approach in Chapter 6. In the context of cloud security, here are some activities that require the contribution of a security architect:

- What will be the level of freedom that the DevOps teams will get? For example, you must decide if they're allowed to create new network subnets as part of application deployments through a CI/CD pipeline.

- The selection of technologies to implement the CI/CD pipelines. As a cloud security architect, you'll have to define the required permissions to integrate the CD tool into the cloud instance(s).

- Also, for the detailed design of the CI/CD pipeline itself, there are security-related design decisions, like where to add security quality gates to the CI/CD pipeline. The goal of these quality gates is to ensure that the automated build and deployment of applications includes security checkpoints before they can run in the cloud. Chapter 10 contains a discussion of the quality gates.

Operations level

A cloud environment changes the way you need to consider security operations. The existing security operations may not be ready to handle the changes in security processes and service level demands placed on them. There will be many additional technologies, increased service response demands, and hours of support needed. Consider whether your organization can meet these new demands. As an architect, you will need to consider the implications of security operations in your solution.

A hybrid cloud environment will further stretch your organization with consideration of where to distribute the security tools needed to protect the applications, data, and infrastructure. You will want to balance the benefits of centralizing the security operations with the benefits of distributing capabilities to optimize the non-functional requirements.

Chapter 11 will further discuss the needs of security operations.

It's clear that a security architect will be very busy the first time a new IaaS cloud gets onboarded. The four domains for organizing security we discussed previously are just a small subset of what will end up on the desk of the security architect. Once a cloud instance is onboarded and DevOps starts to deploy workloads in the cloud instance, there are still other activities to fulfill. One of them typically comes from the CSP itself. Every CSP updates the capabilities and functionalities of their technology and services. This is true for the security functionalities as well. On a regular basis, the CSP adds new features or deprecates some older capabilities. The security architect should follow these evolutions and adapt the current design if needed. A recent technology update in the public cloud might be more beneficial for the organization or even required to address new threats.

Another dynamic component in an IaaS context will be the network. Thanks to SDN capability, the reality is that after one year, the number of subnets might have tripled or more. As the network setup continues to evolve, it's important that the overall network design is coherent and remains consistent during expansion. The organization must monitor to ensure that the growing complexity of the network doesn't create security flaws that might go unnoticed. Also, here, the security architect should perform a continuous follow-up. Creating some architecture patterns that the architects should adopt will help keep alignment. We will talk more about this in Chapter 9.

Lastly, independent of the technology evolution and configuration changes, there should be a scheduled review of the security architecture to ensure there are no gaps or design updates needed. The table in Table 8-3 sums up some of the security architect activities for the solution lifecycle stages (Day 0, 1, and 2) as well as per scope (enterprise, cloud instance, DevOps).

Table 8-3. Security architect activities during solution lifecycle

Level	Initial setup	Changes and improvements	Steady state
Enterprise level	• Contribute to the overall design • Update/define security policies • Select enterprise-wide products and services	• Validate design changes	• Yearly quality assurance review • Revalidate selected enterprise-wide products and services
CSP level	• Design for security-as-a-code • Establish governance model • Create cloud architecture diagram	• Follow up CSP level updates and improvements • Validate network changes	• Synchronize with platform and product teams • Follow up noncompliance and incidents (root cause)
CI/CD level	• Cloud resource certification processes	• Review onboarding of new third-party components and libraries	• Review "special" network connectivity requirements (firewall policies)
Operations level	• Perform a security operations gap analysis	• Update organization to handle enhanced response and hours of service • Deploy new cloud security tooling and processes	• Perform performance and capacity management • Monitor service levels and perform continuous improvement

Now let's continue with the description of cloud architecture using a cloud architecture diagram.

Cloud Architecture Diagram

When creating a cloud architecture diagram (CAD) for the different CSPs, you will discover different terminology for the same type of building blocks or cloud resources. That hasn't been a big issue, but it's important to use the right terms when speaking to different teams and when selecting solution components. More important than a different name are the exact capabilities of each component type. The same type of component at different CSPs won't have the exact same capabilities or configuration parameters. It's important to keep these differences in mind, as one parameter can make a huge difference. In Table 8-4, we've listed some common building blocks used in a CAD with their names per CSP.

Table 8-4. Public cloud resource naming conventions

Building block	AWS	Azure	GCP	IBM Cloud
Network segment (VLAN)	Virtual Private Cloud (VPC)	Virtual Networks (VNet)	Google Virtual Private Cloud (VPC)	Virtual Private Cloud (VPC)
Direct connection	AWS Direct Connect	Azure ExpressRoute	Google Cloud Interconnect	Direct Link (Dedicated or Connect)
Network peering (between VLANs)	VPC Peering Connections	Virtual Network Peering	VPC Network Peering	Transit Gateway
Network routes	Route Tables	Azure Virtual Network Routing	Routes	Route Tables
Private endpoint	PrivateLink	Private Endpoint	Private Service Connect	Virtual Private Endpoint
Network ACL	Security Group (instance)	Network ACL (subnet)	Network Security Group	Firewall

Now there are, of course, more differences than just the resource names. Every CSP has its own particularities and constraints. All publish best practices and reference architectures that you should review in detail. We made a summary in Table 8-5 of some best practices from the CSPs about network design as an example, but you can also find information on other aspects of the solution on their websites. In Chapter 9 we provide more information on these best practices.

You'll see that for the same use case, the CSPs might come with different approaches and patterns. At the network level, there isn't a one-size-fits-all approach. A standardized approach among different CSPs could be more easily achieved at the platform level, for example, using Red Hat OpenShift as the compute platform in all the different instances (cloud and data center).

Table 8-5. Public cloud network design

Solution topic	AWS	Azure	GCP	IBM Cloud
Overall network structure	Combined model with a VPC per group of workloads	Hub-spoke architecture	VPC networks are global resources spanning multiple regions	In a region where a VPC can span an MZR, the attachment of resources will take place on one of the subnets in the VPC.
North-south traffic and east-west traffic	A central Ingress VPC and a central Egress VPC	All ingress and egress internet traffic goes through hub	Internet traffic via dedicated VPC; east-west traffic via a shared VPC	The configuration of all ingress and egress internet traffic will take place to enforce the use of the transit VPC.
Separation of production and non-production environments	Most granular segmentation: Create an OU per environment and an account per application	Most granular segmentation is achieved through creation of a subscription per environment and per application; a more coarse-grained network segmentation is, for example, the set up of a PRD subscription and a non-PRD subscription	Environments are represented as Folders under an organization. Production resources are separated from non-production resources in a separate folder.	Multiple options for separation including Cloud Accounts within an Enterprise Account. Resource groups can be used to separate resources with Access Groups or Trusted profiles to grant access. VPCs can also be used to separate workloads.

The development of the CAD may come from a different team, and as a security architect, you will have contributed to it. You should keep in mind that realizing an IT architecture in general consists of 50% technical activities and the other 50% communication. The same applies to security architecture. If you create diagrams like the examples used in this book, then these are the most important vehicles for communication with other stakeholders. That's true at the conceptual and logical levels as well as at the technical level, for example, with this CAD. It will help you explain the current solution, the future solution, the options for integration, and other aspects of solution design. Without such diagrams, it will be difficult to have an informed discussion with the different stakeholders. We'll provide an example of a CAD in the case study later in this chapter.

Now, thanks to the evolution of automation solutions, the CAD has another purpose as well. Today, tools exist that can create deployment configuration files from this diagram. That means that from the CAD, you could initiate the infrastructure setup, configuration, and deployment of all the elements in the diagram. The prerequisite is, of course, that the CAD has all the required configuration information and is properly stored as metadata. The build process will take the information from the CAD and adapt the configuration so the application complies with the company standards and guidelines. Such a level of automation requires supporting processes and governance to ensure all steps are clearly articulated with the required input and expected output. Diagrams without additional metadata aren't sufficiently detailed for a fully automated deployment, but with the addition of sizing parameters, it's still enough for a SRE to configure the resources (or create the deployment files).

One of the benefits of using a cloud platform is the use of a multi-zone region containing three or more zones to support high levels of availability. Let's go on to discuss how this affects the design of security.

High Availability

While availability is a critical aspect of a security solution, it's, in many cases, not addressed primarily by the security architects themselves. That doesn't mean a security architect isn't contributing to the high availability design, as the availability of applications depends on the availability of security services. This is an important part of the role of a security architect and requires continuous communication between all solution architects. In this book, we won't address this topic in a detailed way, but we will provide a short overview of the possibilities in the public cloud.

Most public cloud service providers, if not all, provide, per region, three or more availability zones. These zones are mostly in separate data centers in the same region with high bandwidth and low-latency network connectivity. Figure 8-11 shows a simplified view of a cloud architecture diagram to show the availability zones without any compute nodes, appliances, or cloud services.

The cloud architecture diagram shows a hub-and-spoke solution with VPCs spread over three zones in a multi-zone region. There needs to be the deployment of critical components over the three zones for redundancy for both the hub and the spoke VPCs.

Hub, Transit, and Edge Are Interchangeable

A hub is normally called a transit or edge VPC when it comes to implementation.

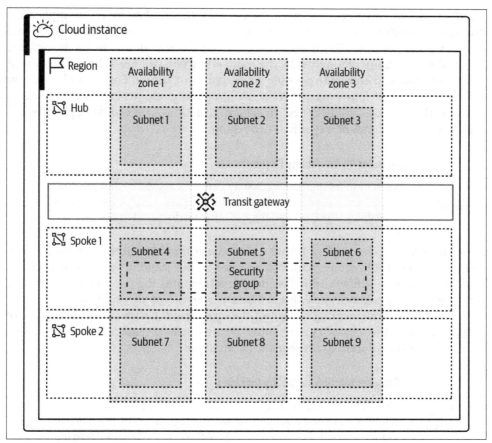

Figure 8-11. Simplified cloud architecture diagram; see the original diagram (https://oreil.ly/SAHC)

If you need a web application firewall (WAF) appliance, you should deploy a WAF instance in each of the three availability zones of the transit VPC. A load balancer should then distribute the web traffic over the three WAF instances in the different zones. In more sophisticated solutions, there will be multiple subnets per zone and per VPC. Making use of the availability zones in a public cloud simplifies the availability design, but it also requires good planning of the network zones and their related IP address ranges.

We discussed in Chapter 5 the need for defining the availability of an application through availability bands or "nines availability," recovery time objective (RTO) and recovery point objective (RPO). High availability is a design discipline on its own; the higher the availability requirements, the more effort you will need during the design and build phases to eliminate possible single points of failure. For example, with an availability band of four nines, that's something you could achieve within a single region with three availability zones. To achieve five nines, you should deploy the full application in a redundant way across two regions.

Consider All Availability Requirements

Keep in mind that the availability band is a key driver, but the final solution will depend on the two other requirements related to high availability: the RTO and the RPO that we discussed in Chapter 5.

For example, the process of restoring a database from object storage is slow, and if you have a low RTO requirement, you will need a hot standby solution instead. An RPO is difficult to achieve with just infrastructure, and the concerned application may need to have rollback capabilities. These requirements also apply to the security solutions you're implementing to protect the application. Last but not least, if you're encrypting data, the loss of keys or other security-critical data could occur, so you should design the solution to prevent such a situation.

Consider Solution Suitability for Cloud

Be careful in your product selection, as an on-premises security solution may not be suitable to provide high levels of resilience in a cloud context. For example, the solution may rely on underlying networking capabilities not available in a public cloud. To validate assumptions, get assurances from the product supplier on the specific configuration and perform a proof of concept early.

Of course, the opposite is true. We have seen a solution that would only boot on AWS and not in any other environment, as it relied on the proprietary security features of the hypervisor.

The availability of the security services needs to meet or exceed the availability of the protected workloads. Cloud-delivered security services can rely on availability capabilities from the cloud, but when you are hosting your own security services on premises, you also need to design the resilience characteristics.

Another view on the required availability of an application is when it's part of the core business of the organization (so the application is part of a minimally viable company). In such a case, you must review the cyber resilience capability of the overall solution, including the supporting security solutions. How could it sustain attacks like DDoS or ransomware? How can you protect it against these threats? How will it recover from such a severe security incident where key infrastructure elements are down or data gets lost?

The analysis of the cyber resilience capabilities for a given solution is sometimes part of threat modeling, but more often this design aspect is a dedicated design activity driven by the overall business continuity strategy plan and the related governance execution.

Cyber Resilience Engineering

A great supporting tool for security architects is the Cyber Resiliency Engineering Framework (CREF) Navigator (*https://oreil.ly/mQl2d*), created by the MITRE organization. It establishes a visual navigation between CREF approaches and the mitigations from the MITRE ATT&CK knowledge base. So the implementation of security controls could serve two purposes: to mitigate threats and to improve cyber resilience.

Let's continue with a look at developing a cloud architecture diagram with the case study.

Case Study: Cloud Architecture Diagram

Let's have a closer look at the cloud architecture diagram in Figure 8-12 for the case study. A full cloud architecture diagram for the case study would be a very complex diagram, so we selected just one aspect of the solution: zero trust network access to the admin console of the Clean Air Guilford application for the staff and the partners (for example, the Guilford Service Desk). This web-based admin application isn't accessible to the public, though it should be accessible from the internet in a secure way.

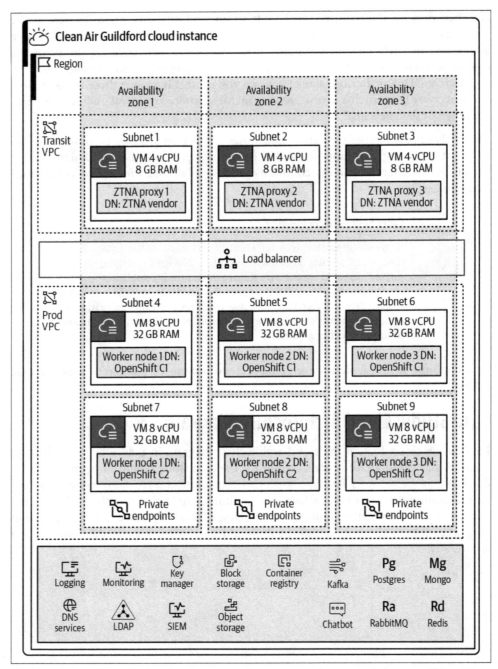

Figure 8-12. Case study cloud architecture diagram; see the original diagram (https://oreil.ly/SAHC)

The implementation of ZTNA implies the setup and configuration of three component types:

End-user device

Many ZTNA solutions require the installation of a specific agent on the end-user devices. This is specifically for the staff of the organization, but agentless solutions do exist via a browser. The capabilities of agent-based versus agentless also vary per product vendor, but they often provide a pre-authentication assessment of the security posture of the device and user location.

ZTNA service provider

When the ZTNA vendor delivers their solution from the cloud, you will have to make the necessary configuration changes so the service meets the needs of your organization. It may also require opening the boundary security devices, such as a firewall, to enable communication with the service provider.

Application landing zones

The landing zones where the private applications are running. That could be a mix of on-premises and public cloud.

In the case study exercise, we only focus on securing public cloud. We assume that the CAG application will run in a dedicated spoke, and the selected application pattern is a typical three-tier approach:

1. A frontend web application running in a dedicated subnet for the administration of the CAG application, only accessible by the staff and some partners.

2. A backend application in the second subnet that performs the critical data processing.

3. A data tier: the CAG application will access the databases available via the PaaS capabilities from the CSP. The databases are accessible via private endpoints in the spoke subnets.

In Figure 8-12 you'll notice the following components to support the application:

ZTNA proxy

We planned the deployment of the ZNTA proxy, hosted on a virtual server, in a redundant way over the three availability zones in the transit VPC. The ZTNA proxy will establish an outgoing network connection to the ZTNA service for the SASE provider, and the proxy will establish sessions to the CAG Admin web application via a load balancer.

Load balancer

The load balancer manages the traffic between the ZNTA proxies and the CAG Admin web application running in the CAG prod VPC in subnets 4, 5, and 6.

CAG Admin web application

This administrator console is running on an OpenShift cluster in the CAG prod VPC and deployed in a redundant way over the three availability zones in subnets 4, 5, and 6.

The CAG backend application

The backend application is running on another OpenShift cluster in a dedicated subnet in the CAG prod VPC in subnets 7, 8, and 9. In the same subnet as the backend app are the private endpoints for a direct network connection to the databases.

If you reflect back to the deployment architecture diagram in Figure 8-10, you will see that trying to represent all the detail in a cloud architecture diagram would be complex and would not fit onto a page. You could draw multiple viewpoints to show a perspective of the application, or you could go directly to the specification of the cloud architecture using automation.

Let's move on to the conclusion of this chapter.

Cloud Deployment QA Checklist

- Review cloud services for their implementation of encryption in transit, mutual authentication, and automated rotation of certificates.
- Match the availability characteristics of the security solutions to those of the workload or application you are securing.
- Ensure the availability characteristics of the cloud services supporting security solutions.
- Check data flows for both primary and failover routes for protection.
- Check all compute nodes have appropriate ZTNA agents and controls in place.

Summary

In this chapter, we took you through the general steps of infrastructure design and how the security architect plays a key role during this journey. A deployment architecture takes the functional design as a starting point in a hybrid cloud context, delivers the non-functional requirements, and makes technology choices based on the blend of inputs. We also provided an overview of possible approaches to network segmentation. The security architect will focus on the security-specific requirements, leverage the outcome of the threat modeling activity, and apply the zero trust principles where feasible and needed.

We've seen the importance of spending a significant effort on zero trust, with an overview of the most common solutions and a deep dive into ZTNA. We've extended the technique we developed for the deployment architecture and integrated the threat modeling we first performed for the component architecture. Research and development are ongoing for the integration of zero trust thinking into compute platforms, both for on-premises data centers and in the cloud. As a security architect, you need to monitor this emerging technology area.

A cloud architecture for the public cloud introduces many additional concepts that add complexity, including the idea of an MZR to enable applications to be highly available. Like in the other chapters, we used the Clean Air Guilford case study to show you a possible approach based on the techniques from the chapter.

Building architectures from a blank sheet of paper isn't the most effective way of developing an architecture. There are many best practices and heuristics included in standard architecture patterns that will be missed, leading to insecure solutions. Building our solutions from architecture patterns enables us to accelerate the architectural thinking process and improve confidence in the effectiveness of the solution. In the next chapter, we will provide you with an overview of architecture patterns and approaches that you can use as a starting point or benchmark for your solutions.

Exercises

1. The architectural thinking technique of placing a functional component onto the chosen compute node is called __.

   a. Hosting

   b. Deployment

   c. Identification

   d. Categorization

2. What documentation would be an input to support the definition of a deployment architecture diagram?

   a. Storage design

   b. A shared responsibility diagram or table

   c. Node description

   d. System context

3. What documentation should be created to help further describe a deployment architecture diagram?

   a. Network design

   b. Non-functional requirements

   c. Architectural decision records

   d. Current IT environment

4. Which key artifact is needed as an input when architecting for compliance?

   a. Non-functional requirements

   b. A shared responsibility stack diagram

   c. A threat model

   d. System context

5. In compute node to compute node communication, what are the types of transaction flow that need to be considered?

   a. Transaction flows triggered by human and system actors

   b. Transaction flows triggered by system events

   c. Transaction flows triggered by threat actors

   d. Transaction flows triggered by the cloud service provider

6. Deployment across many compute platforms is assisted using what artifact?

   a. A component interaction diagram

   b. A shared responsibility diagram or table

   c. A component architecture diagram

   d. System context

7. A zero trust network access (ZTNA) solution is a more secure remote access solution than a virtual private network (VPN) because _____. Select all that apply.

   a. It uses more advanced encryption algorithms.

   b. Identity and access policy enforcement occurs before establishing the network connection.

   c. It inhibits malware lateral movement between end-user devices and target systems.

   d. It isolates internal enterprise applications from the internet.

8. What are the different domain levels that you should consider for cloud security? Select all that apply.

   a. Enterprise level

   b. The cloud service provider (CSP)/landing zone level

   c. Application and continuous integration (CI)/Continuous deployment (CD) level

   d. Operations level

9. True or false: An on-premises software solution architecture will always work in a cloud environment.

   a. True

   b. False

CHAPTER 9

Architecture Patterns and Decisions

As a security architect, you won't create a security architecture from a blank page; that would be a rather exceptional case. Luckily, there are a lot of sources of information you can reuse to create or update the security architecture you need. One of the artifacts you would be looking for most are security-related architecture patterns. These patterns will give you a kickstart when creating a security architecture. You should save valuable time when making use of such patterns, and you'll get the assurance that the pattern will deliver the expected functionality because someone has tested it before.

In this chapter, we first take a closer look at the term "pattern" itself. What do we mean by the term *pattern*, and is there a definition for it? Next, we will review what kinds of security pattern types exist and direct you to or show you some examples. We're then going to talk through layers of core security design patterns that demonstrate the need for patterns written as code for automation of the solution deployment using *deployable architectures*.

The next topic in this chapter is one that's close to the authors' hearts and fundamental to architectural thinking: architectural decisions. In general, IT architecture is created under time pressure. The shorter duration of development sprints for some projects doesn't leave much time for solution architects and security architects to create detailed documentation. You'll have to make some choices on which type of artifacts you'll work on and what their level of detail should be. No matter how little time you have as a security architect, you should always prioritize the documentation of architectural decision records. You should record the choices you make during solution design. You'll learn more in this chapter about why it's the most important artifact and how you should document your decisions.

Both patterns and architectural decisions will be key elements you'll rely on during the design of security architectures; hence, we grouped these two topics in this chapter.

Chapter Artifacts

The artifacts described in this chapter are either inputs to your security architecture, deliverables you'll create, or both (see Figure 9-1).

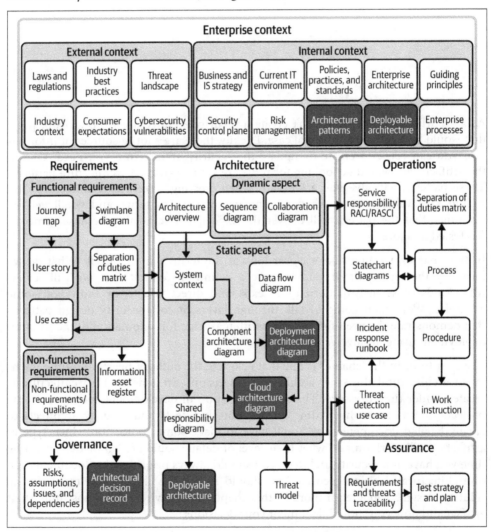

Figure 9-1. Architecture patterns and decisions chapter artifacts

Let's walk through the list highlighted in Figure 9-1:

- *Architecture patterns* are typically inputs that you'll leverage with the goal of speeding up the design of your solution architecture as they enable you to apply proven best practices. Sometimes, your final result might be a new pattern for possible reuse in your organization and even something to share with a wider audience.

- Based on the examples in this chapter, you'll notice that there are patterns available for various artifact types. In the solution architecture domain, you'll be looking for the availability of both *deployment architecture diagrams* and *cloud architecture diagrams* as possible patterns supporting your solution.

- A similar type of artifact is the *deployable architecture*. These artifacts are automation patterns derived from architecture patterns, which you can deploy with minimal configuration changes. These types of patterns are common in a public cloud context. Also here, a deployable architecture might be one of the artifacts created as part of the project; hence, you'll find it back on the artifact dependency diagram as both input and output.

- Last but not least, there is the document or repository where you maintain the *architectural decisions*.

Before we start exploring the security-specific patterns, let us begin with a better definition of a pattern in an architectural context.

Architecture Patterns

The best place to explore for the definition of an architecture pattern is the TOGAF® Standard from The Open Group®. TOGAF® is the most prominent enterprise architecture standard as it sets the standards, methods, and taxonomy. You can consult the Standard's chapter about architecture patterns (*https://oreil.ly/EdVO5*).

The standard has the following description:

> In the TOGAF Standard, patterns are considered to be a way of putting building blocks into context; for example, to describe a re-usable solution to a problem. Building blocks are what you use: patterns can tell you how you use them, when, why, and what trade-offs you have to make in doing so. Patterns offer the promise of helping the architect to identify combinations of Architecture and/or Solution Building Blocks (ABBs/SBBs) that have been proven to deliver effective solutions in the past, and may provide the basis for effective solutions in the future.

This description helps us to better understand what a pattern means in the context of IT and enterprise architecture. You can easily find more definitions for patterns, though the emphasis on certain pattern attributes will vary based on the context and the goal of the pattern.

Another viewpoint on patterns comes from The Hillside Group (*https://oreil.ly/glDek*), who refer to an introduction from Brad Appleton called "Patterns and Software: Essential Concepts and Terminology" (*https://oreil.ly/TEHEY*) using Jim Coplien's criteria for a *good pattern*:

It solves a problem.
Patterns capture solutions, not just abstract principles or strategies.

It is a proven concept.
Patterns capture solutions with a track record, not theories or speculation.

The solution isn't obvious.
Many problem-solving techniques (such as software design paradigms or methods) try to derive solutions from first principles. The best patterns generate a solution to a problem indirectly—a necessary approach for the most difficult problems of design.

It describes a relationship.
Patterns don't just describe modules, but describe deeper system structures and mechanisms.

The pattern has a significant human component.
All software serves human comfort or quality of life; the best patterns explicitly appeal to aesthetics and utility.

You'll notice the focus on the applicability and practicality of the pattern in the context of software development.

Most of the patterns in IT focus on the functional aspect of a given solution architecture, like the functional components of an application to support a business process. Such a pattern will probably have little content that describes the required security solution, and you have two principal choices to include security:

Integrate
Integrate the security into the existing pattern for the workload so you can add the security measures at the right place in the pattern. Also, you should add both the descriptions for the security components integrated into the documentation for the workload components and the security-specific ones that you've added. The result could possibly become a new pattern or an improvement to the original one once you have been able to deploy and test it.

Overlay
Overlay the security components on the existing pattern as an extra layer and document the security-related information in a separate document. This may happen if you don't have enough time to update the pattern. While this might work for one project, it probably won't be something that's ready for reuse

outside the project, and there is a risk that it's not maintained to match the changes made to the underlying solution. This approach, where security still gets handled as an afterthought, is clearly not the preferred solution, yet sometimes it could be the most pragmatic one. We mention it here for the sake of completeness.

In Chapter 2, we described the different types of security-related architecture activities, including enterprise architecture and solution architecture. We're going to focus on solution architecture patterns in this chapter.

Solution Architecture Patterns

This is the core topic of this chapter. When you review all the activities needed to build a security architecture as part of the solution architecture process, you'll identify patterns that could accelerate the building of your security architecture. You have probably also seen that there are many other sources of information besides patterns. It's your responsibility as a security architect to identify and select the sources of information you need.

In an ideal situation, the most relevant security patterns for your organization are already available from a repository maintained by an enterprise security architecture team. For solution architecture teams, security patterns that contribute to a secure design could be, for example:

- Authentication for customers accessing internet-facing web applications
- Product implementation patterns from the vendors
- Cloud deployment patterns from the CSPs
- Secure configuration of a Kubernetes cluster set up in the data center

So a pattern describes the solution for one specific security aspect, like authentication, or addresses security in a more holistic way for a given context (a cluster, a landing zone, etc.).

CSPs are an important source for security patterns. While these patterns are a very good base to start with, you should adapt them to the needs of your organization. The cloud governance model of your organization should include the necessary processes to adapt the vendor patterns, and the cloud center of excellence team should publish the updated patterns in repository for reuse by the DevOps teams. You'll read more about this in Chapter 10.

As the CSPs are updating these web pages continuously we can't provide an up-to-date list. The kind of sources for CSP patterns that you should look for are: their well-architected framework, the related reference architectures, and the security-specific patterns. Following are some examples from the CSPs; for the most recent versions, you should consult their websites.

Well-architected framework

As a starting point, CSPs offer a set of principles, practices, and guidance for the effective development of a cloud architecture to support workloads. CSPs usually call this a *well-architected framework*, and it's organized using domains aligned to non-functional requirements such as:

- Security and compliance
- Resiliency and availability
- Operations and service management
- Performance and scalability
- Financial operations
- Sustainability

These may contain design patterns for adoption in the development of solution architectures.

Reference architectures

CSP reference architectures are normally solution architecture patterns that support specific cloud workloads based on a set of environmental assumptions with specific architectural decisions. They may have options to support variations of workloads.

Open Group TOGAF (*https://oreil.ly/k89DA*) suggests that as a starting point, the table of contents of an architecture pattern should include:

- Name
- Problem statement
- Context or applicability
- Quality attributes
- Solution description
- Resulting context
- Implementation examples
- Rationale
- Related patterns
- Known use cases

We suggest you supplement the information to meet your needs.

Deployable architectures

Deployable architectures are the next step in developing an architecture pattern for cloud with automation to deploy a predefined reference architecture. Such assets are available from CSPs, as well as from some security vendors. You get the necessary scripts and templates to deploy the solution in your cloud environment. It saves a lot of time and, even if you need to adapt it, it will be faster than if you have to create the deployment scripts yourself. A deployable architecture could be your starting point, as well as a deliverable of your project.

Each of the major CSPs host their own frameworks and architectures, as shown in Table 9-1.

Table 9-1. CSP frameworks and architectures

CSP	Well-architected framework	Reference architectures or patterns
AWS	*https://oreil.ly/ttfDA*	*https://oreil.ly/K6Z5t*
Azure	*https://oreil.ly/XyzvX*	*https://oreil.ly/8ah56*
GCP	*https://oreil.ly/TkKQs*	*https://oreil.ly/eLIeA*
IBM Cloud	*https://oreil.ly/XF7OK*	*https://oreil.ly/ybbjL*

We'll talk more about deployable architectures later in this chapter. For now, let's talk about design patterns.

Solution Design Patterns

Solution architecture patterns describe a high-level view of a software system, showing the major components, whereas solution design patterns are lower-level for parts of a system that aren't a complete solution. Architecture patterns are often made up of multiple solution design patterns that are the building blocks of an implementable solution. You can implement architecture patterns by adding some context.

The development of architecture and design patterns has come from many years of experience and provides best practices in the development of solution architectures. We're going to talk through some security solution design patterns and discuss some architectural decisions that you will need to make as you develop your own solutions.

Each of these design patterns we discuss comes from a set of architectural decisions shown in Table 9-2. Each of the decisions supports the separation of workloads for risks relating to security and resilience.

Table 9-2. Architectural decision records

ID	Decision	Rationale	Implication
AD01	Segment the application into as many tiers as components.	• Segmentation to the lowest level reduces the risk from lateral movement of attackers. • The scaling of each network segment is independent and resources distributed.	Applications need to use microsegmentation for separation with access control lists at every segment boundary to reduce attack surface and reduce the risk of lateral movement.
AD02	Separate each type of development, test, and production environment.	• There is a reduction in the risk that one environment interferes with another, such as if a component in development isn't fully secured.	Create an environment for each stage of the development, test, and production stages with each containing the n-tier application (as needed).
AD03	Centralize external and internal network inter-connection.	• Reduces duplicate security components that would increase cost and complexity. • Simplifies network security with centralized policy. • Makes it easier to detect and respond to security incidents.	Create a network segment containing a network security appliance to secure all north-south traffic.
AD04	Separate operations and management workloads from business workloads.	• Management workloads often have privileged access across many workloads and need isolating and additional controls as they span workloads. • Ensures that system admins can only gain access to workloads via infrastructure that controls and records all actions.	Create a network segment hosting systems management components.
AD05	Use components for test/dev environments separate from production environment.	• Changes in the test/dev environments must not impact production environments. • This reduces the risk of attackers jumping from dev/test to production environment. • Separate dev/test and operations teams supports separation of duties.	Create dedicated transit and management VPCs separating dev/test and production workloads.

We'll now talk through each of the design patterns derived from these architectural decisions. These are decisions that you may wish to record for your organization.

N-tier applications

The 3-tier application architecture pattern has been around since the late 1980s as an expansion of client/server architecture, splitting server functions into presentation, application, and data tiers, as shown in Figure 9-2. Each of the tiers has its own compute platform to scale independently, with the components separated by firewalls to protect sensitive data from attackers.

Figure 9-2. 3-tier application

It worked for simple applications at the time, but the cloud has introduced additional components such as global and local load balancers, streams for buffering data and messaging, and many data sources. Each provides additional resilience and performance benefits but with that comes added complexity. We ended up with n-tier applications from architectural decision record AD01, resulting in the example architecture shown in Figure 9-3.

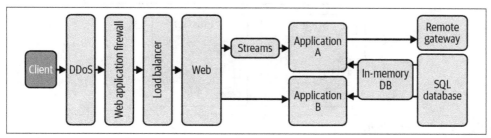

Figure 9-3. N-tier application

The example n-tier design pattern is the foundation for many cloud applications or workloads. It requires many interconnected network segments and cloud services, all of which require security. The network segments and services are likely to be different for each application. Each stage of development will require a copy of the n-tier pattern.

Route to live environments

We don't develop, test, and run production on one instance of an n-tier pattern; we create a sequence of environments that have a different purpose and with isolation from each other. It's likely some earlier environments were insecure at some point during their lifetime, as that's the nature of development.

This sequence of environments has many different names, such as "Route to Live," "Route to Production," or "Path to Production." They all follow the same principle with a sequence of environments with copies of the n-tier architecture in each environment. We therefore made the architectural decision record AD02, resulting in the architecture shown in Figure 9-4.

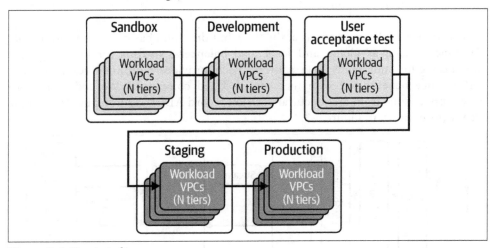

Figure 9-4. Route to live

Each of the environments will have an assigned purpose and include different tools to support the stages of development, testing, and production. To ensure rapid build and configuration of the environments, you'll need to build the environments using automation. We'll talk more about the importance of automation later in this chapter.

We've now discussed the route to live and n-tier architecture used to host the primary workload and need to add the supporting infrastructure into the picture.

Hub and spoke

So far, our workloads aren't set up to support external communication or management of the workloads. This is where we come onto the hub and spoke architecture from architectural decision records AD03 and AD04, resulting in Figure 9-5.

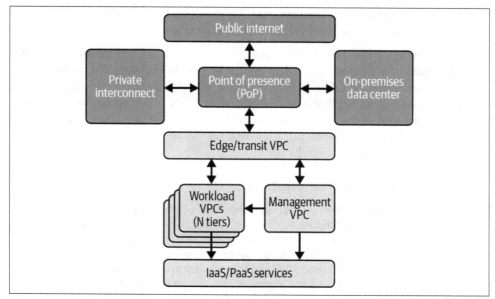

Figure 9-5. Hub and spoke

In this diagram, the hub is known as the edge or transit VPC and the spokes are the workload VPCs. Let's discuss each of the building blocks on the diagram:

Workload VPCs

The workload VPCs in this diagram represent both the route to live and n-tiers of the application. It's getting all too complex, which is why we simplify the picture at this point for the workloads as our focus is on what supports the workloads. The workloads need connectivity to external systems and operations management.

Point of presence (PoP)

The PoP is a network data center that's a concentration of different networks, including public internet connectivity and private connectivity to SaaS providers or other data centers, including cloud data centers. The network data centers are normally owned by a third-party network provider who also owns global or national backbone networks.

Edge/transit VPC

The edge, or transit, VPC provides the interface between the workload VPCs and the external networks or other cloud accounts. North-south traffic contains the network connections that pass in and out of the cloud account. This VPC will contain a security appliance or firewall that controls the traffic in and out. For in-bound application traffic this may be a web application firewall (WAF), and for outbound traffic there may be data loss prevention (DLP) capability to detect and block exfiltration of sensitive data. We're not going to discuss the capabilities in-depth but have discussed the architectural principles.

The hosting of the transit VPC may be in the cloud, but hosting may also take place in a POP network data center or the on-premises data center of an organization. These other locations enable the sharing of network protection and monitoring of applications that may span CSPs and on-premises. Don't just assume hosting of the transit VPC in the cloud, as there are alternatives. Even if the transit VPC is in the cloud, it's worth recording an architectural decision to validate the decision among the team.

 Independent Security Appliance

Security appliances built into the cloud platform could potentially use the same technology as the VPC. For this reason, some organizations prefer to use NextGen firewall technology from providers independent of the cloud platform. This provides defense in depth with a mix of cloud VPC and independent security technology. On the other side of the argument, smaller organizations that don't have specialist security skills may be better off using cloud technology, as it's easier to administer.

Management VPC

The management VPC hosts the set of development, testing, operations, service, and security management tooling used to support the development and operation of the cloud workloads. The management VPC is different from the workload VPCs in that it connects to multiple workload VPCs and environments. It needs careful design of the networking and management workloads to ensure threat actors can't use them to jump to other workloads. Given the diverse set of tools, it's likely that an organization will split the management VPC into multiple VPCs, each managed by a dedicated team providing operations support.

IaaS/PaaS services

At the bottom of the diagram, we show the cloud native IaaS and PaaS services for the workloads in the different VPCs to consume.

You should apply this pattern to all your workloads in the cloud, and you will have seen we already used these design patterns in Figure 8-7.

However, there are still single points of failure.

Resilient hub and spoke

In the previous pattern, we saw the sharing of the transit VPC, PoP, and management VPC between development, testing, and production. A change or failure in any of those shared components for testing and development may cause a failure in the production component. For a resilient infrastructure, we need to fully separate development and testing from production, so we made the architectural decision record AD05, resulting in the architecture shown in Figure 9-6.

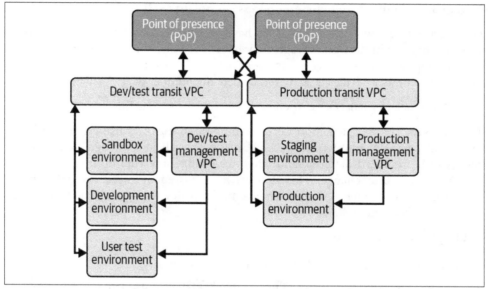

Figure 9-6. Resilient hub and spoke setup

In this pattern, we've split the transit VPCs and management VPCs into two so that changes made to the dev/test environment can't impact production and there is resilience with the POPs.

Changing Design Patterns

We chose this set of design patterns to show the challenges of securing an enterprise at scale. The field is changing rapidly, and we suggest you keep abreast of the latest practices. There are many other books that discuss design patterns and architectural decisions, such as *Hybrid Cloud Security Patterns* (*https://oreil.ly/qbAn7*), which provides a good starting point for hybrid cloud security patterns.

You'll notice we've not included all dimensions in each diagram, only the perspectives necessary to demonstrate a design pattern. How do we draw diagrams for a large-scale enterprise environment?

Scaling for the enterprise

We need to think about how architecture and design patterns scale in an enterprise, as they can become unmanageable without some planning. At the lowest level, we need to define multiple rules for each access control list (ACL).

Let's start with a few calculations. If we have an organization with 100 applications and they have eight tiers on average, they have four environments for their route to live: development, testing, staging, and production. At each tier, there is one ACL and the average number of rules is 20. Let's calculate the number of ACL rules:

100 applications × 8 tiers × 4 environments × 20 rules = 64,000 individual ACL rules

This is a very simple calculation for a medium-sized business using the cloud, and there will be many more rules needed in the firewall at the edge. Many of the rules will be standard patterns, and when we change one rule in an ACL, we will have many more to change. This is why we discussed the need for policy-based management in Chapter 2, where a change to the policy would make a change to all instances of the same ACL.

At this point, there are two challenges:

- A single diagram won't scale to represent this complexity.
- The security configuration can't be effectively managed using manual processes.

This is where an architect needs to bridge into being an engineer and use automation to describe the architecture. Let's move on to discussing deployable architectures.

Deployable Architecture

We always say that documentation is good but given the complexity, there is a need for automation to describe the solution. Architecture diagrams aren't able to describe the complexity of the solution. This is where we move into the engineering of the deployment architecture diagram using automation. This code that describes the architecture is a *deployable architecture*, which is sometimes called a *landing zone*.

Automation for deployable architecture uses three main components:

- A distributed version control system (DVCS)
- A continuous integration/continuous delivery (CI/CD) pipeline
- An infrastructure as code (IaC) toolchain

Let's discuss each of these components.

A Distributed Version Control System

A DVCS is a tool for software development that manages the lifecycle of a repository, which includes code, other text files, and images. Each developer receives a copy of the code to work on, which is then version-controlled and merged into a single codebase. This allows developers to work together to create code for projects. In this case, the code will define the automation needed to deploy the specified deployment architecture.

Git (*https://git-scm.com*) is a widely used DVCS tool providing a source code repository that's used as the single source of truth for the storage of infrastructure configuration and deployment commands. The tooling enables collaboration while maintaining control over the code. Git is often wrapped in a SaaS application, such as GitHub (*https://github.com*) and GitLab (*https://oreil.ly/YyKWT*), to provide a user interface supporting collaboration.

Reading for Git

For Git, we suggest some further reading in *Learning Git* by Anna Skoulikari and *Head First Git* by Raju Gandhi (both O'Reilly).

Continuous Integration/Continuous Delivery (CI/CD) Pipeline

A CI/CD pipeline provides the automation to build, test, and deploy code through the different development, test, and production environments. One key responsibility of the pipeline is to ensure the quality of the code, including scanning for misconfigurations and vulnerabilities that may impact the security of the code.

The pipeline begins with the CI process bringing code together from the different developers using a DVCS tool, such as Git. This frequent integration by the different developers reduces the divergence of code and makes integration easier. It goes on to support testing the code through automation, enabling the rapid fixing of issues. The CD stage of the pipeline then takes the validated code stored in the Git repository and passes it on for deployment using the IaC toolchain.

There are a large number of tools to choose from to automate the CI/CD pipeline, such as Jenkins, Tekton, and Travis CI.

Infrastructure as Code Toolchain

Infrastructure as code (IaC) is the process of managing and provisioning infrastructure resources through code rather than a manual process. In effect, the code describes the architecture of the solution you would like to deploy. The files are in a text format that's easy to edit, and they enable you to document a precise specification of the solution architecture.

The IaC deployment code is either declarative or imperative. Declarative code documents *what* the end state of the deployable architecture should be. The tooling will understand the current state of the infrastructure and automatically work out what needs to change between the current and required states. Imperative code documents *how* the provisioning of the deployment architecture to the infrastructure will take place. The code contains a set of commands to perform the deployment. Tooling used for automating infrastructure deployment will normally operate in both modes but have a preference for one.

Popular IaC automation solutions include Chef, Puppet, Red Hat Ansible, Terraform, and AWS CloudFormation.

Reading for IaC

For infrastructure as code, have a read of *Infrastructure as Code* by Kief Morris, and for Terraform, look at *Terraform: Up and Running* by Yevgeniy Brikman (both O'Reilly).

Using a Deployable Architecture

We've discussed the components used for automating deployable architectures, and earlier we discussed the availability of reference architectures. Figure 9-7 shows how this all comes together.

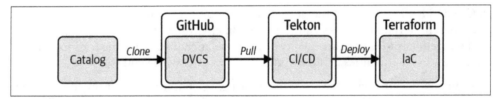

Figure 9-7. Deployable architecture components

The documentation of a deployable architecture in a catalog will include a reference architecture with code for automated deployment. You will be able to clone code for storing in your DVCS repository, where you can customize it to meet the needs of a specific workload. A CI/CD pipeline can pull the automation for testing before passing onto the IaC tooling for deployment. We've used GitHub, Tekton, and Terraform tooling in this example.

Major CSPs provide deployable architecture or landing zone catalogs including AWS (*https://oreil.ly/QbHCA*), Azure (*https://oreil.ly/Sgcfr*), GCP (*https://oreil.ly/ViwaJ*), and IBM Cloud (*https://oreil.ly/y4-7r*).

Book CI/CD Pipeline

We used the same automation principles for continuous integration and continuous deployment of this book and the book companion website (*https://securityarchitecture.cloud*), but we're building a book and a website, not a cloud infrastructure.

We wrote the book in AsciiDoc (*https://asciidoc.org*) and it's stored in a private GitLab repository with automation to build the book into an EPUB and PDF document.

We wrote the book companion website in Markdown (*https://www.markdownguide.org*), with extensions, and stored it in a private GitHub repository with automation to generate a GitHub Pages (*https://pages.github.com*) site using Material for MkDocs (*https://oreil.ly/sfJWf*).

If you haven't used Git or Markdown before, have a go at building a Material for MkDocs website using GitHub. It's a great way to learn the underlying principles of using Git to write architecture documentation before you have a go at IaC.

Let's move on to the core of architectural thinking, making architectural decisions.

Architectural Decisions

When developing an architecture, we make many architectural decisions about the design of architecture components, such as high-availability approaches, authentication mechanisms, protocols, etc. Those decisions can have significant immediate and future consequences, for example, additional costs or constraints on the ability to extend the solution in the future.

You should document all architectural decisions in architectural decision records (ADRs) whenever a decision has an impact on a solution's fundamental structures. This is what we call a decision with architectural significance. Because of the significance of the decision, specifically its consequences, it's important to have documented traceability.

New team members might join the project or you might inherit a solution from someone else, and you will find it beneficial to understand why someone made a decision and the alternatives considered while making the decision. It can avoid revisiting the decision many times over the duration of a project and result in better decisions. This encourages improved stakeholder participation and helps remove emotion from contentious decisions.

Removing Emotion from Decisions

Often, there will be a decision on a project where the arguments for one side or the other can get heated. The decision-maker may be a senior leader or a client, and you believe the decision should be something else. Sometimes the emotion surrounding the decision is due to the decision not being fully considered or communicated. Writing the discussion down as an architectural decision can help better communicate the options with benefits and drawbacks.

Even if the decision goes against what you believe, the person who made the decision is now accountable for the outcome. Remember, we all have to sometimes take a risk and make decisions based on incomplete information. It's our job to communicate effectively for others to make those decisions.

Recall the definition from Grady Booch we discussed earlier in Chapter 2 that "architecture represents the set of significant design decisions." During the development of the design documentation, we frequently make decisions that aren't significant due to their low change impact and don't need detailed documentation.

Everyone involved in the architectural process can make or propose architectural decisions. A design authority is a group where a domain architect will propose an architectural decision for approval by leading architects in the organization. It's good practice to document who was part of the decision process and finally sign off on the decision.

Documenting Architectural Decision Records

To enable a sound decision and to allow for enough traceability in the future, the ADR should include relevant information when you document it. In Table 9-3 we've listed the most important elements for an ADR.

Table 9-3. Architectural decision record

Subject area		The area of concern
Decision title		Overall title of the decision
Description		State the to-be decision as a question
Problem statement		A short description of the problem
Assumptions		What's believed to be true about the context of the problem, constraint on the solution
Motivation		Why this decision is important
Alternatives	Description	Description of this alternative
	Advantages	Advantages of this alternative
	Disadvantages	Disadvantages of this alternative
	Expected effort/cost	Qualitative expression of the expected effort and/or costs
Decision		The decision taken
Justification		Justification for the decision taken
Consequences		What impact the decision will have
Derived requirements		A list of requirements derived from this decision
Related decisions		A list of related decisions

You are likely to add other fields specific to the overall governance, such as who drafted the ADR, who the approver is, the status of the ADR, and the approval date.

Not all decisions need this level of detail as they're important but easy to understand decisions, and therefore we suggest you use a short-form architectural decision record, made up of a decision, rationale, and implication, as shown in Table 9-4. The earlier table Table 9-2 contains additional examples.

Table 9-4. Short-form architectural decision record

ID	Decision	Rationale	Implication
AD01	Standalone NextGen firewall	• We want to follow the defense-in-depth principle by using vendor technology and built-in cloud technology. • The security operations team will use the technology they have the skills and experience to maintain. • We can maintain separation duties with the security operations team running the NextGen firewall and the cloud platform team running the VPC network security configuration.	• Complete onboarding process for the NextGen firewall to the security operations team.

Forms of Architectural Decision

Architectural decisions can have a different scope and therefore impact depending on where they're made, such as at the organization level, program level, or within an individual project. We suggest layering different types of architectural decisions that have a different scope and impact, as shown in Table 9-5.

Table 9-5. Architectural decision scope

Scope	Type of decision	Discussion	Example
Enterprise	Architecture guiding principle	Architecture guiding principles guide the decision-making process; they don't make specific changes to the architecture. The CXO level in the organization documents these principles within the business or information systems strategy.	Managed Service before Open Source before Licensed Product before Bespoke Solution.
Program	Architectural decision	A decision that's made for an overall program will apply to all project work streams. A design authority will make a decision at the level of the program and keep a program log of architectural decision records.	There is a preference for agentless technology over the use of an executable agent.
Project	Design decisions	These are significant design decisions where the impact of the decision isn't outside the scope of the project. You will make decisions within the project for recording within the solution architecture documentation.	The system will use an integrated security appliance.

This provides a hierarchy of decision making across an organization. Guiding principles should guide architectural decisions. Architectural decisions then need to either demonstrate compliance with the principles or justify why they deviate from them. We introduced guiding principles in Chapter 3.

We've a format for the decisions, but where should we record the ADRs, together with an audit trail of decisions?

Managing Architectural Decisions

It's good practice to document the ADRs in a common repository, where everybody involved in making decisions can access them. In the past, the approach was to record them in a document owned by the design authority "gatekeepers." This often slowed the process of decision making, and now projects are adopting more Agile practices with a strong audit trail of discussions and changes. Here are a few ideas for documenting ADRs:

Document or spreadsheet
> The traditional way of documenting ADRs has been to record them in spreadsheets or documents with meeting minutes and document sign-off regarding the agreement. This records a static point in time and often loses the important

discussions that take place. The documents are under the control of the document owner or formal governance board, which doesn't encourage collaboration.

Kanban board

In an Agile environment, the use of tooling, such as a kanban board, often tracks the state of the program and project ADR. There are kanban boards available on tooling platforms such as Zenhub (*https://www.zenhub.com*) with GitHub or Trello (*https://trello.com*) to manage them in different states. They start in the new decisions column, move to the design authority review, and when approved, move to the decisions agreed, as shown in the wireframe example in Figure 9-8.

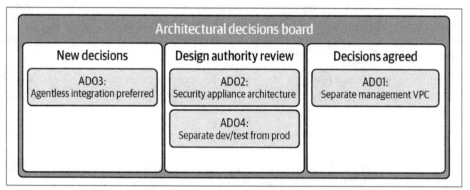

Figure 9-8. Architectural decision records kanban board

The cards can record a history of discussion, changes, and decisions that form an audit trail. At the speed required by the project, these discussions can occur without the restrictions of a design authority. There will be some decisions that need discussion by a design authority, but it allows a dialog to take place before the meeting for a fast decision when everyone does meet.

However, this isn't the best place to store a catalog of approved decisions that are easily read. You may go back to the document approach, but a more recent approach is the use of GitHub Pages.

GitHub Pages

Using a GitHub Pages site, a project is able to build documentation with tracking of change through issues and pull requests. We find that combining Zenhub for a kanban board and a static website such as Material for MkDocs (*https://oreil.ly/sfJWf*) enables professional documentation with full lifecycle management of the content.

A great source of information about ADRs is the ADR GitHub organization website (*https://adr.github.io*). The site has information on what's a good ADR, tools for capturing decisions, and many other references to written work on the subject of ADRs.

So how does this work in practice? Let's use the case study to discuss the creation of an architectural decision record.

Case Study: Architectural Decision

The project has been through several iterations of the solution when someone notices there is an API gateway for API protection but nothing for Layer 7 application security, such as a WAF. The lead application architect has asked the security architect and the lead infrastructure architect for options.

The infrastructure architect is suggesting it's not a problem, as he has used WAF services from a security-as-a-service provider before. It can be easily enabled without delay for the project.

The security architect is saying CAG must run its own WAF as the organization can't allow a third party to decrypt the TLS sessions for inspection because CAG has a data protection obligation. The CISO team will need additional resources for the security operations team, and there will need to be a delay to the go-live date.

The program manager asks two architects to write an ADR for review at the design authority tomorrow. They came up with the ADR in Table 9-6 after discussing the overall business risk with the project sponsor.

Table 9-6. Case study architectural decision record

Subject area	Application security
Decision title	Web Application Firewall Solution
Description	Implementation and operation of a web application firewall are a balance of risk, cost, and timescales.
Problem statement	A SaaS service is easier to support and lower cost, but the service terminates the TLS session for inspection, and there is a risk the SaaS supplier can use the decrypted data for purposes other than intended. Whereas a WAF appliance built into the transit VPC enables only CAG security staff to manage the device and ensures data isn't intercepted by a third party, but it will take too long to implement and CAG couldn't supply the resources.
Assumptions	• There is a SaaS supplier available to support the type of workload required to meet legal obligations to protect sensitive data in the required timescales.
Motivation	Using an appliance may exceed the project timelines and be beyond the skills of CAG to manage.

Alternative #1	**Description**	WAF Appliance in Transit VPC
	Advantages	• Termination of TLS sessions takes place in networks controlled by CAG, reducing the risk that third parties can intercept sensitive data.
	Disadvantages	• Requires a team of around six skilled SMEs available 24×7 to provide support. • Requires the installation and testing of highly available WAF appliances. • The installation will take longer than the go-live date required.
	Expected effort/ cost	• Would require up to six skilled and experienced WAF SMEs for 24×7 support (including vacation and sickness)
Alternative #2	**Description**	WAF as SaaS
	Advantages	• A specialist security team with extensive skills and experience can manage the WAF. • Easily set up through configuration.
	Disadvantages	• Risk of the supplier being able to intercept unencrypted sensitive data
	Expected effort/ cost	• Lower costs to deploy and run
Alternative #3	**Description**	MSSP WAF Appliance in Transit VPC
	Advantages	• Termination of TLS sessions takes place in networks controlled by CAG, reducing the risk that third parties can intercept sensitive data.
	Disadvantages	• Reduced effort than an in-house managed appliance but will still require solutioning and ongoing management. • Requires the installation and testing of highly available WAF appliances. • The installation will take longer than the go-live date required.
	Expected effort/ cost	• Would require monitoring of MSSP, including access to the device, to detect changes • Would need investment to install, purchase a license, monitor infrastructure, and manage MSSP
Decision		WAF as SaaS
Justification		CAG doesn't have the skills to support a WAF appliance; the cost would be higher for an appliance, and implementation timescales for an appliance would delay go-live. A risk assessment has determined that the lack of skills and experienced SMEs is a risk far higher than the risk of third-party interception.
Consequences		We will need to evaluate and contract a WAF SaaS supplier.
Derived requirements		Add responsibility for solution architecture and delivery to CISO architects, and Day-2 ops support to the Security Operations team.
Related decisions		None

In the end, the project sponsor, who is accountable for the business risk, decided maintaining a team of six skilled SMEs wasn't viable. Even if they did have the resources, the maintenance would be so infrequent that the SMEs wouldn't be able to maintain their skills with such a low frequency of change. If there was an emergency, the team would be unlikely to handle the response fast enough. They decided that there was a need for a third-party managed service from a specialist security company.

They also determined that a delay to the project was unacceptable because there are penalty clauses associated with the project delivery, and that it needs to be a SaaS with simple configuration and not a WAF appliance. The sponsor agreed that a review of the decision could take place after 12 months of operating the service.

The scenario we've discussed is common, with the security team asking for something that's not viable and can become a bigger security risk to the business. This is something you will need to consider when architecting security for a system. Documenting an architectural decision record enables the consideration of options and allows the business sponsor to make a decision with an audit trail.

You may think the SaaS solution is the right one, but it's still useful to document the options you have ruled out in the event the service provider does intercept the traffic. You aren't responsible for making business-risk decisions. Allow the owner of the business to make significant decisions. The ADR is an important artifact in the "kit bag" of an architect for aligning an organization.

The updated deployment architecture diagram in Figure 9-9 highlights the WAF with shading for the public internet traffic.

Note that the connection between the driver and the firewall now has a WAF. It's placed on the internet rather than the transit VPC because we made the decision to use SaaS rather than an appliance.

Look out for a further update to the deployment architecture diagram in Chapter 11.

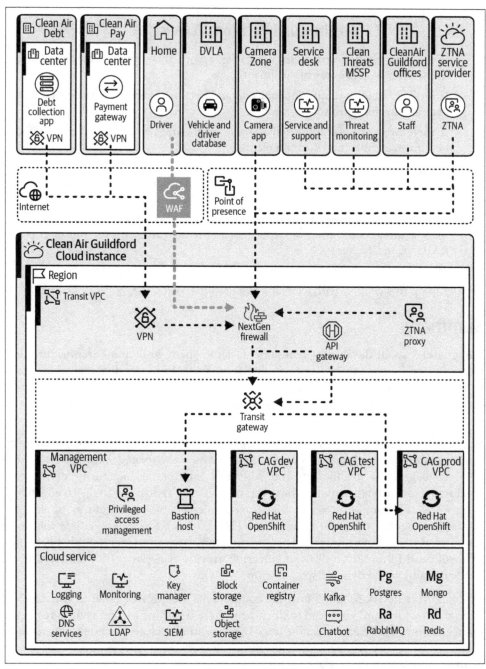

Figure 9-9. Deployment architecture diagram with WAF; see the original diagram (https://oreil.ly/SAHC)

Architectural Decision QA Checklist

- Is there an existing architectural decision record that should take precedence over the one you propose to document?

- If you have made a significant choice in architecture, have you documented it in your architectural decision record?

- If there are multiple options that some might not agree with, then use the long-form architectural decision record.

- Ensure the review and approval of all architectural decisions is recorded in either the solution architecture document or the overall program architectural decision records log.

- Have you documented the impact of the decision and raised any appropriate risks, assumptions, issues, or dependencies for the program? We will discuss a RAID log in Chapter 10.

Let's wrap up this chapter with a closing discussion.

Summary

We've talked about developing component, deployment, and cloud architecture diagrams in previous chapters, and we discussed in this chapter that you don't have to start from nothing each time. The use of architecture and design patterns will accelerate your architectural thinking with associated diagrams and architectural decisions.

With the increasing number of environments to support route to live, n-tier architectures, and the separation of different applications into isolated network segments, a single diagram is insufficient. You will need multiple architecture patterns and diagrams to describe the solution but even then, it's not specific enough. To effectively specify the solution, we need to make use of deployable architectures or landing zones documented through automation. This further accelerates getting solutions into a production environment. As an architect, it's becoming increasingly likely that you will need to understand the engineering aspects of deployment architectures to create or validate the detailed specification.

You will make decisions about how the components integrate together as you develop your architecture, and you need to document these decisions to gain wide agreement, reduce rework, and create an audit trail. Documenting architectural decision records is an architect's core artifact and technique. If there is one artifact you must document as an architect, then this is the one.

Now that we've gathered the requirements and documented the architecture, we need to consider how this integrates into the development lifecycle and the essential project governance for the delivery of a solution architecture, including security. Read on to the next chapter for a discussion about these topics.

Exercises

1. In the TOGAF Standard, patterns are considered to be a way of putting building blocks into context, for example, to describe _____.

   a. A solution architecture for a problem

   b. A reusable solution to a problem

   c. Solution architecture meeting requirements

   d. A reusable solution to mitigate threats

2. What are the characteristics of a deployable architecture? Select all that apply.

   a. It is based on a reference architecture or architecture pattern.

   b. It is automation for the deployment of an architecture pattern.

   c. It uses a set of best practices, principles, and guidance.

   d. It can be deployed without changes on any cloud platform.

3. True or false: A solution design pattern can be deployed as a complete, reusable solution to a problem.

   a. True

   b. False

4. True or false: A 3-tier architecture pattern is found in a cloud environment.

   a. True

   b. False

5. What are likely locations for an edge or transit virtual private cloud (VPC) in a hybrid cloud architecture? Select all that apply.

   a. In a cloud environment

   b. In a point of presence (PoP) network data center

   c. In an on-premises environment

   d. In a co-lo data center

6. What dimensions define the complexity of security rules for a cloud enterprise architecture? Select all that apply.

   a. The number of tiers in each application

   b. The number of applications

   c. The number of environments in the route to live

   d. The number of security rules per host

7. What are the essential parts of a simple architectural decision record? Select all that apply.

   a. Decision

   b. Rationale/motivation

   c. Implication/consequences

   d. Assumptions

PART IV

Build

Once we've designed a solution architecture, we continue with the build phase by considering the development lifecycle from DevOps to DevSecOps and the importance of security assurance in this process.

CHAPTER 10

Secure Development and Assurance

Throughout the course of this book, we've covered how to design a secure solution based on the external and internal requirements of the solution as well as the threats that it's exposed to. With that we've addressed *design* with regard to the design-build-run framework.

Automating major elements of the building process can significantly reduce the time it takes development teams to go from design to production. In other words, we're getting newly developed functionality into production at a much quicker rate, which is a pretty good outcome. Because these automated processes eliminate a significant amount of manual gatekeeping, the likelihood of a vulnerable solution and the probability of the introduction of insecure code into production increases.

In this chapter, we will discuss how we can overcome this challenge by incorporating security measures into the development and building process.

Chapter Artifacts

We will discuss the development and assurance processes in order to determine what kinds of security tests and assurance measures we ought to incorporate into the process and whether or not it's even possible to do so. We're documenting the results of this in the test strategy and plan artifact as outlined in Figure 10-1.

The risks, assumptions, issues, and dependencies (RAID) artifact is where we will discuss how we can document and manage risks, assumptions, issues, and dependencies not of the solution itself, but rather of the process or project that's developing the solution. But let's first have a look at the software development lifecycle (SDLC).

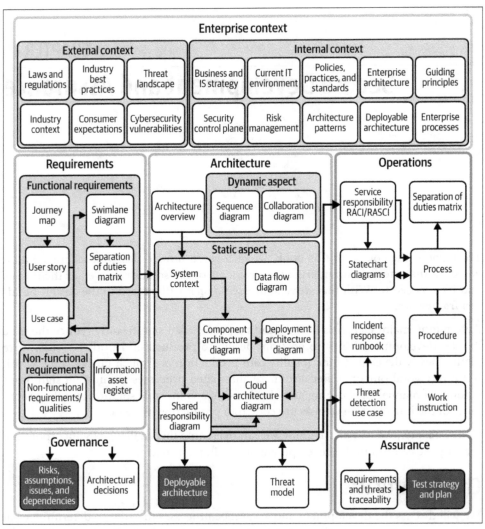

Figure 10-1. Secure development and assurance chapter artifacts

The Software Development Lifecycle

Almost all information system architectures have components or elements that require the development of code, be it the development of comprehensive applications from scratch, the extension of existing software, developing automation scripts, or infrastructure as code (IaC) configurations. In any case, we run through a set of steps from the initial requirements until we have the intended functionality running in production. These steps typically include analyzing the requirements, designing the solution architecture, coding and testing the functionality, and finally deploying and operating the solution in a production environment. This is what we call the software development lifecycle. The terms used for the different steps might differ in your organization, but the idea behind it remains valid.

We're, of course, interested in software that's running in a production environment with a broad range of vulnerabilities that have been reduced to an acceptable level and remain at that level. Implementing a solution free from vulnerabilities is, in most cases, not realistic.

We've worked with organizations that deploy and run solutions with vulnerabilities with a low Common Vulnerability Scoring System (CVSS) (*https://oreil.ly/mIB38*) score and without known exploits supported by the Exploit Prediction Scoring System (EPSS) (*https://oreil.ly/jsgL4*). The traditional approach to this is to have a security gate at deployment time where organizations perform manual or automated security tests. These tests evaluate the solution's vulnerabilities and potential security gaps. However, this approach is time-consuming and can lead to delays in the software release. Moreover, relying solely on a security gate at deployment time doesn't ensure continuous monitoring and protection against evolving threats. As a result, organizations are now turning toward integrating security measures throughout the development process.

We also talk about a shift-left approach, as illustrated in Figure 10-2, with the objective of identifying as many security issues as early as possible in the development lifecycle.

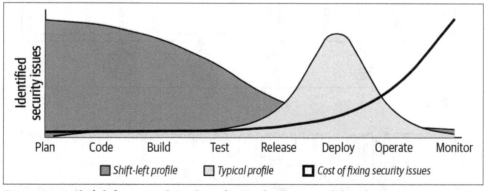

Figure 10-2. Shift-left approach in the software development lifecycle

The later we detect security issues, the more costly and time-consuming they can be to fix. By integrating security measures early on, organizations can identify and address vulnerabilities before they become major risks. This shift-left approach not only improves the overall security posture of the software but also saves resources by reducing the need for extensive post-deployment security patches and updates. In an ever-evolving threat landscape, it's essential for organizations to prioritize security from the beginning of the design and development process to ensure the protection of sensitive data and the integrity of their systems.

This is the voice of a security professional, but in reality it's easier said than done. Security is often considered by the rest of the organization as friction in the system, complicated, delaying, and difficult to understand; although everybody will acknowledge its necessity.

In Figure 10-3 we're illustrating where the friction in the different software development practices occurs and what the impact of it is.

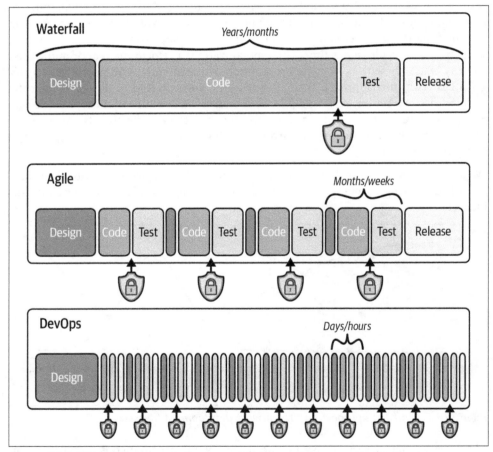

Figure 10-3. Waterfall versus Agile versus DevOps and the security friction

Let's go through each practice in more detail:

Waterfall

In the waterfall model, we operate with very siloed teams: developers, testers, and operations. Each team has its own responsibilities, and there is often little collaboration between them, making it difficult to address security concerns effectively. As mentioned previously, security concerns are often first identified during the testing phase. In addition, it takes many months to realign development that has happened in a different context to operations. This can result in additional development to add the operational hooks into the application to be ready for production. The application may have been developed on a different build to the one that's supported. Either development needs to change or operations need to change. Either way it takes significant time as the application needs to be regression tested, increasing the friction.

Agile

The Agile model following the Agile Manifesto (*https://oreil.ly/KmoyF*) reduces friction by introducing multidisciplinary teams that include developers, testers, and operations working together throughout the entire development process. This allows for regular communication and collaboration, which helps in identifying and addressing security concerns early on. The development cycle is in the dimension of months and weeks. Any remaining frictions will have a visible impact on the velocity of the team.

DevOps

The DevOps model removes the remaining friction between development and operational teams by introducing a high degree of automation. By automating tasks like provisioning, configuration management, and deployment, the DevOps model enables development and operational teams to work seamlessly together. This automation not only saves time and effort but also reduces the chances of human error. Additionally, the DevOps model promotes a culture of continuous integration and continuous deployment, allowing for faster releases and quicker feedback loops. Test-driven development is a common approach that focuses on writing tests before writing the actual code, which helps to improve code quality and results in faster development cycles and better collaboration between developers and testers. As a result, the velocity of the team increases, and it can identify and resolve issues more efficiently, leading to improved security and the overall success of the project.

We recommend reading *The Phoenix Project* (*https://oreil.ly/ g2sad*) by Gene Kim, Kevin Behr, and George Spafford, as well as *The Unicorn Project* (*https://oreil.ly/Q8xm8*) by Gene Kim (both IT Revolution Press), where the authors describe the benefits of DevOps in an illustrative way. The same authors have also released *The DevOps Handbook* (*https:// oreil.ly/QSNbX*) (IT Revolution Press).

We've now separately introduced the concepts of Waterfall, Agile, and DevOps. In practice, teams often apply, for example, Agile and DevOps in a complementary way.

DevOps focuses on removing friction and automating the software development process; integrating security throughout the process transforms DevOps into DevSec-Ops. In the next section we will discuss what makes up the *Sec* in *DevSecOps*.

From DevOps to DevSecOps

A DevSecOps approach ensures that security measures aren't an afterthought but rather an integral part of the software development lifecycle. This approach allows for the early identification and mitigation of potential security vulnerabilities, reducing the risk of security breaches. With DevSecOps, security becomes everyone's responsibility, fostering a culture of collaboration and accountability among developers, operations teams, and security professionals. DevSecOps is a collaboration of technologies and different teams, as illustrated in Figure 10-4.

Often underestimated is the human side of the development process. Some might think it's the security team that's responsible for the security of the developed code, but we've worked with organizations with thousands of developers while the security team has only a handful of team members. It's pretty obvious that this doesn't scale. Every single developer, architect, product owner, etc. is responsible for security though we also acknowledge that not everybody is a security expert. The concept of security champions helps to address the scalability problem. In many development teams, there will be someone with a security affinity. This person can become the *security champion* in the development team, trained and supported by the central security team.

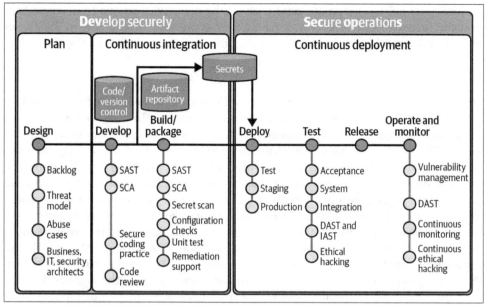

Figure 10-4. DevSecOps reference model

Security Champion

A security champion is an individual who promotes and advocates for security practices in DevOps teams. A security champion should ideally have experience in security architecture and software development. The security champion's goal is to incorporate security practices into the development process and to give continuing advice to help project teams to promote secure by design and secure by default principles.

Security champions typically provide the following practices:

- Application security training to development teams
- DevSecOps workshops and advisory as needed
- DevSecOps framework design
- Application security requirements analysis
- Threat modeling and architectural analysis
- Application security testing planning
- Application vulnerability remediation guidance

Technologies help to automate large parts of the security measures to decrease friction and increase velocity. Let's now have a look at the security activities in the phases of the development lifecycle and discuss the different supporting technologies.

Design

During the design phase, business analysts, IT, and security architects are building the backlog of functional and non-functional requirements. In Chapter 4 and "Threat Modeling" on page 177 we've discussed how we develop and document those requirements. This is also the phase where the development team prioritizes requirements and defects from the backlog, and it's here where we meet the first friction. The pressure on the development team to deploy functionality frequently results in the deprioritization of preventive work and security features or defects from the backlog. Functional requirements are frequently prioritized over security requirements because their release is highly visible, whereas the realization of security requirements may be less visible to the organization right away. In "Prioritization of Controls" on page 192 we've discussed how we can prioritize security controls based on risk to the organization. In *The Phoenix Project* (*https://oreil.ly/g2sad*), the authors describe how they have made the development teams more efficient by spending 15% of the developers' available time on preventive work to solve the friction between the competition of function versus preventive work.

In addition to the definition of functional and non-functional requirements, the definition of abuse cases helps detect application business logic flaws during later testing. The OWASP SAMM project (*https://owaspsamm.org*) defines misuse and abuse cases (*https://oreil.ly/mQu6p*) as:

> Misuse and abuse cases describe unintended and malicious use scenarios of the application, describing how an attacker could do this.

Abuse cases define the abuse of functionality and are also called *business logic attacks*. We define abuse cases based on functional requirements, which define important business rules, by experimenting to see if the application properly enforces the business rules.

Ecommerce Shopping Cart Abuse Case

Let's look at the scenario of an ecommerce shopping cart, where an attacker attempts to acquire discounts by exploiting the business logic of an ecommerce website. We can identify the following abuse cases:

Abuse of time-limited offers
    If the website offers time-limited promotions or discounts, the attacker may employ system clock manipulation or other techniques to extend the period of

---

the promotion, allowing them to profit from the lower rates beyond the specified time frame.

Manipulation of item prices

Consider an ecommerce website where consumers may add things to their shopping baskets, examine the total price, and check out. The business logic of the system is intended to correctly compute item pricing, apply discounts, and manage the shopping cart. An attacker, on the other hand, may attempt to manipulate the pricing in order to exploit program flaws. An attacker might intercept and manipulate client-server communications to change the price of products in their shopping cart. This may entail changing the amount or unit pricing of things to pay less than the actual price.

Abuse of weak discount codes

Many websites offer discount codes for their customers. Some websites validate only the code's syntax, not the actual code itself. An attacker would only need to understand the underlying syntax to gain discounts.

These are three possible abuse cases and you can very likely develop even more. The better you understand the business logic, the easier it is to identify how you can abuse it.

Abuse cases are ideally developed jointly by a business analyst and a security architect after the business analyst has defined the functional requirements as they build on them. The abuse case then triggers the definition of a countermeasure requirement.

Develop

In the development phase, developers are developing the actual code and require education in secure coding practices. Establishing secure coding practice guides specific to the programming language in use is a good practice. Developers can integrate many static application security testing (SAST) tools into their IDE to identify potential vulnerabilities already at the development stage. Manual secure code or peer reviews are an additional effective measure to identify potential security problems during the development phase. Standards like the Payment Card Industry Data Security Standard (PCI DSS) v4 (*https://oreil.ly/38sbi*) are requiring code reviews of bespoke and custom code. The OWASP Code Review Guide (*https://oreil.ly/x4e0c*) outlines a number of factors to consider when developing a secure code review process:

Risk

As it's not realistic to review 100% of the source code, the team should apply a risk-based approach in selecting the components and methods for the manual review.

Purpose and context

Another consideration as part of the risk-based approach is to understand the purpose and context of the application. A payment service requires a higher security standard than a canteen menu website.

Lines of code

Define the effort required but also provide an indication of the number of possible errors, as a program with many lines will also have many possibilities for errors.

Programming language

Some programming languages (e.g., Java, C#) are less vulnerable to certain bugs versus others like C or C++.

Resources, time, and deadlines

Time is, of course, critical to consider, as the required time for a manual review is directly connected to the amount of code.

Use of Generative AI Tools During Development

Generative AI tools are becoming increasingly popular in the developer community, as they can significantly increase the efficiency of developers. We might assume that this approach actually improves code security, but multiple studies reveal that this isn't the case. AI generates code based on *historic* data and does not necessarily supply best practices. Cornell University (*https://oreil.ly/_CNbL*) identified that participants who had access to an AI assistant wrote significantly less secure code than those without access. Additionally, participants with access to an AI assistant were more likely to believe they wrote secure code than those without access to an AI assistant. Researchers at New York University (*https://oreil.ly/ziShz*) discovered that 40% of the generated code in a security-relevant context had vulnerabilities. The ability of generative AI to generate code quickly can lead developers to have a false sense of security; they tend to blindly accept what the AI assistant is generating without applying a critical eye to the generated code and context.

Next to secure coding practices, it's also important to establish traceability of changes to the code during the development phase. It's common practice for small to large development teams to use code repository tools such as Git to ensure traceability of code changes and to enable collaboration across developers.

Build and Package

During the build and package phase, developers use various scripts and tools to automate the compilation, testing, and packaging of the software. We employ technical, automated security tests within the CI/CD pipeline. Those tests, listed next, focus on the source code, container configuration, and images:

Static application security testing (SAST)
> The source code of an application is analyzed to identify potential security vulnerabilities. This type of testing can help detect common coding mistakes, such as buffer overflows or SQL injection vulnerabilities, prior to the application's deployment. SAST tools scan the source code line by line, looking for patterns or code snippets that could indicate a security issue. Once vulnerabilities have been identified, developers can take appropriate actions to fix them.

Software composition analysis (SCA)
> It's rare you develop software without leveraging open source components. It's critical to have an overview of where you use those components and whether those components have vulnerabilities that you incorporate into your application by using them. SCA helps in identifying any vulnerable or outdated components used in the software that may pose a security risk. Additionally, it also allows for the detection of any licensing issues or compliance violations that may arise from using certain software components. Ultimately, SCA plays a crucial role in ensuring the security, reliability, and legality of the software you develop or use.

Software Bill of Materials

SCA tools can assist in the creation and maintenance of software bills of materials (SBOMs), which contain information on every third-party component utilized, including version and license information. SBOMs received a lot of attention after the US government issued an executive order (*https://oreil.ly/aJ9j_*) on improving the nation's cybersecurity, which requires firms that wish to do business with the US government to produce a thorough inventory of all components that make up an application to increase the level of security. The EU has also created a requirement for SBOMs in the EU Cyber Resilience Act (*https://oreil.ly/Iv1cn*). Another example is the critical vulnerability known as "Log4Shell," which was discovered in the widely used logging module Log4j in 2021. Log4j is used in many enterprise products as well as open source software. Many businesses had significant difficulty determining where the module was used. For more information about SBOM, see CISA SBOM (*https://oreil.ly/mlMQh*).

Secrets scan

Secrets like passwords or API keys are often hard-coded by developers into the source code. This creates vulnerabilities, which adversaries can exploit. Scanning code repositories and other data sources for sensitive information like passwords and access keys is known as secret scanning. This may be accomplished through the use of a variety of tools and approaches, such as regular expressions, to discover patterns that match certain categories of sensitive information. Secrets can typically be found in source code, container images, configurations, and infrastructure as code.

Secure configuration check

Once the code is compiled, it's typically deployed in containers. The container images and their configuration will be scanned for vulnerabilities, verifying the integrity of the image and ensuring that it adheres to the organization's security policies and hardening guidelines. Many organizations use CIS Benchmarks (*https://oreil.ly/nqxKg*) as a basis for their hardening guidelines.

The built artifacts produced in this phase are finally stored in an artifact repository for later, automated deployment to testing, staging, and production environments.

Deploy, Test, and Release

We use the deploy phase to deploy the code in different environments in order to perform different levels of testing to validate the software against the requirements. To ensure the effectiveness of security controls, we must prepare for the completion of security assurance efforts prior to service go-live as well as continuous Day-2 operations. We must plan for numerous cycles of security and compliance checks, as well as time for corrective actions. As a security architect or security champion you need to ensure the inclusion of security assurance activities in the overall test strategy and plan, which we will discuss in the following:

Test strategy

The test strategy, as shown in Table 10-1, outlines in detail how a solution will undergo testing to ensure its quality and functionality. It includes information about the testing objectives, scope, as well as approach.

Table 10-1. Test strategy

Objectives and scope	Clearly define the overall goals and objectives of the testing effort. Outline the scope of testing, specifying what will and what won't be tested.
Risk analysis	Identify potential risks to the testing process and establish strategies for risk mitigation. Prioritize risks based on their impact and likelihood.
Entry and exit criteria	Define the prerequisites for testing (entry criteria). Specify the conditions under which testing will be considered complete (exit criteria).

Test levels and types	Identify different levels of testing (e.g., unit, integration, system, acceptance) and types of testing (e.g., functional, non-functional). Specify the criteria for when each type of testing will be conducted.
Test execution strategy	Detail how test cases will be executed, including the order and frequency of test cycles. Address any specific test execution considerations.
Test metrics and measurement	Identify key metrics for measuring the effectiveness and progress of testing. Define how and when these metrics will be collected and reported.
Approval and sign-off	Specify the criteria for obtaining approval and sign-off at various stages of the testing process.

Test plan

The testing plan specifies the resources and timelines required, the types of testing to be conducted, such as functional testing, performance testing, and security testing, and provides guidelines for defect tracking and reporting. The information shown in Table 10-2 is typically included in a test plan.

Table 10-2. Test plan

Test resources	Identify the roles and responsibilities of individuals involved in testing. Specify the skills and expertise required for each role. Address any training needs for the testing team.
Test schedule	Develop a detailed schedule that includes testing milestones, timelines, and dependencies. Align the testing schedule with the overall project timeline.
Test automation strategy	Define the approach to test automation, including which test cases will be automated and the tools and frameworks to be used. Outline the criteria for selecting test cases for automation.
Defect tracking and reporting	Specify how defects will be logged, tracked, and managed. Define the process for reporting and communicating defects to relevant stakeholders.
Test environment	Describe the test environment, including infrastructure, software, network configurations, and other dependencies. Ensure that the test environment mirrors the production environment as closely as possible.
Test data	Define the test data requirements, including input data for various test scenarios. Specify how test data will be generated, acquired, and managed. This is specifically important because the use of production data for testing can introduce a significant risk. Strategies for test data generation include careful scrambling of production data to meet the testing purpose, but without the risk of exposing sensitive information. Another strategy is to use generative AI to generate synthetic test data.
Test deliverables	Enumerate the documents and artifacts that will be produced as part of the testing process (e.g., test plans, test cases, test reports). Define the format and frequency of test deliverables.

Tailor these components to the specific needs of your project, and keep the test strategy and plan up-to-date as the project evolves. Regularly review and revise the plan as necessary to adapt to changes in requirements, technology, or project scope. Overall, a well-structured and comprehensive test strategy and plan are essential for effectively identifying and resolving defects, ensuring a successful solution release.

Operate and Monitor

System maintenance, monitoring, and optimization are the primary goals of Day-2 operations. Day-2 operations continue throughout the product lifecycle since system behavior must be regularly examined and fixed. In the following section, we'll look at critical processes that assure the solution's security controls at the transition point from *deploy, test, and release* to *operate and monitor*, as well as continuously throughout *operate and monitor*. In Chapter 11, we will discuss in more depth further security operational aspects.

Security Assurance

We've discussed how we develop security requirements and how we build them as security controls into our solution. Before we release the solution into production we must ensure that the security controls are effective at the time of go-live, but we also need to ensure that they stay effective during the lifetime of the solution. This is what we call security assurance. In NIST SP 800-39: Managing Information Security Risk (*https://oreil.ly/_JRU-*), NIST defines security assurance as the "grounds for confidence that the security functionality is effective in its application."

Systems Operations Phasing

The terms *Day-0*, *Day-1*, and *Day-2* operations are often used during the implementation of new systems, processes, or technologies:

Day-0 Operations
> This phase includes the initial planning and preparation activities prior to the implementation of a new system or technology. In Figure 10-4, this is the Plan phase.

Day-1 Operations
> Day-1 operations begin on the day that the new system or technology is activated or becomes operational. This phase focuses on system deployment and activation. In Figure 10-4, this is at the point of Release.

Day-2 Operations
> Day-2 operations begin after the initial deployment, usually on the second day following implementation. In Figure 10-4, this is the Operate and Monitor phase.

These terms can vary slightly depending on the specific context and organization.

Only the combination of functionality *and* assurance in the end delivers effective security controls with a high level of confidence. Assurance provides that extra layer of confidence to the controls. It's critical to plan for assurance activities early in the project because they extend the timeline. You should also plan for multiple iterations of these activities. During Day-2 operations, it's essential to maintain all assurance activities either when processing a change or at regular intervals.

We've already covered a number of assurance activities in this chapter, but we'd like to emphasize the significance of these processes by documenting when they're required during Day-0, Day-1, and Day-2 operations. We consider the assurance processes shown in Table 10-3 as foundational to ensure effective security controls.

Table 10-3. Assurance activities

Activity	Description	Day-0/1 operations	Day-2 operations
Documented and approved solution	All key stakeholders must review and approve formalized requirements, high-level design, low-level design, and implementation standards.	Required	At every change
Documented processes and procedures	All key stakeholders review and approve formalized processes, procedures, and work instructions.	Required	At every change
Requirements traceability	Complete a traceability matrix from requirements to design, implementation, and testing to ensure that all required controls are in place and operational. We discussed requirements traceability at the end of Chapter 4 and we'll discuss threat traceability at the end of Chapter 11.	Required	At every change
Functional and non-functional testing	In the previous section we've described different test types that test functional as well as non-functional requirements and how they relate to those requirements in the V-model. Test processes for functionality and non-functionality to ensure they work properly. Perform non-functional testing, such as checking the continued availability of security services after a component failure.	Required	At every change
Supply chain risk assessment	Examine the supply chain risks for software, hardware, and services. Projects introduce new locations, suppliers, products, and technologies, which necessitate a risk assessment: are organizational policies and standards being followed; are new risks being introduced; are new management controls required; and how do we assess, secure, and mitigate open source supply chain risks?	Required	In regular intervals
Vulnerability management	Conduct automated vulnerability scans with tooling to detect flaws in the implemented solution, such as missing security patches. To perform this process, you can use tools such as SAST, DAST, IAST, SCA, as well as traditional infrastructure and container image vulnerability scanning tools. Prioritize the identified vulnerabilities based on risk, plan their remediation, and carry out the remediation by patching to an agreed-upon timeframe.	Required	In regular intervals

Activity	Description	Day-0/1 operations	Day-2 operations
Ethical hacking	Penetration tests or bug bounty programs that employ both manual and automated attack strategies against the implemented solution supplement automated testing tools. This measure may not be required for all systems. The system's criticality is an important deciding factor.	Required	In regular intervals
Continuous configuration monitoring	Continuous configuration monitoring, also called continuous compliance, ensures that accidental or intended changes in the configuration of the system or the underlying platform aren't violating the organization's policies.	Required	In regular intervals

At the end of Chapter 4, we discussed the need for requirements traceability to ensure the completeness of design, implementation, and testing. We will now look into a model that implements this traceability.

In software testing, the V-model is a development and testing technique that focuses on a phased approach to software development and testing. The model in Figure 10-5 gets its name from the visual depiction of the development and testing phases, which create a "V" shape. The model depicts the link between each development step and its associated testing phase.

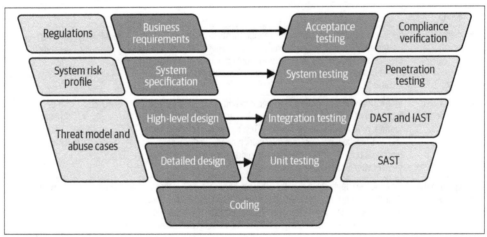

Figure 10-5. V-model

The V-model typically consists of the following phases, with each development phase having a corresponding testing phase. The left side of the V represents what we described in the *design* phase in this section:

- Business owners and business analysts define *business requirements*, which provide input to the acceptance testing planning.
- The system risk profile drives the required security controls into the *system specifications*.
- The threat model as well as abuse cases shape the system's *high- and low-level design*. Testers are creating detailed test cases based on the design specifications.
- During *coding* the actual implementation of the software occurs.
- Developers perform *unit testing* to ensure that each unit functions as intended. This is also the time where SAST scans will be executed during the build process.
- *Integration testing* verifies that the integrated components work together as expected. During integration testing, test automations typically perform dynamic application security tests (DAST) and interactive application security tests (IAST).
  - — *DAST* scanners evaluate an application's security vulnerabilities in real time. DAST involves sending various types of input to the application and analyzing its responses to determine whether any security flaws exist.
  - — *IAST* can identify security vulnerabilities by actively monitoring an application during runtime. This involves analyzing the traffic and data inputs to uncover potential vulnerabilities and exploit them. By actively scanning an application while it's running, IAST can capture vulnerabilities that are only apparent in specific runtime conditions, improving the overall effectiveness of security testing.
- *System testing* validates the entire system against the defined requirements. This is the phase where ethical hackers perform penetration tests. They use a combination of different tools and their experience to try to break the system.
- The business users perform *acceptance testing* to verify whether the system meets their expectations. This includes the verification of regulatory compliance requirements.

We just discussed how we incorporate security activities into the development process to ensure that we identify and address weaknesses as early as possible. The application is running on a platform and is leveraging services from the platform. In the next section, we discuss how a cloud security operating model helps to ensure that the platform gets and stays in a secure state.

Cloud Security Operating Model

Adoption of cloud capabilities in many businesses began in one business area and has gradually moved to more and more business areas. Sometimes teams want to experiment with how they might exploit the cloud, and soon test configurations become production setups, and business processes begin to rely on it. In other cases, local IT was too slow to meet the demands of the business areas, and because cloud computing is so *simple*, business areas could achieve their goals quicker than relying on their IT teams. Both situations frequently occur without the engagement of security procedures, and without taking into account an organization's security standards, which raises many risks for the organization including, but not limited to, the following reasons:

- Organizations might accidentally expose sensitive data to the internet through misconfiguration.
- Teams might store data in cloud locations, which might violate regulatory requirements.
- Business areas might forget to remove access for users when they change job roles or leave the organization.
- Teams might be unfamiliar with security gaps in different cloud services.

A structured approach considering people, processes, and technology in the form of an operating model helps mature organizations leverage the cloud in an effective and secure manner. A cloud security operating model is a framework that organizations use to establish and maintain effective security practices in cloud environments. The purpose of a cloud security operating model is to provide a structured approach to managing and enhancing security in the cloud.

The cloud security operating model, outlined in Figure 10-6, is made up of five key functions (dark shading): the CISO office, enterprise architecture, cloud center of excellence (CCoE), the platform, and the DevOps teams. These functions may be structured and referred to differently depending on the terminology and organizational structure used in your organization. These functions work with the cloud marketplace and configuration, through the CI/CD pipeline with the cloud instances (the lighter shaded technology).

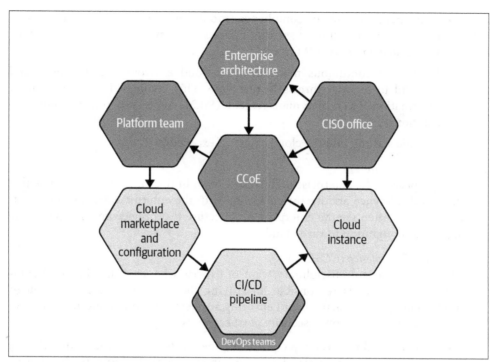

Figure 10-6. Cloud security operating model

Let's look at each of these functions:

CISO office

In this context, the CISO office consists of one or more enterprise security teams composed of strategy- and risk-focused teams as well as operational security teams. Their purpose is to:

- Issue the organization's security policies to ensure that security measures in the cloud align with the overall business objectives and goals of the organization.

- Identify, assess, and manage risks associated with cloud services and infrastructure to protect sensitive data and critical business operations.

- Align security investments with business priorities and manage security costs effectively. Optimize security measures to provide the necessary protection without unnecessary expenses.

- Contribute to the enterprise architecture by developing the enterprise security architecture.

- Implement continued compliance monitoring in the cloud to ensure enforcement of technical security policies. This involves cloud security posture management (CSPM) tools.

- Implement continuous monitoring of cloud environments to detect and respond to security threats in real time. This involves the use of security information and event management (SIEM) tools and other monitoring solutions.

- Provide staffing into the cloud center of excellence.

Enterprise architecture

The purpose of the enterprise architecture team in this context is to validate that the cloud reference architecture is in line with the enterprise architecture strategy. We also often see the enterprise architecture team reviewing and approving application migration toward cloud.

Cloud center of excellence (CCoE)

The CCoE is a multidisciplinary team of experts who specialize in cloud computing. This team is responsible for driving the organization's cloud strategy, implementing best practices, and ensuring successful adoption and utilization of cloud technologies. From a security perspective its purpose is to:

- Establish a cloud security control framework for compliance with relevant regulations, industry standards, and internal policies. Ensure that governance structures are in place to maintain control over cloud resources.

- Achieve consistency in security practices and policies across multiple cloud service providers or environments, reducing the risk of misconfigurations and vulnerabilities. Benchmarks and standards like the CIS Benchmarks (*https://oreil.ly/RGR4B*) can form a valuable basis for the application and enforcement of best practices.

- Define and establish architecture patterns to speed up the creation of solution architectures and applying best practices. We discussed *Architecture Patterns and Decisions* in Chapter 9.

- Establish criteria for selecting and managing cloud service providers based on their security practices. Ensure that third-party services meet the organization's security standards.

- Establish criteria for selecting and managing cloud products and capabilities and certify the same for inclusion in the cloud reference architecture.

- Enable security measures that are adaptable to the dynamic and scalable nature of cloud environments. Support the rapid deployment and scaling of applications while maintaining security.

- Define and establish landing zones for the selected cloud providers to enable fast deployment of workloads by a defined set of infrastructure and security capabilities.

- Ensure that teams responsible for managing cloud resources are well-trained in security best practices. Foster a security-aware culture within the organization.

- Foster a culture of continuous improvement in cloud security. Regularly assess and update the cloud security operating model to address emerging threats, technologies, and organizational changes.

- Define processes and procedures for incident response and recovery in the cloud. Establish mechanisms for detecting and responding to security incidents effectively. We'll discuss this in more detail in Chapter 11.

Platform team

The platform team consists of technical cloud SMEs whose purpose is to deliver platform build services and in this context:

- Leverage automation and orchestration tools to implement and enforce security controls consistently. This helps in reducing manual errors and improving efficiency.

- Make certified security products and configurations available in the cloud marketplace and the infrastructure pipeline.

Cloud marketplace and configurations

The different cloud providers typically provide a marketplace where organizations make certified products and configurations available to implement the actual cloud security architecture and security policies for use in the CI/CD pipeline.

CI/CD pipeline

The pipeline, as illustrated in Figure 10-7, consumes the certified products and configurations from the cloud marketplace and provisions them to the cloud instances. Provisioning is only possible through automation to prevent manual access to cloud instances.

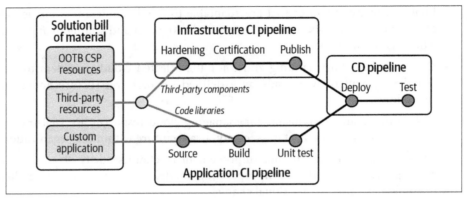

Figure 10-7. CI/CD pipeline

If we look a bit closer into the pipeline, we see that it's not one pipeline, but in reality a composition and collaboration of multiple pipelines. A solution bill of material shows that the solution is based on out-of-the-box (OOTB) cloud service provider (CSP) infrastructure resources, third-party resources, as well as custom developed applications:

- Within the infrastructure CI pipeline, the platform team provides the hardened and certified cloud and third-party resources.

- On the application CI pipeline DevOps teams are developing, building, and unit testing the custom application, including external code libraries.

- The combined infrastructure and custom application resources will be joined-up and deployed in a selected environment via the continuous deployment (CD) pipeline.

Cloud instances
The solution is automatically deployed in the cloud instance without direct manual intervention on the cloud instance itself.

DevOps teams
As we've described in the previous section, the DevOps teams are working with the pipeline and consuming products and configurations from the marketplace to implement their solution.

Implementing a cloud security operating model helps organizations navigate the complexities of cloud security, mitigating risks, ensuring compliance, and allowing for the secure and efficient utilization of cloud resources. It serves as a strategic guide to achieve a well-architected and resilient security posture in cloud environments.

In Chapter 11, we will discuss further aspects relevant to security operations. In the next section, we will discuss a simple yet very powerful tool that we use during the design, build, and handover to run phase of a project.

Risks, Assumptions, Issues, and Dependencies

A RAID log is a project management tool used to track risks, assumptions, issues, and dependencies. It provides a systematic approach to managing these elements throughout the project lifecycle. By updating and reviewing the RAID log on a regular basis, project teams can identify potential roadblocks, take proactive risk-mitigation measures, and ensure that all necessary dependencies are included. This helps in improving project efficiency, reducing surprises, and increasing overall project success.

It's good practice for project teams to maintain a RAID log and document each RAID item as outlined in Table 10-4. The emphasis here is on *team*, as not only the project manager should document RAID items but everybody in the project team should contribute RAID items throughout the project.

Table 10-4. RAID log

RAID item	Description	Action
Risk	There is a risk that *<risk>*, caused as a result of *<cause>*, which may result in *<impact>*.	Avoid or reduce or transfer or accept or share
Assumptions	There is an assumption that *<assumption>*. If assumption is not validated or turns out to be invalid, there is a risk that *<risk>*, which may result in *<impact>*.	Validated or owned
Issues	There is an issue that *<issue>*, which has resulted in *<impact>*. This has been caused because *<cause>*.	Solution or plan changed (e.g., to avoid)
Dependencies	There is a dependency on *<name>* to *<action>*. If not delivered against and/or in the required timeframe, there is a risk that *<risk>*, which may result in *<impact>*.	Communicated, agreed, and tracked

The RAID log provides a central place to document these items. Documenting RAID items creates transparency; next to that it's important that the responsible owners action the documented RAID items:

Risks

Risks in a RAID log are project-related risks, not solution-related risks. In Figure 6-13, we covered solution-related risks and how to record them. Risks are anything out of the ordinary, unforeseeable, or unexpected that might have a negative influence on the project if they occur. The assigned owners are responsible for the treatment of the identified risks. Table 10-5 shows an example of how we propose to document a risk item.

Table 10-5. Risk example

Date raised	01. Feb. 2024
Raised by	Mark
Risk description	There is a risk that *existing IT support staff may leave before knowledge transfer is complete,* caused as a result of *the outsourcing agreement,* which may result in *reduced delivery quality.*
Risk severity	Medium
Risk mitigation strategy	Reduce
Mitigation owner	Carsten
Risk mitigation plan	Increase team that's shadowing existing IT support staff to be able to document activities in high quality.
Status	Open
Financial impact when occurs	Cost of 5 extra FTE
Date closed	Open

Assumptions

An assumption is anything that hasn't yet been confirmed, but is relevant for the success of the project. The action owner should validate and remove the assumption as soon as possible. The client or the project sponsor should ideally own it. Table 10-6 shows an example of how we propose to document an assumption item.

Table 10-6. Assumption example

Date raised	01. Mar. 2024
Raised by	Stefaan
Assumption description	There is an assumption that *no sensitive personal information is processed by the system.* If assumption is not validated or turns out to be invalid, there is a risk that *important security controls are not considered in the solution,* which may result in *regulatory compliance violations.*
Action owner	Mark
Action to validate assumption	Validate with the business owner of the system that no sensitive personal information is processed by the system.
Status	Closed
Date closed	24. Apr. 2024

Issues

An issue documents conditions that exist, such as when something has gone wrong on the project and needs management or escalation. Issues can occur at any moment and may need adjustments to the solution or plans. Table 10-7 shows an example of how we propose to document an issue item.

Table 10-7. Issue example

Date raised	01. Apr. 2024
Raised by	Carsten
Issue description	There is an issue that *many developers don't have access to the source code repository*, which has resulted in *significant delays in developing the new solution*. This has been caused because *the business owner who needs to approve the access got sick*.
Action owner	Stefaan
Action plan	Identify a stand-in to perform the access request approvals.
Status	Closed
Date closed	07. Apr. 2024

Dependencies

A dependency is a link in the plan to an external factor that needs to be managed for a successful project result. It might be a third party's property or links between projects. Table 10-8 shows an example of how we propose to document dependency items.

Table 10-8. Dependency example

Date raised	15. May 2024
Raised by	Carsten
Dependency description	There is a dependency on *a third party vendor* to *configure required firewall changes*. If not delivered against and/or in the required timeframe, there is a risk that *integration tests can't be performed*, which may result in *delay of the overall schedule*.
Solution description	Seek early confirmation from the third party vendor that they're available to perform the firewall changes at the required time.
Action owner	Mark
Status	Open
Date Closed	Open

You have seen that a RAID log is a relatively simple but powerful tool. The difficulty is in the daily practice. We're making a lot of assumptions and identifying risks and dependencies throughout our daily work. It requires a lot of discipline from us to get them documented in the RAID log so that we can properly treat them. Let's have a look at how we can use the RAID log in our case study.

Case Study: RAID Log

Within the case study you are a security architect with the ask to develop a security solution in an already running project. As you are now part of the project team and are understanding the ask to you, the overall solution ideas, as well as the project setup and progress, you are naturally identifying RAID items that you enter into the simplified RAID log in Table 10-9.

Let's have a look at the case study to identify obvious RAID items. We've highlighted those parts of the case study that provide us with that information.

Marked-Up Case Study

The project deployment approach agreed upon between the CIO, Business Sponsors, and the Project Executive (PE) leading the integration is as follows:

- Start with a development environment using Red Hat OpenShift to build a cloud native container application using DevOps practices on a public cloud platform.
- Then build a full route to live with preproduction and production environments in the public cloud.

- Clean Threats, a threat management company, will manage all the security services from their security operations center (SOC).
- The solution will be fully hosted in the cloud and will need to be resilient to availability zone failures.

The program manager would like a high-level solution architecture that provides a minimum viable product (MVP) solution based on the preceding information.

The project is already installing the IT infrastructure, and the staff will be joining in six weeks' time.

We can now translate the highlighted parts into RAID items, as illustrated in Table 10-9. Throughout the discussion of the architectural thinking process, as well as the discussion of the case study within this book, we've referred to typical steps where you commonly identify RAID items.

Table 10-9. Case study RAID log

RAID	Statement	Action
R.1	There is a risk that the critical security controls are not reflected in the overall solution, caused as a result of the MVP approach of the project, which may result in exposure of sensitive information.	Prioritize security features in the development backlog based on risk.
A.1	There is an assumption that the already started DevOps practices already include security practices. If assumption is not validated or turns out to be invalid there is a risk that security issues are not identified and addressed early in the development process, which may result in additional costs to the project.	Verify with the development team that the development process is addressing security practices as described in "The Software Development Lifecycle" on page 326.

RAID	Statement	Action
I.1	There is an issue that IT infrastructure is already installed, which has resulted in a solution without segmentation and the right level of security controls. This has been caused because no security solution was defined before the installation.	Define the infrastructure security solution, assess the gap to the current installation, and adjust the installation.
D.1	There is a dependency on Clean Threats to manage all security services. If not delivered against and/or in the required timeframe, there is a risk that the security solution is unmanaged, which may result in undetected threats.	Confirm with Clean Threats that they agree to the timeline and the scope of services that they're expected to deliver.

It's never too late to start a RAID log. When you get into a project and no RAID log exists, create one and work with your team so that it becomes a daily routine to use and maintain it. A RAID log is also very useful when you hand over a solution to another team, as it provides a solid documentation about the risk, issues, assumptions, and dependencies that went through the project lifecycle.

RAID QA Checklist

Use this checklist to improve the quality of your RAID entries.

General

- Does a risk, assumption, or issue depend on a third party with whom you will have a contract or internal agreement? If so, this should be a *dependency*, as it will depend on an agreement. This ensures everything that needs an agreement is on one list.

- Ensure every RAID entry has actions with owners and dates for completion.

- Check that the recorded actions will close out the RAID item.

Risk

- Has this risk already happened? If so, it should be an issue.

- Ensure there is an owner for the overall risk according to the process of your organization.

- Document at what stage in the project the mitigation needs to be in place, ensure it's in place before proceeding, and record the agreement of the risk owner.

Assumption

- Ensure validation of all assumptions before signing off on a solution or document that it depends on.

- If validation of an assumption can't happen before the appropriate phase of the project, identify the risk of not validating the assumption and raise it as a risk for sign-off.

Issue
- Has this issue not happened yet, or have you phrased the issue as something that might happen? If so, change the issue to a risk.

- If remediation of an issue can't happen before the appropriate phase of the project, identify the risk of not remediating the issue and raise it as a risk for sign-off.

Dependencies
- Ensure every dependency has an action to ensure written responsibilities are in a contract or internal agreement.

- Before the project goes live, check that there is coverage for all dependencies in a contract or agreement. If not, identify the risk of not having the agreement and raise it as a risk for sign-off.

Summary

With the completion of this chapter, we've concluded the transition from solution architecture and design to Day-2 operations. We investigated how to include security activities into a highly automated development process without adding frictions.

The staged assurance strategy not only assists us in identifying and resolving security issues early in the development process, but it also assures that the entire solution that you will hand over to the business owner fulfills all functional and non-functional requirements.

You've learned about the RAID log as a powerful tool for managing risks, assumptions, issues, and dependencies throughout the project lifecycle. No project should run without a RAID log, it provides you with control and structure and is one of the key tools to enable a successful project.

In the next chapter, we will dive deeper into the security aspects of the Day-2 operations. We will investigate the best ways to ensure that we're able to identify and counteract any potential threats that may arise during *run*.

Exercises

1. What's the objective of the shift-left approach?

   a. Implement DevOps, as shift left is only possible with a DevOps approach.

   b. Identify and address security issues as early as possible in the software development lifecycle.

   c. Perform penetration tests as early as possible in the development lifecycle.

   d. Make the development team responsible for security.

2. Who is responsible for security in practicing DevSecOps? Select all that apply.

   a. The security team

   b. The Chief Information Security Officer (CISO)

   c. The developer

   d. Everybody involved in the development process

3. When are security assurance activities required? Select all that apply.

   a. At the start of the development process

   b. At the transition from development to operations

   c. Throughout the development process

   d. In regular intervals during Day-2 operations

4. What's a valid risk to document in a risk, assumptions, issues, and dependencies (RAID) log? Select all that apply.

   a. There is a risk of unauthorized access by customers, caused by improper input validation, which may result in exposure of sensitive data.

   b. There is a risk that the project team is not available in time, caused by a delayed project start, which may result in project timelines not being met.

   c. There is a risk that network traffic can be sniffed as a result of unencrypted traffic flows, which may result in sensitive data exposure.

   d. There is a risk that the security appliance does not fully meet requirements, caused by a lack of time to perform a comprehensive evaluation, which may result in missing functionality or delays due to a new solution being identified.

5. Why does security introduce less friction in the DevOps approach compared to the waterfall model?

   a. The waterfall model is applying less efficient security testing tools.

   b. In DevOps, all team members are physically located in the same place, increasing collaboration between team members.

   c. In DevOps, a separate testing team ensures that all security tests are executed in a very efficient way.

   d. DevOps employs a high degree of automation between development and operational teams.

6. Which of the following security testing activities can be automated? Select all that apply.

   a. SAST (static application security testing)

   b. SCA (software composition analysis)

   c. Secret scan

   d. Ethical hacking

7. True or false: Security assurance activities are only required during Day-0 and Day-1 operations.

   a. True

   b. False

8. The technique for defining business logic attacks is called _____.

   a. Threat modeling

   b. Abuse case

   c. Business use case

   d. User story

9. What is the role of the cloud center of excellence (CCoE) from a security perspective? Select all that apply.

   a. Certify products for inclusion in the cloud reference architecture.

   b. Achieve consistency in security practices and policies across cloud service providers.

   c. Implement continuous compliance monitoring in the cloud.

   d. Make certified security products and configurations available in the cloud marketplace.

PART V

Run

Finally, we need the system to remain secure after it's live, so we discuss the operational aspects of the system as shown in the run phase. We are discussing operational processes and procedures and how the outcome of the threat modeling process in the design phase helps to produce threat detection use cases and incident response procedures that build threat traceability.

CHAPTER 11

Security Operations

Now we need to consider how to securely operate the solution in production, also known as Day-2 operations. It's the stage where an operations team maintains, monitors, and optimizes the system for continued operation. Effective Day-2 operations need clarity around the operational responsibilities for the security controls to ensure continued protection of the information assets, detection and response to threats, and recovery from any outages that might occur. We can start to achieve that by defining responsibilities and the required processes for the successful operation of the controls.

The chapter starts by discussing the definition of responsibilities together with the documentation of processes, procedures, and work instructions. For effective operation of the controls, we enhance the swimlane diagram, discussed in Chapter 4, by discussing decomposition and providing additional detail for recording audit trails.

The chapter continues with exploring two specific processes that utilize threat modeling, from Chapter 6, to identify threats that may require threat detection. We use the identified threats to define how the detection of threats and the response to incidents should take place. As architects, we need to be able to support the definition of threat detection use cases and incident response runbooks. We need our solution architecture to describe how we provide information for protection and automation for response activities.

As you consider the techniques discussed in this chapter, you may start to identify new requirements that will result in new updates to the architecture to support the operational aspects we're now examining. Completion of these activities must take place before you sign off your solution architecture as complete.

Chapter Artifacts

This chapter's main goal is to discuss the definition and documentation of security processes. At the top right of Figure 11-1, we have the enterprise processes that apply across an organization. We use enterprise processes to develop processes, procedures, and work instructions that support the operations of the solution, as shown in the operations domain on the right. A Responsible, Accountable, Consulted, and Informed (RACI) table supports the definition of responsibilities for processes with a separation of duties matrix to enable the avoidance of high-risk combinations of activities.

To support the detection and response to threats, the top left of Figure 11-1 shows the threat landscape and cybersecurity vulnerabilities that feed the threat model down at the bottom. The threat model then feeds the development of the threat detection use case and the incident response runbook.

We're going to start with defining the shared responsibilities required for the secure operation of security services.

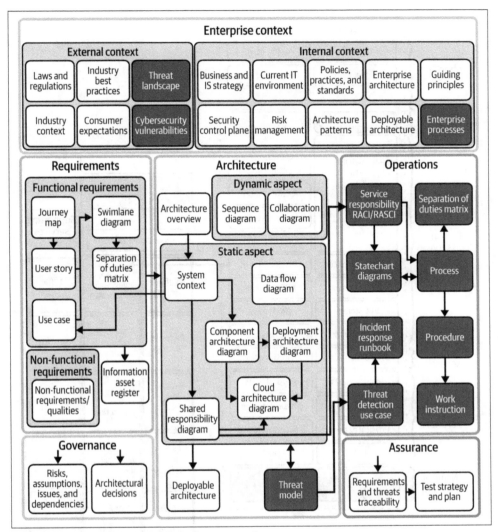

Figure 11-1. Security operations chapter artifacts

Shared Responsibilities

We started building up to this chapter in Chapter 7, where we discussed the functional layers of the cloud platform, including a layer for security services. Using the enterprise security architecture we discussed in Chapter 2, we decomposed the security services layer into domains, categories, and then security services. The diagram in Figure 11-2 illustrates the connection between the shared responsibilities diagram and the enterprise security architecture.

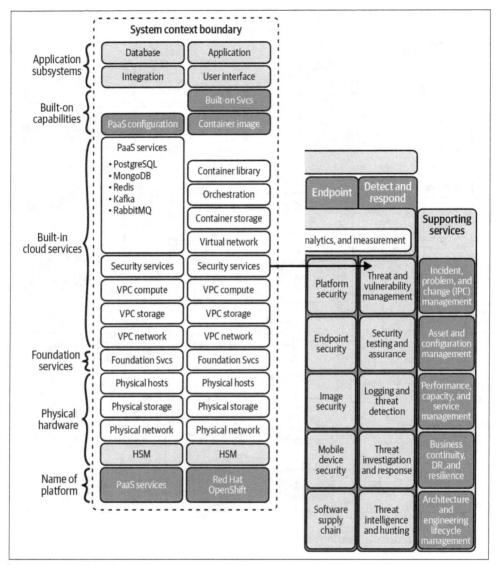

Figure 11-2. Shared responsibilities to security services

On the left side of the diagram we've included part of the shared responsibilities diagram from Figure 7-8. It shows the shared responsibilities stacks within the boundary of the system context. On the righthand side we show a slice of the enterprise security architecture diagram from Figure 2-6.

The arrow from the *security* layer in the shared responsibilities diagram to the *threat and vulnerability management* category of the enterprise security architecture diagram shows the decomposition of the security layer. Within that category is a service called *vulnerability management*, which is the service we discussed in Chapter 4, when building a set of requirements for a vulnerability management service.

A New Requirement: Vulnerability Management

By this point, you may have noticed there is no requirement for vulnerability management in the case study, but it's essential to managing the continuing security of the running system. That's where the enterprise security architecture in Figure 2-6 becomes a useful checklist. Especially when it is also filled out to contain a list of security processes or services, as in Figure 2-7.

In Figure 11-3, we show another way of looking at the decomposition from the security layer to vulnerability management. It shows the decomposition from security services to the detect and respond domain, to the threat and vulnerability management category, and then to the vulnerability management service. This approach to consistent decomposition enables clear communication of security services and easier identification of gaps in controls.

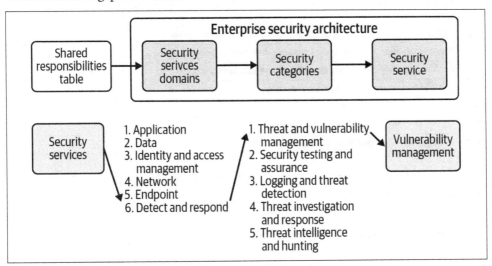

Figure 11-3. Decomposition example for vulnerability management

We've gotten to the point where we have a high-level name for a security service. It needs a description of the security service defining what security capabilities the workloads can consume and the share of responsibilities between the provider (the security service) and the consumer (the workload). We describe these responsibilities using a RACI table to describe who is responsible, accountable, consulted, or informed for each activity related to the service.

We've split the RACI table into two parts, starting with a header for the RACI in Table 11-1, including a title and short summary.[1]

Table 11-1. RACI table—header

2. Vulnerability management
Summary   A service to identify vulnerabilities in an information system and track their lifecycle to closure or risk acceptance.

The RACI continues with the numbered responsibilities in Table 11-2, with a split between the provider and consumer of the service.[2]

Table 11-2. RACI table—content

ID	Responsibility	Provider	Consumer
3.1	Provide vulnerability scanning for networking, hosts, containers, and applications.	R/A	I
3.2	Provide API, CLI, and web console interface to configure and use the vulnerability scanning capabilities.	R/A	I
3.3	Provide vulnerability management capability to track and manage risk lifecycle for the results from the vulnerability scanning.	R/A	I
3.4	Keep all records from the vulnerability scanning and management for a period of at least 90 days.	R/A	I
3.5	Update vulnerability scanning to detect new vulnerabilities, weaknesses, and threats.	R/A	I
3.6	Provide notification within 24 hours of updated vulnerability scanning capabilities.	R/A	I/C
3.7	Provide a capability to create and schedule customer vulnerability scans.	R/A	I
3.8	Create and schedule regular vulnerability scanning.	I	R/A
3.9	Create and schedule custom or ad hoc scans.	I	R/A
3.10	Manage lifecycle of vulnerability scanning results.	I	R/A
Key	R=Responsible, A=Accountable, C=Consulted, I=Informed		

R, A, C, or I denotes the type of responsibility for each of the responsibilities listed in the table. They represent:

Responsible
  Defines who is responsible for performing an activity or task

Accountable
  Defines who is accountable for delivering, but not performing, an activity or task

---

1 You may be asking why we split the tables in this chapter. We did this so the book can be searchable and available in print, EPUB, and online. In practice, the header and content will be combined into one table.

2 This is an example and isn't a complete set of responsibilities. As an exercise, perhaps you would like to extend this list of responsibilities.

Consulted
Defines who to consult on the performance of the activities or tasks

Informed
Defines who to inform about the activities or tasks

In our table, we've shown just two owners, the provider and the consumer, but often there is a need to show the sharing of responsibilities between multiple teams on the consumer side for one activity. This could leave us with multiple teams marked as responsible, without clarity on who takes the lead for the delivery of a responsibility. For example, for 3.9, either the vulnerability scanning team or the penetration testing team could perform this activity.

In this case, we can define a RASCI by splitting the responsibility for performing a service into those that are responsible for _leading_ and _supporting_:

Responsible
Defines who is responsible for _leading_ the performance of an activity or task

Supporting
Defines who is responsible for _supporting_ the performance of an activity or task

Table 11-3 shows an example of a RASCI activity split between vulnerability management and penetration testing teams.

Table 11-3. Example RASCI table activity

ID	Responsibility	Provider	Vuln Mgt	Pen testing
3.9	Create and schedule custom or ad hoc scans.	I	R/A	S

This implies the team responsible will need to specify the solution and lead the activity, while the supporting team will perform some parts of the activity. Both teams will need to provide the resources required to deliver their activity.

Another way of dealing with this is by splitting a responsibility into different responsibilities so there is only one team responsible. If there are quite a few roles supporting and performing the same activity, the use of a RASCI may be the best approach.

At the end of developing the RACI or RASCI, you will have a clearer idea of the split of responsibilities. Otherwise, there is a risk that the delivery of the activities won't happen or be correctly resourced, as the responsibilities are unclear. In this case, the penetration testing team knows they have to schedule their scans and the vulnerability management team doesn't need to provide the resources to perform this activity.

A RACI also helps communicate responsibilities so that teams requiring a security service know who to work with. If there is a need for an activity, it's now clear who to request the service from. For example, the project team should engage the penetration testing team to perform ad hoc scans and not the vulnerability management team.

You will see cloud or managed security service providers using similar RACIs. For security services delivered internally via a security operations team or via a custom managed security service, convert this RACI into an internal agreement or a contract for an external service.

One-Sided Shared Responsibilities

Beware of one-sided shared responsibility agreements with only one party having documented responsibilities and the other assuming anything not described is their responsibility.

Take the case where an organization hires a service provider to design, develop, and run a workload on the cloud. However, the organization retains the core security services as they want control and full transparency for security and compliance. The resilience of the workload now relies on the service levels, functionality, scalability, and resilience of the retained security services.

With a one-sided agreement, there is no formal way of communicating and agreeing on the requirements for the security services before the signing of the contract. We've seen this result in misunderstandings, service failures, and contractual disputes.

Considering the responsibilities of each of the security services will make you consider how the operations are to take place and may result in architecture changes. Completing the definition of a RACI allows you to move on to the next stage of definition: defining the processes, procedures, and work instructions for the operation of each service.

Shared Responsibilities RACI QA Checklist

- Identify from the requirements and existing security services the set of security services required to support the operation of the workload.

- Where a security service RACI doesn't exist, develop a new RACI for each security service.

- Where a security service RACI does exist, if required, split the consumer into multiple owners.

- Embed the RACI into contracts for external security services and an internal agreement for internal security services.

Defining Processes, Procedures, and Work Instructions

To establish auditable controls for consistent application across an enterprise, there is a need for processes to define the implementation of the security policy. Without processes, it's not clear who performs the individual activities. Processes are necessary to define the order of activities, the control points or decisions, and the records that require storage.

For instance, the policy might state that authorization is necessary before accessing a system, but it might not specify that the line manager and application owner are the next two people to give authorization. Writing the order of activities and control points into policies and standards isn't the most effective approach, which is why there is a requirement for documented processes.

ISO 9001:2015 Quality Management Systems

We've used a documentation structure that will enable an organization to meet the requirements of ISO 9001:2015 Quality Management Systems (*https://oreil.ly/obr3o*). Using processes, procedures, and work instructions can be the basis of a Quality Management System (QMS) for an organization.

For enterprise-wide consistency with different layers of abstraction, the top layer will be a written *process* that's independent of technology and application-specific rules. We write the mandatory control requirements for a whole organization into the top-level process. For security processes, the Chief Information Security Officer (CISO) team may document them to ensure consistent execution of the security controls across an organization.

At the next layer, the written *procedures* will define the execution of a process that's specific to a line of business or application. Perhaps it adds additional detail to the process. For example, the IT systems operations team may have a process where the line manager and technology platform manager are the approvers, with an additional application approver required for access to sensitive data. For security procedures, the Business Information Security Officer (BISO) team may document them to include the line of business-specific control requirements.

This procedure may then have an impact on automation. An organization-wide identity lifecycle management system may control the execution of this process. The approval of the line manager and technology manager is in the standard management system, with a custom approval mechanism built into the application that manages the approval of the application approver. The procedure, but not the process, would include information on the additional approval and the use of tooling.

CISO and BISO

Larger organizations split the role of a CISO by assigning line of business, division, geography, or subsidiary responsibilities to a BISO. They may take the policies, processes, and practices developed at an organization and translate them into documentation specific to that part of the organization. If a BISO isn't necessary, it might be an indicator that the organization could consolidate its processes and procedures into a single set of documentation.

We still don't have the step-by-step keystrokes documented. This final level of documentation is in a *work instruction*. For work instructions, the technology or applications operations team may document them as they understand the specific technical implementation.

We've summarized the process, procedure, and work instruction artifact layers with organization scope, definition, description, and examples in Table 11-4.

Table 11-4. Processes, procedures, and work instructions

Artifact	Organization scope	Definition	Description	Example
Process	Enterprise— whole organization	A process states *what* needs to be performed and why.	This is a high-level process flow, using a swimlane diagram or flowchart, that defines the roles, activities, control points, and separation of duties that's described independent of technology.	Process to request a user ID
Procedure	Line of business or business application	A procedure states *how* a process is to be performed.	This is a set of step-by-step activities that specify the steps specific to a business and may include additional activities needed for the business. They're insufficient to use as they don't have details of the specific commands or steps for entering at a keyboard.	User ID request procedure for the payments line of business
Work instruction	Specific technology or application	A work instruction explains *how* to carry out a procedure.	This is a set of step-by-step instructions that specify the specific commands and parameters used to execute the activities. It will include configurations specific to the environment, such as IP addresses and security configurations.	User ID request work instruction for the payment application in the user ID request portal

While there is likely to be a need for all three layers in large global enterprises, it may be sufficient to merge layers for smaller organizations where there are few lines of business and where there is a small range of technologies with little variation.

Clearly defining documentation ensures consistent execution of the control process across an enterprise, with automation of control points, compliance checks, and successful recording of audit events.

But how does this work in practice? Let's show an example of how to document the vulnerability management processes we discussed earlier in the RACI.

Case Study: Vulnerability Management Service

Earlier in this chapter we identified a new derived requirement for a vulnerability management service for the case study. We documented, in Table 11-2, a RACI for a vulnerability management service to describe the provider and consumer responsibilities. Within the responsibilities, there is responsibility 3.3, which says the security service provider must:

> Provide vulnerability management capability to track and manage risk lifecycle for the results from the vulnerability scanning.

We'll now continue by discussing the description of the process, procedure, and work instructions for the risk management lifecycle to support this vulnerability management capability.

Process Definition

We begin to think about the steps a vulnerability needs to go through when managing the risk, from the identification of a new vulnerability to the confirmation of its removal or risk acceptance. The statechart diagram in Figure 11-4 illustrates the vulnerability's various state changes. Every state change entails a process that may involve human intervention or complete automation.

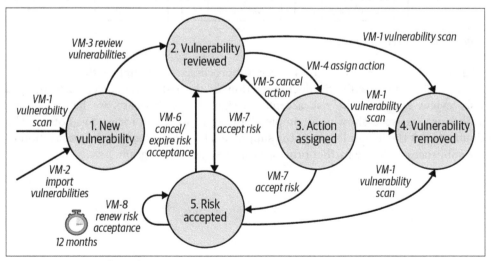

Figure 11-4. Statechart diagram

We started with the state change VM-1, where a vulnerability scan identifies a new vulnerability or an import of vulnerabilities takes place in the state change VM-2. This moves the vulnerability record to the first state of a new vulnerability. The import could be from external tooling or manual checking that identifies a vulnerability. At this point, the vulnerability is new and a review hasn't taken place.

The completion of a vulnerability review automatically moves the vulnerability to state 2, where either there will be a re-run of the scan (VM-1), an assignment of a remediation action (VM-4), or the risk is accepted (VM-7). Where there is an acceptance of a risk (VM-7), the renewal of the risk (VM-8) will be at an interval defined by a security standard. We've included a timer graphic with a renewal period of 12 months on the diagram. The statechart lifecycle continues with state changes until the vulnerability reaches state 4, where the removal of a vulnerability has taken place.

Each of these state changes happens through a process that's a mix of automated and manual activities performed by one or more actors. We need a way to describe the processes and we suggest using the swimlane diagram that we discussed in Chapter 4. However, many of the processes we're now describing are a sequence of processes with multiple layers of process description. We suggest starting with a simple layer 1 process flow, as shown in Figure 11-5 for the VM-7 accept risk process (or state change).

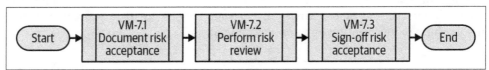

Figure 11-5. Level 1 process flow

The level 1 process flow shows three subprocesses to complete the VM-7 state change. This starts with the documentation of the risk acceptance, performing a risk review, and then the risk acceptance sign-off. In this case, we haven't drawn swimlanes, as we're showing a simple chaining of one subprocess to another. The double bar at the left and right of the subprocess box indicates that the description of the subprocess is in the further process flow or swimlane diagram.

Figure 11-6 shows the subprocess VM-7.1 as a swimlane diagram.

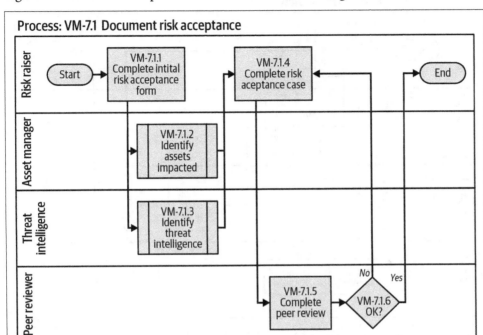

Figure 11-6. Level 2 process flow—VM-7.1 Document risk acceptance

The process shows the different roles involved in its execution. The implementation of the process, VM-7.1, isn't fully defined until the documentation of the two subprocesses, VM-7.1.2 and VM-7.1.3. Decision VM-7.1.6 doesn't generate any audit records because it's not an important control decision.

When VM-7.1 is complete, the overall process will move on to VM-7.2, as shown in Figure 11-7.

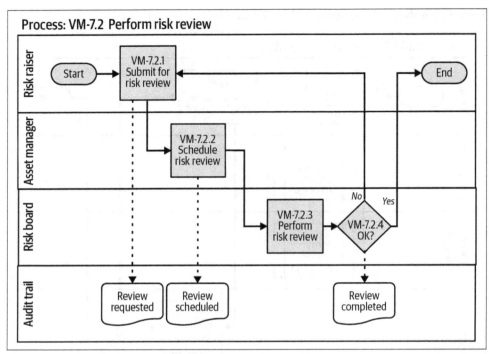

Figure 11-7. Level 2 process flow—VM-7.2 Perform risk review

Here you will see the risk raiser role in the swimlane for VM-7.2 with a different set of supporting roles from those in the process VM-7.1. The risk review stage is an auditable process, with the generation of an audit trail for the auditable activities. There is no information on the implementation of the audit record at this stage.

When VM-7.2 is complete, the overall process will move on to VM-7.3, as shown in Figure 11-8.

In this subprocess, VM-7.3, we have the risk raiser role with another new set of roles. Splitting the overall process into stages removes the need to have all the different roles in one process flow and makes each stage easier to comprehend.

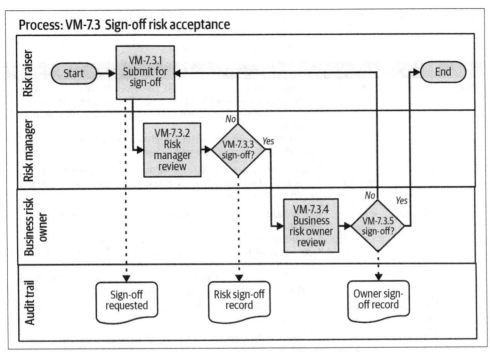

Figure 11-8. Level 2 process flow—VM-7.3 Sign-off risk acceptance

With each of the swimlane diagrams or process flows, we need a more detailed description to explain each of the steps. We're going to use the VM-7.3 swimlane diagram as an example for a process description.

We've split the description into two parts, starting with the header in Table 11-5.

Table 11-5. VM-7.3 Sign-off risk acceptance process—header

Process definition: VM-7.3 Sign-off risk acceptance description	
Description	Sign-off of a risk acceptance for continued risk from a vulnerability with compensating controls by the line of business risk managers and the business risk owner.
Inputs	Risk acceptance form—proposed
Outputs	Risk acceptance form—approved

The description continues with the process activities in Table 11-6.

Table 11-6. VM-7.3 Sign-off risk acceptance process—activities

Activity	Title	Role	Description
VM-7.3.1	Submit for sign-off	Risk raiser	The completion of the preparation and risk board review for the risk acceptance has allowed submission of the risk for formal sign-off. The submission of the risk takes place to the risk manager for approval. The request must include mitigation for the vulnerability. *Record in Audit Trail:* Date and time of sign-off requested, name of approver, risk ID, risk details, and free text message given to approvers.
VM-7.3.2	Risk manager review	Risk manager	The risk manager reviews the risk to confirm the inclusion of all details, that there is sufficient information to assess the risk, and that there is a proposal for appropriate risk mitigation.
VM-7.3.3	Risk manager sign-off	Risk manager	After reviewing the submission, the risk manager either approves or rejects the submission. If rejected, return to activity VM-7.3.1 with the reasons for rejection. If approved, record the approval and move on to activity VM-7.3.4 for the business risk owner review. *Record in Audit Trail:* Date and time of approval or rejection, name of approver, risk ID, and free text comment on the approval or rejection.
VM-7.3.4	Business risk owner review	Business risk owner	The business risk owner reviews the risk to assess whether this is a risk they're willing to accept.
VM-7.3.5	Business risk owner sign-off	Business risk owner	After reviewing the submission, the business risk owner either approves or rejects the submission. If rejected, return to activity VM-7.3.1 with the reasons for rejection. If approved, record the approval, and the VM-7 process moves on to completion. *Record in Audit Trail:* Date and time of approval or rejection, name of approver, risk ID, and free text comment on the approval or rejection.

The process description provides additional details about the decision criteria and the content of the audit records because the swimlane has insufficient space to record this information. This example is simple and the description may be more detailed in reality.

Some detail is still missing, as we haven't determined which combination of activities each role can and can't perform. We created a separation of duties matrix to show this in Figure 11-9.

SoD combination	
✗	Elevated risk
❋	Low risk
✓	Combination allowed
Role	
1	Risk raiser
2	Risk manager
3	Business risk owner

Process step	Role	ID	Submit for sign-off (1)	Risk manager review (2)	Risk manager sign-off (3)	Business risk owner review (4)	Business risk owner sign-off (5)
Submit for sign-off	1	1		✗	✗	✗	✗
Risk manager review	2	2	✗		✓	❋	❋
Risk manager sign-off	2	3	✗	✓		❋	❋
Business risk owner review	3	4	✗	❋	❋		✓
Business risk owner sign-off	3	5	✗	❋	❋	✓	

Figure 11-9. Separation of duties—VM-7.3 Sign-off risk acceptance

The activity steps are numbers to the right and below the *ID* label. Avoid combinations marked with a *cross*, as they pose an elevated risk. For example, the person who submits the risk for approval must not be the risk manager or the business risk owner. Where there is a *star*, this is low-risk and ideally shouldn't be the same person. If the business risk owner is the risk manager, this combination can take place only if there are no other suitable options. Lastly, the combination of activities with a *tick* can take place.

We've been through the architectural thinking and core artifacts used to describe a process flow, including:

- A statechart diagram
- A level 1 process flow
- A level 2 process flow using a swimlane diagram
- A process description
- A separation of duties matrix

The process still has no detail specific to a line of business, application, or technology. We therefore need to continue with the development of procedures and work instructions.

Procedures and Work Instructions Definition

Now we need to expand the process into a procedure by defining content specific to an application or line of business. There may be little change from the process to the procedure. The business leader might just sign off on a controlled document that records the specific names of the approvers in the business. The document may also record the delegates for the application owner in the event they're not available, such as on vacation.

Sometimes, there is a need to rewrite the statechart diagram, swimlane diagrams, and process descriptions for that line of business. If the line of business uses its own specific tooling or adds to the overall enterprise process, it will enhance the process into a line of business procedure.

The procedure will still include the different roles in the swimlane diagrams, but when you get to work instructions, you may split them into documents that specify the individual instructions or commands for a particular role. For example, each of the three roles in process VM-7.3 has a dedicated work instruction.

At this level of detail, documenting a process flow or swimlane diagram is unnecessary due to the presence of separate work instructions for each role. You may record the work instructions in a user manual or online help portal with a series of numbered activities.

Practical Quality Management Systems

As we discussed earlier, these layers of documentation can make sense in a large enterprise environment that's in a regulated industry, but for smaller organizations, it would be impractical to require all this documentation. If you are going down the route of implementing a Quality Management System, we suggest you take some time to read guidance such as *Implementing ISO:9001:2015* (*https://oreil.ly/dRDNM*) (IT Governance Publishing) by Andrew W. Nichols.

In the first half of the chapter, we used the vulnerability management requirements we talked about in Chapter 4 to document who is responsible for what activities in a RACI. We then went on to create processes, procedures, and work instructions, as seen in Figure 11-10. Clear traceability is shown from one step to the next helping to ensure there are no gaps in the solution.

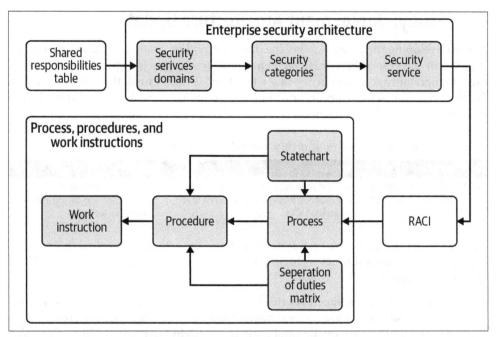

Figure 11-10. From a security service to work instructions

Process, Procedure, and Work Instructions QA Checklist

- From the identified security services and RACI, identify the lifecycle for the management of information and the process transitions through documenting a statechart diagram.
- Identify what processes exist already and what new processes need development.
- Where processes already exist, add the development of procedures and work instructions to the project, where they require development.
- Where there is a need for new processes, add the development of processes, procedures, and work instructions to the project.

Before we move on to the next section, the vulnerability management supplier provided a new requirement that needs discussion.

Case Study: Deployment Architecture Update

While developing the process swimlane diagrams and separation of duties matrix, the supplier of the vulnerability management services adds a new requirement for locating a vulnerability scanning proxy in a VPC that has access to all the workload VPCs. We then documented a short architectural decision record, as shown in Table 11-7, to place the proxy in the management VPC.

Table 11-7. Vulnerability scanning architectural decision record

ID	Decision	Rationale	Implication
AD15	Vulnerability scanning proxy in management VPC	• The management VPC is designed to hold all operational tooling that needs access to all workload VPCs.	• Update the deployment architecture diagram and assess the impact on the project.

The update to the deployment architecture diagram includes the vulnerability scanning proxy and communication highlighted with shading in the management VPC, as shown in Figure 11-11.

This is typical of the architectural thinking process, where considering operational aspects of a solution introduces new components into the deployment architecture. Have a think about other operational aspects we might have missed from this solution that will require an update to the architecture.

Now we're going to move on and focus on the development of documentation to support threat detection and response. We will use the threat modeling discussed in Chapter 6 to further define the threat detection and incident response requirements.

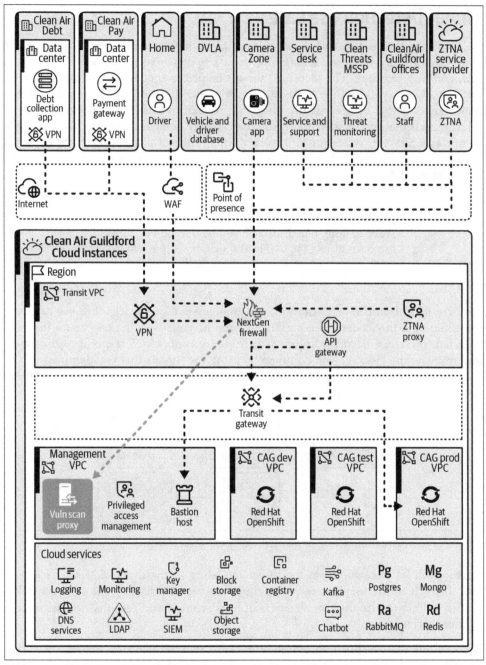

Figure 11-11. Vulnerability scanning proxy update; see the original diagram (https://oreil.ly/SAHC)

Threat Detection Use Case

We earlier performed threat modeling on a component architecture diagram and a cloud architecture diagram, identifying threats to sensitive data while in transit, at rest, and in processing. The identified threats helped to specify the countermeasures, but not all risks will be fully mitigated, and the identification of a new vulnerability may take place that can expose the workload. We can also use the identified threats to select threats that require detection. You may require detection because it's impossible to mitigate a threat, you want to be aware when a threat actor is trying to exploit a potential vulnerability, or because there is a significant risk from the identification of a new vulnerability.

Limited Threat Detection Scope

We're limiting our discussion to identification of threat detection use cases during the design and delivery of a workload. There are many other ways in which the identification of threats for detection takes place.

Perform identification, prioritization, and implementation of detection use cases for the setup of a threat detection service to support your workload. When a threat is detected, there is a need for an incident response runbook to respond to the threat and mitigate the risk. We will continue by using the threats that we identified earlier to define use cases for threat detection and incident response runbooks, as shown in Figure 11-12.

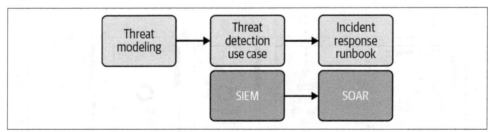

Figure 11-12. Threat modeling to incident response traceability

Threats will be traceable from the threat modeling to the threat detection use case and through to the incident response runbook. We will discuss using a traceability matrix to help ensure the completeness of the detection and response for the system later in this chapter.

Automation of the threat detection use case can take place in a tool such as a security information and event management (SIEM) system, and incident response runbook automation can take place in a security orchestration, automation, and response (SOAR) system. As this automation is specific to the technology, we won't be discussing that in this book.

A threat detection use case communicates what the threat is and how the detection is to take place. As an architect, you may create or support the creation of a use case that's specific to your workload. The use case will need to include:

Title
> Give the use case a short title to convey the threat detection capability.

Description
> A description of the use case discusses what threat detection needs to take place and how the detection of the threat may take place. The level of detail in the description will depend on who is completing the use case and their level of understanding of the potential detection mechanisms. It could be high-level, expressing the use case in a non-technical way or very technical if the author understands the specific details of the threat detection approach.

Rationale
> The rationale helps to understand the context behind the use case and the detail behind the detection mechanism. We suggest that, as a start, you should include information about the application, the sensitivity of the processed data, and the impacted business processes in the event that a threat actor exploits a vulnerability or weakness. This will enable the request for a detection mechanism to be better prioritized.
>
> Some additional background on the threat is important, such as that obtained from threat intelligence sources. If the use case is to detect a specific threat actor that's particularly active or seen as a significant threat, this again helps give an idea of the priority and the effort needed. Include links to open source information containing more detailed descriptions of the threat and how to implement detection. The external information may change over time, so don't just copy the content and not include a link.

Requester
> The name of the requester provides the source of the request. It's likely there will be a need for additional clarification on the development. Once the implementation of the detection mechanism is complete, it will need integration and testing with the requester to ensure its effectiveness.

A use case may consist of one or more detection rules that may need integration and tuning to an appropriate level of sensitivity. For each detection rule, we suggest the following content:

Detection rule
> Give the detection rule a short name that summarizes the purpose.

Description

Provide a longer description of the detection rule that gives more detail.

Event sources

The triggering of an event may come from a recorded log event or an alert. Record the source of this event.

Event fields

Record the required information from the event source needed to detect a threat.

Exceptions

To reduce false positives, you should limit the detection rule's scope. Make a note of what you don't want the rule to apply to.

Dimensions

Define what the focus is so that you only include resources that are at the highest risk.

Notes

Include additional information, such as prerequisites for preparation.

Let's continue by applying the concepts we've discussed to the case study we've been using in Appendix A.

Case Study: Threat Detection Use Case

In the case study, we've used a number of different databases that contain sensitive information related to the driver and vehicle. The data needs protection from threat actors, including controls for protection, detection, and response. Let's think about a threat detection use case to detect the attempted exfiltration of data from the database.

EasyPark Incident

In December 2023, the Swedish parking firm EasyPark had data stolen from its parking systems, including names, mobile numbers, addresses, emails, and parts of credit card numbers. Its US-focused app, ParkMobile, was previously compromised in 2021. This example reinforces the need for you as an architect to identify threat detection use cases specific to your application or workload and it's the role of the threat detection engineering team to design the detection. Don't think that it won't happen to your application.

In developing security for a solution architecture, you will come across threat detection use cases in two contexts:

Generic use case

These are widely applied use cases that need a simple setup or configuration to apply to an infrastructure or workload. For example, a use case for detecting a change to a file just needs configuration to include new files related to your workload.

Using a generic use case may require updates to your solution to enable support for threat detection. For example, it may require the installation of additional code within your servers or containers.

Before spending time developing your own unique new use cases, think about how your solution should support generic threat detection use cases from the threat detection engineering team's existing catalog.

Workload-specific use case

These are use cases that are specific to the development of a workload or application solution architecture. They're not generic use cases that are widely applied and may require new development to deliver automation.

A solution architecture for a security service may need new use cases, such as identity lifecycle management, as they're domain-specific security applications.

We will focus on the development of a threat detection use case for the case study by using threat T05, which we identified earlier in Table 6-3 and is shown in Table 11-8.

Table 11-8. Case study threat

STRIDE category	Threat	Control
Information disclosure	T05—An attacker exploits a vulnerability by performing a mass data exfiltration of the database.	C05.1—Detect mass exfiltration of database (detective). C05.2—Implement separation of duties and the least privilege principle for application components authorized to query the database (preventive).

Using the threat T05 and the guidance discussed earlier, we've split the threat detection use case into two parts, starting with the header in Table 11-9.

Table 11-9. Threat detection use case: Mass database exfiltration detection—header

Threat detection use case: Mass database exfiltration detection	
Description	Detect the mass extraction of data from a database.
Rationale	If a threat agent were to extract data from a database, the characteristics of the queries and processes performing the queries would suggest a potential exfiltration of data, indicating a system compromise. The extraction of personal information would be a notifiable incident and could result in reputational damage, loss of customers, and a substantial fine.
Requester	Project X—security architect

We set the context of the threat to the organization. Note that it still has a major impact, even if you think the recovery or destruction of the stolen data is possible. The duplication of data has likely already taken place and spread among the hacker community.

The use case continues with a description of the suggested threat detection rules in Table 11-10.

Table 11-10. Threat detection use case: C05.1—Database exfiltration detection—Rules

Rule	Description	Event sources	Event fields	Exceptions	Dimensions	Notes
Extensive query	Detect database queries that are pulling a substantial number of records	Database event log	Query source, query performed	None—will detect both trusted and untrusted processes	All databases	The baseline configuration for the number of records to trigger an event will take place after monitoring database queries.
Unauthorized process	Monitor for processes that try to open database and fail	Database event log	Query source, query performed	None—will detect even if untrusted processes	All databases	The database will only be open to trusted processes, but detection should detect a query that fails.

A Detailed Threat Detection Use Case

We gave a simple example of a threat detection use case. With a complete set of rules, you should provide as much detail as possible so that the threat detection team understands how to detect a threat with as little research as possible. This makes it easier to get your threat detection rules implemented faster.

We proposed two rules, but there could be many others, such as detecting new files with privileged execution permissions or new processes. The threat detection team would look for a combination of these events and other existing generic use cases to indicate a potential threat to the system.

The rules may require the installation of a software agent or script on systems to detect ransomware or other malicious code. This is information you should record in your solution architecture.

Once the threat detection team has received the use case, they will enrich the information with the detection of other weaknesses, vulnerabilities, tactics, and techniques. Sources for this information include:

Weaknesses

Software developers may include weaknesses in the development of their products, and it's not something that can be completely tested for in advance when you don't have access to the code. You should assess your workload for these weaknesses to develop use cases to monitor for an attempt to exploit those weaknesses.

The Open Web Application Security Project (OWASP®) Foundation Top Ten (*https://oreil.ly/y6X4Z*) is a useful list for developers to watch out for in their development. The threat detection engineering team may use these as a starting point for developing some threat detection use cases.

MITRE has made a more comprehensive and specific list of weaknesses available in their Common Weakness Enumeration (CWE) list (*https://oreil.ly/pu_sj*), including the top 10 Known Exploited Vulnerabilities (KEV) Catalog. Threat detection for these vulnerabilities is something to consider in the development of the workload.

Vulnerabilities

Over time, the identification of vulnerabilities takes place and is often fixed with patches or configuration changes. The fixing of vulnerabilities isn't always possible and an attempted exploit will need blocking. The attempted exploit may also indicate a threat actor has taken an interest in your system and further threat detection use cases may require development.

There are several databases that track vulnerabilities. The NIST National Vulnerability Database (NVD) (*https://nvd.nist.gov*) is a repository of vulnerabilities for the US government stored in the security content automation protocol (SCAP) format. The MITRE Corporation also hosts the Common Vulnerabilities and Exposures (CVE) (*https://www.cve.org*) list. Both of these lists may contain vulnerabilities that you can mitigate by a change in architecture and are therefore worth reviewing as part of your architectural thinking.

Tactics and techniques

Threat actors have a set of tactics and techniques they use to exploit weaknesses and vulnerabilities. A list of these is available at the MITRE ATT&CK knowledge base of adversary tactics and techniques (*https://attack.mitre.org*). Review this list to see how you can architect your system to be resistant to these tactics and techniques used by threat actors.

Threat Detection Engineering in Depth

The purpose of the threat detection use case is to enable an architect to help document requirements for a threat detection engineering team. Megan Roddie, Jason Deyalsingh, and Gary J. Katz give a far more comprehensive description of threat detection engineering in *Practical Threat Detection Engineering* (*https://oreil.ly/MGLNU*) (Packt Publishing).

We suggest you review these data sources to help identify potential use cases needed for your solution. For example, the threat detection engineering team may not know about every software component you have and what their weaknesses are. This is for you to help identify and build protection mechanisms to remove the weakness.

Threat Detection Use Case QA Checklist

- Review the existing threat detection use case catalog to identify any use cases that need updating to include workload-specific rules.

- Review existing threat detection use cases that apply and need detection capabilities added to the solution.

- From threat modeling, identify the need for any new threat detection use cases and send an outline use case to the threat detection engineering team for their consideration.

- Review external data sources for weaknesses, vulnerabilities, tactics, and techniques that you could remove from your system or detect as threats.

Incident Response Runbook

Now that we've developed a threat detection use case, we need a process for responding to an alert from the threat detection service about a potential security incident. The process used by the industry normally aligns to the Incident Response Lifecycle proposed in NIST SP800-61r2 Computer Security Incident Handling Guide (*https://oreil.ly/y_DF2*) and shown in Figure 11-13.

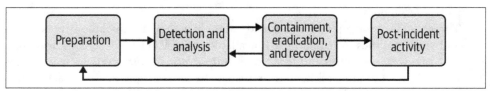

Figure 11-13. NIST SP800-61r2 Incident Response Lifecycle (detection and analysis)

The response to an incident follows these steps:

Preparation

The preparation stage includes the development of a solution architecture, including security controls to protect the workload. The hardening of the deployed solution is next, using baseline standards. Security testing follows to ensure the controls have been effectively deployed.

The work also includes the deployment of threat detection and incident response services, as well as the processes and education needed to respond to a security incident. There should be testing of the incident response processes to provide assurance that they're effective.

Identification (detection and analysis)

The threat detection service will automatically raise alerts when the detection of a potential threat occurs. The alert needs investigation to validate whether the threat is a false positive or if it needs further investigation. This stage often involves collecting together the details, including the source of the threat, and entering them into an incident record for the next stage.

Containment

Once the identification of a threat has taken place, it may need containment to stop the impact. Malicious code, such as ransomware, will need rapid containment, but other threats may need further monitoring. Containment may tip off sophisticated threat actors who may take more aggressive action to destroy data and the environment, making things worse, and moving on to eradication may be the better approach.

Eradication

At this stage, the objective is to not only contain but also remove the threat. Removal of vulnerabilities and weaknesses will be a priority by updating software to remove vulnerabilities, undoing changes to the security configuration, and removing malicious code across the environment. In addition, there will need to be a change of all secrets, encryption keys, and passwords.

Recovery

Actions taken during eradication may have reduced service levels across the whole environment. Those services need recovery through actions like refreshing server operating systems. In a cloud environment, it may mean running automation to deploy the infrastructure from the ground up again. There may be a need for emergency improvements to the security controls before the closure of the incident.

Post-incident activity (including lessons learned)

After completion of the service recovery, the organization can learn many lessons to improve the detection capabilities, incident response process, and security of the information systems. There may be a need for some long-term projects for improvements that require significant investment as their completion can't take place during the recovery activities.

For incident response, we use the identification, containment, eradication, recovery, and post-incident activity stages in the development of an incident response runbook. The development of a runbook will include a wide range of different stakeholders, as it may need to include incident response, security operations, service management, operations teams, legal, communications, and the CXO team.

The organization's incident response department typically oversees the incident response process and distributes responsibility among different teams in accordance with their qualifications, experience, and responsibilities. The division of incident response depends on the approach an organization uses. Following is a description of the incident response teams that one organization uses:

Tier 1: First responders

These are the first responders who perform the initial review of security alerts and decide whether an alert is something that requires further investigation. They might collect extra information together and record it in an incident record for further investigation. Many of the activities at Tier 1 are increasingly automated and assisted by AI to identify patterns to match against known threats.

The next activities of containment, eradication, and recovery get passed on to teams with more skills and experience. It also enables Tier 1 to continue looking for new threats and not get distracted by ongoing incidents.

Tier 2: Incident responders

The Tier 2 incident responders perform further investigation and start to contain the threat. They have further experience and are able to work on incidents that haven't had a wide impact across the organization.

Tier 3: Major incident responders

The Tier 3 team handles major incidents that could have a wide impact across the organization. They lead and coordinate the incident across the different operations teams supporting the information systems.

They take on more long-running incidents that may involve automating the investigation and remediation of a wide number of on-premises and cloud resources. They may also perform forensic activities as a part of their investigation for use in later legal actions.

Tier 4: Computer Security Incident Response Team (CSIRT)
> The CSIRT team provides more of a leadership and coordination function, including review and approval of major changes. They coordinate with other business functions, including legal, communications, and data privacy teams.

Let's continue by applying the concepts we've discussed to the case study from Appendix A.

Case Study: Incident Response Runbook

Earlier in this chapter, we discussed a threat detection use case derived from a threat T05 mass data exfiltration that was identified during threat modeling of the component architecture diagram in Chapter 6. If we detect a threat related to this use case, we would need an incident response runbook.

We will now discuss an example runbook created specifically for the threat of mass data exfiltration. We've split the incident response runbook into two parts, starting with the header in Table 11-11.

Table 11-11. Incident response runbook: IR10—Database exfiltration incident response—header

Incident response runbook: Database exfiltration incident response	
Description	Respond to suspected mass exfiltration of database.
Detection use case	Database exfiltration detection

The header includes a title and description, followed by a link back to the threat detection use case that will trigger this incident response runbook.

 Your organization may already have templates for incident response runbooks for you to use as a starting point. They're likely to be more detailed, including details on specific tooling and commands to follow within your organization.

The incident response runbook continues with a description of incident response stages in Table 11-12. It's split into five sections:

- Identification[3]
- Containment
- Eradication

---

3 Called Detection and Analysis in NIST SP800-61r2.

- Recovery
- Post-incident activity[4]

Table 11-12. Incident response runbook: IR10—Database exfiltration incident response—Stages

	Activity	Description	Tier 1	Tier 2	Tier 3	CSIRT
Identification	1.	1. Review results from event records associated with the raised incident record.	✓			
		2. Review network traffic monitoring for increased data export and record screen shots in the incident record.				
		3. Identify the external network destination and record it in the incident record.				
		4. Research network destinations and record information in the incident record.				
		5. Review other recorded events and tag potentially relevant records against the incident record.				
		6. Retrieve additional database logs from the database analyst and get them to validate whether they expect the database query.				
		7. Assess whether a false positive exists: either cancel the incident record or forward it to Tier 2 for continued investigation.				
	2.	1. Review the record passed from Tier 1 and validate the external network address.		✓		
		2. Confirm the network address doesn't match any known trusted external service for the specific workload or generic list of services.				
		3. Complete the Tactics, Techniques, and Adversary Research runbook.				
		4. Send a request to the CSIRT team notifying them of a potential data protection breach.				
		5. Decide whether to use containment or eradication, then move on to the next stage.				

---

4 This section is often called Lessons Learned, but it's much more than that.

	Activity	Description	Tier 1	Tier 2	Tier 3	CSIRT
Containment	1.	1. Create a request for a network block for the CSIRT team to review and approve. 2. Continue monitoring while waiting for confirmation.		✓		
	2.	1. Review the network block request and ask for further information if needed. 2. Approve the network block.				✓
	3.	1. Implement network block. 2. Review related network and workload monitoring for any impact on services. 3. Confirm network traffic monitoring shows a reduction in network traffic. 4. Review to see if the attack switched to an alternate network address. 5. Pass to Tier 3 for further investigation.		✓		
	4.	1. If the threat actor is now using an alternate IP address, perform further investigation and response using the Adaptive IP Threat runbook. 2. Move to eradication phase.			✓	
Eradication	1.	1. Review database logs to establish the extent of data exfiltration. 2. Identify vulnerabilities that enabled exploits using the Extended Exploit Investigation runbook. 3. Notify the press office, legal department, and Chief Privacy Officer of the ongoing incident. 4. Build threat eradication plan. 5. Request CSIRT team review and agree to threat eradication plan.			✓	
	2.	1. Review the threat eradication plan and ask for further information if needed. 2. Approve threat eradication plan.				✓
	3.	1. Raise change tickets for the implementation of fixes for the remediation of vulnerabilities. 2. Raise change tickets for the changing of all secrets, encryption keys, and passwords.			✓	
Recovery	1.	1. Develop recovery plan. 2. Propose a recovery plan and send it to CSIRT for agreement.			✓	
	2.	1. Review the recovery plan and ask for further information if needed. 2. Approve recovery plan.				✓
	3.	1. Raise problem or change tickets for the implementation of the recovery plan.			✓	

	Activity	Description	Tier 1	Tier 2	Tier 3	CSIRT
Post-incident activity	1.	1. Review incident response records.				✓
		a. Effective threat detection use case?				
		b. Effective identification, containment, and eradication?				
		c. What was effective?				
		d. What needs improvement?				
		e. Any future consequences?				
		2. Record incident response investigation.				
		3. Raise problem tickets for post-incident improvements.				
		4. Handover incident report including scope of data breach to Chief Privacy Officer and legal.				
		5. Track post-incident improvements.				

Table 11-12 includes a simple form of a RACI matrix to show the handover between different members of the incident management team who will own different stages of the incident. It could be extended to include the full RACI or RASCI designation. Many others could assist in supporting the incident.

During the identification stage, data is collected from sources immediately available to the Tier 1 incident handler, but the extraction and examination of additional logs may need to take place with the help of the database analyst, who will have full privileged access. The database analyst may also be useful to validate that the query is an unexpected activity for the application.

The incident progresses between different tiers of incident management teams, depending on the stage of the incident and the level of skill needed. Depending on the type of threat, for example, if the threat is widely embedded across the environment, the incident response team may skip over the containment stage and proceed with eradication.

Outside the incident management team, the incident response team will involve a wide variety of stakeholders. The team won't have full privileged access or the skills for every technology and will therefore need operations teams, including security, to support the incident. In this case, it's a potential data protection incident with personal data extracted by the threat actor. The Chief Privacy Officer and legal team will likely have to notify the authorities of the data breach, and the press office will need to communicate with those affected.

This runbook is a foundation for a workload-specific set of instructions. Throughout the runbook, there will be call-outs to other runbooks that are more generic and detailed in their approach to the investigation, containment, and recovery.

Incident Response in Depth

To find a more detailed description of incident response, consult *Intelligence-Driven Incident Response* (O'Reilly) by Rebekah Brown and Scott J. Roberts.

The incident response runbook that we describe is an illustration of a runbook template that a security operations center (SOC) uses. It gives you an idea of the required information needed while responding to an incident. You may have access to many other existing runbooks for consideration when developing your solution architecture.

As an architect, you may need to add capabilities to the solution to enable effective incident response. For example, are logs available to the incident response team from the database and other components in your solution? Ensure the documentation of the required logs within your solution, along with any automation required during an incident.

Incident Response Runbook QA Checklist

- Review the existing incident response runbook catalog to see if any runbooks need updating to include workload-specific activities.

- Review existing incident response runbooks that apply and require data collection capabilities that need adding to the solution.

- From the threat detection use cases, identify the need for any new incident response runbooks and raise a request for their development.

- Identify event logs that need forwarding to support the incident and ensure integration with the threat detection system.

- Identify automation for use in a security incident and integrate it with the threat detection and response systems.

Threat Traceability Matrix

At the end of Chapter 4, we discussed the use of a traceability matrix to ensure the completeness of design, implementation, and testing. At the beginning of our discussion on the threat detection use case, we also suggested the use of a traceability matrix to ensure coverage for threats. We propose that you create a table in a spreadsheet, such as shown in Table 11-13, to demonstrate full coverage with the detection, response, and testing of all threats.

Table 11-13. Threat detection and response traceability matrix

Threat ID	Threat	Detect ID	Detection use case	IR ID	Incident response runbook	IR test ID
T05	Mass data exfiltration	C05.1	Database exfiltration detection	IR10	Database exfiltration incident response	Test_IR_003

There is unlikely to be a one-to-one mapping of threats to detection in the incident response runbook, and you may need to extend the table to support multiple mappings. Separating the identifiers from the titles makes it easier to filter and find mappings.

Summary

This chapter starts by examining how a RACI table, processes, procedures, and work instructions can describe security services. This is an activity that an architect will get involved with and is extremely important to ensure the continued operation of security and compliance for a system. You may get help but as a technical leader, you are accountable for ensuring their development and that teams accept ongoing ownership before handover to operations teams.

We continued by looking at the development of a threat detection use case and incident response runbook. As an architect, you should identify workload-specific use cases for development and identify generic use cases that need integration with your solution architecture. They may result in changes to your solution to ensure effective threat detection and incident investigation. The threat detection engineering team will develop the automation and is likely to need your help to develop or adapt the automation. You will need to ensure there is effective integration and the completion of testing.

When the threat detection team identifies a potential threat, the incident response team will follow the corresponding incident response runbook. The incident response team will likely lead the development of the runbook, with your support limited to the inclusion of workload-specific activities. The runbook discussed provides an example to give you an idea of what an architect needs to deliver. As the technical leader for the workload, you will have the responsibility to ensure this runbook is in place. Supporting activities such as the development of automation to collect data and reconfiguration of parts of the system to contain threats are yours to ensure implementation and testing.

Consider Operations Early

Don't leave the discussion of operational processes until the end of the architecture. The documentation of human and system actors and their use cases should start with the documentation of the system context diagram. They're likely to require consideration of additional components and integration throughout the architectural thinking process. Applications or workloads may require additional work to add instrumentation to support the operational processes.

We've now been through the requirements definition, architecture development, secure development practices, and operational thinking for the solution architecture. We're now moving on to the closing chapter of the book to provide some reminders about some basic principles you need to consider, perspectives about the overall development lifecycle, including control maturity, and a few thoughts on using AI in the development of a security architecture.

Exercises

1. Why might a Responsible, Accountable, Supporting, Consulted, and Informed (RASCI) matrix be used rather than a Responsible, Accountable, Consulted, and Informed (RACI) matrix? Select all that apply.

   a. A RASCI matrix ensures there is only one owner responsible for leading the delivery of the activity by splitting those Responsible and those Supporting.

   b. Rather than decomposing into multiple activities, the activity is split into those that lead the delivery activity and those that support delivery by performing part of the activity.

   c. A RASCI matrix ensures there is only one owner responsible for leading the delivery of the activity by splitting those Responsible and those Supervising.

   d. The S defines who is responsible for summarizing the activity.

2. True or false: A Responsible, Accountable, Consulted, and Informed (RACI) matrix that only defines the responsibilities for one party in an agreement is the best form of responsibility definition.

   a. True

   b. False

3. True or false: A process states how to complete a set of activities.

   a. True

   b. False

4. A statechart diagram is useful to identify _____ needed to perform state changes of data.

   a. Processes

   b. Requirements

   c. Architectural decisions

   d. Work instructions

5. What artifact is used to ensure that activities in a process that are high-risk cannot be performed without another party agreeing to the activity?

   a. Statechart diagram

   b. Process

   c. Separation of duties matrix

   d. Shared responsibility table

6. True or False: Threat modeling is used to identify security countermeasures and what threats should be detected.

    a. True

    b. False

7. Why is a threat traceability matrix required? Select all that apply.

    a. To ensure there is a use case for detection of a threat

    b. To ensure there is a response runbook for responding to a threat

    c. To ensure detection and response are tested for a threat

    d. To ensure a threat actor is identified for a threat

PART VI

Close

What more? To conclude, we will provide a refresher on the basics of security. Following that, we will offer some final thoughts on the emerging issues around AI in security and securing AI.

CHAPTER 12

Closing Thoughts

We've discussed a range of architectural thinking techniques and artifacts to use during the development of a hybrid cloud solution architecture. With a focus on artifacts rather than documents, the principles we went through apply to both traditional waterfall and Agile approaches to solution delivery.

There are other good practices that will help you on your journey to become proficient in architecting security into your solution architecture. We will take you through some of these guidelines as well as some thoughts around AI as our closing thoughts for the book. Let's start with the basics.

Getting Started

You may be thinking this is all a bit overwhelming, and where do I start with something simple? We'll discuss a few different perspectives to start with, including starting with some basic security controls, starting with a minimum set of artifacts, iterating to improve maturity, and getting the balance of risk right.

Don't Forget the Basics

We talk about performing a comprehensive analysis with control compliance and threat modeling with assurance to provide confidence in your solution, but you can remove a large proportion of the risk rapidly by performing the basics, including:

Use supported software
> Using supported software ensures the availability of security patches. This includes open source software that requires regression testing with all the different integrated components. Open source software isn't free; it still needs support.

Patch vulnerabilities

Software isn't free of vulnerabilities, and software suppliers release regular security patches to their supported software. Understand what software you have in your organization and ensure that patching takes place within a timeframe appropriate to the risk.

Harden software

Disabling services that aren't required, changing default passwords, enforcing strong passwords, and enabling encryption in-transit and at-rest are fundamental secure configuration practices that significantly reduce the threat surface.

Use multi-factor authentication

Multi-factor authentication reduces the risk of a compromised password for a user account. The mechanism is broadly available and relatively simple to implement, increasing the level of protection significantly.

Restrict administrative privileges

Users with administrative privileges pose a significant risk, as they usually have a wide range of access and the ability to make significant changes to the configurations or bypass critical security controls. Don't use privileged accounts for daily business. Limit the privileged account's access rights to the bare minimum, and ensure that only users with a clear business need can access a privileged account.

Back up your data

Should a disastrous event happen and your data becomes the victim of a ransomware attack or is otherwise made unavailable, it's crucial to have backups available to recover your business. We've seen businesses severely impacted because there were missing, outdated, untested, or inappropriately stored backups.

Maintain employee hygiene

Raising awareness about avoiding phishing emails, practicing safe browsing habits, and recognizing social engineering tactics can significantly reduce the risk of falling victim to cyber threats within your organization or household.

Once the basics are in place, what next?

Minimum Viable Artifacts

We often get asked—there are many artifacts but what's the minimum we can get away with? We suggest you start with two artifacts:

Architectural decision records (ADRs)

As we discussed earlier in Chapter 1, architecture represents a set of significant design decisions. If you don't make architectural decisions, you aren't performing architectural thinking. All the other artifacts are just a way of describing requirements and the architectural decisions you make. You should record your decisions in an ADR.

A threat model

As we're talking about security and risk, we need to identify the threats and corresponding countermeasures. We do this by looking at the data flows and performing threat modeling. Without threat modeling, we're not looking at appropriate countermeasures for inclusion in a solution architecture.

You will soon discover that this isn't enough, as you will use other artifacts to describe architectural decisions and countermeasures. You might be doing this free-form and not separating the system context, functional components, and deployment layers. This is why having standard formats for the system context diagram, component architecture diagram, and deployment architecture diagram becomes useful.

You will then want to have a way to track important items about the project, which is when a RAID log becomes useful as well.

As you start to describe different aspects of the requirements, architecture, and operations, you now have a "kit bag" of different artifacts and techniques to support your architectural thinking. Use these artifacts, as you find them useful, to support your thinking and communicate different aspects of your solution.

What you may find is that you start with a small set of artifacts and iterate with increasing numbers of artifacts as the maturity of the solution increases.

Increasing maturity also applies to the number and strength of the security controls.

Iterate for Maturity

Once the basic controls are in place, that's not the end. You'll need additional layers to provide defense in depth so you aren't relying on a single layer of controls. Capability maturity models help you to assess, measure, and structure the process of iteratively improving the maturity of your solution. The following activities help you use the maturity approach to improve your security:

Select the reference framework

Reference frameworks provide you with a structure for the capabilities that represent good security practices. We've discussed a number of common frameworks in Chapter 2. For most frameworks, the authors will have defined maturity models as part of the framework or they may have been created by other organizations.

A maturity model consists of a definition of levels and a description of the capabilities associated with those levels. Many maturity models use the Capability Maturity Model Integration (CMMI) definition of maturity levels (*https://oreil.ly/GcitD*): Level 1: Initial, Level 2: Managed, Level 3: Defined, Level 4:

Quantitatively Managed, and Level 5: Optimizing to define the steps on the maturity staircase.

In *Rational Cybersecurity for Business* (*https://oreil.ly/lxXNn*) (Apress), Dan Blum describes a generic cybersecurity maturity model that establishes high-level maturity levels for the capabilities of people, processes, and technology, as illustrated in Figure 12-1.

	Initial	Developing	Defined	Managed	Optimized
People	Activities unstaffed or uncoordinated	Security leadership established, informal communication	Security roles and responsibilities established for security functions	Increased resources and awareness, clearly defined roles and responsibilties	Culture supports continuous improvement to security skills, process, technology
Process	No formal security program in place	Basic governance and risk management process, policies	Processes in place, but only in some areas with manual verification	Formal infosec committees, verification and measurement processes	Processes more comprehensively implemented, risk based, and quantitatively understood
Technology	Despite security issues, few or no controls exist	Some controls in development with limited documentation	More controls documented and developed, but over-reliant on individual efforts	Controls monitored, measured for compliance, but uneven levels of automation	Controls more comprehensively implemented, automated, and subject to continuous improvement

Figure 12-1. The rational cybersecurity maturity model

This simple model illustrates the foundation of most security maturity models.

Define target maturity

We need to define the target maturity level for each capability, as the target isn't to achieve the highest maturity level in all capabilities. The size, industry, and level of acceptable risk of your organization influence the target maturity level you should strive for. Often, a comparison to similar organizations' maturity levels via industry benchmarks can also help you define the target maturity level.

If your organization is a member of the Information Security Forum (ISF), you have access to the ISF Benchmark (*https://oreil.ly/Cfpam*), which provides a framework with the Standard of Good Practice for Information Security (*https://oreil.ly/UrNVI*) and corresponding benchmark data.

Assess current state

Through document reviews, interviews, or system assessments, you can capture the current state and identify the current level of maturity. You can do this as a self-assessment, or if you want a more independent result, you can ask another team or organization to do the assessment for you.

Plan the activities

You now have the current and target maturity. This provides you with a gap, and this gap drives the definition of activities to close the gap and, with that, achieve the target maturity level. If your current maturity is on Level 1 and your target maturity is on Level 4, then it's good practice to define some interim activities to achieve incremental improvements, as you will typically not be able to raise the maturity level in one go by more than one level.

As you focus on security, there are many other factors to consider, and you need to get the balance right.

Get the Balance Right

In previous chapters, we've discussed that the foundation for implementing security controls is to reduce risk for the organization. We've also discussed that, in cases where a security control is more expensive than the benefit, i.e., the risk reduction it provides, it's either not an appropriate security control or the implementation approach of the control isn't ideal. In other words, we need to balance *security* (risk) and *cost*. But these aren't the only elements that we need to consider, as security can have an impact on non-functional requirements.

Usability is another important element we must take into consideration. As humans, we have a tendency to take the path of least resistance, and we become creative in achieving this. We all know the examples of too-complex password rules and short password change intervals, which make it very difficult for us to remember passwords. As a result, we choose passwords where we only rotate some numbers or use sticky notes to remember them. Luckily, the security industry is adopting password-less technologies, which increase usability and, in fact, security. As a security architect, you need to keep usability in mind, as it can affect the effectiveness of the security controls you are designing.

Irrespective of the controls that we design to protect our assets, we need to assume that compromise of our solution will occur. This is one of the principles that we also discussed in the context of zero trust. A fast detection of a compromise allows the organization to initiate actions to contain the incident and stop the compromise. Once we contain the compromise, it becomes important to return to normal operations as fast as possible. This is what we collectively call *cyber resilience*.

Cyber Resilience KPIs

Often used key performance indicators (KPIs) in this context are:

Mean time to detect (MTTD)
MTTD is a key metric to measure the average time it takes your security operations team to detect a potential security incident.

Mean time to contain (MTTC)
MTTC measures the average time it takes for your organization to contain the identified attack vectors across all endpoints and systems from the time of initial detection.

Mean time to resolve (MTTR)
MTTR represents the average time it takes your organization to fully resolve and recover from a security incident after its initial detection.

Throughout this book, we've discussed all these elements in detail. As a security architect, it's your responsibility to balance security, cost, resilience, and usability. So how can you get the balance right?

You need to keep the goal in mind. The objective of security architecture is to reduce the risk that the organization faces. Because of this, you can't make compromises on the controls that decrease the risk. You must carefully evaluate the control implementation by working with other stakeholders in technology and service selection to ensure the most cost-effective solution possible. One of the most important factors that determines the implementation and ongoing costs is the selection of the technology and the services that will support it.

From the point of view of usability, you should strive to achieve the minimum objective, which is that the implementation of security shouldn't result in a decrease in the user experience. The effectiveness of your resilience solution often depends not only on which detection, response, and recovery elements you are designing but also on what capabilities your organization provides for you to integrate those solution-specific elements.

As an example, you will likely not design a security monitoring service only for your solution, but you will integrate it with the existing service in your organization. If this service doesn't provide effective detection and triage capabilities or the organization isn't prepared to respond to and recover from security incidents, it will directly affect the time to detect, respond, and recover.

The design, build, and operation of effective security can't be done in silos but require integration and coordination across technical and organizational boundaries.

Security Silos

Security has been and is often still an afterthought. As security professionals, we're working to integrate security as much as we can into relevant activities. This book and the method we're describing are an approach to achieving this. We suggest that not only security professionals should apply architectural thinking to security, but every IT professional should.

We've often faced organizations and teams where application and infrastructure architects are doing their architecture work and, independent of that, a security architect is developing their own solution. Security often becomes disconnected with this approach. Integration of security into the architectural thinking process must be done from the start to the end to ensure the best possible risk reduction and the most cost-effective way of achieving this.

Even within security teams, we've seen silos, where the vulnerability management team doesn't talk to threat management teams, etc., and often security only comes together in the SIEM tool when logs aggregate and correlate from different sources. You won't get the most out of your security solutions with this approach. In Chapter 2, we've described how an enterprise security architecture can help ensure the tight integration of all security capabilities.

Security can get handled in silos with security from different delivery teams. Security services require tight integration. Even if someone else is responsible for a service, think about how your solution integrates with other services and start with developing a RACI as discussed in Chapter 11.

Artificial Intelligence in Security Architecture

We couldn't finish the book without some thoughts on the impact of AI. First, we will discuss the role AI plays in security controls, how we can use AI for the development of a security architecture, and some current limitations. We will then follow on with a discussion on securing AI.

AI for Security

Since the 1950s, researchers have been working on artificial intelligence (AI), a technique that allows machines to simulate cognitive functions associated with human minds. Foundational models materialized in the late 2010s. The release of ChatGPT (*https://chat.openai.com*) democratized this technology and generated a wide interest in foundational models in the form of a Large Language Model (LLM). The use of LLMs in generative AI (GenAI) has lead to a revolution in the generation of content.

We can use AI to assist in the process of designing security and to enhance the implementation of security controls. Let's start with AI in architectural thinking.

AI in architectural thinking

The use of GenAI will become part of the architectural thinking process to accelerate the development of a solution architecture. However, as we show, it still relies on the architect to ask for the right information, rephrase the content, and add context.

We had a go at using several different GenAI systems with the objective to increase efficiency in the architectural thinking process. We used two different approaches, starting with asking a broad question:

> Could you provide me with a list of actors for a system context diagram for a system to charge polluting cars to enter a city?

The system generated a list of system actors but didn't have enough context to include the cameras to detect vehicles. It also didn't include human actors other than vehicle owners, such as the staff to manage the IT infrastructure.

The second approach was to enter part of the case study to identify actors.

> From the following text, identify the list of actors for a system context diagram: << insert case study text>>

It did well at extracting actors but also included Clean Air Guildford, which is part of the system and not an actor. As with the first request, it was missing human actors and so we asked a follow-up question:

> Can you add to that the human actors needed for managing and supporting the system?

This generated a comprehensive list of human actors to add to the system context diagram. We then wanted a list of use cases for each of the actors, so we asked for them:

> For all the actors previously suggested for the system context diagram, can you identify the use cases that are required for each actor?

It did suggest some use cases, but they weren't specific enough to be useful.

Overall, AI gave us a more complete list of actors, but you will notice it relied on us asking the right questions and spotting gaps in the response before asking for more detail. Actors will be missing and the use cases need further definition. You will need to add more context and organize the information into something that's useful. Architectural thinking skills and experience are still needed.

Generative AI Is a Significant Risk

The use of GenAI is a risk to your organization, as often everything you enter into the system for processing is now reused to generate further content, with the risk that confidential data can leak from your organization. Ideally, you need to work with a provider that enables the protection of your confidential data during processing. Consult with your CISO or cybersecurity team before using generative AI.

AI in security controls

The application of AI technologies can provide efficiency gains in a variety of use cases and open up previously unavailable capabilities. Businesses are realizing these benefits and adopting AI at a rapid pace. Meanwhile, adversaries are realizing the possibilities that AI offers them. In addition to the conventional threats that apply to all solutions, AI introduces a series of new threats and alters the characteristics of some conventional threats.

We can use AI to become more efficient at detecting and responding to threats. This is, for example, used in SIEM and SOAR solutions:

- In SIEM solutions, the ability for an AI system to learn is used to improve detection quality by reducing the number of false positives. Some SIEM solutions use LLMs based on a broad body of knowledge about adversary techniques, tactics, and procedures, which enhance the automated event analysis with external context information. The same approach can also help threat analysts quickly get contextual information during the triage of an incident.

- SOAR solutions use AI to summarize the incident for security analysts, provide remediation and protection recommendations, and automate decision-making in certain use cases, with the objective of increasing the response time.

There are many more use cases, where AI can enable and enhance security controls. In addition to the efficiency gains that we can achieve from using AI, we need to be aware that AI introduces a set of new threats that we haven't faced so far. These threats are very difficult to detect and respond to. We want to illustrate this with the following examples of AI-specific threats:

Voice deepfakes
With only a very short voice sample, GenAI is capable of generating a speech of any text in any language using that voice. It's almost impossible for a human to distinguish the artificially generated voice from the original.

Image or video deepfakes

You can apply a similar technique to images or videos. A few sample pictures are enough to generate an artificial image of a person, or, combined with a voice that's a deepfake, an artificial video.

Misuse of these deepfakes can have a significant impact, ranging from breaking into banking accounts that use voice authentication to political influence through social media to offending people with fake nude videos.

Traditional techniques aren't sufficient to detect these types of threats. This is where we can benefit from using AI to analyze image and video data for artificially generated content. But not only for artificially generated content; AI also allows, for example, the police to find sequences in a huge amount of surveillance video data where a certain event is happening.

Prompt injections

The adversary crafts malicious prompts to induce unintended behavior in the model, enabling it to comply with their instructions and circumvent the system's safeguards. This is essentially a semantic attack, using words in the knowledge itself to bias the output.

Traditional input validation is one of the OWASP Top 10 Proactive Controls (*https://oreil.ly/Br0r7*), which we apply in conventional application development and is basically based on pattern matching. In order to defend against a prompt injection attack, we need to understand the intent of the prompt; this isn't possible with pattern matching. Technologies available today are using specific LLMs to analyze the prompt for malicious intent and, by doing so, defend against prompt injection attacks.

With the preceding examples, we want to illustrate that, in addition to traditional security controls, we need to apply AI-based security controls to defend against AI threats. The security industry is actively working on developing and releasing AI-based security technologies.

Securing AI

In the previous section, we discussed how we can use GenAI to support the security architectural thinking process (AI for security). GenAI solutions in themselves provide a new set of threats, which we also need to address (security for AI).

We will take a brief look at how you can apply the methods and techniques that we've described throughout this book to secure a GenAI solution. For that purpose, we need to understand the high-level building blocks of a retrieval-augmented generation (RAG) GenAI solution. RAG is an AI framework that enhances the accuracy of responses generated by a LLM by incorporating external knowledge sources to complement the LLM's internal representation of information. In Figure 12-2, we've illustrated the conceptual architecture of a RAG solution, which we've seen implemented. We've kept this at a very high level, as the development in this space is rapidly progressing.

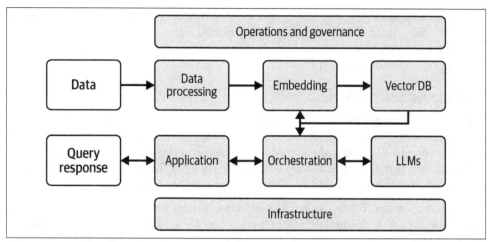

Figure 12-2. Conceptual RAG architecture

Let's have a look at the building blocks of a GenAI solution and what security considerations we need to make. This is by no means a comprehensive description, but it should give you enough starting points when you face a GenAI solution.

Data processing/embedding/vector DB

These functional components, at the top of Figure 12-2, are about transforming enterprise data (unstructured and structured) to train and tune the model for later retrieval. AI engineers, together with supporting technology, break data sets down into chunks, which are then passed through an embedding model before they're stored in a specialized database, known as a vector database.

Some of the GenAI-specific threats we need to consider to secure the design for this part of the solution are:

Data poisoning
Poisoning of data sets by modifying data sets or labels with the objective that the model later produces bad or unintended results.

Exfiltration
An adversary breaks into the system and exfiltrates data. A characteristic of GenAI solutions is that large amounts of data, which are otherwise distributed throughout the enterprise, are now concentrated in one place to train and tune

the model to make it more accurate. The data sets might contain large amounts of sensitive data, which makes them a very interesting target for adversaries.

We establish key countermeasures by understanding and classifying data based on the data collected, its origin, and how it was secured before consolidation. The classification will allow us to derive the required controls, e.g., access controls, multi-factor authentication, and encryption. Including monitoring allows us to rapidly identify and respond if exfiltration occurs.

Application/orchestration/LLMs

The AI application provides the interface to the end user of the GenAI solution. The user enters queries and receives the responses via the application. When the user has entered the query, the application formulates the prompts for the LLM. The orchestration component retrieves contextual data from the vector database to enrich the already-formulated prompts and execute the final prompts against the LLM.

LLMs play a central role in a GenAI solution and perform tasks related to language understanding, generation, and interaction across various applications and domains. There are various models with different capabilities for use with different objectives. Be it text, image, or speech generation; programming code conversion or generation; or many more. The model, specifically the trained model, is one of the key valuable assets in a GenAI solution. It takes a lot of time, processing power, and investment to build and train these models.

Some GenAI-specific threats we need to consider when we secure the design of this part of the solution are:

AI supply chain attack
  Compromise of components of the AI supply chain, e.g., GPU hardware, data, the ML software stack, or the model itself. Few organizations will develop their own models, as this is computationally expensive. Most organizations are relying on existing models, either open source or commercial. Understanding where you get the models from makes a huge difference, as in the end, you need to trust the model that you are using. Adversaries might create copies of existing models, manipulated for their malicious intent, to introduce bad data or malware. You need to manage the supply chain of the sources you are using for your solution.

Prompt injection
  Crafting malicious prompts to make the model behave in an unintended way so that the model follows the adversary's instructions, bypassing the guardrails of the system. This attack type can lead to:

Data leak
  Crafting of prompts that make the model leak sensitive information.

Model theft

Gaining full access to the model, its architecture, parameters, and class ontology by crafting queries that generate results for mining the model. This might allow an adversary to build their own version of the model.

Model evasion

Crafting of data that prevents the model from correctly identifying the content and data, for example, evading a ML-based malware detection solution.

Denial of service

Where the adversary is crafting prompts that overwhelm the system so that it can't keep up anymore.

To address these threats, you need to monitor the inputs to the solution and put so-called guardrails, or AI firewalls, in place, which are typically implemented in the orchestration component. Current AI firewalls analyze the intent of a prompt and can apply input and output controls, like blocking prompts or masking data. It will be very difficult to address all kinds of semantic attacks. This is an area where a lot of development is happening in the market.

Different vendors are emerging that develop and provide controls to counter these threats. They use similar controls as traditional software development, such as input validation and output encoding. Pattern matching alone isn't enough when the input and the output aren't predictable. Vendors use other LLMs to verify whether the input prompts and the output result are in line with the organization's policy.

Infrastructure

Every IT solution runs on one or another form of infrastructure; this is no different with a GenAI solution, which can be running on a cloud, on premises, or in a hybrid mode. All the practices we've described in this book apply here as well. This includes at least hardening of the infrastructure and application, role-based access controls, strong authentication mechanisms, vulnerability scans, and continuous monitoring.

Operations and governance

We use traditional continuous monitoring solutions like SIEM combined with a SOAR solution to automate response processes. Those kinds of solutions are, of course, also recommended for a GenAI solution to identify and respond to traditional threats. In addition, a new type of technology is evolving: Machine Learning Detection and Response (MLDR). The objective of this technology is to detect specific ML threats we've mentioned previously, for example, model theft, denial of service, supply chain, data poisoning, etc.

Finally, we need a governance function to ensure functional operation and the correct results of the solution. We need to ensure that the solution acts fairly, isn't biased, and that the model doesn't drift over time because someone has introduced some incorrect information. In addition, we must make sure that the solution complies with ethical standards and regulations and that we stay up to date on any issues.

Summary

You can apply the architectural thinking methods and techniques we've described in this book to GenAI solutions, as they're just applications running on infrastructure that stores and processes data. So all traditional approaches and considerations also apply to GenAI solutions.

In addition, GenAI solutions introduce new types of threats, different types of assets that we need to secure, and new types of countermeasures, as we described previously. OWASP has created the OWASP AI Exchange (*https://owaspai.org*), where they collect guidance and professional alignment on how to protect AI against security threats. MITRE has established MITRE ATLAS (*https://atlas.mitre.org*), where you can find more details about adversary tactics and techniques toward AI. We recommend following at least these two initiatives, as there is a lot of development ongoing in this space.

The examples we've given here are around GenAI, but there are certainly many different other AI and ML solutions where we also need to apply security practices. As these are emerging technologies, the industry, governments, and organizations are still in the early phases of maturing good practices and frameworks. It's a good idea to follow organizations such as ENISA, which has published "Multilayer Framework for Good Cybersecurity Practices for AI" (*https://oreil.ly/1AwKB*) and the UK NCSC, which has released "Machine Learning Principles" (*https://oreil.ly/goVwv*).

That concludes our exploration of security GenAI solutions. As we said, this is still a relatively immature space from a security perspective. We expect that a number of *new* companies will pop up that will provide advanced technologies to address many of the *new* threats.

Go Learn, Practice, and Share

> Without good architecture, security is difficult, if not impossible.
>
> —Unknown

We asked a team member to analyze and define the security aspects of a solution that should enable collaboration between different organizations. The solution should enable use cases for remote access, source code exchange, etc. We received a list of security technologies associated with the use cases. We didn't expect this, as the response didn't consider the solution's scope, functional components, actors, and data, or what the rationale behind certain security control decisions was.

We sat together and started drawing diagrams, understanding what components are relevant in the solution context, identifying the type of data involved, in which directions it's flowing, and in which locations the components and data reside. This visual representation helped us then develop alternatives and appropriate security controls. We also used this diagram for the dialog with the customer to finally make a joint architectural decision about which alternatives were the best fits in the overall context.

Designing a solution is a collaborative effort that requires communication. Pictures say more than a thousand words; this is especially true in architecture. This simple example should demonstrate that you can't design good security without going through the architectural thinking process we described in this book. Now it's your turn to get started. Whatever level or proficiency of the techniques and artifacts you have, only through practice will you be able to build up experience. We recommend you get involved not only in *Plan* and *Design* but also in *Build* and *Run*, as only there will you see whether whatever you architect is actually effective and working.

As you develop your skills and experience in using the method for the development of your products, projects, and programs, you can make your organization more effective at architecting security by sharing your experiences with your colleagues. We encourage you to set up or join a security architecture community to build on what you have learned by sharing experiences and learning from others. We'll be adding content to the book companion website (*https://securityarchitecture.cloud*) to help you on your journey.

Go learn, practice, and share.

Exercises

No quiz questions included. Further, summative questions and answers can be found on the companion website (*https://securityarchitecture.cloud*).

Case Study

The book uses a case study to enable you to see how to apply the tools and techniques discussed. The case study may use terms you are unfamiliar with, but a quick search on the internet will give further details about a clean air scheme.

To get the most out of the book, read and think about the security implications behind the case study. Some descriptions may be unclear and have inaccuracies, but that's standard with every project. The architectural decision records and RAID log become useful in managing this uncertainty and project risk.

Clean Air Guildford Case Study

The local authority has hired Clean Air Guildford to design, construct, and manage a system to charge polluting car drivers to enter the city. Cameras will monitor cars entering the city to detect the number plate on the car. To enter the city, the car drivers will need to pay a charge within 48 hours or receive a fine.

The project has already started to build the new hybrid cloud solution, with the core application hosted using PostgreSQL on a public cloud platform. As a security architect, you have received a request to urgently develop a security solution for the system.

The project deployment approach agreed upon between the CIO, Business Sponsors, and the Project Executive (PE) leading the integration is as follows:

- Start with a development environment using Red Hat OpenShift to build a cloud native container application using DevOps practices on a public cloud platform.
- Then build a full route-to-live with preproduction and production environments in the public cloud.

- With the Clean Air Application containing:
  — Systems of engagement using Open Liberty running on OpenShift at the center
  — Cached and state data stored in MongoDB and Redis cloud databases
- Connected to on-premises systems:
  — A payments gateway connecting to Clean Air Pay using Apache Kafka Streams
  — Integration to a debt facility using RabbitMQ
- The solution should use a hub-and-spoke architecture.
- Future developments will be in the public cloud infrastructure.
- github.com stores the code, and trello.com helps manage the project.

The program manager has sketched an architecture overview, as shown in Figure A-1, and talked you through the solution, but you haven't received the documentation yet.

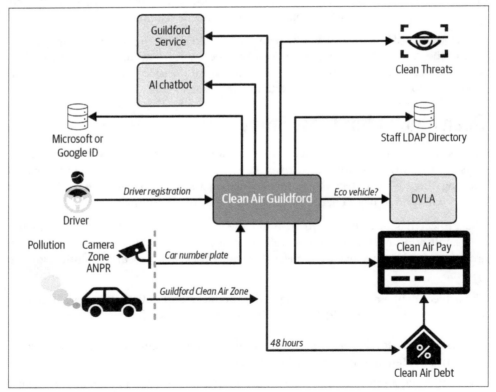

Figure A-1. Architecture overview

After talking to the program manager, you have determined that:

- The installation of Automatic Number Plate Recognition (ANPR) cameras has taken place on the roads leading into the clean air zone. Camera Zone reads the number plates of vehicles and sends information to Clean Air Guildford (CAG). CAG checks the type of vehicle in the Driver and Vehicle Licensing Agency's (DVLA) database. Camera Zone provides an outsourced service for the running of the ANPR cameras and does the same service for other clean air schemes, police, and security services.

- Vehicle owners with higher emissions will pay a £10 fee to enter the clean air zone during peak hours of 07:00 to 19:00 Monday through Saturday. Within 48 hours of entering the clean air zone, they must pay this fee via a payment portal that the scheme will provide. They have selected Clean Air Pay as their payment provider. As this is a payment service, the design of the application must include PCI DSS requirements.

- For those vehicle owners who don't pay the fee at the end of the 48-hour period, a debt collection agency, Clean Air Debt, will receive information on the driver. They will send out letters notifying the vehicle owner of the fine and, after a period, pursue collection of the fine.

- The vehicle owners will be able to use their Google or Microsoft IDs to log into the portal and register their car with the program so that, upon entering Guildford, the payments are automatically made.

- The scheme uses the Guildford Service SaaS application in a service center to respond to queries by phone and take payments.

- An AI chatbot, provided as a cloud service by the public cloud provider, will handle driver queries more rapidly without waiting for telephone support via the service center.

- Clean Threats, a threat management company, will manage all the security services from their security operations center (SOC).

- The solution will be fully hosted in the cloud and will need to be resilient to availability zone failures.

The program manager would like a high-level solution architecture that provides a minimum viable product (MVP) solution based on the preceding information.

The program manager has no security solution but has identified one high-level security requirement:

IAM_001 Integrate single sign-on by using the Staff LDAP Directory as an Identity Provider for staff.

He would like you to document 10–20 high-level requirements (in the preceding format) that he can focus on with his team within the next six weeks and would like the requirements traced back to the NIST Cybersecurity Framework that the local council uses for compliance.

He has confirmed that Clean Threats has a comprehensive threat management system in place to detect and respond to intrusions. Clean Air Guildford will be responsible for securing the core system, and he wants assurance the company can detect if there is a compromise in the application. By creating a detection use case and response playbook that are applicable to Clean Threats' threat management service, the program manager hopes to gain some assurance.

The project is already installing the IT infrastructure, and the staff will be joining in six weeks' time. There is a need for the service center employees to complete a background check by an external company and obtain HR approvals for access to the core application.

Artifact Mapping

You're probably already using another method that contains its own artifacts, and the artifact names in this book don't exactly align with the names you are using. We've tried to use a generic set of names that are easily mapped to different methods. In the following tables, we've mapped our artifact names to methods that are publicly available either as open source or in published books.

The methods we've used are:

1. *Unified Modeling Language (UML) 2.5.1* (*https://oreil.ly/OMaKB*) from the Object Management Group

2. *C4 Model* (*https://c4model.com*) from Simon Brown

3. *arc42* (*https://arc42.org*)

4. *Practical Software Architecture* (*https://oreil.ly/tXa3J*) from Tilak Mitra

This should help you map to any methods you may be using. Feel free to adapt our artifacts to your method.

Table B-1. Requirements artifact mapping

Artifact name	Unified Modeling Language (UML) 2.5.1	C4 Model	arc42	Practical Software Architecture
Use case	Use case diagram	-	-	Use case diagram
Journey map	-	-	-	-
User story	-	-	-	-
Swimlane diagram	Activity diagram	-	-	-
Separation of duties matrix	-	-	-	-

Artifact name	Unified Modeling Language (UML) 2.5.1	C4 Model	arc42	Practical Software Architecture
Non-functional requirements[a]	Non-functional requirements	Non-functional requirements	Quality goals/quality requirements	Non-functional requirements
Information asset register	-	-	-	-

[a] Also sometimes called quality attributes or architectural characteristics

Table B-2. Architecture artifact mapping

Artifact name	Unified Modeling Language (UML) 2.5.1	C4 Model	arc42	Practical Software Architecture
Architecture overview	-	-	-	Architecture overview
System context	-	System context	Context and scope	System context & system landscape
Shared responsibility diagram	-	-	-	-
Component architecture diagram	Component diagram	Container diagram & component diagram	Building block view level 1/2/3	Component model
Data flow diagram	-	-	-	-
Deployment architecture diagram	Deployment diagram	Deployment diagram	Deployment view	Operational model
Cloud architecture diagram	-	-	-	-
Sequence diagram	Sequence diagram	-	Runtime view	Component interaction diagram
Collaboration diagram	Communication diagram	Dynamic diagram	Communication diagram	Collaboration diagram
Threat model	-	-	-	-
Deployable architecture	-	-	-	-

Table B-3. Operations artifact mapping

Artifact name	Unified Modeling Language (UML) 2.5.1	C4 Model	arc42	Practical Software Architecture
Shared responsibility RACI/RASCI	-	-	-	-
Separation of duties matrix	-	-	-	-
Process	-	-	-	-
Procedure	-	-	-	-

Artifact name	Unified Modeling Language (UML) 2.5.1	C4 Model	arc42	Practical Software Architecture
Work instruction	-	-	-	-
Statechart diagram	State machine diagram	-	-	-
Threat detection use case	-	-	-	-
Incident response runbook	-	-	-	-

Table B-4. Governance artifact mapping

Artifact name	Unified Modeling Language (UML) 2.5.1	C4 Model	arc42	Practical Software Architecture
Risks, assumptions, issues, and dependencies (RAID) log	-	-	Risks and technical debt	-
Architectural decision record	-	-	Architecture decision record	Architecture decision

Table B-5. Assurance artifact mapping

Artifact name	Unified Modeling Language (UML) 2.5.1	C4 Model	arc42	Practical Software Architecture
Requirements traceability matrix	-	-	-	-
Threat traceability matrix	-	-	-	-
Test strategy	-	-	-	-
Test plan	-	-	-	-

Exercise Solutions

Here are the answers for the exercises at the end of each chapter:

Chapter 1. Introduction

1. A, B, D, and E. We talk about four foundational security techniques used within the book: data-centric security, secure by design with threat modeling, zero trust architecture, and compliance management. Data-centric security involves tracing data throughout its journey in transit, at rest, and in processing. Secure by design with threat modeling takes a risk-based perspective on developing a solution architecture. Zero trust architecture assumes implicit trust is removed from an internal network and a breach has already occurred, so data is fully protected through all stages of its journey. Compliance management is included, as compliance with legal and regulatory requirements is required for all organizations.

2. A and C. Two characteristics of secure by design include: i) threat modeling to identify the risk to data; and ii) being primarily targeted at the design of technology products.

3. A and C. Zero trust architecture follows a number of principles, including "Never trust, always verify." The zero trust model assumes that all business transactions and data flows, whether originating from inside or outside the network, are potentially malicious. Every interaction in a business transaction or data flow must be continuously validated to ensure that only authorized users and devices can access sensitive business data. In effect, it moves the perimeter from the system boundary to the point at which identification, authentication, and authorization take place, resulting in identity becoming the new perimeter.

4. C. Only a security champion role is specific to an Agile or DevOps development environment.

5. D. The governance section in the artifact dependency diagram covers all stages of development with recording of the risks, assumptions, issues, and dependencies (RAID) log and architectural decision records.

6. A, C, and D. Diagrams, automation, and tables are all types of artifacts. There are many diagrams, including system context diagram, the swimlane diagram, the deployment architecture diagram, and the statechart diagram. The deployable architecture artifact is automation. Tables include the information asset register and incident response runbook.

7. C. A solution architecture decomposition diagram contains the system context, component architecture, and deployment architecture.

Chapter 2. Architecture Concepts

1. A, B, and D. Design thinking is an empathetic, human-centered process that is iterative, using experimentation to build a solution in steps while refining the requirements.

2. False. Architectural characteristics or non-functional requirements need to be included in the scope to ensure the system being considered is ready to scale, resilient, and secure for a production service. This would be a proof of concept, not an MVP.

3. A, B, and C. In a tweet from 2021, Grady Booch says, "All architecture is design, but not all design is architecture. Architecture represents the set of significant design decisions that shape the form and the function of a system, where significant is measured by cost of change."

4. True. A consultant would need to use architectural thinking, including making architectural decisions about non-functional requirements, to ensure a system is resilient, scalable, available, adaptable, secure, and compliant.

5. False. Architectural thinking is about making significant design decisions, whereas specifying firewall configuration is an engineering activity that doesn't make significant design decisions.

6. False. A security champion supporting DevOps performs a mix of architecture and engineering activities as decisions are made to integrate security services. If architectural thinking is missing from DevOps, no significant design decisions are made, which is unlikely during the development of all but the simplest information systems.

7. A and C. An enterprise architecture is aligned with business objectives and goals. It provides a holistic view of architecture for an organization and doesn't describe a specific solution.

8. A, C, and D. A solution architecture solves a specific business problem using an information system that includes technology, processes, and people. It specifies how technologies will deliver the required capabilities of the system. An architect will use architecture patterns, enterprise architecture, and enterprise processes to guide the development of a solution architecture.

9. C. A policy engine (PE) makes security policy decisions and passes the results to the PEP to enforce the connection between the subject and the enterprise resource.

10. A and C. The term service should be used for security capabilities rather than alignment to a process or control framework because: i) a service consists of technology, processes, and people, not just a process and ii) a service needs a service design to ensure quality of delivery, including hours of service, availability requirements, etc.

11. False. As we demonstrated with the Cloud Security Alliance (CSA) Cloud Controls Matrix (CCM), the list of required security services may be incomplete even for a basic set of controls. In addition, the specific risks for each workload need to be assessed to identify additional controls.

Chapter 3. Enterprise Context

1. A, C, and D. Laws and regulations are a minimum baseline that organizations need to add to based on their risk environment and tolerance. They provide high-level guidance to be interpreted. Justification is needed if the guidance isn't followed. Laws and regulations can apply globally, but also to each region, country, or state.

2. D. NIST SP 800-53 is a detailed catalog of security control requirements.

3. A and C. A business strategy should contain a vision and mission, along with a value proposition for the organization.

4. B and D. A network PoP data center or a co-location data center could be considered an independent location, provided that they're not co-located with the cloud data center being used for workloads.

5. A, B, and D. Separation of duties is used in financial transactions where one person requests a transaction and another person approves it for prevention of fraud. The control is used for critical security controls configuration, such as a request and then approval of a firewall change, reducing the risk of introducing a vulnerability that compromises the system. Separation of duties is also used for activities such as development of code, where one person performs the development and another person performs quality assurance checking, including looking for security vulnerabilities.

6. C. Secure by default is the principle that the default configuration of a system or piece of software should provide a high level of security without requiring the user or administrator to make additional modifications or settings.

7. B, C, and D. A process is independent of technology; the next level of procedures and work instructions will introduce technology. A process should remain unmodified even after implementation changes, which is what the audit and compliance processes should test. Each of the process activities should be assigned to roles, not specific people, so that they remain valid even if the organization changes and should record what control points should be measured when it comes to an audit or compliance test.

Chapter 4. Requirements and Constraints

1. A and C. A functional requirement defines the primary functionality, or what a system should deliver, of a workload or application.

2. A, B, and D. The term non-functional requirements represents those requirements that are not functional. However, the term architectural characteristics is sometimes used to represent those requirements that are not functional. For instance, Mark Richards and Neil Ford use it in their book, *Fundamentals of Software Architecture* (O'Reilly). ISO/IEC 25010:2023 on systems and software engineering uses the term product quality properties.

3. D. The loss of availability for cloud services like secrets or certificate management can result in almost immediate failure of workloads, so security services often need to be more resilient than the workloads they support.

4. B and D. This refers to a circular dependency that cannot be resolved unless there is an alternative way to retrieve the encryption keys. If there aren't multiple routes to retrieve the encryption keys, we can't resolve a circular dependency.

5. C. Specific, measurable, attainable, relevant, and time-bound (SMART) is the set of qualities used to measure how good a requirement is.

6. B and D. The best functional requirements definition techniques for identifying end-user functional requirements are a journey map and user story. A journey map originates from design thinking and is a human-centered approach to understanding the needs, pain points, and goals of personas. It's a good starting place, with user stories further detailing the activities. User stories originate from the extreme programming (XP) methodology as a way to improve software quality and be more responsive to changing customer requirements. A journey map might serve as their guide.

7. C. The best functional requirements definition technique for the formal definition of the sequence of security-enforcing activities taking place between different end users is a swimlane diagram. A swimlane diagram provides a formal

approach to documenting a sequence of activities for security-enforcing activities as it shows the relationship between activities, and a separation of duties matrix is available.

8. B and D. Quality is a factor that is balanced against time and cost of a project. The risk of loss of confidentiality, integrity, and availability is balanced against the cost and time of the project.

9. A, B, and D. It might be necessary to rearchitect around a different component with a higher cost of change later in the design and development process if other components of the solutions do not support particular versions of products and services.

10. B. Dimensions are used to externalize the scope and get you to think about a list of different types to include in a scope.

Chapter 5. System Context

1. C. SPI relates to data concerning a person or identifiable individual that's so sensitive that its disclosure could cause irrevocable harm. This includes information on racial or ethnic origin, sexual life, political opinions, criminal records, religious beliefs, trade union activities, and physical or mental health.

2. B and C. Aggregation is the integration of data from multiple sources into a single dataset. Aggregation may increase the sensitivity of the resulting information. Generation is the creation of new data through processing or analysis of existing data, which may increase the sensitivity of the resulting information.

3. A, B, and D. A system context diagram shows the boundary of the system, the human and system actors interacting with the boundary of the system, and interactions of the actors show where the data flows in and out of the system.

4. B and D. A database administrator is responsible for the administration of the database used in the online store, whether it is software running on a compute host or a cloud service. The service desk agent would need to access the online store to provide support.

5. A and C. A parcel logistics system would be run by the parcel delivery company, which would provide an external system used to schedule parcel collection and delivery. A card payment system would be external and accessed via a payment gateway by the online store.

6. True. An employee with internal access and an employee with remote access reside in different threat environments, may use different security controls, and may have different access restrictions to the data being accessed. Consider them separate to identify the differences.

7. B. A service that requires single-zone resilience has an annual availability of 99.99% and falls in Category B.

Chapter 6. Application Security

1. B and C. The component architecture is the first iteration of identifying building blocks that represent the functionality the solution should implement and creating an abstraction of the system architecture, omitting details.

2. A and C. Threat modeling is an iterative process that changes at each iteration of the solution, and into Day-2 operations, where the threats continually change. The level of detail and the areas of the solution where you perform threat modeling can often be expanded. At some point, you will have reached a satisfactory level of detail for the first major iteration based on the joint agreement of the threat modeling team. As threats and vulnerabilities change, further threat modeling will be needed for Day-2 operations, where the threats continually change. Therefore, the process is never really complete.

3. A, B, and D. Through the threat modeling process, you define controls that mitigate threats. Only identified security controls that reduce the risk to the organization are useful and relevant. Identified threats will then feed into threat detection use cases, as further described in Chapter 11.

4. B and C. An initial threat model should certainly be developed as part of the shift-left approach to identify security issues as soon as possible in the development lifecycle. Significant changes to the solution can drive further changes to the threat model.

5. B. Justification of the importance of identified security controls, which reduce the risk to the organization, receives high priority because they have a positive business impact.

6. C. Following the flow of the data through the system will help you identify places with threats and a need for corresponding controls.

Chapter 7. Shared Responsibilities

1. A, B, and D. Key benefits of cloud computing include provisioning of cloud resources on demand, rapid deployment of resources to support peak business events and sharing of resources, and enabling pooling of resources with lower costs.

2. False. SaaS service security still requires some consumer involvement, such as configuring access to data and role-based activities. You need to assume someone will need to manage the SaaS service and include them as a system or human actor.

3. A, B, and D. A cloud service provider is responsible for all things physical in a cloud data center, including a cloud data center's physical security, storage subsystem security, and network device security.

4. A, B, C, and D. A landing zone package will contain all of these elements. An enterprise pattern describes the organization of the cloud environments for an enterprise with many different lines of business, workloads, and projects. An architecture pattern is best practice for the construction of types of workloads or single workloads of a particular type. A resiliency pattern shows how to achieve the required service levels to deliver the desired resiliency for workloads. Principles guide the decision-making process for the deployment of the solution to the landing zone. They cover topics like resilience, performance, reliability, sustainability, operations, security, and compliance.

5. False. Cloud services aren't necessarily more cost-effective than on-premises services. It depends on the type of workload and how they use resources. If cloud resources are not required much of the time, you have the opportunity to turn them off and not be charged for their use. Cloud computing provides flexibility for workloads that have spikes in resource utilization, and the rate card will include a share of the cost to maintain unused resources.

6. True. A hybrid cloud architecture can combine one or more cloud services and on-premises data centers to support workloads that span on-premises and cloud.

7. A, B, and D. A hybrid cloud environment will consist of multiple compute platforms with varying shared responsibilities for each technology architecture and cloud service provider. Security services will be built into the cloud platform, with each of the cloud providers having a different security operations team, and the consumers of the services will also perform security operations.

8. True. Although the cloud service provider is responsible for some of the underlying security, the user must administer the security services offered by the cloud platform.

9. B, C, and D. You ensure that all parties within an organization understand their shared responsibilities by defining a document of understanding (DoU) as it defines who is responsible for each activity; a shared responsibility diagram or table as they define who is responsible for each major service; and documenting processes and procedures as they define who is responsible for each activity.

Chapter 8. Infrastructure Security

1. B. The architectural thinking technique of placing a functional component onto the chosen compute node is called deployment. Deployment refers to identifying the appropriate compute characteristics for the functional component and placing it on the compute node.

2. B and D. An input to the definition of a deployment architecture diagram is a system context diagram and a shared responsibility diagram or table. A system context diagram describes the boundary of the system with the actors and interfaces to help define the deployment architecture diagram. A shared responsibility diagram or table is an input that describes the technology stacks needed for the deployment architecture diagram.

3. A and C. Documentation that should be created to help further describe a deployment architecture diagram includes network design and architectural decision records. Network design documentation describes the detailed network solution for a deployment architecture diagram. Architectural decision records would be recorded as part of the architectural thinking to further describe the deployment architecture diagram.

4. A. Compliance needs to be demonstrated using a catalog of non-functional requirements. If security requirements are part of the primary functionality, there may be some functional requirements that need to be considered as well.

5. A, B, and C. In compute node to compute node communication, the types of transaction flows that need to be considered are those triggered by human and system actors, system events, and threat actors. Transaction flows triggered by system events are a secondary set of flows that frequently go unnoticed because they may be the result of incidents, mistakes, or timed batch transactions. Transaction flows triggered by threat actors that should never occur need to be considered.

6. B. A shared responsibility diagram or table is used to describe the compute platforms and is used when deploying functional components onto compute nodes.

7. B, C and D. A zero trust network architecture (ZTNA) solution is a more secure remote access solution than a virtual private network (VPN) because identity and access policy enforcement occurs before establishing the network connection, it inhibits malware lateral movement between end-user devices and target systems, and it isolates internal enterprise applications from the internet.

8. A, B, C, and D. The enterprise level considers how all the different environments are integrated together to secure the whole cloud environment. CSP/landing zone level considers the controls related to a specific data center or cloud environment. The application and CI/CD levels consider the controls needed in the application development environment. The operations level considers the requirements for the security operations needed to support the cloud environment.

9. False. An on-premises software solution may use an architecture that relies on capabilities only available in an on-premises environment, such as network latency and underlying storage capabilities. Due to such dependencies on the

on-premises environment, an on-premises software solution might not be able to deliver as a cloud solution.

Chapter 9. Architecture Patterns and Decisions

1. B. A pattern is considered to be a reusable solution that solves a specific problem.

2. A, B, and C. A deployable architecture is automation based on a reference architecture or architecture pattern that's reusable and uses best practices, principles, and guidance.

3. False. A solution design pattern solves an individual problem but is insufficient to provide a complete solution. Many solution design patterns, each solving an individual problem, must combine together into an architectural pattern to solve a problem, providing an implementable solution.

4. False. A 3-tier architecture pattern is a pattern used previously on-premises, but normally cloud applications are n-tier architectures.

5. A, B, and C. In a hybrid cloud architecture, an edge or transit VPC is normally located within a cloud environment but may be in a point of presence (PoP) network or on-premises data center to remove the need to manage multiple locations for network protection and monitoring. Using a co-lo data center would add complexity to the architecture with the support of a new location.

6. A, B, C, and D. There are many applications, each with a number of tiers, hosted in multiple environments, that each require security rules per host to be configured, adding complexity.

7. A, B and C. An architectural decision record needs a decision to be recorded (otherwise there is not a decision). The rationale documents why the decision was made and the implication documents how the decision changes the solution and how it is delivered.

Chapter 10. Secure Development and Assurance

1. B. The earlier in the development lifecycle that security issues are identified, the cheaper it is to address them.

2. A, C, and D. The security team might provide a security champion to the development team, which takes on some responsibilities for security activities, but not all and not alone. Developers take on responsibilities including the application of secure coding practices, code reviews, and static application security testing (SAST) scans during unit testing. The different roles of a development team have mostly a security responsibility in the development process.

3. A, C, and D. Secure assurance activities are required throughout the development process, from plan to release, including the start, to ensure that requirements are documented and approved. Then, during Day-2 operations, certain assurance activities need to be repeated at regular intervals.

4. B and D. They are project risks and should be a proper RAID item. The others are solution risks that are addressed in the solution risk register or during threat modeling.

5. D. Automation and the culture of continuous integration and development are the foundations for an efficient development process.

6. A, B, and C. SAST, SCA, and secret scanning tools are integrated into the build process. SAST tools scan the source code for vulnerabilities based on defined policies. SCA tools scan the components for vulnerable and outdated components. Secret scans scan the source code for hardcoded secrets.

7. False. Assurance activities are required during Day-0 and Day-1 operations but are also required with every change during Day-2 operations.

8. B. Abuse cases define flaws in the business logic and lead to respective countermeasures and tests.

9. A and B. A Cloud Center of Excellence (CCoE) certifies products for inclusion in the cloud reference architecture and drives consistency in security practices and policies across cloud service providers.

Chapter 11. Security Operations

1. A and B. A Responsible, Accountable, Supporting, Consulted, and Informed (RASCI) matrix splits the responsibility for an activity into the person who is responsible for leading and one or more people responsible for supporting the activity. The delivery of some activities may be performed by multiple people, but the operations team don't want to add complexity by decomposing further into multiple activities, so one person leads and the others support the activity.

2. False. The best form of RACI for two parties is an agreement where both parties have their responsibilities explicitly described; otherwise, it can lead to confusion and disputes.

3. False. A process defines what needs to be performed and why. It is the procedures and work instructions that define how activities are completed.

4. A. A statechart diagram is useful to identify processes, not work instructions, needed to perform state changes of data.

5. C. A separation of duties matrix identifies risks associated with a party performing an activity without the approval of another party.

6. True. Threat modeling is not just for identifying countermeasures; it is also used to identify threats that should be detected as part of the threat detection and response system.

7. A, B, and C. A threat traceability matrix is to ensure there is a use case for detection of a threat and a response runbook for responding to a threat, then ensure detection and response are tested for a threat.

Chapter 12. Closing Thoughts

No quiz questions included. Further, summative questions and answers can be found on the companion website (*https://securityarchitecture.cloud*).

Index

security awareness training, 187
security by obscurity principle, 84
security categories, 52
security champions, 9, 12, 331
Security Content Automation Protocol (SCAP), 71, 383
security controls compromise, separation of duties, 82
security controls implementation, deployment architecture, 246
security domains, 50
security information and event management (SIEM), 43, 187, 344, 378, 407
security operations, 21, 357-393
    artifacts, 358
    case study, 367-376, 380-384, 387-391
    deployment architecture, 247
    incident response runbooks, 384-391
    processes, procedures, and work instructions, 365-374
    shared responsibilities, 359-364
    threat detection, 378-384
    threat traceability matrices, 391
Security Orchestration, Automation, and Response (SOAR) system, 379, 407
security services, 53
    designs, 58-60
    processes versus, 49
    responsibilities, 54-56
    security service management, 53
security silos, 405
Security Technical Implementation Guides (STIGs), 71
security techniques, 2-8
    compliance management, 7-8
    data-centric security, 3-4
    secure by design with threat modeling, 4
    users of, 8-9
    zero trust architecture, 5-7
self-messages, sequence diagrams, 167
sensitive personal information (SPI) asset class, 134
separation of duties principle and matrices, 82, 109-111
sequence diagrams, 166-167, 239
server virtualization technologies, 213
serverless platforms, 213
service availability, security service design, 59
service catalogs, security service design, 58

service continuity, security service design, 59
service level management, security service design, 58
service level objectives (SLOs), 59
service performance and capacity, security service design, 59
shared responsibilities, 21, 205-234
    artifacts, 206
    case study, 228-234
    cloud computing, 208-219
    cloud security policy responsibility, 227-228
    cloud service provider responsibilities, 223-225
    cloud user responsibilities, 225-227
    one-sided shared responsibility agreements, 364
    QA checklist, 234
    security operations, 359-364
shared responsibilities stack diagrams, 220-223, 231-234
Sherwood Applied Business Security Architecture (SABSA), 26
Sherwood, John, 26, 49
shift-left approach, software development lifecycle, 327
Shifting the Balance of Cybersecurity Risk (CISA, et al.), 5
short-form ADRs, 311
Shostack, Adam, 8
SIEM (security information and event management), 43, 187, 344, 378, 407
single capability non-functional requirements, 92
Skoulikari, Anna, 307
SLOs (service level objectives), 59
SMART framework, 98
SOAR (Security Orchestration, Automation, and Response) system, 379, 407
Software Architect Elevator, The (Hohpe), 76
software as a service (SaaS), 211, 229
software bills of materials (SBOMs), 335
software composition analysis (SCA), 335
software development lifecycle, 326-330
software development proactive controls, 188
software versions
    dependencies, 97
    identifying, 115
software-defined networking (SDN), 256, 279
software-defined perimeter (SDP) pattern, 264

About the Authors

Mark Buckwell is a cloud security architect, thought leader, speaker, and trainer with 30 years of experience architecting and delivering security solutions. He is known for leading the successful delivery of global security solutions to protect business-critical enterprise workloads. With an emphasis on regulated environments, he has worked with organizations to develop their security strategies, enterprise architectures, and solution architectures across a variety of industries. He has also been using his extensive experience to help develop the next generation of security architects through training security professionals globally and students through an assessed cyber security master's degree module at two UK universities.

Stefaan Van daele is CTO at IBM Cybersecurity Services in the northern, central, and eastern Europe region and he is a trusted advisor to CISOs and their teams. He is also IBM architect profession leader for the Benelux region. In that role he guides IBM architects with their architect certification journey. As a senior certified security architect, he led several security transformation projects at organizations in Europe. He is also an instructor in security architecture classes, both internally at IBM and externally. In his current role he is the lead architect on a multiyear security project.

Carsten Horst is an associate partner and Open Group certified senior security architect. In his more than 25 years of experience, he has helped organizations across a variety of industries to develop and implement their security strategies and security architectures. In his role, he has been leading security transformation projects across Europe. He is also an instructor and coauthor of security architecture classes at IBM. In his current role as associate partner with IBM Security, he is helping clients with the design, implementation, and management of security solutions within a hybrid cloud context.

Colophon

The animal on the cover of *Security Architecture for Hybrid Cloud* is a crested eagle (*Morphnus guianensis*), a neotropical eagle living throughout Central and South America.

The crested eagle has a large head, enhanced by the crest of feathers that gives it its name, a long tail, and short wings. Its small wingspan allows it to move through forest environments. The birds' plumage varies from a light brownish-gray to mostly black.

The crested eagle eats mostly small mammals, rodents, snakes, and smaller birds. Like most raptors, they are solitary birds. They build relatively large nests and typically produce two eggs; however, only one eaglet hatches. Juveniles remain dependent upon their parents for up to thirty months, which indicates that parents do not breed every year.

Crested eagles have a large distribution, but the population of breeding adults is estimated to be only 1,000 to 10,000 birds. The IUCN lists their status as Near Threatened. Many of the animals on O'Reilly covers are endangered; all of them are important to the world.

The cover illustration is by Karen Montgomery, based on an antique line engraving from *Iconographia Zoologica*. The series design is by Edie Freedman, Ellie Volckhausen, and Karen Montgomery. The cover fonts are Gilroy Semibold and Guardian Sans. The text font is Adobe Minion Pro; the heading font is Adobe Myriad Condensed; and the code font is Dalton Maag's Ubuntu Mono.

9 781098 157777